American Legion

American Legion Baseball

A History, 1924–2020

WILLIAM E. AKIN

McFarland & Company, Inc., Publishers

Jefferson, North Carolina

ISBN (print) 978-1-4766-8574-8
ISBN (ebook) 978-1-4766-4389-2

LIBRARY OF CONGRESS AND BRITISH LIBRARY
CATALOGUING DATA ARE AVAILABLE

Library of Congress Control Number 2021051194

On the cover: Keeter Stadium, in Shelby, North Carolina, opened in 1976
and served as home to various minor league teams. Beginning in 2000
it hosted various Legion tournaments. In 2008 it hosted the Legion World Series
and won the right to host on a trial basis beginning in 2011. The Series proved
so successful, breaking attendance records each year, that the Legion happily
made Shelby and Cleveland County the home of its World Series. Player introductions
are always a highlight of the event (courtesy Brittany Randolph, *Shelby Star*).
Background © 2022 Suzanne Tucker/Shutterstock.

Printed in the United States of America

*McFarland & Company, Inc., Publishers
Box 611, Jefferson, North Carolina 28640
www.mcfarlandpub.com*

To the memory of William J. "Bill" Stout

Table of Contents

Acknowledgments

Some years ago, having completed a book on *The Middle Atlantic League, 1925–1952* (2015), I was on the lookout for a new research project. My good friend Bill Stout suggested we collaborate on a book-length study of American Legion baseball. A native of Gloucester City, New Jersey, next door to Brooklawn's powerful Post 72 Legion team, he brought enthusiasm and, indeed, passion to the project. It did not take long to determine that such a book would, indeed, fill a gaping hole in baseball literature. Besides, it sounded like fun. He volunteered to do the grunt-work, and I could write it up. So, I signed on.

A trip to the National Baseball Hall of Fame in Cooperstown, where we dug into the Giamatti Research Center, got us into the project. Then we made a serious road trip to the American Legion Library and Archives in Indianapolis, Indiana. Shortly thereafter, my co-author bailed on me. Of course, it was not Bill's fault that he contracted cancer. It was brave, maybe even heroic for him to forgo chemotherapy, but … damn, why did he have to die just when we were getting underway? After Bill's death, my heart went out of the project. It took many months for me to figure out that I owed it to Bill to finish the research and writing. So here it is, brother Stout!

My personal experience with American Legion baseball began in a less than heroic manner. When I was a 14-year-old lad aspiring to a career in major league baseball, I was called up to the local Legion nine from the Boys Club midget team. With that call-up I got my first real uniform. That heavy gray wool flannel might as well have been woven out of gold fabric. On the back of the jersey was spelled out "Berwyn Fuel and Feed." I could not have been prouder if it had said "New York Yankees."

Those halcyon days proved short-lived. Although I did not play in the first game after my call-up, I did warm up the pitcher and managed to get grass stains (quite on purpose) on that beautiful uniform. My grandmother, "Mama," whom I loved dearly, decided the uniform needed bleach to get it clean. The problem was that my beautiful uniform came out with white splotches all over it. I sucked it up, no matter how embarrassed I was, and went to the next game, knowing I would start. To complete my humiliation, that game was against a nasty curve-ball pitcher, good enough to sign a professional contract the next season. I will never forget the first pitch heading right for my head. I hit the deck, only to hear the umpire shout "strike one." Humiliation. On pitch two I held my ground, but my left foot was far in the bucket. "Strike two." Pitch three, I flailed at, but did not come within a foot of the ball. At that moment I knew my dream of reaching the majors was over. After that, I stuck to fast-pitch softball, where, at least, I held my own. Perhaps, this book will atone for my personal experience in American Legion baseball.

Very little history, baseball or otherwise, comes totally from individual effort. This book is no different. It benefited from the contributions of numerous people. Several people read and commented on portions of the manuscript. For this, I especially thank my former colleagues at Ursinus College, Jon Volkmer, Dave Sherman, and Rick DeFeliciantonio, as well as my old grad school friend, the late John Wiseman. Dave Sherman, John Teter, and Devon Schuler provided help in tracking down photos. Ruth Sprague, Ursinus User Support Specialist, saved the day by correcting a serious flaw.

The internet has made baseball research much more accessible than it was when I first began writing about baseball, but libraries and their staff remain necessary for serious research. I have found librarians anxious to help. I am especially thankful for the staff of Myrin Library at Ursinus College, the Lewes, Delaware, Public Library, and the Charles C. Wise Jr. Library at West Virginia University. The American Legion Library and Archives in Indianapolis, Indiana, was invaluable. The National Baseball Hall of Fame and its Giamatti Research Center is a must stop for any baseball research.

My family continues to tolerate my obsession with baseball with good cheer, and once a year joins me for a trip to see the Delmarva Shorebirds in Salisbury, Maryland. For this, and for dozens of other reasons, I thank daughter Lynn Akin, Adana, Sydney, and Chloe Brauer, and the Coverts, Binker (aka Denton), Jacqui, Brenden, and Griffen. More than ever, I cannot imagine how I could function without my wife/life-partner/friend/literary critic/love of my life/and computer assistant, Elizabeth Teter Akin. Thanks Babe!

1

Americanism and Baseball, 1924–1932

Whether it was true or not, large numbers of Americans in the early to mid–1920s came to believe that baseball was rapidly declining, perhaps beyond redemption. The Black Sox scandal of 1919 had created a scar on the American psyche. At least eight members of the Chicago White Sox had conspired to lose the 1919 World Series. When the scandal broke in 1920, the National Pastime had been shown to be corrupt. America's innocence was laid bare. The public response to the scandal was, perhaps, best summarized by the story of the little boy on the courthouse steps who looked up to his hero, Shoeless Joe Jackson, and said, "Say it ain't so, Joe." How could baseball ever recover from such a dastardly attack on all that American boys held dear?[1]

In fact, the condition of baseball, at least major league baseball, was not as dismal as it might have seemed. True, even before the reality of the fix was known, attendance at major league games fell from 9.1 million in 1920 to 8.3 million in 1922. That, however, was well above the 6.5 million who had attended major league games in 1916, even before the Great War. Moreover, the flamboyant Judge Kenesaw Mountain Landis had taken charge as commissioner of baseball in 1920 with sweeping powers which he quickly used "to clean up the game." After suspending the eight Black Sox fixers for life, Landis pronounced the game clean. At the same time, Babe Ruth's home run explosion announced the end of baseball's Dead Ball Era. The game quickly morphed from a pitchers' game to a hitters' game. The opening in 1923 of mammoth Yankee Stadium breathed renewed optimism into the game.[2]

Baseball below the major leagues, especially in the minor leagues, on the other hand, continued to suffer. The first decade of the 20th century had been a boom period in minor league baseball. By 1914, at the outbreak of World War I in Europe, the number of minor leagues peaked at 43 leagues. The Federal League (1914–1915), an upstart organization which operated as a "third major league," lured many major league and numerous minor league players to its ranks. World War I (1917–1919) devastated the minor leagues. The number of leagues had declined to ten at the beginning of the 1918 season; by Armistice Day at the close of that season, only one, the International League, survived. Through all of this, the major leagues remained deaf to the problems of the minors. Even so, after the end of World War I, the minor circuits, like the majors, showed some signs of renewed life. Although minor leagues would continue to struggle until the mid-1920s, by 1922 the number of leagues had jumped to 30 and promised to go higher.[3]

Even African American professional baseball flourished as never before. Andrew

"Rube" Foster, himself an outstanding pitcher, now owner of the Chicago American Giants, put together the Negro National League in February 1920. The league initially consisted of Foster's team plus the Chicago Giants, Cuban Stars, Dayton Marcos, Detroit Stars, Indianapolis ABCs, Kansas City Monarchs, and St. Louis Giants. In March 1920, the short-lived Negro Southern League was formed. After one year, that league joined Foster's Negro National League. The Birmingham Black Barons and the Memphis Red Sox from the Negro Southern League not only survived the merger but even managed to prosper. In segregated America, most whites remained unaware of this black world.[4]

The issue really bothering most American men was what was happening or, more to the point, what was not happening on the sandlots and city streets where boys without a team played. No doubt as men grew older, they tended to romanticize their youth. Before the Great War, boys of all ages joined in pickup games, playing until darkness sent them home. Country boys might play barefooted in pastures without fences, backstops, or real bases. Town kids found vacant lots on which to play. City boys in knickers played in streets where fire hydrants and manhole-covers served as bases. Even if there were not enough kids to pick teams, the rump could always play varieties of the game called "knockers" (one, two, or three), "one old cat" or some other variation of the game. Or they could always have a game of catch. Following the Great War, the thinking went, boys were not playing those informal games that developed skills and instilled a passion for the National Game. That drop-off appeared in high school and college baseball, both of which showed a sharp decline beginning in 1922.

This perception became widespread in the mid-1920s. One person who bought into this concern was young Jennings Randolph, later a long-serving Senator (1958–1985) from West Virginia, then a reporter in his first job out of college. He remembered his boyhood before the war, when "we played baseball from dawn to dark and beyond." No one did that anymore, he lamented. "Kids don't take to baseball like they did when you and I were kids." Now, he moaned, dozens of other attractions—golf, tennis, swimming, movies, cars, girls—"take up time he could devote to baseball." That perception was hard to dispute.[5]

John L. Griffith, among others, shared Randolph's concern, and he quickly became the leader of those men worried about baseball's future. Griffith, a well-known figure in the sport world of the United States, had been in that world for most of the new century. After graduating from Beloit College in 1902, Griffith held positions at Yankton (1902), Morningside (1905), and Drake (1908) Colleges. At each of these small Midwest schools, Griffith coached football, track and baseball. At Drake in 1910, he created the famous Drake Relays, a multi-day carnival centered around track and field. When the United States entered World War I in 1917, Griffith resigned his position at Drake and joined the army. He coached football and baseball teams at Camp Dodge in Kansas and took charge of recreation for the base. Before war's end, Griffith became physical training director for the entire army, with the rank of major.

Following the Great War, Griffith accepted a position as physical education instructor at the University of Illinois. While there, in 1921 he established and edited *Athletic Journal,* an academic journal aimed at physical education teachers and coaches. That same year he became executive vice president of the National Amateur Athletic Federation. His appointment in 1922 as the first commissioner of the Western Athletic Conference ... which morphed into the Big Ten Conference ... gave him a significant national platform from which to speak and to be heard.[6]

Griffith bought into the widespread concern about the decline of baseball and arranged for the Amateur Athletic Federation to undertake a study to test the prevailing belief that baseball was in decline. The Federation announced its findings at its annual meeting in December 1925. The report confirmed the worst fears of people like Jennings Randolph. The study concluded that 50 percent fewer boys were currently playing pickup baseball games than played them before World War I. This was, indeed, a significant decline![7] Not surprisingly, with fewer boys playing the game, the sales of baseball goods—bats, balls, gloves—had also dropped sharply. The report attributed much of the decline to lack of space to play in cities and large towns, as vacant lots disappeared before urban development and growth. The report also documented an increase in the number of boys playing tennis and golf. Those sports, once seen by boys as games for "sissies" and for the country club elite, had moved into back yards and to public courses where all could play. Football, of course, had been popular, but before the war it was confined largely to college campuses. In the 1920s, football exploded in popularity; younger boys were drawn to the game producing Saturday's heroes, and older men became subway alumni. Basketball, even if played in those then-controversial short pants, was finding

more and more participants and fans, especially at the high school level. Overall, the study confirmed the general belief that baseball was in serious trouble both as a participation and spectator sport.[8]

Griffith and others in the business of training, coaching, and directing youth would not be satisfied with merely increasing baseball play on the sandlots, streets, and pastures. Early in the 20th century, educated and "respectable" Americans had developed confidence in organized youth activities. Luther Gulick, who in 1903 had founded the New York Public School Athletic League, after over a decade of running the YMCA Training School at Springfield, Massachusetts, had the reputation as the foremost physical educator in the country. He expounded the theory that organized athletic competition *with strong adult supervision* possessed the unique ability to promote physical fitness, democratic living, sportsmanship, and "the overall character development of children."[9] The YMCA and the Boy Scouts adopted and

John L. Griffith. In the 1920s he taught and coached at the University of Illinois where he established the *Athletic Journal* and served as vice president of the Amateur Athletic Federation before becoming the first Commissioner of the Big Ten Conference. He was a prime mover in getting the American Legion to adopt a baseball program (Library of Congress).

exploited the notion that character could best be developed through close adult supervision. As Gulick exclaimed, *"play could no longer be left in the hands of children."* Following this logic, for baseball to be restored to its rightful place as America's National Pastime, it would have to be in an organized and supervised fashion.[10]

Griffith believed it would take a nationwide organization to adopt and sponsor the effort to restore baseball to its pre-war eminence. He imagined an organization, which he termed a "league," whose play culminated in a national tournament to crown a sandlot champion of the entire United States. He attempted, albeit with limited success, to interest various fraternal organizations in the undertaking, especially organizations in which he held membership, including the Elks and Rotary Clubs.[11]

Then, in 1925, Griffith ran into Frank McCormick, who had played football for him at Camp Dodge during the Great War and who, following the war, briefly played professional football. McCormick at the time coached baseball and football at Columbus College in Sioux Falls, South Dakota. He later became baseball coach (1930–1941) and athletic director (1932–1950) at the University of Minnesota. In addition to coaching, the friendly and outgoing McCormick was in 1924 the Commander of the South Dakota American Legion. On his way to a Legion meeting in Indianapolis, he stopped in Chicago to meet with Griffith. His old coach explained his concern about the present and future of baseball and his hope for reviving interest in baseball among teenage boys. McCormack took the bait and asked Griffith if the American Legion would be the appropriate organization to develop such a program. That assumed, of course, that McCormick could sell the idea to the Legion. Griffith, himself an active Legion member, happily agreed, and the two began to make plans for converting the Legion to their cause.[12]

In the mid-1920s, the American Legion was far from the powerful organization it became after World War II. Its membership of 610,000 veterans in that decade seems minuscule compared to its peak of 3,325,000 in 1946. There had been veterans' organizations after the Civil War (The Grand Army of the Republic, and the Spanish-American War, the Veterans of Foreign Wars) that served as models. The Legion dated its beginning to a Paris meeting in February 1919 attended by some 20 officers selected by Lt. Colonel Theodore Roosevelt, Jr., and others. A member of the 1st division, Roosevelt commanded attention as the son of the recently deceased former President. That group included, among others: Lt. Colonel George S. White from General Headquarters of the American Expeditionary Forces, who had the ear of commander-in-chief John J. Pershing; Major Eric Fisher Wood, former editor of the *Portland Oregonian,* from the 88th Division; Lt. Colonel Franklin D'Olier, later president of the Prudential Insurance Company; and Lt. Colonel William "Wild Bill" Donovan, who later founded the O.S.S, the forerunner of the CIA. General John J. Pershing selected others to attend. The soldiers saw a need to improve morale among the war-weary members of the American Expeditionary Force and to establish a post-war veterans' organization.[13]

The initial group called for a general meeting in Paris on March 15, 1919, to formalize an organization. *Stars and Stripes* publicized the call to American soldiers in France. Nearly 2,000 officers and enlisted men met for what was at the time termed the Liberty League Caucus, but which came to be known as the Paris Caucus. Wood chaired that meeting initially but was replaced by General William G. Price. They agreed to a name: the American Legion beat out Veterans of the Great War. They approved a temporary constitution which called upon the organization "to perpetuate principles of Justice, Freedom and Democracy for which we fought," and created an Executive Committee to plan a general meeting in the United States. That meeting took place May 15–17, 1919, in St. Louis. It proved to be a rather disorganized affair, but it managed to confirm the principals set out at the Paris Caucus, adding "to perpetuate 100 percent Americanism" and attacking Bolsheviks and the Industrial Workers of the World (IWW). It set up offices in New York City and planned to obtain a charter from Congress. The Legion charter came from Congress in September 1919. In November 1919, a date selected to correspond to Armistice Day, the first anniversary of the end of hostilities in France, the formal founding convention met in Minneapolis. Among things accomplished at that first convention were an agreement to remain nonpartisan in American politics, the establishment of an Americanism Commission, and a vote to move the organization headquarters to Indianapolis, Indiana, where it remains. Officially the Legion would be a patriotic and mutual help organization. After Teddy Roosevelt, Jr., made clear he did not want the post, Franklin D'Olier of Pennsylvania was elected as the first National Commander of the Legion.[14]

The Legion was founded on "four pillars." These included veterans' affairs and rehabilitation, national security, Americanism, and children and youth. It eventually became a powerful lobbying group for veterans' rights and opposed to anything that could be considered "Bolshevism" or un–American. The preamble to the Legion constitution called upon its members "to foster and perpetuate a 100 percent Americanism." No one was quite sure what "Americanism" meant, but it did not include Bolsheviks, radicals, leftists, and immigrants who worked to subvert "the American way of life." Initially, the Legion maintained an isolationist position in world affairs and officially opposed a large standing army, although it supported military preparedness including universal military training. The Legion pushed for and gained Congressional approval for additional payments to veterans and the creation in August 1921 of the U.S. Veterans Bureau, a forerunner of the Department of Veterans Affairs.[15]

The Legion gained a certain notoriety at about the same time as the Minneapolis convention. In Centralia, Washington, an armed conflict between local Legion members and the local Industrial Workers of the World (IWW) put the Legion on page one of most American newspapers. In that conflict, four Legion members were killed and one "Wobblie" was lynched. Subsequently, 12 IWW members were convicted of murder. Throughout the 1920s, the Legion continued as a leader in attacking left-wing politics. The national organization, however, left issues of race to state and local groups, thereby assuring segregation and exclusion of African Americans in much of the country.[16]

Throughout the 1920s, the Legion served a strong social function. Members kept busy building, buying, and decorating clubhouses in cities and towns across the country. There veterans could gather, drink, network, and socialize. The Legion gained publicity as local Legion groups campaigned against speakers and publications it considered un–American. Locals worked to deny public forums to speakers whose views it considered seditious or un–American. But most members busy putting their lives back together after the war were simply happy to have a place of their own to socialize. Membership continued to grow.[17]

Frank McCormick, true to his word, first took the proposal he and Griffith had worked out to the 1925 South Dakota American Legion convention meeting in Milbank, South Dakota. There he asked the state group to pass a resolution urging the national American Legion to create a summer baseball league for young boys. McCormick argued that a baseball program would allow the Legion to take "a bunch of softies" and to "transform them into a bunch of hard-fisted fellows." Griffith attended the meeting to speak for the proposal. He asked the Legion to "assist in the training of young Americans through our athletic games." Such a program would "teach courage and respect, sportsmanship and citizenship." McCormick, Griffith, and like-minded supporters of sandlot baseball for teenagers held unspoken assumptions. They aimed their program at boys, specifically white boys, aged 14–17. The South Dakota convention approved the proposal with little debate. McCormick did not stop there. In neighboring Minnesota, he urged the state Legion convention to approve and support the program. Since scattered American Legion posts around the Gopher state had organized baseball teams since 1923, the state convention readily agreed to sponsor a statewide program of what it termed "junior baseball."[18]

While lobbying the South Dakota Legion convention, McCormick brought in Leonard B. "Stub" Allison, a former football, basketball, and baseball great at Carleton College, who was head football coach at the University of South Dakota (1922–1926). In the 1930s, he became coach of the University of California football team, winning the Rose Bowl and the unofficial national championship in 1937. Allison proved crucial in rounding up the necessary votes. He proved especially effective in convincing the Americanism Commission of the Legion to support the program. The resolution establishing American Legion baseball referenced the arguments of both Allison and Griffith. The authorizing legislation, Resolution 482, read:

> Athletic competitions conducted under proper direction are the best-known means of teaching boys good sportsmanship, an essential of good citizenship, and in addition have genuine civic value. Whereas a more physically fit citizenship can be obtained by extending the benefits of athletic training to the greatest possible number of boys and young men, a large percentage of whom are not receiving adequate athletic training at present.

The resolution obligated the Legion to "inaugurate and conduct base ball [*sic*] leagues and tournaments for local championships, and that the local champion be given opportunity to compete in departmental [state], sectional and regional tournaments." At the pinnacle of these tournaments would be "a junior world championship baseball series to be conducted at each national convention."[19]

Legionnaires, however, needed a higher justification for spending their time and money than either supporting the revival of baseball among teenagers or turning them into real men, even though both of these were worthy goals. A more stirring goal was the "promotion of positive Americanism and teaching our young people love of country." "Americanism" had become a watchword in Legion circles since the 1919 Red Scare, and it was posited in opposition to communism and Bolshevism. Many Legion members clung to the anti-radical, anti–Bolshevik concerns even after the return to normalcy. National Legion Commander James A. Drain had no trouble backing the resolution once it linked baseball and Americanism.[20]

Given its new purpose, responsibility for implementing and running the Legion baseball program logically went to the Americanism Commission of the Legion. The goal of the Legion's Junior Baseball program would not be to develop baseball players for organized baseball, or to revive the game, although those might be acceptable by-products. Rather, the desired result was to develop citizens through a program that would teach boys to play by the rules and to know how to win or lose with dignity. It would "instill discipline, the type of discipline one doesn't learn in schools, the church, the home." Frank Clay Cross, director of the Legion's Americanism Commission, gladly accepted the Legion's new baseball program, but he had little interest in the details of the program.[21]

Given Cross's lack of interest, for all practical purposes the Legion baseball program fell into the hands of Dan Sowers, Assistant Americanism Director, and Griffith, who continued to involve himself in Legion affairs. Many loose ends remained to be decided. To aid the Legion, in August 1925, Griffith appointed Harry Butler, an officer in the National American Athletic Federation, to work out the organizational structure for the Legion's embryonic baseball program. At that time, among other things, confusion reigned about who would pay for what. McCormick, Griffith, Sowers, and others involved in establishing the program very much wanted a tournament that would culminate during the American Legion's national convention. "Junior World Series" seemed a good name for this event. No "world" was actually involved, of course. The term was used in the same metaphorical way as the major leagues' World Series, actually meaning "American" but on a grander scale. The Legion would assume the costs of this final culminating event. Initially, teams could join Junior Baseball without any affiliation with a Legion post. Teams would need a sponsor to cover the costs through a series of local, state, regional, and sectional tournaments that the national office would arrange, but not pay for. Ideally, that would be a local Legion post, but not necessarily so.[22]

Griffith, Sowers, and McCormick prepared to make the presentation to the American Legion's national convention in Omaha, Nebraska, in October. Griffith clearly wished "to stimulate interest in baseball among boys 14–17." Beyond that goal, he believed the program would "develop patriotism, citizenship, courtesy toward opponents, qualities of fair play, sportsmanship and respect for law." These goals remained dear to Griffith's heart. Americanism was not high on Griffith's list, but he had no profound objection to the use of the term to facilitate baseball's revival.[23]

South Dakota and Minnesota got the jump on the rest of the country, being the first to declare teams in the new system. In South Dakota, Legion baseball got underway in 1925. At the urging of McCormack and Allison, posts in South Dakota sponsored no less than 925 teams. In doing so, the state established a pattern of local sponsorship that eventually swept the nation. Minnesota already had a strong system of boys' town teams dating to the turn of the century and a state amateur tournament organized and sponsored by the *St. Paul Pioneer Press* in 1924. So in Minnesota, Legion Junior Baseball initially functioned as feeders for the town clubs. In February 1926, the Minnesota Legion appointed Karl Raymond as its first Athletic Director for the state. He quickly established the first state American Legion Junior Baseball tournament in Mankato, where the state Legion convention was to be held. The Clarence A. Nelson Post 154 of Crosby proudly claimed the first Minnesota championship after beating St. Paul Navy-Marine.[24]

Outside the upper Midwest, more often than not, the first Junior Baseball teams existed outside the Legion post system. In Kentucky, for example, the first clubs to make application to appear in the Junior baseball league were church teams and Boy Scout teams. None of the teams in the first few Kentucky state tournaments had Legion affiliation. The *Louisville Courier Journal* underwrote the costs of the tournament, but each team arranged its own transportation. Louisiana, among other areas, had a strong system of YMCA-run baseball leagues. These teams arranged for local Legion posts to sponsor existing YMCA teams in the first few years of Legion baseball. The Playground and Recreation Association of America, which Luther Gulick and Henry Curtis, director of the Washington, D.C., playground system, had founded in 1905, adopted a broader agenda and urged municipal recreation systems to organize sandlot teams for boys. In many urban areas, especially in the Northeast, city recreation departments did organize teams and then searched for posts that would sign off on their application to participate in the tournament. Over 500 recreation departments around the country organized teams. The National Amateur Athletic Federation estimated that over 2,000 teams had been created in 1926.[25]

American Legion Junior Baseball officially began in 1926. The 2,000 teams from 15 states took the field under the auspices of the American Legion. They engaged in playoffs to determine local champions, then state, regional and sectional champions. That process winnowed the 2,000-plus down to four teams, who gathered in Philadelphia from October 11–15, 1926, for the first American Legion Junior Baseball World Series.[26]

The team from Yonkers, New York, took the first championship. Even before the concept of American Legion Junior baseball reached the New York suburbs, a group of Irish boys with names that included O'Brien, Fitzgerald, McDonald, Goodwin, Leahy, and McCormick organized a team at the Yonkers Recreation Department field. The Recreation supervisor, James E. McCrudden, found out about the Junior Baseball program and approached Cook Post 321 of Yonkers about sponsoring the team. Post commander James Arbuckle and Fred Kampfer, chairman of a newly created post baseball committee, agreed to sponsor the local boys. The post allowed the team to retain its nickname, the "Recs," but insisted on naming one of its own, William T. "Bill" Grieve, as coach. He proved a fortunate choice. A knowledgeable baseball man, Grieve made the game his career, and he eventually became an American League umpire (1938–1955). He insisted on holding his own tryouts. Some 75 boys showed up at Yonkers Recreation Department Field, but the final squad he selected consisted mostly of the original tough Irish boys, spiced by a couple of Italian kids.[27]

Donning new uniforms purchased by the post, with "YONKERS" in block letters across the shirt front and Yankees pinstripes highlighting their uniforms, the Recs were on their way. In college and professional sports, teams played a regular season schedule and then moved into playoffs. For Yonkers and others in the initial playoff, there was no regular season as such. They went directly to playoff games, where they either won or went home, single elimination style. To get to Philadelphia, the Recs first sailed through the New York state tourney, which they did with ease, beating a team from Southfield in the final. They moved on to Belmar, New Jersey, where they beat Passaic, New Jersey (11–5), then destroyed the Rhode Island champs, 7–1, on a no-hitter by pitching ace Ray House. A 12–11, ten-inning squeaker against Rutland, Vermont, provided Yonkers with its only close call. Finally, they knocked off St. Anthony's of Wilmington, Delaware, to win a trip to Philadelphia.[28]

The Recs enjoyed fine pitching from Maurice "Mary" O'Brien, Ray House, and Joe Fitzgerald. The rest of the lineup, largely Irish toughs, included catchers George Godwin and John Ferris; first baseman Jeff McDonald; second baseman Francis "Banky" Leahy; shortstop and captain Norbett "Bass" Landy; third baseman Johnny Dauterman; and outfielders John "Babe" McCormick, Arty Brill, John "Ruzz" Figura, and Patty Leahy. McCormick was their big bopper.[29]

The second team to qualify for the final four came from Springfield, Ohio, representing the Central States Region. The Springfield Eagles, as the team was known, dominated the Ohio state playoffs, toppling Hamilton, Armco (American Roller Mill Co.) of Middletown, tiny Ludlow, and Richmond. Springfield won its way into the Regional finals at

Parkway Field in Louisville, home of the American Association Colonels. The Eagles beat Chicago by the slimmest of margins, 6–5. The hometown favorite Ninaweh club of Louisville had defeated Indianapolis, 7–4. Springfield then downed the Louisville-based club to reach the Legion World Series.[30]

At the Western Regional in Sioux Falls, South Dakota, Post 81 of El Dorado, Kansas, emerged as champions. Located in south-central Kansas, El Dorado, with a population of 10,000, had been a booming oil town since the El Dorado oil field opened a decade earlier. Coach Russell Gill selected his team from boys on local teams from the company town of Oil Hill, and the hamlets of Towanda, Midian, Roselia, and Leon, as well as El Dorado itself. The team adopted the nickname Wildcats, a reference to oil rather than felines. Perhaps reflecting the dirty work of oil derricks, the team always looked grimy and dusty in their gray, wool uniforms with "LEGION 81" on their shirt fronts. The Wildcats captured the southern Kansas title, beating Independence by 7–3 and 6–4 scores. That earned them a spot in a best-of-three series for the state title against Hays. Two games were all El Dorado needed, beating Hays 9–5 and 12–7. Then they moved on to Sioux Falls, where they ran through Decatur, Texas, Crosby, Minnesota (7–4), and Beresford, South Dakota. Against Beresford, the Wildcats had to score six runs in the ninth inning to take a 9–7 victory.[31]

The fourth team in the Philadelphia World Series came out of the Pacific Northwest regional, where Pocatello, Idaho, captured the final spot. The Pocatello Razorbacks beat Idaho Falls in the state final and barely slipped past Salt Lake City in the sectional, 3–2 in 12 innings. Their modest coach, Ralph "Dube" Bisine, declared, "I don't know whether I manage them [the boys] or not." Although not certain about his influence, the boys did quite well and looked sporty in their pinstriped uniforms with a giant "P" on the left of their uniform shirtfronts. Pitcher/outfielder Clyde Raidy, outfielder Jack Crawford, shortstop Tim Wilson, outfielder Charlie Wilson, and first baseman Mike McGaugh carried the team.[32]

The first American Legion World Series was scheduled at the Sesquicentennial Exposition in October 1926. The idea for an Exposition had originated in the mind of department store magnate John Wanamaker (1832–1922), who was the last remaining member of the Centennial Exposition Planning Committee from the 1876 World's Fair. Wanamaker said its purpose was to celebrate the 150th anniversary of the Declaration of Independence. World War I, the Spanish flu of 1918, and internal dissention retarded planning for the event. Mayor J. Hampton Moore and Chamber of Commerce head Alba B. Johnson favored a commercial fair, while Edward W. Bok, editor of *Ladies' Home Journal,* and Cyrus H. K. Curtis, publishing magnate, wished to emphasize Philadelphia's role in American history and industry. When W. Freeland Kendrick became mayor in 1924, little planning had been accomplished, and whatever public enthusiasm had existed continued to wane. Kendrick and Republican political boss William Vare moved the site to South Philadelphia, north of the Navy Yard.[33]

An impressive array of buildings was ready by the Exposition's opening in May 1926. Five large exhibition halls provided indoor space for 31 states and nine countries. An 80-foot-high replica of the Liberty bell greeted visitors at the park's northern entrance at Broad Street and Packer Avenue. In addition, the exhibition boasted a 10,000-seat auditorium. Unfortunately, the planned 175-foot-tall "Tower of Light" did not get completed before funds ran out.[34]

The most impressive structure was the horseshoe-shaped Municipal Stadium (renamed John F. Kennedy Stadium in 1964). In September 1926, 125,000 rain-soaked fans attended the Jack Dempsey–Gene Tunney heavyweight boxing match there. The clean-cut Tunney upset the champion in a 10-round decision. Although the Dempsey-Tunney bout drew the largest crowd to an American sporting event up to then, attendance at the fair proved disappointing. The city lost $5.8 million on the venture.[35]

The first American Legion World Series (ALWS) took place in the rainy and disappointing summer of 1926. With almost no one in the stands of the massive stadium, the ALWS opened with a doubleheader on October 1. The boys' game proved far less attractive than a heavyweight boxing championship. Only 1,100 fans paid the admission price. Connie Mack, manager and owner of the Philadelphia Athletics, threw out the first ball and shook hands with all the players. In the first American Legion World Series game, Pocatello scored two runs in the ninth to top El Dorado, 9–7. Tim Wilson and Charlie Wilson paced Pocatello with two hits each. In the second game, Yonkers beat Springfield by an 8–2 score, thanks in large part to the 13 walks issued by Springfield pitchers. The

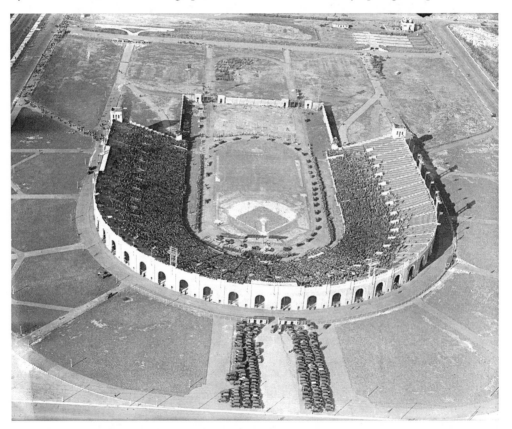

Sesquicentennial Stadium (1926), later renamed Municipal Stadium and still later JFK Stadium, held over 110,000 to see Gene Tunney capture the heavyweight boxing title from Jack Dempsey in the summer of 1926. Later in the summer, only 3,000 turned up for the first Legion championship won by Yonkers, New York. This photograph showing the diamond was taken a year after the first Legion World Series. The crowd is gathering to welcome Charles Lindbergh after his solo flight across the Atlantic (courtesy of the Hagley Museum and Library, Wilmington, Delaware).

Rec's pitching ace, Ray House, threw a tidy five-hitter. Jack McCormick, who collected two singles, was the only Rec with more than one base hit.[36]

Yonkers and Pocatello both won again on the second day. With just 200 people watching in the giant stadium, Yonkers enjoyed an 18–1 laugher in destroying El Dorado. McCormick slammed two home runs and scored four runs. Pitcher John Fitzgerald, relying on his curve ball, threw a three-hitter. Pocatello, in its second tight game, slipped by Springfield, 8–7. First baseman John Fitzgerald picked up three hits. Tim Wilson scored the winning run on an infield out. Springfield, however, gave the game away by committing eight errors.[37]

For the final game, attendance jumped to 3,000, including Major League Baseball Commissioner Kenesaw Mountain Landis. Yonkers clearly established its preeminence in teenage baseball as the Recs clobbered Pocatello, 23–6, to take the Junior Baseball title. Yonkers pounded out 17 hits, including another home run by McCormick, who earned his nickname, "Babe." No most valuable player was selected, but had it been, the clear choice would have been McCormack, who batted .583 for the tournament. That average stood as the World Series record for the highest batting average until 1972.[38]

Despite the relative success of Legion Junior Baseball in 1926, the future of the program remained uncertain. Rather quickly after the first of the year, Legion leaders made clear their intention to hold the Legion's national convention for 1927 in Paris, France. The leadership understood there would not be enough funds both to go abroad and to underwrite a national baseball tournament; there was no question that baseball would have to go. Nevertheless, in December 1926, the Legion's national office issued a press release that the Junior baseball program would continue. Exactly how it would continue was not made clear.[39]

Even without financial support or a World Series to entice teams, several states managed to play through the summer of 1927. In Kentucky, the *Louisville Courier-Journal,* a strong supporter of Junior Baseball in 1926, sponsored a state "Junior Baseball Tournament." Teams in the tournament had no affiliation with any Legion post, and there would be no further play beyond the state finals. South Dakota prided itself as the origin of "Junior Baseball," but its 1927 tournament, like that of Kentucky, had no affiliation with the Legion.

Despite the interest demonstrated in 1927 and the relative success in 1926, it was not a given that Legion baseball would continue in 1928. Fortunately, during the empty year of 1927, Legion leadership changed. Responsibility for the baseball program shifted to the new Director of the Americanism Commission, Auburn Dan Sowers (no one ever called him Auburn), who had run the Legion baseball program since its inception, without the title. He quite rightly has been called the "father of American Legion Baseball." Born in Pocahontas, Virginia, in 1895, and raised in West Virginia, he attended Emory and Henry College in southwestern Virginia before enlisting in the Army during World War I. Following the war, he graduated with a law degree from Cumberland College in Tennessee. He stayed in the Cumberland mountains area of south-central Kentucky, where he practiced law in Burkesville. In the summer of 1926, he went to Indianapolis as the Legion's assistant director of Americanism.

Despite his life in the mountains, Sowers was no hillbilly. "Portly and aggressive," one historian called him. Players referred to him as "very bright, confident, delightful." During the Great War, he had served in the ambulance corps before becoming an editor for *Stars and Stripes,* the Army newspaper. "Stout," the Army labeled him; "corpulent," some called him. He may well have topped 325 pounds. Sporting granny glasses and a bow tie, he looked the part of a college English professor. Upon his ascension to leadership of the Americanism division, he advised the whole organization to quit trying to prevent public speakers and asking public authorities to look after suspected treason. Never a player himself, Sowers loved baseball. Despite his weight, Sowers possessed boundless energy and a salesman's knack for getting others to accept his ideas. In 1927 and 1928, he threw himself into the task of creating a viable baseball program.[40]

Boys in the 14–17 age group remained Sowers' target audience. He advanced the notion that Legion ball should "give every lad ... who wants to play the opportunity." The reality of competition quickly ended that ideal. He had greater success with his desire to teach sportsmanship

Dan Sowers, often called "the Father of American Legion Baseball." As the Legion's Americanism Commission's director, he orchestrated Legion ball and its World Series in its first years. He returned in the depth of the Depression to put the World Series on sound financial footing (courtesy the American Legion).

and citizenship through respect for rules, fair play, loyalty to the organization, teamwork, and what he called "gameness." He believed the most valuable product of the sport was the development of *character* in the boys. Baseball, he opined, provided "a sufficient attraction to interest the American boy and implant in his character those elements of good citizenship." Players learned tolerance, respect, teamwork, and loyalty while at the same time developing virile and strong bodies. Nothing could be more important for the future because those youngsters "are steadily marching on to manhood to take over the reins of this country."[41]

Sowers did not mind travel and spent days on the road, talking up the new product. His efforts brought results. By the end of summer 1927, teams had formed or re-formed in 15 states. Then he committed his energies to reviving Junior Baseball in 1928. Along the way, he assigned each state a quota for the 1928 World Series. He understood that Legion ball needed outside funding to keep going. He turned to Major League Baseball. Sowers had met Commissioner Kenesaw Mountain Landis at the 1926 Legion World Series, and so knew that Landis liked the Legion and supported its anti-radical political agenda as well as its baseball agenda. Sowers, an aggressive salesman, approached Landis, who arranged a meeting with the presidents of the American and National Leagues in mid–February. Sowers made his pitch, and he knocked it out of the park. The country was experiencing unparalleled prosperity in 1927, leaving the major leagues on sound financial footing and with a generous spirit. The two major leagues agreed to donate $25,000 each to support sectional, regional, and national tournaments. That number coincided with what Sowers needed. For good measure, the majors agreed to pay for the winner of the American Legion Junior World Series to attend two games of the major leagues' World Series. Sowers was delighted.[42]

With funding assured, Sowers took to the road in the spring and early summer of 1928. He attempted to visit every state, always expressing confidence in the coming season. He spoke to civic groups including Rotary and Elks clubs, fire departments and police departments. He spent March and April on the road, visiting places as diverse as Phoenix, Los Angeles, San Francisco, Spokane, Seattle, Salt Lake City, Denver, Louisville, Atlanta, Richmond, Wilmington, Philadelphia, and Boston. In May he anticipated that 175,000 boys would participate in the 1928 World Series tournament. State championships were played in 44 states. Connie Mack, the "Grand Old Man of baseball," became an outspoken supporter. Legion ball, Mack opined, "would do more for the future of baseball in America than anything I can imagine." Mack's longtime rival, Charles Comiskey, owner of the Chicago White Sox, offered the use of his park, Comiskey Park, as site for the 1928 American Legion World Series.[43]

In June of 1928, the Legion featured Sowers in an Abian "Wally" Wallgren cartoon that appeared in *The American Legion Monthly*. In the first frame, boys are running wild in the sandlot with no organization, chased both by the police and housewives with rolling pins. Sowers says, "It's a shame. These boys need our help. This is a job for the Americanism Commission." In the second frame, Sowers says, "Say boys! How would you like to be formed into a real team in the American Legion Junior Baseball league?" The boys jump on the idea with enthusiasm. Sowers intones, "Now that you've helped to clean up and make a regulation diamond out of this old lot ... what say we get down to real ball playing." The boys in uniform are ready to go. In the final frame, Sowers, now with a big cigar in his mouth, tells the uniformed players, "the Code of Sportsmanship, fair play, team work and honest effort must prevail."[44]

To encourage more entries, Sowers made it clear that teams could enter the Legion playoffs even if unrelated to Legion posts; but, of course, he worked to hook such teams up with a local post. Civic organizations of all kinds, church groups, boys' clubs, and city playgrounds organized teams. In Lafayette, Kentucky, for example, the city tournament consisted of a variety of teams: the Hoosiers, Lafayette Cubs, Seventh Street Sluggers, South End Cubs, St. Ann's Juniors, and St. Ann Wildcats. With 19 Legion posts in the city, it proved easy to hook one of these squads up with a sponsoring Legion post. In Louisville, 120 teams entered the local Junior baseball tournament. Beyond the local level, lining up sites for 48 state tournaments, 12 regional, and two sectional tourneys kept Sowers traveling through the summer. To his surprise, he found no shortages of men willing, indeed anxious, to volunteer for the program. Sowers estimated that over 300,000 boys were enrolled on Legion teams. He lined up regionals at Seattle, Oakland, Salt Lake City, Saint Paul, Omaha, Shreveport, Cleveland, and Louisville, as well as Meridian, Mississippi, Wilmington, Delaware, Central Falls, Rhode Island, and Worcester, Massachusetts. He made the decision to reduce the number of teams in the kids' World Series from four to two, one from east of the Mississippi River and the other from the west. This two-team final would more closely align the American Legion World Series [ALWS] version with the major league World Series.[45]

Even before the playoffs got beyond the state level, Sowers came face to face with his first serious crisis. At a Vermillion County, Indiana, playoff game between the Blanford Cubs and the Clinton Baptists on June 18, the issue of girls playing raised its head. The game went 12 innings before Blanford's second baseman won the game with a walk-off single. Clinton lodged a formal protest because the game-winning hit came off the bat of Margaret Gisolo. Because she was undeniably a girl, Clinton maintained she was an ineligible player, hence they should be awarded the victory. The protest worked its way to A. V. Springfellow, director of the Indiana tournament, who did not want to deal with the prickly issue and passed it along to Robert W. Bushee, state athletic director for the Legion. He suspended Gisolo for six days, an irrational decision, and handed it off to Sowers. Although Judge Landis had nothing directly to do with American Legion baseball, Sowers reasoned that Landis was the *commissioner of baseball,* so he took the issue to the highest authority. Landis, noting the contribution of women to the war effort and finding nothing in the Legion rules to prohibit girls from playing, decided that Gisolo should be allowed to play. Landis and Sowers issued a joint statement saying the American Legion did not "contemplate the participation of girls but nothing in the rules bar them." With the support of baseball's czar, Sowers denied Clinton's appeal, thus allowing Gisolo to continue playing for her Cubs.[46]

Margaret Gisolo was a 14-year-old girl who choked halfway up on the bat, but who was a natural athlete. Once reinstated, she helped Blanford win the district and the Indiana state championships. After Blanford beat Terre Haute, 6–5, for the state title, the losing team gave their uniform jerseys to the scruffy victors. At the Legion World Series, the National Americanism Commission unabashedly and unapologetically prohibited girls from playing. Margaret Gisolo went on to graduate from Indiana State University and later earned a Master's degree at New York University. In summers from 1930 through 1934, she played on a girls' traveling baseball team, the All-Star Rangers out of Chicago. During World War II, she served in the WAVES. She eventually became a university teacher. After a short stint at Indiana University of Pennsylvania, she turned her athletic talents to tennis and dance, and she put together what became recognized as one of the country's top dance programs at Arizona State University.[47]

Sowers established the 1928 East regional at Louisville, his favorite venue, for August 22–24, and a West regional at Denver for August 28–30, each with six teams. The six teams that gathered at Parkway Field in Louisville included Browder-Hoskins of Louisville, Central Falls, Rhode Island, Worcester, Massachusetts, Meridian, Mississippi, Cardinal of Wilmington, Delaware, and a team from Panama. The Panama boys, sons of Americans working there, gained a spot because they made an appeal to Sowers, just as a team from Cleveland, who seemingly gained the right to be there by beating Chicago Marine, was disqualified for using an over-age player. Central Falls, Rhode Island, got to Louisville by knocking off defending champion Yonkers. The Rhode Island team, however, quickly fell to the hometown Louisville boys, 5–1. Louisville then pounded Panama, 12–2. Worcester, however, came out of Louisville as the champions of the East. They beat Meridian, victors over Wilmington in the first round, behind pitching ace Wilson Dunlap, who threw a two-hit shutout. Then they faced the tough Browder-Hoskins team of Louisville. Worcester slipped past Louisville, 3–2. Third baseman Eddie Curran, shortstop Andy Kazlankas, and Wilson Dunlap, the winning pitcher, provided big bats for Worcester.[48]

At the Western playoffs in Denver, it quickly became apparent that the Oakland club, sponsored by Montgomery Ward department store, stood head and shoulders above

Margret Gisolo, a 14-year-old girl who led Blanford to the 1928 Indiana state championship, becoming a cause célèbre in the process. The attention she garnered led to the Legion formally excluding girls from playing American Legion baseball (courtesy the Gisolo Family).

the rest. They outscored opponents in the tournament, 186 to 6, and batted over .310 as a team. Before the season started, when coach Leroy Sharpe put out the call for try-outs, over 100 boys had shown up. The 14 who made the cut were from Fremont High School and Oakland Tech. Sowers, who spent a great deal of time with the Oakland team, thought they embodied the best of Legion ball because the team included Protestants,

Catholics, and Jews, and it included boys from nine different national backgrounds. The Ward's pitching aces, righty Al Silva and hard-throwing lefty Charles Hardt, chalked up a combined 14 shutouts in 19 games. Oakland went to the World Series as the clear favorite. In addition to the strong pitching, they had six players hitting .333 or better, and they owned a tight defense. Their best hitters were third baseman Einar Sorenson, who batted .422 during the season and .500 in the ALWS and who would spend six years in the minors; outfielder Dan "Bud" Hafey, who made the big show for three seasons; captain and center fielder Weido Lancione; and catcher Arleigh Williams, who went on to become a football All-American at the University of California, where he later became Dean of Students.[49]

Sharp's Montgomery Ward club went undefeated on its way to Comiskey Park. Oakland marched through the California tourney in Los Angeles. At the Phoenix regional, they beat the best from Nevada, Arizona, and New Mexico, knocking off Reno Rotary in the final game. They then took the train to Denver for the Western finals against teams that included teams sponsored by the *Seattle Times* and the *Salt Lake City Telegram*, John D. Parcq Post 406 of St. Paul, Tesar and Tesar of Omaha, and Lowe-McFarlane from the Shreveport YMCA League. Oakland continued its domination. Tesar beat Shreveport, 10–6, but lost to Oakland, 12–0. Oakland next faced St. Paul Post 406, winners over Salt Lake City (13–5) and Seattle (6–4). Oakland's pitching again dominated as the Wards prevailed, 5–0, over St. Paul, behind Al Silva's five-hit pitching.[50]

On paper, Oakland had the stronger team in the ALWS as the Wards and Worcester prepared for the best-of-three finals in Chicago. Both teams had spent an extra four days in Indianapolis, resting and practicing. Unfortunately for Oakland, their catcher, Albert Swick, had to be hospitalized in Indianapolis due to a leg infection. Both teams threw their aces in the first game. Worcester's Wilson Dunlap brought a record of 21 wins and just a single loss while averaging 10 strikeouts per game. Oakland's Silva had allowed only two runs in 67 innings of tournament play. In addition to Dunlap, Worcester brought four players with batting averages over .500 for the tournament. These were third baseman Eddie Curran, shortstop Andy Kazlanskas, first baseman Paul Shannon, and center fielder Mallett, who hit .510. What they lacked was a strong second pitcher.[51]

The Oakland club started out the 1928 World Series with its nerves showing. They committed errors on the first two batters. First, the shortstop flubbed a ground ball; then the first baseman dropped a routine throw. After that, they settled down. Silva got the next three batters and proved to be the better pitcher. He allowed just five Worcester hits and no runs in a 4–0 shutout, while he contributed an RBI double to help his own cause. Oakland picked up two runs in the third inning on Sorensen's double, and two more in the fourth on RBIs by Hafey and Silva.[52]

In game two, before 3,000 fans, Oakland proved even more dominant than in game one. Williams got four hits, Sorenson went three-for-four, and right fielder Hans Hansen batted in three runs to lead the offense. Hardt walked six but allowed only two runs, just his third run allowed in 77 innings of tournament play. He pitched a four-hitter. Oakland captured the 1928 national championship by a 12–2 score. That left Oakland undefeated for the entire season and playoffs. Oakland's 177 runs for the tournament, against six by their opponents, left little doubt of their dominance. After the Junior Series, the team traveled to New York, courtesy of major league baseball, to see a World Series game. The experience had created strong bonds and memories the team members never forgot. For at least the next 30 years the team held an annual reunion to which they always invited Sowers.[53]

In the off-season and through the summer of 1929, Sowers spent most of his time on the road. His efforts to spread Legion ball from coast to coast led him to visit all 48 states. In his talks around the country, he reiterated his commitment to developing good men with respect for rules and law, who learned "sportsmanship, teamwork and democracy." He set the goal of enrolling over 300,000 boys, double the number who played in 1928, by giving each state a quota to meet.[54]

The issue of race did arise during Sowers' years, but he managed to brush it aside. In his February 1929 article in *American Legion Monthly,* he stated that there is "no standard of human excellence save merit." He continued: "Legion principles are certainly that there is no such thing as segregation." This statement, of course, would not withstand even cursory critical scrutiny. When Sowers was pushed by St. Louis post commander Walter Lowe, who knew that the Michigan state champion had an African American catcher, Sowers responded, "there has never been any ruling from this office barring Negro players from our tournaments." That seemed to resolve the issue for the moment.[55]

Sowers had reasons to be quietly proud of his product. In 1929, for the first time Junior Baseball had teams in all 48 states and the District of Columbia. In a major public relations coup, Sowers lined up the National Broadcasting Company (NBC) to broadcast the 1929 finals coast-to-coast over 38 stations. Graham McNamee, the country's premier play-by-play announcer, happily agreed to man the microphone for the series. As an adopted son of Kentucky, it was not surprising that Louisville was Sowers' favored site, or that he again selected Parkway Field, home of the American Association's Louisville Colonels, as the host for the 1929 Legion World Series.[56]

The New Orleans White Sox, composed of boys from Samuel T. Peters High School, was led by a 19-year-old coach, Chester Frest, a pre-med student at Loyola University of New Orleans. Frest relied on first baseman Leon Antoine, second baseman/pitcher Frank Frederico, and pitcher Savvi Carboni. New Orleans came through tough regionals in Shreveport, Louisiana, in mid–August and sectionals in Colorado Springs, Colorado. At the Southwest Regional, the White Sox fought their way past state champions from Oklahoma City, Little Rock, and Waco. Moving on to Colorado Springs, they cruised past Albuquerque and Mill Valley, California, before squeaking past Portland, Oregon, by the slimmest of margins, 6–5. In the Western final, Carboni pitched three-hit ball for seven innings in relief and collected three hits himself.[57]

In the 1929 World Series, New Orleans faced a team from South Buffalo, New York, Post 721, known as the South Buffalo Burkes, after its sponsor, Burke Brothers Men's Store, an institution in South Buffalo. The southern third of Buffalo was a tough, industrial area with a population traditionally Irish and working class. Work, as well as dust and grime, came at Bethlehem Steel and Republic Steel. Nine of the 14 Burkes players attended St. Joseph Collegiate Institute, a college preparatory school run by the Christian Brothers. The Burkes' coach, Joe Brown, doubled as coach at Saint Joe's. The South Buffalo boys sailed through New York Legion competition, beating Syracuse 8–0 in the state final. Regionals at New Britain, Connecticut, came next. Then they moved on to the Eastern finals, played in Washington's Griffith Stadium. Teams from Atlanta, Browder-Hoskins of Louisville, and Lisbon Falls, Maine, joined Buffalo in the capital. Lisbon Falls bested Louisville, and South Buffalo slipped by Atlanta, both by 5–4 scores. South Buffalo then topped Lisbon Falls, 6–4, to gain a berth in the Junior World Series.[58]

Previous Legion World Series had been scheduled as best two out of three games, as was the case in 1929, but winners had always swept in two straight games. The 1929

Series was the closest to date. Burke Brothers took the first game, 6–4, before a modest crowd of 2,217. Captain Bill Joyce picked up the win and contributed a strong bat as well. New Orleans came back with power in game two. New Orleans got four runs in the first inning, but Burke Brothers scored five of their own. Not to be outdone, New Orleans put up six more runs in the second. After giving up ten runs in two innings, the White Sox called second baseman Frank Frederica to the mound, and he proved the difference in the game. He held the Buffalo lads scoreless for seven innings while his teammates posted six more runs to salt away the win. Buffalo brought Bill Joyce, who boasted a 14–0 record, back to pitch the deciding game of the 1929 American Legion World Series. The Bisons scored six runs in the third inning to break a 2–2 tie, and this time they never looked back. Burly catcher Joe Smith had four hits and four RBIs, second baseman Ray Charmat chipped in three hits, and Joyce drove in two runs. New Orleans contributed four errors to the losing cause. The win gave South Buffalo a final record of 25–1.[59]

Following the series, Sowers presented the winning team with a trophy, now named the Howard P. Savage Trophy in memory of the past National Legion Commander. The South Buffalo team included first baseman Coral Wojtkoniak; second baseman Ray Scharmach; third baseman Don Jacobi; shortstop John Ford; and outfielders Fran Russert, Walt Krocznski, and 14-year-old Cy O'Connell. Russert was the uncle of popular television newscaster and long-time moderator of "Meet the Press" Tim Russert. Other team members were catcher Joe Smith and pitchers Bill Joyce, Joe Berger, and James "Mugsy" Flynn. who later became Father James of Batavia, New York. In addition to trophies, they received gold watches and would get to see four World Series games.[60]

After the stock market crash in the fall of 1929, Sowers announced that he was resigning effective January 1, 1930, to take a position with the Henry L. Doherty's Cities Service Oil Company in New York. He could look at his work as head of the American Legion baseball program with great pride. He had seen the program expand to all 48 states and pull in over 300,000 players. He had put Legion baseball on sound financial footing. The *Louisville Courier-Journal* described Sowers as "jovial, talented, capable, master of men, boys and difficulties." He was, according to the paper, "responsible almost singlehandedly for the rapid spread of the sport from coast to coast." Now he resolved to enter industrial public relations. In truth, he had to be exhausted from three years crisscrossing the country from tiny hamlets to big cities. The Legion elected him to the Board of Directors of the Americanism Commission in the hope of keeping him involved, and under some pressure he agreed to stay on until March 1, 1930.[61]

Russell Cook, former athletic director of Central Normal College (Canterbury College after 1946) in Danville, Indiana, succeeded Sowers as director of Americanism. A native of Boswell, Indiana, Cook had graduated from DePauw College in Greencastle, Indiana, before enlisting in the army during World War I. Thirty-five years old, he had logged eight years as coach and athletic director at Central. He brought a special interest in public education, both in increasing literacy and fostering "Americanism" in schools. Charles M. Wilson served as assistant national director under Cook.[62]

In the off-season of 1929–1930, a novel by Harold M. Sherman titled *Batter Up! A Story of American Legion Junior Baseball* shone a bright spotlight on Legion baseball. Sherman credited Sowers for the philosophical grounding of his story, which he saw as a "counterattack on jealousy, fraction, selfishness and class rivalry." At its best, Legion baseball managed "to imbue in the youth of the nation unselfishness, teamwork and cooperation." It was the story of a fractious team from Traverse City, Michigan. The fictional team, however, was split between the Factory District—sons of working-class families—and the Lincoln Boulevard crowd—the "nice" side of town. After class divisions and jealousy threatened to rip the team apart, they persevered and actually won the national championship. Speaking on nationwide radio, the team captain proclaimed, "from now on Lincoln Boulevard and Factory Avenue are going to be one street." Legion leaders never liked the concept of class; it threatened to turn into class warfare. For his part, Sowers had to love the endorsement.[63]

Junior baseball reached new heights in 1930. Russell Cook estimated that a record 500,000 boys participated in Legion play that summer. That represented a 66 percent jump from the pre–Crash total. By the middle of the 1930s, graduates of Legion ball were appearing on the rosters of major league clubs. Clearly, Legion ball was on its way to becoming an established institution. NBC, with Bill Munday at the mike, broadcast the ALWS live.

In 1930, teams from Baltimore and New Orleans met for the American Legion World Series at Russwood Field in Memphis, August 28–30. Russwood was home to the Memphis Chicks of the Southern Association from 1901 until destroyed by fire in 1960. Both Legion clubs came out of solid, established programs. The Baltimore and Ohio Railroad Post 81 team, known as the Railroaders, had won Maryland state titles in 1928 and 1929. In 1930 they disposed of Elkton, 6–0, for the state title. The Railroaders featured an outstanding pitcher in Charlie "Bullet" Burrows. The hitting came from slick and quick first baseman Norm "Nutty" Weiner, leadoff hitter George Reichart, cleanup man Andy Bolognese, third baseman Bill Steiner, and captain and right fielder Herb "Lefty" Newberg.[64]

The New Orleans team had a new sponsor in 1930, Sizeler Brothers, a real estate company, but was essentially the Samuel T. Peters High School team that had finished second in ALWS the previous year. Their leading slugger, first baseman and captain Leon Antoine, was the most notable returnee from the 1929 club. Second baseman Erwin Breaux came on strong once the tournament got underway to give the Eagles a second big bat.[65]

The B&O team, after beating Elkton for the Maryland state title, had a short jaunt to Hagerstown, Maryland, for its regional tournament against Clayton, the champions of Delaware, Morgantown, West Virginia, Uniontown, Pennsylvania, and Spengle Post of the District of Columbia. Uniontown, Pennsylvania, and its African American pitcher, Hasco Talley, gave the B&O club its toughest game before the Railroaders emerged with a 4–2 victory. In the Eastern Sectional at Charlottesville, Virginia, they had an easy time knocking out Manchester, New Hampshire, by a 9–1 score.[66]

New Orleans Sizeler Brothers experienced a tough time reaching the finals. They took out Tulsa (13–3) and the Galveston Pirates (5–3) in the Shreveport Regional. Breaux homered against Tulsa and drove in three runs in the Galveston game. At the Sectional in Colorado Springs, New Orleans came from three runs down in the ninth inning to beat Salina, Kansas, 7–6, in 11 innings. In the final they squeezed past Long Beach, 6–5.[67]

In the opening game of the 1930 American Legion World Series at Memphis, New Orleans and Baltimore finished regulation play tied 4–4. New Orleans got two runs in the first inning, but Baltimore knotted the score with two in the seventh. Both teams scored two runs in the eighth. In the tenth inning, Nutty Weiner led off for B&O with a single. He advanced to third on consecutive singles and came home with the winning run on Charlie "Bullet" Burrows' squeeze bunt. Their captain, Leon Antoine, had three hits for

New Orleans, and George Reichard had a like number for Baltimore. In the second game, Weiner continued his heroics. He contributed five RBI in Baltimore's 10–4 win. The Railroaders scored five runs in the fourth inning to break open a 3–3 game. With the bases loaded, Weiner singled home two runs. His theft of second allowed a third run to score. Weiner scored when catcher Roland Kaun tripled. Kaun then scored on a wild pitch. Herb Newberg had three hits for the Railroaders. Baltimore's B & O Railroaders had won the 1930 Legion championship, two games to none.[68]

The following year, 1931, the American Legion World Series moved to Houston, Texas. It witnessed the greatest pitching performance in Legion history, the first night game, and the largest crowd in ALWS history to that date. South Chicago Post 493 looked the favorite going into the ALWS. The South Chicago lads beat Marine Post of Chicago, as captain and pitching ace Jimmy McKirchy struck out 18 opposing batters. They finalized their state title by first beating Berwyn for the Cook County crown. Then they ousted downstate winner Zeigler, the defending state champ, in a two-of-three series at Wrigley Field. In the regionals at Ottumwa, Iowa, they had little competition, beating Highland Park, Iowa, 15–0, and St. Louis, 11–1, in the finals of the four-state tourney. In the Western finals at Colorado Springs, they took out Albuquerque, 4–0, and Seattle, 4–2. In the regional final they met Stockton, winner over back-to-back Western champion New Orleans. South Chicago took out Stockton, 8–6, to advance to the ALWS. Chicago Coach G. D. Applegran had the luxury of calling on two outstanding pitchers. McKirchy possessed a sharp breaking curve. His second pitching ace, slim, bespectacled Al Lawler, threw hard and had good command of his pitches.[69]

Columbia, South Carolina, Post 6 became the first Southern team other than New Orleans to make the World Series. Columbia had beaten Charleston, South Carolina, by a 2–1 margin in 11 innings. Columbia struggled in their Regional before beating Gastonia, North Carolina, 6–5. Roanoke Rapids, North Carolina, and Danville, Virginia, fell by the slimmest of margins, 5–4, Danville in 13 innings. At the Sectionals in Manchester, New Hampshire, Columbia enjoyed a 9–0 laughter against the host before beating Bridgeport, Connecticut, 5–2, on pitcher Kirby Higbe's two-hitter. In the final, they sailed past Jackson, Mississippi, 13–1.[70]

In 1931 the World Series organizers in Houston scheduled the opening game for the evening of August 28 to show off their new state-of-the-art lighting system. The previous summer, in July 1930, the Houston Buffs had installed one of the earliest lighting systems in baseball, and they were understandably proud of the new technology. The Columbia boys, never having played under lights and fearing arc lights would put them at a disadvantage, protested the decision. In the end, cooler heads prevailed, and Columbia agreed to play at night. The night game attracted a record 7,000 howling fans. Columbia's fears proved well founded as South Chicago scored six runs in the first inning. After that explosion, Chicago pitcher Jimmy McKirchy cruised to a 13–4 romp.[71]

To Columbia's delight, the second game was scheduled for the afternoon. They sent a tough kid named Kirby Higbe to the mound. Higbe, however, was not a poster child for Legion ball. His biographer described him as "a hell raiser all his life" who had "a taste for alcohol and a lust for living." He had dropped out of school after the seventh grade to work as a messenger boy for the Southern Railroad and pitch in the local National Guard league against older boys and men. By age 16 he had developed his lifelong taste for alcohol which the Legion coach, Paul Autry, saw as reason not to want Higbe on the team. The youngster threw fast, but he was not always sure where his pitches would go. His talent, however, proved hard to resist. Autry relented after the season started and brought Higbe on as the ace of his pitching staff.[72]

In the 1931 ALWS, South Chicago countered with rail-thin, bespectacled Al Lawler. The two pitchers dueled through 13 scoreless innings. Higbe struck out 10 but Lawler whiffed an ALWS record 17 batters, while allowing just five hits. In the 14th inning, South Chicago catcher Wally Holem led off with a sharp single to right. He stole second and moved to third on a throwing error by the catcher. Two walks loaded the bases. Red Harrassingovicz, a Polish-born second baseman, bounced a high hopper through the mound that scored Holem for the game-winner. South Chicago merited the title of 1931 champions of sandlot baseball.[73]

Despite losing, Higbe was the main show in the ALWS. One sportswriter wrote, "It was a brand of baseball seldom seen outside the big leagues. Time and again Higbe fought out of holes with cool courage." As soon as Higbe got home to Columbia, the 16-year-old signed a contract with the Pittsburgh Pirates for a $500 signing bonus. Exuding confidence, he promised the hometown folks, "I'm going up there and do just like I did down here." His 16-year-old self-assurance jarred with the reality of professional baseball. At Tulsa of the Texas League, he was wild and ineffective before being sent home. After that disappointment, he knocked around the South Carolina Textile Leagues and minor leagues until late in the 1937 season, when the Chicago Cubs signed him and brought him to the Big Show. He pitched only one inning in 1937, but he returned the next spring. He stayed in the majors until 1950, winning 118 games against 101 losses. He had his best seasons in 1940 and 1941, when he made the National League All-Star teams and helped Brooklyn to make the 1941 World Series. That year he won 20 games for the only time. Higbe, however, is best remembered for objecting to playing with Jackie Robinson in 1947 and organizing Southern-born Dodgers in a failed effort to prevent Robinson from playing.[74]

The Depression had not yet impacted the ALWS. It would be another year before Legion ball felt the full effect of the economic disaster that had affected the rest of the country. By 1932 the country's manufacturing production was 50 percent of its 1929 level. One-fourth of the labor force remained unemployed. Commodity prices had fallen by 55 percent, leaving farmers a pittance of what they received in 1929. Banks called in loans as depositors withdrew their savings. Personal income fell by more than half. Bread lines began to appear in cities. President Hoover had tried to get businesses to voluntarily maintain wages and production. They agreed but quickly went back to their old ways as the Depression sank deeper. Out of work men and women took to the road and poured into shantytowns on the edges of cities, which quickly came to be termed "Hoovervilles."

As the Depression arrived, American Legion baseball appeared firmly established. It had not yet become a source for major league players, but before the 1930s ended it would achieve that role. Preparing professional ballplayers had not been a goal of any of the founders of Legion ball. They wished to combat the decline of sandlot and amateur baseball, following the Black Sox scandal. Due to the work of Sowers and thousands of volunteers across the country, Legion baseball had managed to accomplish that goal.

2

It's True What They Say About the South, 1932–1940

By 1932 the country faced the worst economic depression in its history. The thriving economy of the 1920s seemed to suddenly collapse after 1929. The reality could be found in income figures. Total national income had registered $82.69 billion in 1929 but fell to $41 billion in 1932. Income from wages fell by 40 percent, and farm income shrank by a whopping 61 percent. One-quarter of the work force, between 12 and 15 million people, were without jobs. Industrial production declined by nearly half between 1929 and 1932. An epidemic of bank failures swept the country; 4,377 failed from 1930 to March 1933, ravaging middle-class savings. Millions were struggling, poor, destitute and homeless. Harsh figures indeed.[1]

The election of Franklin D. Roosevelt in 1932 lifted the spirits and hopes for the future of Americans, if not their incomes. "Happy days are here again" could be heard everywhere. Roosevelt had been none too specific about his plans for the country, promising only "a new deal for the American people." His "fireside chats" connected Americans with the head of state as never before, and he offered reassurance that the man in the White House cared about poor and unemployed Americans. Although FDR's rhetoric often outpaced his programs, one piece of legislation followed another in the President's first 100 days in office.

Yet baseball in general and American Legion ball, in particular, not only survived, but expanded in the years of the Great Depression. After all, there was little else for kids and young men to do. Baseball more than ever was the game that boys played. Charles Alexander's excellent study of baseball in the 1930s argues that "more Americans were probably playing baseball in the 1930s than at any time since." Baseball had returned to the role it enjoyed before World War I and the Black Sox scandal. No longer was there talk of baseball declining as a participation sport for boys or as a spectator sport. None argued its place as the National Pastime.[2]

New Orleans had failed to place a team in the American Legion World Series in 1931. What made that worthy of note was that in the first decade of Legion baseball, the Crescent city was the center of the sport. New Orleans was back stronger than ever in 1932. The players on the Zatarain Papooses, as the team called itself, continued to come out of Samuel T. Peters High School, a long-established public school for commerce built in 1912. The team sponsor, Papoose Pure Food Products, had been founded by Emile Zatarain as Papoose Root Beer in 1889. Papoose, by 1932, had become an economic powerhouse in Louisiana. Son Charles Zatarain now ran the company, and he delighted in the Legion team's success. Elderly coach A. J. Park followed the pattern of Philadelphia A's skipper Connie Mack; he always dressed in a business suit for games, and he did not venture beyond the dugout or bench. The team featured pepper-pot second baseman Emile "Moon" Mounes, its leadoff hitter, slick-fielding and hard-hitting shortstop Jimmy Fraiche, outfielder Bobby Maniapane, a hitting machine, and the strong pitching of Joe Graffagnini.[3]

To get to the 1932 World Series, the Papooses of Crescent City Post 134 started by beating Baton Rouge and DeQuincy for the state title. In the sectional tournament, they beat teams from Austin, Texas (3–1), and Oklahoma City (8–2), the latter on pitcher Bill Schonacher's three-hitter. In the regional at Omaha, they thumped teams from Minneapolis (8–6), Seattle (3–1), and Los Angeles (11–6). Los Angeles Leonard Wood Post 125 was loaded with talent. It boasted a 14-year-old infielder named Bobby Doerr, who would eventually be inducted into the Baseball Hall of Fame, and an outstanding catcher in Mickey Owen, who played for the Cardinals, Dodgers, Cubs, and Braves. Their pitching, however, let them down, issuing 16 walks. After state, regional, and sectional tourneys, but before the World Series, three Papoose players—lead-off hitter Emile Mounes, a rail-thin outfielder Alex Diaz, and pitcher/outfielder Joe Graffagnini had batting averages over .500.[4]

New Orleans' World Series opponent, Springfield, Massachusetts Post 21, was no slouch. The team's sponsor, City Services Gas, outfitted the club with sharp new uniforms and provided first-class transportation from the state tournament through the World Series. Springfield prided itself on the strong battery of pitching ace Silvio "Moonie" Giovanelli and team captain and catcher Pete Siciliano. Both went on to professional careers short of the majors. Springfield beat Milford in the state title game. In the four-state tourney, they beat Barre, Vermont (12–2), and Manchester, New Hampshire (8–0). Giovanelli took home the Most Valuable Player trophy for that series. In the Eastern regional at Cumberland, Maryland, Giovanelli shut out Alexandria, Virginia (1–0), then after beating Gregg Post of Reading, Pennsylvania, 4–2, Giovanelli struck out 14 batters in a 6–2 win over the Baltimore and Ohio Railroad Post 34 of Baltimore in the final game of the sectional.[5]

The 1932 World Series, played in Manchester, New Hampshire, proved to be close, hard-fought, and the best attended to date. Games were played at Athletic Field, whose concrete and steel grandstand made it one of the first modern parks in the country, built in 1913. Only Rickwood Field in Birmingham and Fenway Park in Boston are older. Initially known as Textile Field, it served the Amoskeag Manufacturing Company, the Manchester Manufacturers League, city schools, and several professional teams in the New England League. The city took over operation of the facility in 1927 and renamed it Athletic Field. In 1967 it would be renamed Gill Stadium. It seated 3,000 under a roof. In game one, New Orleans came back from a 2–0 deficit to score three runs in the ninth inning for the win. Team captain and shortstop Jimmy Fraiche started the rally. Third baseman Peter Constancy drove in the first run. The big hit, however, was a two-run double to center field by Joe Graffagnini. The hitting hero also was the winning pitcher. A hearty crowd of 8,000 attended the game, and NBC carried the game, as it did the entire American Legion World Series.[6]

Following a solar eclipse, which excited players and fans alike. Springfield came right back to take game two by a 5–1 score. Giovanelli pitched the complete game for

Springfield and tripled in the first run before scoring the second run on a New Orleans error. Springfield first baseman Vince Raffaelo had three hits and two RBI. Springfield's win meant the series would go to the third game for only the second time. In game three, the teams seemed like heavyweight boxers slugging it out for 12 innings. Fraiche's homer in the sixth inning had given New Orleans the lead, but Springfield came back to tie the game. Both teams scored in the tenth inning, but neither could break the game open. With the game tied 5–5 after the 12th inning, the umpires called the game on account of darkness.[7]

In the 1932 championship game, neither team could settle matters in regulation time. Springfield had taken the lead in the third on catcher Pete Siciliano's three-run double. New Orleans picked up two runs in the fourth inning and tied the game in the fifth on Bobby Mangiapane's single. In the tenth inning, the Papooses' second baseman Emile "Moon" Mounes led off with a walk, followed by Pete Constancy's infield hit. Jimmy Fraiche slashed a single to left, scoring Mounes with the winning run. Constancy was out at home, but Graffagnini singled to right to score Fraiche with the final run of the game. Joe Schonacher pitched the first seven innings for New Orleans, but Graffagnini came in to pitch in the bottom of the eighth inning, pitching three shutout innings, to save New Orleans' 5–3 victory and the championship. At the end of the series, over 40 innings, both teams had scored 17 runs, a measure of how evenly matched they were.[8]

New Orleans' Jimmy Fraiche batted .450 in the national competition and fielded flawlessly. He staked a strong claim to being named outstanding player for the Series. The first individual trophy given at an American Legion World Series, presented by New York Yankees manager Joe McCarthy for the most valuable player, went instead to Springfield pitcher Silvio Giovanelli. Over 30,000 attended the Manchester World Series. The Papooses got windbreakers and pocket watches, while the losers received wrist watches. A huge welcoming celebration awaited the team when they arrived back in New Orleans. An estimated 25,000 fans and four bands awaited them at Union Station. Later they were spectators at the Yankees-Cubs World Series in Chicago, and then got to ride in the Pennsylvania Railroad's World Series press car from Chicago to New York.[9]

The Great Depression caught up to the American Legion Junior Baseball program in 1933, when it nearly ended the season and the entire Legion baseball program before it began. For five years, since Dan Sowers obtained a financial commitment from the major leagues, the Legion had started out on sound financial footing. In 1933, however, the major leagues notified Russell Cook of their inability any longer to support Legion baseball. Attendance at major league games had begun to decline in 1930, the first summer after the Great Crash, and continued to fall each season. In 1932 only the pennant winners made any money. No team drew a million fans. For Connie Mack, things were so bad that he broke up his great 1929–1931 Athletics team. Other teams looked for ways to cut expenses. Reducing their minor league affiliates was a simple and popular way to limit expenses. The subsidy to Legion baseball proved an easy target for the number crushers.[10]

Without the gift from the majors, it was unclear how the Legion tournament could go on. Sowers, who had been lying low for several years, now became active in the effort to raise funds for Legion ball. Frank Knox, publisher and part-owner of the *Chicago Daily News* and an important operative in the Republican Party, cautioned Sowers about relying on big business for support. Instead, Knox pointed Sowers and Cross to newspapers friendly to the Legion. Knox ponied up $5,000 from his paper. Sowers asked and received donations from the *Omaha World-Tribune*. Omaha was, after all, the site of the largest Legion post in the country. Indianapolis was home for the American Legion headquarters, so it was logical that the *Indianapolis News* would come through for the Legion. New Orleans, the Crescent City, was the hotbed of Legion baseball in the late-1920s and early-1930s, so the *New Orleans Item-Tribune* also appeared logical. Other papers that gave to Sowers' fund included many of the most respected papers in the country. The *Chicago Daily News, San Francisco Chronicle, Atlanta Journal,* and *Louisville Courier Journal* fell into that group. The newspapers' contributions totaled $28,000, but that did not make up for the lost subsidy from the major leagues.[11]

By August it became clear that the initial contributions would not be enough to transport teams from regionals to sectionals and from sectionals to the World Series, which was scheduled for New Orleans. Cook requested and was granted $4,000 from the Athletic Goods Manufacturers Association to go toward transportation costs. Spalding, Reach, Wright & Ditson, Wilson, and Rawlings opened their purse strings just enough to allow Cook to announce the playing sites for sectional and regional tournaments and the American Legion World Series in early August.[12]

The final piece came shortly before the start of the Legion World Series. Sowers approached his boss, Henry L. Doherty, president of City Services Gasoline Company, who presented Sowers with a check for $6,500 to defray costs of transporting teams from Sectionals to New Orleans. The total in gifts failed to match the majors' contribution, but a bit of belt tightening allowed the Legion to carry on. Cook extracted promises from regional sites for reduced costs for transportation, lodging, and food, and to kick in a few dollars of their own. His sites were Minneapolis; Springfield, Missouri; Ada, Oklahoma; North Platte, Nebraska; and Pocatello, Idaho, in the West. Lewiston, Maine; Allentown, Pennsylvania; Gastonia, North Carolina; Springfield, Ohio; Richmond, Indiana; and Gainesville, Georgia, hosted the Eastern Regionals. Springfield, Ohio, and Topeka, Kansas, were Sectional sites. The 1933 American Legion World Series was scheduled to be held in New Orleans at Julius Heinemann Park, aka Pelican Park, home of the New Orleans Pelicans of the Southern Association and the New Orleans Black Pelicans. It was a monstrosity of a field. It measured 427 feet down the left field line, a modest 405 to center, and 418 to the right field foul pole. No Legion player would hit a ball out of this park.[13]

Chicago Post 467, sponsored by the National Tea Company, a Chicago-based, Midwestern grocery chain, arrived at the ALWS undefeated in 21 games and a slight favorite to beat Trenton, New Jersey. At the Western Sectional in Topeka, Kansas, August 25–27, Chicago had racked up victories over Woodburn, Oregon (20–3), Oakland (6–2), and Stockton, California (6–2). The Chicago players came mostly from Lane Technical High School. Their captain, 140-pound, pesky center fielder/pitcher Phil Cavarretta, provided Chicago with both its best hitter and top pitcher. Third baseman Nick Polly (aka Polachamin), who had a "cup of coffee" in the majors, and left fielder Ted Swed added pop with their bats. Trenton had a nice little team but lacked star quality. At the Springfield, Ohio, Regional, Trenton slipped by Gastonia, North Carolina (4–3) and destroyed Springfield, Ohio (12–5).[14]

The 1933 Series started with Dan Sowers, now referred to as "Uncle Dan," throwing out the first ball at Heinemann Park. The home of the New Orleans Pelicans of the Southern Association, the park was named after A. J. Heinemann, stadium owner and club president, who shot himself at the park after suffering losses in the stock market crash. The ball ground was renamed Pelican Stadium in 1938. A cozy place, its dimensions were

292 feet to left field, 294 to right, and 409 to center. Once play started, the series became the Phil Cavarretta show! As a pitcher, he won both games of the series. In the first game, he opened on the mound and collected the win as Chicago coasted to a 14–5 victory. In the second game, Ted Swed took the mound and Cavarretta moved to center field. Trenton took an early lead when first baseman Jigg Corrado launched the only home run of the series. In the second inning, Cavarretta's triple with the bases loaded keyed a six-run inning to give Chicago the lead. Trenton managed to tie the game 6–6 in the sixth inning. Cavarretta got the call to change places with Swed. For the rest of the game, he pitched one-hit ball. Chicago's win came in the bottom of the ninth with two outs when second baseman Dan Krause singled and came home on Swed's long double off the right field wall to give Chicago a 7–6 victory.[15]

A year after his heroics in the American Legion World Series, Cavarretta was wearing the uniform of the Chicago Cubs. Chicago signed him quickly following the championship Legion season. He did not take that uniform off for the next 20 years. In 1934 the Cubs sent him to Peoria for 23 games and then to Reading, Pennsylvania, where he batted .310. The Cubs brought him up to the big leagues in September. He failed in two pinch-hitting appearances in Boston but homered for the only run to win his first game in Chicago. Still only 17, he was the youngest player in the majors.[16]

A decade later, in 1945, Cavarretta, now a first baseman, enjoyed the best season of his career. He led the National League in batting with a .355 average, on-base percentage with .449, and base hits with 197. He led the Cubs to the National League pennant. In recognition of his accomplishments, Cavarretta was awarded the National League Most Valuable Player trophy for 1945. That autumn he played in his third World Series. His other Series had been in 1935 and 1938 against Detroit and the Yankees. In the three Series, he batted .317. For his 22-year big league career, he posted numbers just below Hall of Fame level: a .293 average and a .372 on-base percentage. Never a power hitter, he hit double digits in home runs only once, but he did play in four All-Star Games. In mid-season 1951, he became player-manager of a second-division Cubs team. After two seasons as manager, the Cubs fired him after he, in all honesty, told reporters that his team was not good enough to finish in the first division. One sportswriter described him as "a throw-back to the 'rugged hell-for-leather days.'" To him the opposition was the enemy, and no quarter was asked, none given.[17]

Cavarretta did not have the honor of being the first American Legion player to appear in the major leagues. That distinction belongs to pitcher John Salveson of Long Beach, who donned a New York Giants uniform in 1933. Salveson did not win a game, but he did get the first major league hit by a Legion grad. In 1934 five former Legion players, including Cavarretta, got to the big leagues. Lee Strine, a pitcher from Long Beach, and Harry "Cookie" Lavagetto, infielder from Oakland, opened the season with the White Sox and Pirates respectively. Before summer ended, they were joined by outfielders Augie Galan of Berkeley with the Cubs and Walter "Kit" Carson from Long Beach in Cleveland. Carson stayed for the preverbal "cup of coffee" but Galan had a strong 15-year career with Cubs, Dodgers, Reds, Giants and Athletics. Galan finished with a .287 batting average in 1,742 major league games. Cavarretta became the first Legion grad to play in both an American Legion World Series and a major league World Series, which he did in 1935, 1938, and 1945. He also became the first Legion grad to lead the league in batting, which he did in 1945 with a .355 average.

American Legion baseball continued to grow in popularity even in the face of the

Great Depression. In 1934 some 400,000 boys participated in Legion baseball. As was the case with the country during the Depression, each year brought a new crisis for American Legion baseball, but it managed to survive. In 1933 finances had nearly spelled disaster for Legion ball. In 1934 racism gave the program a black eye, and the issue refused to go away. Sowers in his day had faced the issue firmly and head-on. Director Russell Cook failed to provide such firm leadership. In 1932, he grudgingly recognized that no rules prohibited African Americans from playing. Nevertheless, Cook favored a separate black league. A year later, Cook's actions suggested that he agreed with segregation.[18]

In 1934 the race issue focused on Springfield, Massachusetts', fine team and its star player, Ernest "Bunny" Taliaferro, a 15-year-old African American pitcher and center fielder. Taliaferro was a gifted all-around athlete. As a freshman at Springfield Tech, he became the first ninth grader to earn varsity letters in football, basketball and baseball. He was all-city in football and baseball, however, baseball was his favorite and best sport. On his high school team, he led the 1934 club in hits, runs, stolen bases, and wins. His Legion team, Springfield Post 21, sailed through the Massachusetts tournament with Taliaferro pitching a three-hit shutout over Lowell in the title game. In the first game of the Northeast Regional at Brightwood, New Jersey, he was the winning pitcher and, in addition, clubbed two home runs. Next Springfield won the right to move on to the Sectionals in Gastonia, North Carolina, by beating St. Albans, Vermont (1–0) in ten innings. At Gastonia, they would face teams from Cumberland, Maryland, Charlotte, North Carolina, and Tampa, Florida.[19]

Trouble started as soon as Springfield's train pulled into Gastonia. The bus driver who was scheduled to drive the team to their hotel took one look at Bunny Taliaferro and drove off, leaving the players with no option but to lug their own baggage to the hotel. At the hotel, Taliaferro was denied a room on the basis of his color; he could not register or stay with his teammates. Local Legion officials, who knew Springfield was bringing a black player, proposed a home stay with a local black doctor and his family. Neither Bunny Taliaferro, his teammates, nor coach Babe Steere wanted to split up the team. Team manager Sydney J. Harris worked out a compromise arrangement of sorts. Taliaferro was allowed to register as the coach's "valet," and the hotel moved a cot into Steere's room for the youngster. To a later generation, this action would be seen as demeaning and unacceptable, but in 1934 the New Englanders were prepared to overlook this inequality of Southern law and play the games.[20]

The real crisis occurred at the practice field when an estimated 2,000 local men and boys showed up to see the African American lad and his teammates. The crowd quickly became a mob. They poured racial filth and venom on Bunny Taliaferro and his teammates. When the taunts turned to threats, and soda bottles and tin cans started raining on the field, the Springfield players' anger turned to fear. They returned to the safety of their hotel with bats in their hands for protection. Coach Steere called a meeting with Harris and Chuck Wilson of Indianapolis, tournament director for the Gastonia event. Word had it that the teams from Cumberland and Tampa refused to play if Taliaferro took the field. Wilson later claimed this was a "misunderstanding," as no team had filed a formal protest or threatened not to play. What Steere and the players wanted was a guarantee of their safety from the rabid and racist fans. Gastonia officials could not or would not guarantee the safety of Springfield players if Bunny Taliaferro was in the lineup.[21]

Steere called a team meeting that night. The coach gave the team a limited choice: they could play without Bunny Taliaferro or they could go home. Even without Taliaferro,

Springfield might well have won the tournament, and he could join the team for the American Legion World Series in Chicago. Team captain and second baseman Tony King spoke for the team. "There is no choice," he said. "Bunny is a member of this team. If he doesn't play, neither do I." All the players agreed with King. As Richard Andersen put it: "This is a story about very ordinary people doing extraordinary things." Without bothering to inform Wilson or any other official, the players headed for the train station. Word of Springfield's withdrawal reached Massachusetts before the players arrived[22]

Over 1,000 fans awaited the team at Union Station in Springfield, and the flap continued. Harold Redden, head of the Massachusetts Legion, telegrammed the national commander, criticizing Gastonia. He demanded a playoff in Chicago between the winner of the East and Springfield. Legion officials quickly began to put the best spin on the situation. Cumberland coach Earl Brooks offered to bring his team to Springfield for a two-out-of-three series or to meet in Chicago. It seemed a gracious offer at first, but, of course, neither Post had the funds for such travel, and the kids needed to start fall classes. Wilson again played his "misunderstanding" card. No team had actually refused to play or made a formal protest. The blame, he maintained, lay with the hotel for not allowing Taliaferro to register.[23]

The Legion had nothing to be proud of, and it did not help itself when it attempted to bury the issue. The Americanism Commission's office readied a press release blaming the hotel's abiding by state law for the controversy. The players' fear of a race riot got shoved into the background. Springfield's mayor, Henry Martens, had telegrammed Frank Sanders, national adjutant of the Legion, to the effect that the Legion had the choice of standing by its principals or giving in to violence. It took the less honorable choice.[24]

At its national convention in Miami, the Americanism Commission of the Legion proposed to avoid conflicts in the future by acceding to Southern folkways embodied in Jim Crow laws and customs of segregation. Specifically, the proposal put forward by the Americanism Committee would pledge the Legion to support "laws [and] social regulations and long-established customs of states in which regional, sectional or Junior World Series Tournament is played." This would eliminate "unpleasantness." That the Legion convention refused to pass the resolution offered no consolation to Springfield. The next season, Springfield Post 21 chose not to revive its baseball team in protest of the Legion's overt support for racism.[25]

Several years after the event, Springfield mayor Billy Sullivan and a local doctor named Tim Murry raised funds for a stone monument titled "Brothers All Are We" to be placed in Forest Park, where Post 21 played its home games. It listed the names of the players—Jimmy Lawler, Fran Luce, Bobby Tiggs, Tony King, Danny Keyes, Kaiser Lombardi, Johnny Coffey, Ray O'Shay, Joe Kelly, Franny O'Connell, John Malaguiti, Louis Grondolski, Freddy Laczek, and Joe Kogut. The plaque states:

> It was an act of loyalty and love for their friend and brother which sent a message that bigotry has no placed in the game of baseball or in the game of life; a message proclaimed by a band of 16-year-old kids a generation before the barrier of racial prejudice of major league baseball was torn down with the recruitment of another black, Jackie Robinson.

The reconciliation slowly continued. In 2010, Post 21 revived its team after 76 years. Tony King and Danny Keyes, the last surviving members of the 1934 team, threw out the ceremonial first balls. The publication of Springfield College professor Richard Andersen's books on the incident, *A Home Run for Bunny* (2013), a children's book, and the more scholarly *We Called Him Bunny* (2014), refocused national attention on Bunny Taliaferro and his teammates. Gastonia's mayor, John D. Bridgeman, sent a letter of apology to Springfield's mayor. In 2014 Gastonia sent a team to Springfield, and the following year two Springfield teams traveled to Gastonia for goodwill games.[26]

After Springfield went home, Cumberland, Maryland Post 13 won the Sectional with a 6–5 victory over Charlotte to advance to the 1934 World Series in Chicago. The team from western Maryland featured two fine pitchers in Ron Tripplett and Phil Fleming. The 6-foot-3 Tripplett intimidated opponents by his size and his sidearm delivery, while Phil Fleming featured a sharp-breaking curveball. In the World Series, they faced an undefeated club from New Orleans, the epicenter of early Legion baseball. Teams from the Crescent City had advanced to the finals in 1929, 1930, and 1932, when they won the national title, and were back again in 1934. Players from Samuel J. Peters High School had filled the rosters of the first two finalists, while the next two, 1932 and 1934, came from Jesuit High School. Jesuit had won the state high school championship earlier in the year. The Legion club took the nickname of Jesuit High, the Blue Jays. In the Western regional final, New Orleans beat Seattle, 10–6. New Orleans had their own pitching tandem, 6-feet-3 but rail-thin Jerry Burke and lefty Jesse "Midget" Danna. Their captain and center fielder, Charlie Gilbert, who played in the majors from 1940–1947, pretty much ran the team.[27]

In the 1934 American Legion World Series, New Orleans appeared on its way to a second title when it scored four runs in the bottom of the seventh inning, aided by sloppy fielding by Cumberland, to take game one, 5–4. Catcher John "Fats" Dantonio, who became a wartime Brooklyn Dodger, contributed two of New Orleans's RBIs with a bases-loaded single. Their big pitcher, Jerry Burke, got the win. Cumberland came back to tie the Series in the second game, which was played at Wrigley Field. The game went 13 innings before Cumberland eked out a 4–3 win. Singles by pitcher Fred Fleming, outfielder and team captain Charlie Clark, and outfielder Ollie Osborn loaded the bases. Then center fielder Walter Hoewatt's game-ending drive off the wall spelled defeat for New Orleans. Hoewatt collected three RBI and Clark had three hits on the day. In the rubber game at Comiskey Park, Cumberland's Triplett dominated New Orleans, holding them to three hits in a 6–1 victory. In the top of the first inning, Charlie Gilbert worked a walk and Shannon Goetz doubled for New Orleans' only run. In the bottom of the first, Osborne tripled, and third baseman George Kraft brought him home. Cumberland picked up two more runs in the fourth when Triplett's walk was followed by Clark's triple and Osborne's sacrifice fly. Cumberland's final run came in the fifth inning when Kraft walked, followed by two sacrifice bunts and Eddie Lewis's RBI single. Cumberland captain Charley Clark reigned as the top hitter in the Series.[28]

At the Legion's 1934 national convention, leadership of the Americanism Commission, and hence of Legion baseball, changed hands. Homer Caillaux (1897–1946), former commander of the California Legion, replaced Russell Cook as director. Caillaux would last for a decade in that office. Cook had seen baseball as a means of Americanizing immigrants. Caillaux, Virginia-born but raised in Indiana, and a University of Indiana engineer by training, had spent over two years in France during World War I and brought home a French war-bride. He showed little interest in baseball. Rather, he was obsessed by fear of communism and spent the bulk of his time as a prolific speaker, railing against the dangers of "radicalism" and in support of the House Un-American Activities Committee. He acted as if the 1934 proposal to abide by Southern Jim Crow laws had passed. He favored rewarding Piedmont mill towns with the Legion World Series, regardless of their racial proclivities.[29]

In mid–June of his first year in office, Caillaux announced Gastonia, North Carolina, as the site for the 1935 World Series. His decision was made less than a year after the Taliaferro affair, and without reference to it or to the blatant racism of Gastonia's citizenry. Gastonia's record of strong attendance at American Legion Regional and Sectional games, and its history of anti-union policies, overrode any concerns that may have existed about Southern racism among Legion leadership, if any existed at all. Gastonia's fame or infamy rested on the violent strikes by the National Textile Workers Union in 1929. The strikes failed, but not before the Loray Mill evicted its workers from their company-owned homes, the state National Guard patrolled the streets, union headquarters were destroyed by goons, the city Police Chief was killed, over 70 strikers were arrested, and two trials took place before six mill workers were found guilty of murder. A second round of nationwide textile strikes occurred in fall of 1934, when 400,000 workers went out. In Gastonia, Legion ball began in the same year as the first strikes. Unlike the textile union, Legion ball prospered through the Carolinas.[30]

The Gastonia Post 23's 1935 team, sponsored by Cramerton Mills, was logically known as the "Threads." They managed to work their way into the fabric of the community. They featured two outstanding players, Lawrence Columbus "Crash" Davis and Howie "the Howitzer" Moss. Crash Davis became one of the best-known names in baseball because of the lead character of that name in the movie *Bull Durham* (1988). The real-life Crash Davis earned his nickname at age 14 for crashing or running into Legion teammates. A slick-fielding shortstop, he went on to play at Duke University, where he became team captain in 1939 and 1940. After Duke, he went directly to the Philadelphia Athletics, where he spent three years as a "good field, no hit" middle infielder before entering the military. After World War II, he played for the Durham Bulls in the Carolina League until 1952, while in graduate school at Duke.[31]

Power-hitting third baseman Howie Moss became one of minor league baseball's greatest power hitter. He spent 13 seasons in the minors where he launched 279 home runs. In the 1940s, he tore up the International League, leading that circuit in home runs four times, garnering a Most Valuable Player honor, and earning selection to the International League Hall of Fame. On three occasions between 1942 and 1946, major league teams gave him a shot, but all were disappointed. His fielding remained suspect, and his major league batting average registered a pathetic .097 in 22 games.[32]

Before the 1935 season, the Legion made changes to the format of the tournament. To reduce long-distance travel, there would now be 24 regional tournaments between neighboring states. Those would be followed by three regional tourneys, each involving eight teams. The winners of the Northeast and Southeast Regionals would then play a best-of-three-game final to determine the right to meet the winner of the Western Regional. They also made the finals a best-of-five-games format.[33]

In the 1935 World Series, Gastonia met the George W. Menhert Post 391 of Sacramento, California. Sacramento had gotten stronger as they moved through the playoffs. The Menherts, as the team identified itself, struggled in the state playoff against Los Angeles, winning game one but losing game two before taking the state title, 2–1 in ten innings. In the Regionals they crushed Reno, 27–4, in a mismatch, then slipped past Tucson, 3–2. In the Western finals, they topped Chicago, 4–1, and Tulsa, 14–4, thanks to Marcel Dutra's four hits. Although some fans wanted a more experienced coach, 24-year-old

Bill Avila managed to get his team of limited talent to play above their heads for the month of August.[34]

Gastonia did not need to worry about talent, they had that in spades. It still took Gastonia five games to win the 1935 Series against Sacramento. After a parade through town, 12,000 fans paid their way into a park that seated 4,000. They witnessed Howie Moss bang out five hits in a 10–4 victory for the Threads. Catcher J. D. Queen, who later played three seasons in the low minors, homered. Left-hander Clyde "Stokie" Dellinger limited Sacramento to five hits. The California team lost shortstop Mel Cole when he was spiked by Dellinger. Only 3,000 fans showed up for game two. It was Crash Davis' turn. He slammed three hits to lead the way in an easy 8–1 Gastonia win. Pitcher Bobby Lee Hamilton threw a nifty four-hitter. After rain postponed game three, a record crowd for North Carolina of 18,000 attended Gastonia's 12–8 triumph. Sacramento jumped out to a 3–0 lead thanks to sloppy fielding by Moss and clutch hitting by Marcel Dutra, second baseman Tony Hansen, and third baseman Carl Youngblood. Gastonia tied the game and blew it open with eight runs in the fourth inning and three more in the seventh. Moss collected four more hits while outfielder Bill Hand had three hits and three RBI, outfielder Hubert Mauney had three hits, and Marion Dellinger chipped in three RBI. Attendance for the three games was a record 28,900. It was the first ALWS championship for a North Carolina team. Moss finished the series with a gaudy .692 batting average, while Davis hit .545 and Hubert Mauney batted .429.[35]

The success of the 1935 World Series at Gastonia and the desire to increase gate receipts led Chaillaux to again award the Series to another Southern cotton mill town, in this case Spartanburg, South Carolina. Duncan Park, site of the Series, offered a traditional minor league setting. Built in 1926, it seated 3,000 under a covered roof, with dimensions of 318 feet to left field, 372 to center field, and 325 feet down the right field line. It did have lots of space outside the foul lines where fans filled in ten-deep. On the outfield fence, logos of Smith's Drug Store and Royal Crown Cola remained the same over the years. In 1936, Spartanburg Post 28, under the direction of coach Bill "Sarge" Hughes, who looked the part of a tough Marine drill-sergeant, was a scrappy group. Hughes had won a state title in 1933, his first year coaching the Legion team, and would run off four consecutive titles from 1936–1939. They beat Bennettville for the South Carolina title. Then they put away Carrollton, Georgia, by a 6–0 score to get to the Sectional in nearby Charlotte. There they took out Charlotte, 9–6, New Orleans, 8–3 when they scored six runs in the ninth inning to capture a come-from-behind win, and Nashville by an 11–7 score. The Spartans then captured two of three from Northeast champion Manchester, New Hampshire. In the finale of that series, Suvern Wright pitched a tidy two-hitter in a 7–2 win. Catcher Pedro Mahaffey had three hits. In the West, a team from Los Angeles, Leonard Wood Post 9, prevailed. In order to get to Spartanburg, Los Angeles had to beat Stockton, California, Tucson, Holdenville, Oklahoma, Omaha, and Seattle, which they beat by the convincing score of 14–1.[36]

Spartanburg and Los Angeles played a tight five-game ALWS in 1937 before record crowds. In the first game, the crowd overwhelmed the capacity of the turnstiles, but the consensus attendance figure was 12,000 in 3,000-seat Duncan Park. The Spartans took game one by a 3–1 score. Little Jimmy Thomas pitched a clean victory, allowing just four hits. However, the Spartans lost shortstop Roy Price with an injured finger. In game two, played before 8,000 excited fans, L.A.'s Wilbur McElroy shut out Spartanburg, 6–0. Shortstop Bud Malone's triple, which scored three runners, was the big hit. Spartanburg went

Duncan Park, Spartanburg, South Carolina, officially seated 3,000, but for the 1936 American Legion World Series final between Spartanburg and Los Angeles, an estimated 20,000 fans piled into the grounds, standing on the hillsides beside the stands and ten-deep in the outfield, necessitating a ground rule double for any ball hit into the crowd (courtesy of www. Ballparkreviews.com).

up by one win in game three, taking a tight 5–4 decision. The winning run scored in the eighth inning when center fielder Guy Hughes scored from third on a double steal. In game four, the Spartans delighted the home crowd by banging out 16 hits to five for Los Angeles, but Los Angeles pitcher Wilbur McElroy scattered the hits and drove in the winning run in a 5–4 victory. In the deciding game of the 1936 ALWS, a record crowd of 20,000 turned out. Fans stacked ten-deep along the foul lines. That record crowd saw the hometown team nail down the championship in convincing fashion, winning 8–1. James "Pepper" Martin was the batting star for Spartanburg with three hits. First baseman Walter "Pete" Fowler collected three RBI; he would take a shot at pro ball in 1945, but the semi-pro ball in the Carolinas was a better fit for him. For the Series, Spartanburg as a team batted over .300. Fowler led the way, batting .550, while catcher Pedro Mahaffey and shortstop Roy Prince hit .500 or better. Attendance for the Series was listed as 60,000, an ALWS record that remained until the 21st century. The Belk department store gave each of the Spartanburg players a new suit, and they received American Legion jackets.[37]

The 1936 event marked a decade of Legion World Series. If any demonstration was necessary, it made clear that the Legion program had become well-established. The just completed series, with 20,000 fans in the park for the final game, stood in sharp contrast to the 1926 series, where 1,000 paid for seats in an 80,000-seat stadium. The year was noteworthy for Legion ball because more and more of its graduates appeared on major league rosters. Among the 1936 group was the Legion's first future Hall of Fame player, Bob Feller.

Despite the record attendance at the 1936 World Series, not all were happy when the Series ended. At the Pennsylvania-Ohio Regional, a dispute had erupted which led to Pennsylvania's withdrawal from Legion tournaments for 30 years. Following Middletown, Ohio's victory over Reading, the Pennsylvania team filed a protest claiming that Middletown used an ineligible player. Smoothing over conflicts was never Chaillaux's strong suit. George E. Bellis, secretary of the Pennsylvania Legion Baseball Committee, notified Chaillaux in mid–August of his state's intention to withdraw from tournament play. Beyond the immediate conflict, Bellis thought the long tournament ran against the purpose of Legion baseball as he saw it. He believed all boys should be encouraged to play ball as much as possible, and the ultimate goal was to mold citizens. The tournaments took too long and excluded too many teams, he thought. Rather than tournaments stretching past Labor Day, he believed that boys should keep playing. When Pennsylvania withdrew from the national tournament, the state fielded 150 Legion teams. Bellis' approach seemed to work; by 1950 over 1,000 Pennsylvania posts sponsored teams. In an interesting move, the Pennsylvania group started up what it termed "Midget baseball" for boys under 12. The new group proved popular, but when Little League baseball started in central Pennsylvania, the Legion's midget game could not keep pace.[38]

At baseball's winter meeting, the major leagues agreed to contribute $20,000 to the 1937 American Legion tournament. Even with this new influx of funds, Chaillaux chose to continue his Southern strategy, which promised greater income. He did arrange for the American Legion World Series to be broadcast live over 3,000 radio stations. Spartanburg appeared to have reloaded after its championship team of 1936 and seemed to be the team to beat in the Carolinas, and hence the nation. Chaillaux would not announce the site of the finals until August, but he set things up to hold the finals where all attendance records had been broken in 1936. Spartanburg Post 26, however, did sail through the tournament to the finals.

For the 1937 season, Chaillaux moved the World Series out of the Carolinas to New Orleans. A plucky New Orleans team managed to reach the finals at Heinemann Park (aka Pelicans Park), home of the Class AA Pelicans of the Southern Association. All but one of the ALWS games would be played under the lights. It was the fifth time a New Orleans team had reached the finals since the Legion World Series began in 1926, and the fourth time they finished as runner-up. New Orleans' Legion Post 197, made up of boys from Fortier High School, featured pitcher Howie Pollet. A classy left-handed pitcher, he would win 131 games over 14 major league seasons, nine with the St. Louis Cardinals. The Zatarains beat Austin, 2–0, to gain the Western finals against Omaha McDevitts in a best-of-three-game series. Omaha dominated game one, winning 14–5, but New Orleans came back to win, 20–5 and 8–6. In the final game, Sidney Crochet drove in the winning run to give the victory to Pollet. Along the way to New Orleans, East Lynn's answer to Pollet, Ray Bessom, and his teammates beat Berwyn, Illinois, 6–1 and 17–3 in the East title game, and Trenton 7–3 in the Northeast final.[39]

The American Legion World Series of 1937 belonged to Ray Bessom, a chunky, 5–9, 170-pound pitcher-outfielder who starred for East Lynn. His blazing fastball froze opposing batters. He won game one, a 12–1 laughter for East Lynn. He was never in trouble, pitching a five-hit, 12-strikeout game. After a rainout, he won game two with a 5–0 shutout, his 27th win of the season. He was also the batting star with four hits and three RBI. Game three proved closer than the first two, but it ended as a 13–5 East Lynn win. When New Orleans staged a rally in the seventh inning, coach Gus Daum sent Bessom to the mound, and he snuffed out any lingering hopes of New Orleans. Bessom's battery-mate, catcher Jim Hegan, starred for East Lynn with four hits, three RBI, and three stolen bases. Hegan caught for the Cleveland Indians for 11 years before playing out the string with four other clubs. Bessom fanned 55 in national competition, 30 in the ALWS.[40]

Bessom finished the year with the unbelievable record of 28 wins and no losses. He doubled as the hitting star of the Series, batting .555, the highest average of the ALWS. The *Charlotte Observer* believed Bessom to be "the best junior pitcher ever seen here." Following the ALWS, he signed a pro contract. Teammate Clint Conaster, who played with Bessom at Springfield, Ohio, in the fast Middle-Atlantic League (Class C), remembered: "I'd stand there and the ball would just go whoosh right past me. I thought, 'what am I doing here?'" He observed both Bessom and Rapid Robert Feller and claimed that Bessom threw faster than Feller. Bessom spent four years in military service, 1942–1945. He never regained his form after the war.[41]

In 1938, two teams, San Diego and Detroit, appeared to be the class of the Western region. San Diego experienced the most physically demanding schedule. After winning the state title at Stockton, they departed immediately for the sectional in Grand Forks, North Dakota. There they took out Okemah, Oklahoma, 7–5, and Portland, Oregon, 16–3, for the Western title. Without a home-cooked meal, they headed for the semi-finals in Charlotte, North Carolina. There they faced Roose-Vanker Post of Detroit, led by pitching great and future Hall of Famer "Prince Hal" Newhouser. Three teams—San Diego, Spartanburg, and Detroit—qualified for the semi-final round. Spartanburg won its Regional by beating Augusta, Georgia, 13–5. At the Charlotte Sectional they had an easy time, beating St. Louis, 6–1, but needed outstanding pitching by Howie Pollet to get past New Orleans, 3–2. Spartanburg won the bye, leaving San Diego to face off against Detroit.[42]

At that point, Chaillaux's Southern strategy came face-to-face again with Southern racism. San Diego Post 6, brought two black players, although neither started. John Ritchey, a chiseled, light-skinned African American, had a load of talent as a catcher and hitter. Nelson Manuel, a Mexican-American, could play both middle infield and outfield. Local officials explained "Southern mores" and pointed to the Americanism Commission's 1934 proposal to respect local custom as justification for excluding black players. Of course, that proposal had failed to pass, but that seemed not to matter to the Legion officials. San Diego coach Mike Morrow wanted a championship and willingly sold out his youngsters. Believing he could win without Ritchey and Manuel and hoping they would have another opportunity, he agreed to hold them out of the final series in Spartanburg, South Carolina.[43]

At Charlotte, San Diego had to face the best pitcher in Legion baseball, Hal Newhouser. A hard thrower with a wicked overhand curve, "Prince Hal" sported a 17–0 record in Legion competition and a streak of 65 scoreless innings. He went on to win the American League Most Valuable Player award in 1944 and 1945, and he was elected to the Hall of Fame. In game one of the three-game series, Newhouser was masterful, throwing a three-hit shutout and striking out ten batters in a 4–0 win over San Diego. Losing pitcher Chet Kehn allowed just five hits. San Diego took game two by a 3–2 count. Bill Morales got the win for San Diego. Newhouser and Kehn faced each other again in the third and deciding game. Although Newhouser allowed just three hits and no earned runs, he lost, 2–1, thanks to four Detroit errors. In the first inning, Harold Albright reached base on an error by the second baseman, went to third on a sacrifice, and scored when catcher Stan

Sharpe's grounder hopped over the shortstop. In the eighth, Post 6 shortstop Bill Williams reached second on an error, took third on a passed ball, and scored on Sharpe's sacrifice fly. Newhouser would be in a Detroit Tigers uniform before a calendar year passed, but San Diego was headed to the American Legion World Series in Spartanburg.[44]

The 1938 American Legion World Series proved nip and tuck before the Californians finally posted the decisive victory. Game one foreshadowed the entire series. Umpires finally called the game after 14 grueling innings and an 8–8 tie because of darkness. In game two, Spartanburg came from behind to score five runs in the ninth inning to win, 9–6. San Diego came back to even the series with a 7–4 win. The Spartans again took the lead with a tight, 5–4 win in game four. San Diego then took control of the Series, winning the final three games 6–3, 10–2, and 4–1. In the final game, second baseman Fernando Parades' two run-producing hits were enough to give Chet Kehn the victory. Kehn's 10 strikeouts and four Spartanburg errors contributed to the win. Kehn got to have the proverbial cup of coffee with the Brooklyn Dodgers in 1942, and pitcher Duane Pillette enjoyed modest success in the majors from 1949 to 1956 for three teams.[45]

Ritchey and Manuel could only watch the ALWS. Manuel never got the opportunity to play professional baseball; he died when the ship he served on during World War II, the *USS Boise*, was struck by a torpedo. He was credited with saving 14 sailors in the torpedo room before the ship went down. Unlike Springfield, San Diego failed to turn out huge throngs to welcome home the "heroes" nor did it issue loud protests about the slights to its players. Coach Morrow promised only that the team would be back in the ALWS next year. For the first time, the Legion claimed that over 500,000 boys played Junior baseball. The tournament began with 30,000 teams competing for the national crown. The list of former Legion players in the majors was growing longer and included future Hall of Famers Bob Feller, Stan Musial, Ted Williams, and Joe Medwick.

It happened that the best team in 1939, the Omaha McDevitts, sponsored by Omaha Post 1, the largest American Legion post in the country, and by insurance man Frank McDevitt. Players came out of South Omaha and Creighton Prep. Their coach, Francis "Skip" Palrang, also came from "the Prep," where he had won the state crown in the spring. Four of his players had been named all-state, including pitcher Clarence "Bud" Blessie, catcher George Dunn, second baseman and captain Ray Henningen, and center fielder Bill Wachtler. The McDevitts had been a strong club for several years, and years of playing together paid off in 1939. In the state tournament, they beat Lincoln (14–2) and Neligh 7–6 (10 innings), then faced the Omaha Red Tops from Omaha South High School in a three-game set. The city of Omaha went baseball crazy; crowds of 15,000 and 10,000 turned out for the two games. McDevitt won two straight for the Nebraska crown by scores of 10–4 and 2–1. At the Regional in Aberdeen, South Dakota, the McDevitts beat Aberdeen (8–4) and Grand Forks (7–4). Moving on to the Western Sectional at Stockton, California, they toppled Topeka and Los Angeles Sunrise Post (6–4), the last in 13 innings. First baseman Frank "Link" Lyman drove in both runs in the final game. Omaha entered the World Series with a perfect 24–0 record.[46]

It helped the McDevitts that the Legion World Series of 1939 was held in Omaha at Fontenelle Park. The ball diamond was located in the 108-acre park in north Omaha, in an undeveloped area of the city. The skinned infield, lack of dugouts, and limited stands down the third base line spoke of its use as a city recreation park rather than a minor league stadium. Unlimited standing room in the outfield and down the first base line allowed 13,000 to cram in for the Series' final game. McDevitt coach Maurice "Skip" Palrang lacked big stars or a shut-down pitcher, but he constructed a solid team from Creighton Prep boys who had played together all their lives. Bud Blessie and Sam Russo gave them competitive pitching. Catcher George Dunn completed a solid battery. Captain and second baseman Ray Henningen solidified the infield. Outfielder Bill Wachter was good enough to play in the Cardinals farm system after his Legion days.[47]

Omaha had little trouble against Berwyn, Illinois, Post 422 (24–2) in the 1939 American Legion World Series. Berwyn, a suburb of Chicago, had captured the Eastern championship at Sumter, South Carolina, by beating Passaic, New Jersey, twice, 14–8 and 12–0. Berwyn featured Eddie Goralski, who hit .500 to lead all hitters in the ALWS, but little else. In game one, Omaha came back from a 6–2 deficit in the ninth inning to win, 7–6. In that inning, Bud Blessie singled, followed by a walk to Lyman, and second baseman Henningsen's two-run double. Wachtler's double scored the winning run. Berwyn knotted the Series in game two, posting a 9–6 victory. Berwyn got four runs in the second on six base-on-balls, a single, and a sacrifice fly. An uncharacteristic six McDevitt errors aided Berwyn's cause. The loss ended Omaha's 26-game win streak. In game three, Omaha managed to slip past Berwyn, 2–1, in 10 innings. Sam Russo got the win and scored the winning run on first baseman Frank Lyman's triple. Henningsen had scored in the sixth inning on Frank Mancuso's RBI. Omaha finished the series with a 6–2 win before 13,000 fans as Clarence "Bud" Blessie cruised to the win and Bill Wachtler pounded out three hits. The game was played in a dust storm the likes of which the boys from the Chicago suburbs had never seen.[48]

In 1940, Chaillaux, for unknown reasons, placed the World Series in the tiny hamlet of Albemarle, North Carolina. Although the town had a Legion team, it was altogether inappropriate for a World Series of any kind. Its population of a mere 4,000 souls lacked cultural capital. Its ball field, Efird-Wiscassett Park, named for two mill companies, had a seating capacity of just 700. For the Series, the local organizers brought in bleachers and more bleachers, and they roped off a sizable portion of the outfield for standing room only. On the positive side, the Legion did have contracts from CBS and Mutual Radio Network to broadcast the games nationwide.

The return of San Diego Post 6, national champions in 1938, dominated the news about the tournament. They returned with the two African American players whose presence had caused trouble two years before, only now they were 16 years old and starters. Catcher John Ritchey and third baseman Nelson Manuel made Post 6 the favored team over whoever they played. In addition, Post 6 had a future major leaguer and multi-talented player in Bob Usher, who could play the outfield, pitch or catch. Pitching did, on occasion, let them down. In the three-game series for the championship of southern California, they lost to the Greayer Clover Post of Los Angeles 9–4, but came back to win, 17–3 and 6–4. In the state final they bested Sacramento Manhart, 1–0 and 9–5. They also lost to Topeka, 4–1, in the Western Sectionals, but again they came back in the double elimination series to sweep a doubleheader, 13–2 and 8–5. Then they were off to North Carolina for World Series games.[49]

Unlike 1938, when he was surprised by Southern "hospitality," coach Mike Morrow demanded a guarantee in advance that his black players would be allowed to participate. He threatened to take his team home if Ritchey and Manuel were not allowed to play. Entering the semi-final series at Shelby, North Carolina, Ritchey had the highest batting average in the competition. There was no serious problem at Shelby. San Diego won the first game, 5–4, from St. Louis on Ritchey's game-winning double in the eighth inning. The California boys from Post 6 then hammered the St. Louis club, 13–4.[50]

Before the first game in Albemarle, Morrow sent his team out to warm up. On seeing Ritchey and Manuel, the crowd estimated at 9,950 went into a frenzy. Abusive language and dire threats poured down on the players. A full-out riot seemed possible. Local officials, apparently knowing the temper of the population, ruled the two players "ineligible." The game was scheduled to be broadcast on CBS radio network, and Chaillaux did not want that publicity. Morrow, fearing for the safety of his players and believing that his team was good enough to win without the two African American starters, did not pull his team off the field. Rather, he sat the two players, one of whom was his best hitter. When asked for his take, Homer Chaillaux stuck to "no comment."[51]

For the first two games of the 1940 ALWS, it appeared Morrow judged correctly. San Diego took the first game by a 6–5 score and the second, 3–2, on Bob Fitzpatrick's three-hitter. Then Albemarle came back. Outfielder Craig "TG" Lisk's two-run triple put Albemarle ahead for a 6–3 victory in game three. Their pitching ace, John W. "Lefty" List, got stronger as the game progressed; he struck out eight but walked none. The next day, Craig Lisk again led the Albemarle hitters, collecting two key hits in a 7–5 win for the home team to even the series at two games each. Clyde Dick went to the mound in the third inning for Albemarle to collect the win. In the fifth game, San Diego blew an opportunity to tie the score in the ninth inning of a 9–8 Albemarle win. The final out came when Albemarle catcher Hoyle Boger called for a pitch-out on a squeeze play, allowing him to nail the runner at the plate.[52]

Following the series, some newspapers criticized the Legion for its decision to bar the Negro players. None spoke more clearly than the *Oakland Tribune*. At Albemarle, the "most un–American of prejudice, racial discrimination, reared its ugly head." As for the Legion, "That this was approved by the American Legion and not censured even mildly is almost incredible." Strangely, in the report on the series he penned for the *Spalding Baseball Guide*, Chaillaux made absolutely no mention of the event.[53]

The series was not the end of John "Hoss" Ritchey's baseball career. His is a redeeming story. After his San Diego High School ball ended, he played on a variety of African American teams, working his way to the Chicago American Giants of the Negro American League. After World War II, he got plenty of attention when he batted .381 with the American Giants to lead the league. The following year, he became the Jackie Robinson of the Pacific Coast League as he integrated that circuit. He spent nine seasons in the highest minor league at San Diego, Portland, Vancouver, Sacramento, and San Francisco. He batted .323 his first season with San Diego, and in 1951 he batted a league leading .343 with Vancouver. In the minors, the left-handed hitter compiled a .300 batting average, but no major league team took a chance on him. In 2005, however, he sort of made the majors when the San Diego Padres unveiled a bust of Ritchey at Petco Park.[54]

The early 1940s brought significant changes to American Legion baseball. Pressure to change the age limit from 16 to 17 or 18 continued from within and without the organization. By 1941 the Selective Service was drafting boys at age 18 to serve their country. So, the argument went, if kids could die for their country, they should be allowed to play for their country. Using 17 as a maximum age proved to be a good compromise and was adopted for 1941.[55]

The blatant unfairness of giving a team that qualified for the World Series the right to host the Series, as had been the case since Chaillaux started the policy in 1935, appeared obvious to all. The unfairness became glaringly obvious in 1938 and 1940, when the visiting club lost the benefit of their African American players because of local custom. Since Chaillaux began the practice of awarding the Legion World Series to one of the teams had begun, the host/home team won four of six times. The racism of small Southern mill towns may not have bothered the Legion hierarchy, certainly not director Chaillaux, but it nevertheless, presented a black eye to Legion ball.

In the first 15 years of Legion play, California teams had captured the ultimate title on only two occasions, Oakland in 1928 and San Diego in 1938. New Orleans won the title only once, in 1932, but a New Orleans team made it to the World Series on four occasions; no other city had played in the World Series more than twice. After the mid-1930s, the Carolina mill towns had dominated the World Series. Teams from these mill towns won the national title in 1935 (Gastonia), 1938 (Spartanburg), and 1940 (Albemarle). Chaillaux and others in the Legion hierarchy clearly believed that these towns were hotbeds of baseball and drew fans better than other places. Their published attendance figures supported that belief. The greatest total attendance figures up until World War II were in Spartanburg, which drew 60,000 in 1936 and 48,500 in 1938. Tiny Albemarle ranked third, drawing 42,500 in 1940. No location would approach those numbers for another 70 years until Shelby, North Carolina, a Piedmont mill town to be sure, broke all attendance records beginning in 2011.

3

The Golden Years, 1941–1951

In the 1940s, the power center of American Legion baseball shifted to California. For the 15 years that followed 1940, teams from the Golden State captured the national title six times; San Diego, Oakland, and Los Angeles each took home two national crowns. San Diego captured the title in 1941 and 1954. Oakland won back-to-back titles in 1949–1950. Teams from Los Angeles took the ALWS titles in 1942 and 1951. Back East, people came to believe that the California weather bestowed an unfair advantage on teams from the "Golden State."

The Captain Bill Erwin Post 6 of San Diego, after being shamefully treated in 1940 at Albemarle, would not be denied in 1941. Coach Mike Morrow's pipeline continued churning out players. The bulk of Morrow's 1940 team returned. Returnees included first baseman Bob O'Dell, third baseman Ed San Clemente, shortstop Nelson Manuel, and outfielders Wallace "Chris" Criswell, Sam Rosenthal, and Bob Usher, the latter also pitching and catching. He provided firepower and passion in 1941. Usher played six seasons between 1946 and 1957 in the majors with Cincinnati, Cleveland, and Washington. San Diego stumbled in the early stages of the playoffs but gained strength as they marched through the tournament. In the state finals, the boys of Sunshine Post of Los Angeles believed they were robbed of the title by the home plate umpire. Nevertheless, Post 6 took the state title by winning game one against Los Angeles, 8–3, and after losing game two, taking the rubber game, 3–2. Gene Mauch remembered, "Pitcher Bill Spacter threw pitch after pitch down the middle of the plate, but the umpire kept calling balls and the tying run and winning run walked in." Spacter was charged with 11 bases on balls. San Diego had the state title, and Mauch's Sunrise Post could only moan.[1]

At the Stockton Regional, Post 6 hammered Helper, Utah, 17–1, thanks to four hits by San Clemente. Their next game proved a bummer for San Diego, losing to Tucson, 13–2, a game in which Post 6 uncharacteristically committed eight errors. They came back to beat Tucson, 6–3, in game two. Then in a 16-inning marathon, Post 6 prevailed, 2–0. In the bottom of the 16th inning, Bob O'Dell, Miles "Griff" Hayes, and Bob Usher all singled to produce the winning run and the key victory. At Miles City, Montana, San Diego became Western champions. Post 6 beat Lewiston, Idaho, 10–5, and Tulsa twice, 10–5 and 6–5. San Diego spotted Tulsa a 5–0 lead before Usher, O'Dell, Hayes, and Rosenthal provided the punch in the 10–5 victory. Post 6 took the second game, 6–5, thanks to a Sam Rosenthal's home run in the eighth inning with two mates aboard. O'Dell, Hayes, Rosenthal, and Usher made the all-tournament team. According to Chaillaux's reasoning, that win gave Post Six home field advantage in the World Series.[2]

First they had to journey to Spartanburg for the semi-final games against Flint, Michigan. Unlike during their previous visits to the South, Post 6 experienced no racist incidents. In the first game, Flint gave the game away by committing six infield errors, allowing San Diego to win, 9–4. Flint came back to win game two by a 2–1 score, despite Usher pitching a three-hitter. Post 6 finished off the series, 9–4, behind catcher Bill LeGrande's two-run homer.[3]

In the ALWS of 1941, Post 6 had the decided advantage of playing on their home turf. Berwyn, Illinois, Post 422 had a solid program but lacked hitters to stay with San Diego. They had made the World Series in 1939, losing to Omaha. Coached by beloved Gil Laeimer, the boys from J. Sterling Morton High had no answer for San Diego in 1941, losing three straight and scoring just three runs in the process. Usher pitched a three-hit shutout in an 8–0 San Diego win in the series opener. The second game was tight. Stocky Wes Kennerly pitched a 1–0 shutout for San Diego. The winning run came in the top of the ninth inning. After Hayes singled, Manuel reached on an error, and Usher walked, San Clemente's roller to short scored Hayes. In the bottom of the ninth, San Diego needed a game-saving catch by Usher to preserve the victory. In game three, Usher and San Clemente banged RBI doubles in the first inning to put San Diego up, 3–0. After Berwyn tied it, Usher moved to the mound and ended the rally to collect the save. San Clemente drove in the go-ahead run. Hayes collected three hits to pace the offense for San Diego, the 5–3 winner.[4]

The 1941 season had been played against the backdrop of mounting world tensions. War in Europe, of course, had started in 1939. By 1941 the war machines of Germany and Japan continued to roll. Germany invaded the Soviet Union in June, driving deep into Russia. Japan struck French Indochina in July. The United States responded by freezing Japan's assets in the U.S. and placing an embargo on aviation fuel. Japan needed rubber and oil; it looked to Southeast Asia to acquire its war needs. In the fall, America and Germany began an undeclared naval war as American merchant ships ferried goods to Britain and Russia across the North Atlantic, where German U-boats lurked. Even after Germany sank the American ship the good *Reuben James*, President Roosevelt refused to declare war. There was no holding back after December 7, 1941, "the day which will live in infamy" as Roosevelt called it. Japan's attack on America's Pacific fleet at Pearl Harbor brought the United States into the war. Germany obliged by declaring war on the United States. Men and boys went in droves to recruiting stations. Others waited for the draft to call their name. None expected to avoid military service.

On the West Coast, fears of Japanese invasion lasted deep into 1942. The course of events generated bewilderment, uncertainty, and fear. It appeared the world would never be the same. And yet, boys continued to play ball. Homer Chaillaux touted the Legion's contribution to the war effort. Legion baseball had achieved its "prime objective of serving national welfare by providing our youth with recreational activity which would foster and develop community spirit and the physical and mental qualities in our boys, for baseball demands and inculcates alertness, physical fitness, the will-to-win, good sportsmanship, team-work—in brief, Americanism." President Roosevelt had advised the American people to "carry on to the fullest extent consistent with the primary purpose of winning the war." Carry on the Legion proposed to do. The Legion, however, did raise the age limit from 16 to 17; specifically, boys who had not reached their 17th birthday before January 1, 1942, were eligible to play Legion ball.[5]

In 1942, the power center of Legion baseball remained in California, where it had been since San Diego won the American Legion World Series in 1938. Players on Los Angeles Sunrise Post 357 felt they had been robbed in 1941 at the state tournament and looked for revenge in 1942. At Sunrise, baseball started with its coach, Mike Catron, a stubby, terse, crusty, and demanding coach. One player described him as 5-foot-4 inches tall and 5-foot-4 inches wide. Second baseman Don Runcie remembered 50 years later that Catron "knew more baseball than anyone I've ever played for," and he played in the Cleveland Indians' and Pittsburgh Pirates' farm systems after the war. For infielder Gene Mauch, himself later known as a crusty manager, "Mike was a rough, crusty little fellow who really was made out of jello. He loved us all like sons." Mauch remembered, "we were a cocky bunch of ballplayers." They had reason to be. They were loaded. Half of the team went on to play pro ball. First baseman and captain Ralph Atkins provided left-handed power. He holds the Southern Association (class AA) career home run record, although he never quite made the major leagues. Second baseman Don Runcie tried pro ball after the war, but he had left his skills in the military. Mauch generally manned third base, but he was happy to play any position, including catcher. He played in the majors from 1947 to 1957 with six different teams. After his playing career, he managed for 26 years in the majors for Philadelphia, Montreal, Minnesota, and the California Angels, winning 1,902 games, behind only thirteen other managers. Vernal "Nippy" Jones, shortstop for Sunshine, played eight years in the majors as a first baseman, six with the St. Louis Cardinals, one with the Philadelphia Phillies, and his final season with the Milwaukee Braves. Outfielders John Bebek and Jim Muhe signed with Cleveland after the war, but neither advanced above class C level. Catcher Dick Kinaman signed with the Dodgers and played 12 seasons in the minors but, like Adkins, never appeared in a big league uniform.[6]

Sunrise struggled to get to the World Series. In the California final, they again faced San Diego Post 6, the defending state and national champions. San Diego won the first game, 10–6, before Sunrise got hot and took the twin bill on August 1, 1942, 9–5 and 19–5. Dick Kinaman had three RBI in the first Sunrise victory. Ralph Adkins pitched a complete game for the win in the deciding game. In Regional play at Stockton, they bested teams from Albany, Oregon, and Ely, Nevada. In Sectionals at Miles City, Montana, they hammered Missoula, 8–0, and Tucson, 8–1, before a 10-inning win over Missoula, 6–5.[7]

In the Western finals at Hastings, Nebraska, they faced Stockham of St. Louis, a club loaded with future big leaguers. Their lineup included Joe Garagiola (St. Louis Cardinals), first base; Bobby Hoffman (New York Giants), second base; Jack McGuire (Giants, Pirates, Browns) at shortstop; Roy Sievers (Browns, Senators, White Sox, Phillies), outfield; and future Hall of Famer Larry "Yogi" Berra (Yankees), outfield. Their mound ace, lefty Jim Goodwin, pitched briefly for the White Sox. St. Louis had beaten, LaCrosse, Wisconsin, 9–2 and 17–10, and Omaha, 21–4. Not surprisingly, St. Louis, "by virtue of its overhelming preliminary play," reigned as the favorite. Dan Brown, however, pitched a shutout in the opening game, as Sunshine coasted to an 8–0 triumph. Stockton came back to take game two by an 8–4 score. In that game, Berra was credited with stealing home. Fans of Yogi Berra find it difficult to imagine the stocky, awkward, and slow-footed Berra actually stealing home; more amazingly, he crossed the plate standing. The play came on a double steal. With Berra on third, the runner on first took off on a steal of second, and Berra beat the throw home with room to spare. In the rubber game, with Brown back on the mound, Sunshine captured the Western title, 13–6.[8]

In the 1942 World Series, Sunshine had little trouble with Manchester, New

Hampshire, even though the Series was at Manchester's Municipal Athletic Field (later Gill Stadium) The field had hosted the 1932 American Legion World Series. At 312 feet, it was short down the left field line, 321 to the foul pole in right field, and 400 feet to center field. Manchester's Sweeney Post had won their regional, beating teams from Norwood, Massachusetts, Winsor Locks, Connecticut, and Newport, Vermont. Then they moved to the Sectional in Charlotte, North Carolina. After losing an opening game to Norfolk, 5–3, they beat Passaic, New Jersey, 8–0, and Norfolk, 5–2. In the Eastern finals back home in Manchester, they won two of three from an up-and-coming Bentley Post 50 Cincinnati team, which had knocked Oakland out in Omaha. Manchester took game one, 5–2, and game three, 1–0, while losing game two by a 6–5 score. So Manchester got to play on its home field,[9]

Manchester, however, was no match for the boys from Los Angeles in the 1942 ALWS final. Sunrise romped to three straight wins by scores of 6–2, 5–2, and 3–0. In the final, shortstop Nippy Jones led the way with three hits for Sunrise. Third baseman Mauch sparkled in the final game, starting the only double play of the day and collecting the only extra-base hit to drive in the first Los Angeles run. Bob Moore hurled the shutout.[10]

In January 1943, Homer Chaillaux announced that the Legion planned to continue the World Series baseball program despite the war effort. Unlike in the past, when he had justified Legion-sponsored baseball as a bulwark against radicalism, now he claimed it contributed to the war effort by improving the physical fitness of American boys and mastering teamwork. The Legion already had the major league's $20,000 contribution in hand. Discussion about raising the playing age got nowhere. If a boy was 16 on January 1, 1943, he was eligible to play. The format of the World Series, however, would be very different, and the site selection system would also be altered. Since the first American Legion World Series in 1926, the tournament had produced winners of the East and the West, who then played a "world series." The new format would involve four teams playing double-elimination format. When a team lost two games, they would be eliminated. The four regionals would be played in Charlotte, Denver, Hastings, Nebraska, and Miles City, South Dakota. It would be unlikely that any team would have home field advantage, the clearly unfair practice that had been in effect since 1935.[11]

Chaillaux's bes- laid plans came unraveled in the Southeastern Sectional. After Birmingham captured the sectional tournament by beating Whiteville, North Carolina, 8–5, and advanced to Regional play at Charlotte. The Alabama team took two games from Springfield, Ohio, to seemingly punch their ticket to Miles City for the final four. Their journey was put on hold when Springfield and then Whiteville filed formal protests, claiming that Birmingham used an ineligible player. Birmingham ended up forfeiting its games in both the regional and sectional rounds. The other three teams who had won their Sectionals, namely Richfield-Minneapolis, Flint, Michigan, and New Orleans, were already in Miles City awaiting the fourth team. Since both Springfield and Whiteville had legitimate claims to advance, logic would have had them play to determine which team would advance to the finals. With little time to spare before the scheduled start of the World Series, Chaillaux decided to bring both Springfield and Whiteville to Miles City. Richfield and New Orleans were the pre–Series favorites. The New Orleans team was known as Aloysius-Jax because their players came from St. Aloysius High School and their sponsor was Jax beer. New Orleans infielder George Bevan Strickland stood out as the best all-around player. Whiteville boasted George "Buck" Hardee, the batting leader with a .657 average for the tournament. The Red Arrow Post of Flint had the best pitcher in Emery Hresko, who had pitched a no-hitter against Lynn in their 8–1 Sectional victory.[12]

Richfield, Minnesota, came to the ALWS with a 27–2 record. They had only one bump coming through state, regional, and sectional qualifying. They completely outclassed the Minnesota competition, winning by scores of 25–1, 8–0, and 4–0. Competition became tougher at the Sectional, but they slipped past Bancroft, Iowa, 2–1, thanks to pitcher Bob Davidson's 15 strikeouts; and Sioux Falls, 4–3, when captain and second baseman Jerry Smith homered. In their Sectional at Miles City, they faced Rincon Hill of San Francisco, a team that boasted a 49–1 record, in a three-game series. Pitchers apparently left their best stuff at home. Richfield won the first game, 12–11, by scoring two runs in the bottom of the 10th inning. Rincon Hill took the second game, 7–5. Richfield had to come from behind to win the final game, 10–9, on shortstop Roger Brown's two-run homer.[13]

Richfield's struggle with its pitching began to change in the World Series. Springfield beat Whiteville, 8–4, on day one, and New Orleans sent Whiteville back to North Carolina on the second day. Flint also went quickly, losing to Richfield, 5–2, behind Bob Donaldson's winning pitching and his two-run homer, and to Springfield, 10–9, as Springfield's Harry Amato collected three hits, four RBIs, and saved the game in relief. On Sunday, day three of the ALWS, New Orleans, behind the stellar pitching of Tom Brennan, beat seemingly unbeatable Richfield, 3–1. The next day, Springfield knocked off New Orleans, 4–3, on Dick Brinkman's walk-off single. The win over New Orleans put Springfield in the driver's seat, but that perch lasted only until the next game, when they dropped a 9–5 slugfest to Richfield. Donaldson got credit for the win and contributed a two-run home run. After buckets of rain washed out Monday games, Richfield, New Orleans, and Springfield all had one loss. On the final day, Richfield eliminated New Orleans, 3–2. The final game of 1943 was a classic pitching duel between Danielson and Springfield's Amato. Minneapolis broke a 2–2 tie in the seventh inning when Amato walked outfielder Paul Otness and second baseman Roger Brown doubled Otness home with the winning run. Minnesota had its first national champion.[14]

Danielson, who won three games in the series and hit .400, garnered the informal Most Valuable Trophy. George "Buck" Hardee of Whiteville was the batting champ with a .657 average. The all-tournament team picked by the *Minneapolis Star-Tribune* consisted of: Bob Danielson (Richfield), pitcher; Harry Amato (Springfield), pitcher; Emery Hresko (Flint), pitcher; Dan Brennan (New Orleans), pitcher; Harry Collias (Richfield), catcher; Leo Rozyla (Flint), first baseman; Jim Bumilla (New Orleans), second baseman; George Strickland (New Orleans), third baseman; Roger Brown (Richfield), shortstop; Jerry Smith (Richfield), utility; Eugene Burg (Springfield), outfielder; Dick Brinkman (Springfield), outfielder; and Buzz Wheeler (Richfield), outfielder.[15]

World War II continued to rage through 1943 and 1944. In February 1943, the Germans capitulated at Stalingrad after the Red Army suffered enormous losses. American troops finished up in North Africa, captured Sicily, and invaded Italy. In the Pacific, Marines took the island of Tarawa in November 1943 and began island-hopping. On the home front, it seemed that everything was rationed—gasoline, coffee, sugar, nylon stockings. Trains gave preference to men in uniform, making the job of transporting teams a Rubik's cube of railroad schedules. The numbers of participants, players, and posts were down, but Legion baseball soldiered on. The major leagues managed to keep their contribution to Legion ball at the $20,000 level. The Ford Motor Company jumped in to help, evidence that American Legion baseball had burrowed deep into the fabric of the summer season around the country. Edsel Ford, before his death, worked out a plan where Ford agreed to donate the trophy to the winner of the Legion World Series and to encourage its dealers to sponsor local teams and support sectional and regional programs.[16]

Up until the late 1930s, Legion ball failed to produce any dynasties. In the late 1930s and early 1940s, San Diego Post 6 put together a mini-dynasty. They won national titles in 1938 and 1941 and finished second in 1940, when it could be argued that they were deprived a third title by the collusion of the Legion's national office and Southern racism. In 1944 a new team that would be a powerhouse into the 1960s appeared on the scene. Cincinnati's west side pipeline began producing star players for Bentley Post 50 at an unprecedented rate. Most of those players attended either Western Hills Public High School or Elder High School, a Catholic boys' prep school. Elder had won the state baseball championship in 1943. Western Hills captured the state title in 1948, 1951, 1967, 1977, and 1986. Those boys fed into the Post 50 program. There they met a short man with a squeaky voice named Joe Hawk. A school principal when not coaching baseball, Hawk knew how to handle boys and impart fundamentals and dedication to baseball. Hawk's 1944 team had two big pitchers, an outstanding catcher, a lineup that seldom beat themselves, and coolness under pressure. Herman Wehmeier was a 6-foot-2-inch, 16-year-old right-hander who went on to pitch 13 years in the majors with Cincinnati, Philadelphia, and St. Louis. Lefthander Dick Holmes, at 6-foot-4 inches, terrorized opposing batters. Holmes went to war after a brief stint in AAA ball, and he left his good stuff in the military. Catcher Norb Ranz handled pitchers like a tailor measuring a suit. Ranz played a few years in the minors, but in the end, his bat let him down. The battery formed the backbone of a talented team.[17]

Bentley gained the attention of other Legion teams at the 1944 sectional in Grand Forks, North Dakota. In a sweltering, mid-continent heat wave, they beat defending national champion Minneapolis-Richfield in a game that put Bentley on the map. Despite this key victory, Bentley gained admission to the World Series without playing a game. Louisville's Shawnee Post 193 failed to show for the sectional final at Belleville, Illinois. The forfeit went to Bentley. Although Louisville's coach Eddie Martin claimed he had a promise from Steve Butler, tournament director, that the Louisville team would not play the day following a hard game, played in 100-degree temperature, Chaillaux refused to allow Louisville's protest.[18]

The 1944 World Series was played at Minneapolis' Nicollet Park. Few balls went out of Nicollet; the dimensions were 334 feet to left, 432 to center, and only 279 to right, but there was a wall 30 feet high to clear. Tucson Post 7 just managed to make the final four. At the Sectional at Billings, Montana, they beat Aberdeen, South Dakota, 4–3 and 5–3, and took two out of three from Portland, Oregon, losing, 8–3, before winning 5–4 and 9–6. Tucson was happy to be at the World Series. They went down on the first day, losing to Albemarle, North Carolina, 5–2, in the afternoon and to Brockton, Massachusetts, 4–1, at night. In the first game, Albemarle pitcher Ed Gibson struck out 15 Tucson batters. Brockton proved a little tougher than Tucson. They touted two decent little pitchers in Mike Kondracki and Dick Columbo and a nice shortstop in Tom Deftus, Brockton's only selection on the all-tournament team. Still, they were easy pickings. In the opening game of the series, they lost to Herm Wehmeier by a 6–3 score as he struck out 11 batters. Second baseman Larry Keller drove in three runs and contributed "sensational plays" in the field. Albemarle then clobbered the Brocs, sending them home bloodied after an 8–1 loss in which Ed Gibson again struck out 15 batters.[19]

Albemarle was clearly the second-best team in the 1944 Series. On day two, the undefeated teams, Albemarle and Bentley, squared off. Dick Holmes, the 6-foot-4 left-hander who started for Bentley, was fast but wild. He struck out 13 batters while walking10. Bentley had to wait until the ninth inning to score the winning run in a 5–4 game. Albemarle came back behind the strong right arm of little Ed Gibson to upset Wehmeier and Bentley, 6–2, and even the series. Gibson struck out 11 and limited Bentley to four hits. Albemarle exploded for four runs in the fourth inning when two walks, a sacrifice, hit batter, and singles by Red Sides and Chuck Wiles gave Gibson a commanding lead, and they cruised to an 8–7 victory. That set up a grand finale. Gibson would take the mound for Albemarle against Holmes of Cincinnati. The only problem was that Holmes came down with a sore arm and was a no go. Rather than pitch Wehmeier, who had struggled in the last game, Joe Hawk chose to pitch his third baseman, Ralph Kraus, even though Kraus had never before pitched for Bentley. In the third inning, Bentley got three runs when Dick Hollstegge, Kraus, and Norb Ranz singled, between two errors, plus a hit by Chuck Brentlinger. Albemarle threatened in the fourth inning but three hits produced just a single run. Kraus went the distance, giving up just two runs.[20]

Sportswriters and fans alike were awed by Gibson's performance. No one objected to his selection as Most Valuable Player of the Series. The rest of the all-tournament team were as follows: first base, Frank Little, Albemarle; second base, Larry Keller, Cincinnati; third base, Ralph Kraus, Cincinnati; shortstop, Tom Deftos, Brockton; outfield, Jim Hirth, Cincinnati; outfield, Blane Noah, Albemarle; outfield, Herm Wehmeier, Cincinnati; catcher, Norb Ranz, Cincinnati; and pitcher, Ed Gibson, Albemarle.[21]

It was 1945! The war ended! In April, President Roosevelt died. V-E Day, the German surrender, took place on May 8, 1945. For America there was a new president, Harry Truman, a short, tough-talking World War I veteran. The war in the Pacific ended with America dropping two atomic bombs on Japan in August and Japan's formal surrender on the *U.S.S. Missouri* on August 13, 1945. The world had entered the Atomic Age, but few yet understood the full import of that. America wanted to return to normal, and normal meant baseball. Before the end of May 1945, some veterans were returning to their major league teams. Later in the year, baseball got a new commissioner, Albert Benjamin "Happy" Chandler, former senator from Kentucky.

American Legion baseball also got a new head. In May, Homer Chaillaux announced his resignation as head of the Legion's Americanism Commission effective June 6, 1945. He planned to return to his home in Inglewood, California, to become the Legion's director of programs and promotions in California. By October he wanted a more active role, and to that end he campaigned for and was elected adjutant for California. In truth, however, he was in poor health when he stepped down and would die within the year, on February 18, 1946. Chaillaux had run the Legion's baseball program since he became head of the Americanism Commission in 1934. Junior baseball grew and flourished under his leadership despite the fact that his interest was almost always elsewhere. Wherever he could, he spent his time combatting communism, radicalism, immigration, unionism, and any form of liberalism around, especially that which he imagined existed in public schools. Chaillaux's successor would not have the complete power he had wielded. A West Virginian named R. Worth Shumaker took the job as acting director of the National Americanism Commission. Shumaker had been superintendent of schools in Upshur County, West Virginia, where he gained a reputation as a strong advocate for more conservative curriculum in public schools. That issue led Chaillaux to select Shumaker as assistant national Americanism director, which put him next in line when Chaillaux retired.[22]

In 1945 American Legion baseball produced a Cinderella story. Shelby, North Carolina, Warren F. Hoyle Post 82 came out of nowhere to capture the American Legion World Series. Shelby, a small city of 14,000 and the seat of Cleveland County, lacked a tradition of strong Legion programs. Shelby had never sent a team to the Legion World Series; only once had a Shelby team reached a sectional tournament, and that was back in 1938. Their greatest success before 1945 was winning a state title in 1942. As their backup pitcher, B. C. Wilson, put it: "we didn't have a bunch of all-stars." That was an understatement. None of their players had a professional career. Theirs was an example of the saying "the whole was better than its parts." What they did have was a whole town behind them. As the future wife of star pitcher Roy "Boots" Kent remembered: "the whole town just lit up. I have never seen Shelby like that before. Everything that summer was around the team." The whole really was greater than its parts.[23]

Going into the Series, the Trenton Schroths of Post 93 (30–4) stood above the rest as the favorites to win the title. Trenton had a long tradition of strong teams; they had won the New Jersey title 11 times in the past 15 years, most recently in 1941, 1943, 1944, and 1945. In 1945 Shelby posted an impressive 25–1 record, but they had played fewer games than the other three teams. The Tucson Cowboys boasted two future pros in third baseman Lee Roy Carrey, the best pure hitter in the Series, and second baseman Chet Vasey. Oak Park, Illinois, had the best pitcher in classy little lefthander Herb Adams, who made it to the Chicago White Sox as an outfielder. They had defeated Little Rock, 1–0, to advance to the Sectional at Mason City, Iowa. There they beat Bancroft, Iowa, 5–4, the New Orleans Blue Jays, 7–6, and Bancroft again by a 7–0 score for the right to play in the World Series. The Series was played at Griffith Park in Charlotte, North Carolina, a traditional minor league park that seated 6,500, with dimensions of 320 to left field, 390 to center field, and 320 to right field.[24]

Shelby Post 82 had two fine pitchers. Harry McKee was the only member of the team to play professionally; he logged two unspectacular minor league seasons. The second pitcher, Boots Kent, married his high school sweetheart, went in the military, and never returned to the mound. Shelby won the state title by beating Laurinburg, 7–0. They had little trouble at the Regional tournament at Sumter, South Carolina, beating Norfolk, Virginia, Woodruff, South Carolina, and Memphis, Tennessee. In the Section Three tournament at Charleston, South Carolina, they beat Meriden, Mississippi, 3–2, and Roosevelt Post of East Chicago, Indiana, 7–1 and 5–1. In the final game, Kent controlled Roosevelt, limiting the Rough Riders to three hits, while collecting three hits of his own.[25]

Trenton, to everyone's surprise, lost its first game, 2–1, to Oak Park. Adams got credit for the win and drove in both of Oak Park's runs. Trenton's ace, George Uyhazi, took the loss. A capacity crowd of over 9,000 showed up to see Shelby in the second game. Shelby did not disappoint its fans, scoring the winning run in the ninth when third baseman Billy Hutchins singled, his third hit of the game, stole second, and came home on shortstop Allan Washburn's single. In the losers' bracket, Trenton bested Tucson, 9–4, to send the Cowboys home. In the winners' bracket, Shelby's Boots Kent pitched a one-hitter for nine innings, but the game went 10 innings. Shelby scored a run in the second inning on a wild pitch, but Oak Park tallied one in the sixth inning on its only hit of the game, a single by Billy Mead. Kent got credit for the win. Trenton's George Uyhazi threw a four-hitter at Oak Park as Trenton rolled to an 8–1 win and the right to play Shelby in the championship game.[26]

Trenton Schroths Post 93 had arrived in Charlotte with a 30–4 record and was the pre-ALWS favorite. They had confirmed their favorite status at the Bridgeport Sectional when they trounced Newark, Delaware, 6–1 and 15–0, and Stratford, Connecticut, 10–1. Mount ace George Uyhazi pitched a one-hitter against Stratford. They then eliminated Tucson and Oak Park, Illinois, at Manchester, New Hampshire. In the opening game of the World Series, the Schroths showed they were beatable, losing a pitching duel between Uyhazi and Oak Park's little lefty, Herb Adams. They returned to form, beating Tucson 9–4. They reached the championship game by beating Oak Park, 8–1, as Uyhazi pitched a four-hitter before 10,250 fans.[27]

On the final day of the 1945 American Legion World Series, an overflow crowd of 10,025 turned out at Griffith Park. A tired Trenton club committed five errors, and Shelby's mound ace, Harry McKee, humbled the Schroths, limiting them to four hits in Shelby's 4–2 win. Shelby still needed center fielder Harvey Bowen's shoestring catch to end the game with the bases loaded. Worth Shumaker presented the newly minted Howard P. Savage championship trophy to Shelby captain Jack Bridges. The Louisville Slugger Award went to Tucson's Lee Carey with a .376 batting average, low for the ALWS. He signed with the Cleveland Indians. The Series drew 41,250 fans, the fifth-highest since the event started 20 years before.[28]

In 1946 Americans realized the war was over. The United States reigned as the only world power. The Soviet Union, Great Britain, Australia, and Canada were also on the winning side, but they had suffered far more than the U.S. The 20th century really did now appear to be America's century. The country moved to convert from a wartime economy and military mind-set to peacetime priorities. Everyone, it seemed, wanted to get the troops home as soon as possible and return to normal. For teenage boys, it was time to put away their model P-51 Mustangs and get out the neatsfoot oil to work on their baseball gloves. Kids signed up for American Legion ball in record numbers. In the past few years, the Legion had bragged that 300,000 boys participated on teams that entered the Junior Baseball Tournament. In 1946 the organization touted a record 800,000 boys who were not age 17 before January 1, 1947. To deal with the financial pressure which had been an annual issue since 1933, the Ford Motor Company committed itself to contribute $500,000 to Legion baseball. Plenty of boys and plenty of money.

The organization also had a change of leadership at the top of the baseball program. Worth Shumaker, who had served as acting director of the National Americanism Commission in 1945, was reduced to assistant director, although his duties changed little. The new director of Americanism became General Elmer W. Sherwood (1896–1978), a World War I veteran, who had served with the Rainbow Division of Indiana troops and who published *A Soldier in World War I: The Diary of Elmer W. Sherwood and Rainbow Hoosier*. He displayed no more interest in baseball than had Homer Chaillaux, and, as Chaillaux had done, focused his attention on the imagined communist danger.[29]

New Orleans had sent teams to the ALWS six times, but a team from the city had managed to win only once, in 1932. The city fielded another strong team from Jesuit High School, known variously as Post 125, the Blue Jays (the school nickname), or Tulane Shirts, the sponsor. Their coach, Eddie Toribio, one of the all-time great prep athletes in New Orleans history while at Jesuit, had never coached baseball before, but he knew how to handle boys. His track team at Jesuit had won the state championship in the spring of 1946. Brother Martin, the headmaster of Saint Aloysius College High, who had hired Toribio as football coach, said, "in him I know I have a leader, a teacher, a gentleman—in a word 'a real man.'" Toribio fielded a well-balanced club devoid of major league prospects, but solid throughout its lineup. Two strong pitchers, Pat Rooney (9–0) and Gus Riordan (6–2), gave them an advantage in most games. Little Joe Mack, all of 125 pounds, patrolled center field, batted leadoff, and hit .415 for the season. First baseman Stan McDermott led the team with a .421 batting average in the playoffs. Shortstop Don Wetzel was the alpha male of the group. He captained the team and aspired to a baseball career. After graduating from Loyola University of New Orleans, he spent four years in the New York Giants' minor league system before deciding that his degree in foreign trade offered him a better living. He went to work for IBM and is credited with creating the automatic teller machine (ATM) in the late 1960s. A teammate, Maurice "Moon" Landrieu, like Wetzel attended Loyola University of New Orleans, but after graduating, he earned a law degree there and went into Democratic politics. He became a two-term mayor of New Orleans, 1970–1978, and then Secretary of Housing and Urban Development under President Jimmy Carter.[30]

The Blue Jays stumbled in the state tourney, losing to Baton Rouge. Fortunately, the loss came in a two-of-three series, allowing Toribio's squad to come back and win the next two games. They then won two from Shreveport Byrd to take the Louisiana title. Post 125 rolled through the Regional, beating Houston, 19–1, and Little Rock, 4–2 and 10–8. Moving on to Sectionals in Gastonia, North Carolina, they beat Kannapolis, the hometown favorite, in a 7–6 squeaker before 9,000 fans. Then they topped Thomaston, Georgia, by the convincing score of 10–1. Pat Rooney threw a three-hitter for the Blue Jays and sparked a seven-run fifth inning with a two-run triple.[31]

The 1946 American Legion World Series had been scheduled for St. Paul, Minnesota, but a polio outbreak in the Twin Cities threatened the viability of that location. When fear of a pandemic threatened the series in St. Paul, seven cities applied to host. In mid–August, Charleston, South Carolina, was chosen as the site for the World Series. College Park, which served as home field for The Citadel, had short dimensions—310 feet to left field and 298 to right field—but it seated 6,200. In the Series, New Orleans Post 125 faced strong opposition in Trenton, Post 93, Cincinnati's Bentley Post 50, and the Los Angeles Vernons. The Trenton Schroths had a rich heritage, having won state titles 13 times since 1930. They had been national runners-up in 1933 and 1945. Their second-place finish the previous year made them the favorites in 1946. Bentley Post 50 of Cincinnati had won the national title in 1944, although none of that team remained on Joe Hawk's 1946 club. Bentley boasted the top batter in Series play in outfielder Vic Kauffman, who batted a resounding .467. Shortstop Don Zimmer garnered support as the top major league prospect in Legion play. Bentley was loaded but was a year away from peaking. The Los Angeles Vernons and their coach, Ed Kelly, were happy to be in the mix.[32]

As they had in the Louisiana state tourney, the New Orleans Blue Jays stumbled coming out of the gate. To everyone's surprise, Los Angeles managed to upset New Orleans in the very first game by a 6–0 count. Los Angeles pitcher Jack Carmichael was exceptionally sharp, pitching a two-hit shutout. Toribio took his team to task after the game. "I can't see how a team could beat you boys," he moaned. Then he went to the positive, saying, "I think you are the most deserving team here." Finally, he turned to a higher power. "I think the Lord will pull us through." Whether help came from a higher power or not, the Blue Jays sailed through the remainder of the series. In the losers' bracket, they faced Cincinnati. Bentley had dropped a 6–4 game to Trenton. The Schroths' first baseman, Dick Geidlin, provided the spark in that game with two hits and four RBI. The

Blue Jays eliminated Cincinnati with ease, 7–2, as Rooney picked up the win. In the winners' bracket, Trenton moved on with a 3–2 win over Los Angeles. New Orleans faced Los Angeles in another elimination game. The game between losers did not prove exciting as only 1,500 fans showed up. Los Angeles manager Ed Kelly held back ace pitcher Jack Carmichael so he would be rested for the anticipated showdown against Trenton. Kelly paid a steep price for overlooking New Orleans. The Blue Jays sent the Los Angeles boys home with a 5–3 victory. Gus Riordan was the winning pitcher.[33]

That left only Trenton and New Orleans standing to compete for the 1946 title. Trenton needed only to win one game to capture the 1946 title, but their manager, Jake Miller, decided to play it safe and hold his pitching ace George Uhaze for the deciding game in the event New Orleans won the first contest. The first game turned into a 15–3 blowout for the Blue Jays. One sportswriter called the game a "comedy of base on balls." Trenton pitchers issued 13 walks. New Orleans pounded out 16 hits, with first baseman Stan McDermott, second baseman Jimmy Nissel, and center fielder Joe Mock providing most of the firepower. In the final game, Riordan opposed Uhaze, who had a gaudy 14–0 record. In the pitching duel, Uhaze allowed just five hits, but Riordan was even better, permitting only two bingles. New Orleans scored all three of its runs in the fourth inning thanks to two costly Trenton errors. McDermott led off with a single. Money Caballero laid down a sacrifice bunt which Uhaze threw away. With runners on first and second, Jim Nissel hit a double-play grounder to the shortstop, whose throwing error allowed McDermott to score. Mack's sacrifice fly scored Caballero. Catcher Terry Ryan's scratch hit brought in the final run. Perhaps because of the last-minute decision to hold the Series in Charleston, attendance at the 1946 ALWS was a disappointing 19,150.[34]

The American Legion Junior Baseball program got a huge boost in 1947 from the Ford Motor Company. The economic future of the Legion baseball program looked tight as the American economy faced the highest inflation in its history. The major leagues still contributed only $20,000 to help defray costs of the American Legion World Series, but those dollars did not go as far as they had in the past, even the previous year. The *Los Angeles Times* derisively called the majors' contribution "pee wee funds." Ford had been urging its dealers to sponsor local posts since 1943. Now, Ford announced its intention to contribute $1,000,000 to support Legion ball. This included giving a trophy to the World Series winner and second-place finisher, hosting final four teams, throwing a banquet before the start of the Series, and contributing to the transportation of teams to the playoffs and World Series.[35]

Ford got the most public relations mileage from bringing Babe Ruth on as a "consultant" to Ford and the American Legion. In April 1947, Ford held a press conference to announce that Ruth had signed a "life contract" to promote Legion baseball. Ruth had entered the hospital in November 1946, complaining of headaches. Efforts to address his problem showed that he suffered from throat cancer. Doctors and people close to him never mentioned the term, preferring to say only that he had "throat surgery." At the press conference, the Bambino appeared gaunt; he had lost 150 pounds, and at one point spoke in a whisper. His pay from Ford was reported to be $10,000 plus bonuses based on the number of appearances he made, which could raise his compensation to $12,000. The major leagues had been trying to forget Ruth for a dozen years, but to American boys he remained an icon if not a god: "The Bambino," "Sultan of Swat," "the Greatest Player of All Time." And he loved the adulation of boys.[36]

Despite his condition, Ruth soldiered on. He traveled over 40,000 miles for

Babe Ruth was hired in 1947 by the Ford Motor Company to be a "consultant" to American Legion baseball. The "consulting" consisted mainly of speaking to crowds at big games, and signing autographs at the Legion World Series. He was dying of throat cancer, and struggled, especially so in 1948, before he died August 16, 1948.

American Legion baseball in 1947. In the spring, he stayed in the warmth of the South, mostly in Florida. In May he moved on to Pennsylvania, Maryland, New Jersey, upstate New York, Ohio, and Indiana. By June, when he entered Mount Saini Hospital, he had his spiel down. His message was: (1) work with your coach; (2) be in top physical condition; (3) play for the good of the team; (4) play hard but play clean; and (5) hard work will make you a better man. By August, he was back on the road. Ford began to arrange appearances, generally in larger cities and in conjunction with all-star games and parades. Even though Ruth's voice remained weak and hoarse, his fans forgave him.[37]

New diversions were hitting American life in 1947. Commercial television arrived in most major cities. The Federal Communications Commission issued some 100 licenses for television stations, licenses to print money, some critics said. TV would eventually cripple minor league baseball and seriously damage the major league variety, but in the beginning, professional teams were anxious for the "free" coverage. Television was only one of the cultural changes buffeting America. World War II veterans were home from the war and going to college in unprecedented numbers, thanks to the GI Bill. Those vets also signed up for the American Legion, packing the rosters of existing posts and creating the need for new ones. They were also buying homes, new ones in suburban areas, and having children in unprecedented numbers, sparking a Baby Boom that lasted until 1964.[38]

Legion baseball enjoyed its most successful season to date in 1947. Rather quietly, leadership in Legion baseball shifted to Dale Miller, who preferred to stay out of the spotlight, but who recognized that the post-war years could be a time of growth for Legion ball. Holding the title of assistant Americanism director, he took over as coordinator of Legion baseball. With Miller's quiet leadership, membership in Legion posts bursting at the seams, and Ford's infusion of money, the number of Legion teams topped 8,000 for the first time. The Legion claimed that the number of boys playing on its teams had reached 1,000,000, up from 500,000 in 1946. The organization, which had downplayed the number of graduates in the major leagues, now took pride in such success. It claimed that 167 major league players had come through Legion baseball. Legion ball got an added endorsement from the *Los Angeles Times,* which said, "Legion baseball program is the greatest single unified drive against juvenile delinquency in America today."[39]

Cincinnati Bentley Post 50, after winning the World Series in 1944 and making it to the ALWS again in 1946 only to meet an early exit, returned virtually their entire team for 1947. To reach the World Series again, they struggled in the state playoff at Delaware, Ohio, to beat Belleville, Illinois, 6–5, in a sloppy game. Bentley committed five errors before winning in the ninth inning thanks to Don Zimmer's triple and George Moeller's bases-loaded single. In the sectionals at St. Paul, Bob Andres held St. Paul to two hits, but Bentley had to go 11 innings to win, 4–3. They had an easier time in taking two games from Davenport, Iowa, 12–5 and 8–2. This team had played together since they were nine years old. The core players started on a Knothole team called Cheviot Building and Loan, which captured the Cincinnati city title. Eleven of the players suited up for Western Hills High School, helping it to win its first state championship the following spring. None of the team members enjoyed the post–Legion real-world success of the 1946 New Orleans club, but Bentley had baseball players. Shortstop Don Zimmer was a baseball lifer. The press anointed him the best prospect in minor league ball and, after he signed with the Brooklyn Dodgers, the successor to shortstop Pee Wee Reese. Unfortunately, the always aggressive Zimmer developed the habit of getting hit in the head by pitched balls. Although he failed to live up to the lofty early expectations, he played 12 seasons in the majors, then managed for 13 more, and coached until his death in 2014. First baseman Jim Frey led Bentley in batting with a .615 average. He logged 14 minor league seasons. Although he failed to even get a cup of coffee" in the majors, he did get to manage five seasons in the big leagues, winning pennants with Kansas City in 1980 and the Chicago Cubs in 1984. He also served as general manager of the Cubs for four years. Third baseman Glenn Sample coached the University of Cincinnati baseball team for 21 years and was official scorer for the Reds for 30 years. Others—outfielders Hal Grote and George Moeller, and pitcher Bob Andres—tried their hand at pro ball but failed to make the big time. Their manager, Joe Hawk, according to the *Cincinnati Enquirer,* was "an inspiration to the boys under his wing"; he continued his day job as a school principal.[40]

In the 1947 World Series, Sweeney Post 2 of Manchester, New Hampshire, San Diego Post 6, and the Little Rock Doughboys of M. M. Ebert Post 1, joined Bentley Post 50. The Doughboys had been Regional champions in 1933 when George "Skeets" Dickey starred, and again in 1939 and 1940, when Pat Seerey led the team. Little Rock experienced bumps in the road before besting the Adamson Leopards of Dallas, 8–0, in the Regional final. "Big Louie" Schaufele pitched the shutout and drove in four runs on two homers. The victory came after dropping a sloppy 5–1 game to Adamson in which none of the runs were earned. In their Sectional at Sumter, South Carolina, they lost to Kannapolis, 1–0, but came back beat Kannapolis, 6–4, and Greenwood, South Carolina, 4–0 and 7–4. Pitcher Ernie Funk and outfielder/pitcher Louis Schaufele led the Doughboys. Both signed pro contracts with Detroit, but neither made the big club.[41]

Manchester's Sweeney Post 2 sailed through the New England Regional, topping Rutland, Vermont, and Medford, Massachusetts. After beating Torrington, Connecticut, they hit a bump in the road, losing to Wilmington, Delaware. Manchester came back to knock Torrington out of the tourney and then took out Wilmington by 4–0 and 7–1 scores. In the Regional, they beat Medford, Rutland and Bath.[42]

San Diego Post 6's trip to the World Series began by knocking off Florin Post 608 of Sacramento for the California title. In the Regional at Tucson, they scored 75 runs in three games, culminating in a 36–6 win over the Hawaii representative. At the Billings, Montana, Sectional, they defeated Boise, 3–1, and Omaha, 12–0 and 11–0. They boasted four .400 hitters, led by shortstop Neil Henderson, who led the club with a .407 average. They brought a 28-game winning streak to the ALWS.[43]

The 1947 World Series, played at Gilmore Field, home of the Hollywood Stars, had all the glamor and glitter of a Hollywood festival. The field, which opened in 1939, had normal outfield dimensions—335 feet down both foul lines and 407 to center. The distance from home plate to the backstop, however, was only 34 feet, unusually short. Gilmore seated 12,987 fans. All the baseball royalty appeared; Babe Ruth was joined by Commissioner A. B. "Happy" Chandler, along with American League president Will Harridge and National League president Ford Frick. Hollywood's idols, including Clark Gable, Betty Grable, Cesar Romano, Lew Ayers, Eddie Bracken, and Lana Turner, wanted to be seen, as did former heavyweight boxing champion Jack Dempsey.[44]

Bentley experienced trouble with Little Rock but otherwise sailed through the field. Bob Andres pitched a five-hitter and pushed his record to 18–1 as Bentley beat Little Rock, 5–2, in their opening game. Outfielder Stu Hein drove in three runs. In the other opening day game, Manchester surprised undefeated San Diego, 3–2. Manchester won it in the eighth inning when it scored two runs on a walk, single, error, walk, infield out, and sacrifice. In the winners' bracket, Bentley left little doubt of where the power lay in destroying Manchester by a dominating 11–0 score. George Moeller limited Manchester to four scattered hits, and Stu Hein homered. In the losers' bracket, Little Rock scored two unearned runs on San Diego errors in the first inning, and Kermit Tracy kept San Diego off the scoreboard the remainder of the game. Their second loss eliminated San Diego. Little Rock had little trouble in beating Manchester, 13–1, to eliminate the New Hampshire boys and set up the final between the Doughboys and Bentleys.[45]

In the 1947 championship game, Bentley won a tight, 3–2 pitching duel between Ernie Funk of Little Rock and Bob Andres. In the third inning, Funk committed a costly error on a double play ball, setting up Moeller's two-run single. Hein and Jim Frey hooked up with their bats in the eighth inning for the final run. Andres was the pitching hero, striking out 10 and scattering eight hits. Moeller's three hits raised his batting average to a tournament-high .500.[46]

Following their victory, the perks piled up for the Bentley boys. Ruth presented them with watches compliments of Ford Motor Company. They had their individual photos taken with Ruth, Betty Grable, and Lana Turner. George Moeller received the Louisville Slugger trophy for compiling the highest batting average in the tournament. When they arrived back in Cincinnati, over 1,000 fans greeted them at Union Station. In October, they went to New York to attend two World Series games between the Yankees and Dodgers.[47]

The 1947 season had been a glorious one for Legion ball. Entering 1948, the American economy had survived the strike-filled conversion year of 1946 and the inflation year of 1947. Now the economy began to hum. Gone was the fear of depression. Post-war prosperity had arrived. The prosperity made people optimistic. That had not occurred for 20 years. Major league baseball finally increased its support of Legion ball from $20,000 to $50,000. Ford, selling cars at a record pace, continued to be the major sponsor of Legion ball. Ford sponsored a special section on Legion ball in *The Sporting News*. Again, it urged its dealers to sponsor local post teams; nearly 4,000, or half the Legion teams, had Ford sponsorship. The company continued to sponsor Babe Ruth's tour, although, near death, he had an abbreviated schedule. He entered the hospital again in July and died on August 16, 1948. No wonder the Legion's optimism found fruition when the 1948 season started with 14,531 teams.[48]

In 1948, for the first time, the Legion World Series was played in Indianapolis, home of the Legion's national headquarters. The 12 Regional winners included: Region one champion Gordon-Bissell Post 4 of Keene, New Hampshire; Region two, Trenton Schroths, Post 93; Region three, Westport Post 33 of Baltimore; Region four, Hickory, North Carolina Post 48; Region five, Edward C. DeSaussure Post 9 of Jacksonville, Florida; Region six, Travis Post 76 of Austin, Texas (aka Austin Buddies); Region seven, George E. Hilgard Post 58 of Belleville, Illinois; Region eight, Fred W. Stockton Post 245 of St. Louis; Region nine, Austin, Minnesota Post 91; Region ten, Omaha, Nebraska Metz Post 1; Region eleven, Logan Wheeler Post 36 of Yakima, Washington; Region twelve, San Diego Post 6. The 12 shook down to four in the Sectionals. Omaha's Metz Post 1, the weakest of the four finalists, came through the Lewiston, Idaho, sectional by beating Yakima, Washington, 14–5. They featured Don Hunter, the finest batsman of the Series, but little else. Belleville, Illinois, brought a 16–1 record to the Series. Known as the Hilgards or Maroons, they boasted the brother combination of Wayne and Alan Grandcolas. Third baseman Al would sign with the St. Louis Cardinals, spending several years in their farm system. Wayne combined with Darrell Thompson to give Hilgard sound pitching. At Sioux City, Iowa, Hilgard beat Stockton Post of St. Louis, 7–2, to reach the ALWS. Last to arrive in Indianapolis was the De Saussure Post 9 of Jacksonville. Their regional tournament in Charleston, South Carolina, had been delayed because of a hurricane before they beat Austin, Texas, in a tight 3–2 game. They brought to the World Series a 31–3 record and pitching ace Don Bessent, whose 20–1 record caused gasps.[49]

For Trenton, 1948 was redemption time. The Schroths, named for Raymond Schroth, a World War I hero and winner of the Distinguished Service Cross and the Criox de Guerre, had failed to gain the title in four previous trips to the World Series, most recently in 1946, when they lost in the final to New Orleans. This was their sixth New Jersey championship in the past eight years. They entered the Series with a 23–3–1 record, armed with two solid pitchers. Don Minnick, a lanky (6-foot-3) right hander brought a jumping fastball that he threw from a slingshot delivery. After attending Duke University, he had a promising minor league career that earned him a cup of coffee with the Washington Senators in 1957. Little Leon "Pete" Millington, the other pitcher, threw a nasty curve ball. Together, they allowed just four runs and 18 hits in the Series. Trenton needed outstanding pitching because they lacked even average hitting, batting a measly .212 for the tournament.[50]

Trenton struggled in the first two rounds. Yonkers beat them, 10–4, in the Regional before the Schroths knocked off Naugatuck, Connecticut, by convincing 17–3 and 8–0 scores. At the Sectional, they lost to Westport Post 33 of Baltimore, 1–0, in 14 innings before establishing their dominance over the B&O club with convincing 14–0 and 9–0 wins. Marty Devlin's grand slam highlighted the first game, and Minnick's three-hit shutout provided the big story of the second.[51]

After a rain delay, the 1948 American Legion World Series got under way with Trenton (23–3) beating Omaha (43–3), 8–3, as Minnick won his 14th game of the year, striking out ten. Joseph "Chuck" Lucarella's daring theft of home in the first inning set the pace for the Schroths. Belleville (17–1) needed ten innings to beat Jacksonville, 10–8, thanks to catcher Bob Nebgen's tenth-inning, two-run triple. Jacksonville then knocked Omaha from the tourney by a 4–3 score. In a pitchers' duel, Trenton bested Belleville, 2–0. Millington gave up just two hits, and both Trenton runs were unearned. After Jacksonville knocked out Belleville, 2–1, the 1947 championship game was set, the Jax versus the Schroths. The Schroths ran wild on Jacksonville's ace pitcher, Don Bessent, stealing seven bases. Bessent later played for the Dodgers (1955–1958), but on that day, Minnick was the better pitcher as Trenton grabbed the title with a 4–1 victory. Lou Limato, Trenton left fielder, doubled in the third inning to score two mates. He scored following an error and a passed ball.[52]

The late 1940s were glory years for both major league and minor league baseball. They were for American Legion baseball as well. In 1949, the number of participating Legion teams reached a record high of 15,912. Ford's continuing involvement was no small reason for the increase in the number of teams. Over 5,000 Ford and Lincoln-Mercury dealers sponsored teams. Mainly they provided equipment, transportation, and uniforms, usually with the name of the local dealer on the back of the uniform shirt. To no one's surprise, the two best teams in the 1949 World Series, Oakland and Cincinnati, were sponsored respectively by Trader-Scott Ford of Oakland and Hamilton Ford of Cincinnati. *The Sporting News* continued to publish a Junior Baseball Edition underwritten by Ford. The site of the American Legion World Series in 1949 was Omaha's year-old Municipal Stadium (renamed Rosenblatt Stadium in 1964). It boasted perfectly symmetrical dimensions. Down both foul lines it measured 343 feet, left-center and right-center were 375 feet, and dead center field was a whopping 420 feet. These were big league numbers. A ten-foot fence ran from foul line to foul line. Officially, the stadium seated 9,416 fans, mostly under one roof. It became famous the next year, 1950, when it started to host the College World Series, which it did until 2005.[53]

Teams from Oakland and Cincinnati battled through the 1949 World Series before Oakland established its dominance. Bentley Post 50, long the king of baseball in Cincinnati, lost its status to upstart George W. Budde Post 507. In Oakland, Captain Bill Erwin Post 337 was coached by the extraordinary George Powles (pronounced "Poles"). In the next decade, Powles tutored an amazing collection of African American players, including Frank Robinson, Curt Flood, Vada Pinson, and Joe Morgan, not to mention basketball legend Bill Russell. In 1949, however, most of his players were white and Mexican-American kids. Powles drew players from McClymonds High School, where he taught, and Oakland Tech. Wherever they came from and whatever their ethnicity, they were recent arrivals in California, hungry, ambitious, and talented. The team did not want for money with two co-sponsors, E. Bercovich and Son Furniture and Trader Scott Ford. The mainstays of Erwin were shortstop Ray Herrera and catcher J. W. "Jay" Porter. Herrera, the team captain, was a slick-fielding, hard-hitting Mexican-American. He batted .400 for the competition and received the first American Legion Junior Baseball

Player of the Year award. That entitled him to become the first Legion player to be honored by the Hall of Fame, which displayed his photo for the next year. After Herrera signed for a $25,000 bonus, he played in the minors from 1952 through 1955. Porter, a 16-year-old catcher, tore up opposing pitching throughout the tournament. In ten games, he batted a remarkable .551, a new record. He banged out 27 hits, knocked in 22 runs, and scored 20 himself, all new ALWS records. He received the Louisville Slugger Award as the top hitter in national tourney play.[54]

Oakland's main competition came from Cincinnati's Budde Post 507. Cincinnati's Bentley Post 50 had won titles in 1944 and 1947 and appeared in the 1946 series, but there was no connection between Budde and Bentley. Budde arrived in Omaha with a record of 27 wins against just one loss. They had two solid pitchers in Charley Tedesco and Jack Herfurt, both of whom pitched in the New York Giants' farm system in the early 1950s. Budde eked out one-run wins against Flint (4–3) and East Chicago (6–5) in the Regional. They lost, 5–4, to St. Louis in the Sectional before coming back with convincing wins that dispatched St. Louis, 5–3 and 11–2.[55]

The other two teams in the 1949 World Series were Atlanta's Lakewood Heights Redbirds of Post 169 and Post 1 of Wheeling, West Virginia. Both teams were just glad to be there. Atlanta, the last to qualify, came in with a 26–4 record. They had lost in the Sectional to Greenwood, South Carolina, 8–1, but came back to take the sectional crown, 5–4. In the Regional at Orangeburg, South Carolina, they lost to Gastonia, North Carolina, 7–2, before prevailing, 3–1 and 8–5. Wheeling, with a 35–5 record, had two fine pitchers in Dick Westfall and Carl Norman. They captured the Regional crown by defeating Baltimore and Bunker Hill of Washington, D.C. This would be the only West Virginia team ever to make the World Series.[56]

Opening night went as expected. Oakland hammered Wheeling, 12–1, before an overflow crowd of 10,430. Cincinnati teed off on Atlanta, 16–7, a game highlighted by outfielder Jim Trefzger hitting the first home run of the Series. On the second day, Wheeling, capitalizing on six stolen bases, sent Atlanta home with a 7–4 victory. That guaranteed Wheeling a third-place finish. The first game between the two favorites went to Oakland, 11–6. Porter collected three hits, including a two-run triple, to lead the Erwins. Vern Killburg collected the win. Cincinnati then eliminated Wheeling by a 5–0 score as Jack Herfurt pitched the shutout.[57]

Cincinnati's win left only Budde and Bill Erwin Posts to fight it out for the 1949 Legion championship. Another record crowd, this one of 11,168, saw Cincinnati just get by Oakland, 13–12. Earl Hemberger collected two triples to lead Cincinnati. The Erwin boys, who were usually slick fielders, came apart, committing seven errors. In the deciding game, Jim Trefzger unloaded a mammoth home run for Cincinnati, but it was not enough as Oakland prevailed, 8–6. Oakland made up for its sloppy fielding in the previous game by turning the first triple play in World Series history. In the second inning, with Cincinnati runners on first and second, shortstop Ray Hererra "lost" an infield fly, even though the batter was out under the infield fly rule. He recovered and threw to third baseman John Statton to cut down the runner from second trying to gain the extra base; Statton then threw to first baseman Dick Moler to catch the baserunner from first in a run-down, and Herrera put the final tag on the runner.[58]

The Legion was delighted with the Series. It drew 45,757 paid admissions and turned a $12,000 profit. Oakland shortstop and captain Ray Herrera was selected as the American Legion Junior Baseball Player of the Year. Herrera batted an even .500, fielded flawlessly, and pushed his teammates to win. Teammate J. W. Porter captured the Louisville Slugger award for the highest batting average, a resounding .551 mark, in tournament play. His RBI, runs, and hits records lasted until 1983. Dale Miller, Junior Baseball's administrator, announced in November that the 1950 World Series would return to Indianapolis, an unprecedented decision.

Common wisdom and the best baseball minds decreed that no team could repeat as champions of American Legion baseball. In the quarter-century since American Legion baseball began, it had never happened. But the 1950 team from Bill Erwin Post 337 accomplished the seemingly impossible feat of winning back-to-back championships. *The Sporting News,* the Baseball Bible, proclaimed in 1964 that the 1950 Bill Erwin team was "the best legion team in history." That pronouncement was hard to dispute in 1964 and remains difficult to argue against. Not only did they become the first to win back-to-back, but in the World Series, they simply overwhelmed opponents.[59] In 1950, a record number of teams, 16,456 to be exact, participated in American Legion baseball. This was 544 more teams than had played in 1949. The Ford Motor Company, which continued to support the program, never backed away from taking credit for the growth. Over 5,000 Ford and Lincoln-Mercury dealers sponsored teams. In addition, Ford continued to underwrite the Junior Baseball Supplement in *The Sporting News.*

The early rounds of the tournament shook the number of teams from over 16,000 down to 12 Regional champs. They were: Region 1, Somerville, Massachusetts, Post 19 Pioneers; Region 2, Kearney Post 6, Bristol, Rhode Island; Region 3, Bunker Hill Post 31 of Washington, D.C.; Region 4, Richmond, Virginia, Post 1; Region 5, Sumter, South Carolina, Post 15; Region 6, Cedar Grove Post 6 of Shreveport, Louisiana; Region 7, Fred W. Beaudry Post 126, Detroit; Region 8, Fred W. Stockham Post 126 of St. Louis; Region 9, North End Post 474 of St. Paul, Minnesota; Region 10, Leyden-Chiles-Wickersham Post 1, Denver, Colorado; Region 11, Logan-Wheeler Post 36, Yakima, Washington; and Region 12, Bill Erwin Post 337, Oakland, California.

The Regionals reduced the teams to the final four in the American Legion World Series. Everyone seemed to understand that defending champion Oakland appeared to be the strongest team going in to the Series. At Hastings, Nebraska, they had beaten Yakima, 3–1, behind Vern Kilburg's two-hitter and 12 strikeouts. Bob Quinn threw a two-hitter against Denver in Erwin's 14–3 win. They finished with Denver, 10–2, as Pepper Wesley contributed the offensive spark. Bristol slipped in by beating Somerville, 10–4 and 7–5, and then took out Bunker Hill. Richmond, led by big first baseman Mel Roach and pitcher Eddie Cordiero, beat Sumter, 4–2 and 4–3, and Shreveport to claim a place in the ALWS. Stockham beat St. Paul, 3–0 and 8–0, and Detroit, 8–4, to get to the final four. If Oakland slipped, the boys from Beaumont High School in St. Louis and Stockham Legion post appeared ready to take charge.[60]

For the Bill Erwin boys, the World Series proved to be a cakewalk. They needed just three games to win the Series, played again in Municipal Stadium in Omaha, Nebraska. Bristol, Rhode Island, was riding a 20-game winning streak going into their game against St. Louis. Eddie Cordiero limited St. Louis to one run and Bristol scored an 8–1 upset in the first game of the Series. Richmond, Virginia, Post 1 fell to Oakland by an 8–2 score. Kilburg allowed Richmond just three hits. St. Louis came back to knock Richmond out 11–9. Mel Roach had three hits including a homer in a losing cause. The first-round winners, Oakland and Bristol, squared off in game four. Oakland ended any doubt about the outcome in the first inning. Oakland sent 15 batters to the plate, scoring 11 runs. Second baseman Vince Sarubbi got two hits in the first inning and five in the game. Porter had three RBI. Oakland won going away by a 22–11 score. Bristol looked hopeless, committing 10 errors and walking 15 batters. Bristol seemed to lose heart and failed to recover following the thumping by Oakland. Fred W. Stockham Post 245 of St. Louis beat Bristol, 14–6. Third baseman Don Hafer, first baseman Mickey Mahon, and shortstop Gary Delgaudo each had three hits for Stockham. Oakland awaited. In the 1950 championship game, Porter got three hits and four RBI in Oakland's 11–0 victory over Stockham. Kilburg pitched a four-hitter. Oakland did not just prevail in the Series, they dominated.[61]

Was the 1950 Oakland team the best-ever Legion team? Other teams have had more players who went on to major league careers, but none had as much Legion experience. The core of the 1949 championship team returned in 1950, except Ray Herrera. That group included two-time batting champion J. W. Porter. Nine others from 1949 were back in uniform, including the Legion's top 1950 pitcher, Vern Kilburg. The infield of first baseman Dick Moler, second baseman Vince Sarubbi, third baseman Milo Sofrance, and shortstop Eddie Rettagliata all tried to make it in professional ball following their Legion days. So did outfielders Leodis "Pepper" Wesley, Don Gonsalves and pitchers Kilburg, Bob Quinn and Rick Herrera. Catcher J.W. "Jay" Porter was the most sought-after amateur player in the country when he signed a bonus in excess of $60,000 with the St. Louis Browns. He played in only 33 games for the 1952 Browns, who promptly traded him to the Detroit Tigers. The Korean War took two seasons out of his career just as he was getting started. He knocked around for the remainder of the decade, playing for Cleveland, Washington, and the St. Louis Cardinals. He had chances to play first base, third base, and outfield as well as catcher, but his bat, which carried him to the top of Legion ranks, let him down.[62]

Erwin did have one future Hall of Fame player in Frank Robinson. Although he was not a regular starter, Robinson was an integral part of the team as a backup third baseman, occasional pitcher, and outfielder. At his induction into the National Baseball Hall of Fame, Robinson singled out Powles for praise. "I learned more from [coach] George [Powles] than I did from anyone in the big leagues." Powles "taught me how to play the game of baseball the way it should be played and that is to give 100 percent at all times. He taught us how to lose and accept it. Not to be happy about it but how to accept it graciously." Robinson was one of only two African American youth on the team, but his background and culture differed little from that of his teammates. Their working-class families, newly arrived in California, retained their ambition and optimism that showed brightly in the glow of World War II. They played ball whenever they could. Robinson remembered, "on weekdays we began playing ball at nine in the morning and continued until dark. After practice George would invite us over to his house for sandwiches and baseball talk. What a student of the game he was."[63]

The competition in the 1950 World Series was not the strongest. Traditional power Stockham Post 245 of St. Louis boasted pitcher-outfielder Lloyd Merritt, who had a brief major league career, but the team was doomed by terrible fielding. Richmond, Virginia Post 1 looked good on paper. They were 24–1 when the World Series began. Their big first baseman, Mel Roach, would collect a $40,000 bonus when he signed with Milwaukee out of the University of Virginia. Because of the "Bonus Baby rule," the Braves had to carry him for two years, after which, as was the case with Porter, the Navy took two years. In 1958 he severely damaged his knee, effectively ending his career. In the ALWS, his Richmond team failed to win a game, losing to Oakland, 22–12, in the opener, and to St. Louis, 11–9, despite Roach's three hits, including a monster home run.[64]

The Captain Bill Erwin (28–1) team of 1950 not only became the first team to repeat as champion, but Porter was the first back-to-back batting champion. He produced a .488 batting average in 1950 to win the Hillerich & Bradsby trophy. He ended his Legion career holding a number of records. In 1949 he established new records with 27 base hits, 20 runs scored, and 22 runs batted in, which he tied in 1950. Oakland finished the 1950 season with a record of 28 wins and just one loss. Over 1,000 fans greeted the team when it arrived at the Southern Pacific Railroad station in Oakland.[65]

While Captain Bill Erwin Post 337 of Oakland was winning the national title and celebrating its triumphs, tiny Crenshaw Post 715 of Los Angeles struggled for survival. Established after World War II, the post membership had stabilized at 65. In 1949 the post had a deal with a local Ford dealer to sponsor its baseball team. That sponsorship amounted only to a $700 donation. By July 1950, when the Ford dealer pulled out, the team's debt was over $1,000. Team business manager and insurance broker Charles H. Wilson told coach Benny Lefebvre, "unless we find a sponsor we'll have to fold up the team." Wilson and LeFebvre hit the road in search of such a sponsor. Before the 1950 season wound down, they found one in Fred Clampett, a wealthy Plymouth-DeSoto-Studebaker car dealer. Initially he agreed to cover the team debt, but the Crenshaw team started winning. They captured the southern California title before losing two games to Bill Erwin Post on its way to the national championship. By the end of the 1950 season, Clampett was committed to the boys.[66]

Lefebvre, a 40-year-old supervisor at Rancho Cienega Playground, tutored baseball players and future major league managers including Sparky Anderson, Norm Sherry, and Marcel and Rene Lachemann. His own son, Jim, became National League Rookie of the Year in 1965. Even though he knew most of the boys from the Rancho Cienega Terriers, the playground boys' team, Lefebvre held a two-day tryout for the Legion team. Most of the players came from Dorsey High School in South Central Los Angeles, which was located across the street from the playground. A handful came from Loyola High School.[67]

Although Sparky Anderson, years later, became the best-known member of the 1951 Crenshaw team, it was Billy Consolo's team. Without question he was the alpha male of the group. The third baseman was named all-city in Los Angeles in 1950–1951 and L.A. player of the year in 1952. The fastest guy on the team, he also ran track at Dorsey. Anderson swore that Consolo was the best high school athlete he ever saw, and his teammates agreed. They all called Consolo "Superman." In 1953 the Boston Red Sox would sign Consolo to a bonus of $65,000, making him a "Bonus Baby." To discourage such lofty signings, the signing team had to keep Bonus Babies on its major league roster for two seasons. Consolo later said he would gladly have given the money back if he could have played full-time. As it was, he blamed his lack of minor league experience for his failure to live up to his potential. He managed only a .221 lifetime batting average. Never a regular, he managed to stick around the majors as a part-time player for ten years with the Red Sox, Senators, Twins, Phillies, Angels, and Kansas City Athletics. When Sparky Anderson, his lifelong buddy, became manager of the Detroit Tigers, he appointed Consolo to his coaching staff, where he remained from 1980 to 1992. There he gained a reputation as a storyteller and humorist.[68]

Anderson, the Crenshaw shortstop, and Consolo became inseparable at age 10.

George, like Consolo, was all-city before he signed with Brooklyn in 1953. As a kid, his oversized ears embarrassed him so much he tried various ways of getting them to lie flat. While playing in the Texas League, George acquired the nickname "Sparky" that never left him. After five seasons in the Dodgers' system, he was traded to the Philadelphia Phillies. As the Phillies' regular second baseman for one year, he batted only .218 and was relegated to the minors. Anderson began his managerial career with Toronto of the American Association in 1963, but he was back in the majors as a coach in 1969. In 1970, he took over as manager of Cincinnati's Big Red Machine. He won two World Series titles with the Reds in 1975 and 1976. Moving to Detroit in 1979, he won another World Series in 1984 before he retired in 1995. He finished with 2,194 wins and was inducted into the National Baseball Hall of Fame in 2000.[69]

Anderson and Consolo were the only members of the 1951 Crenshaw team to make the majors as players, but they were not the only ones to dream of doing so. Catcher Bill Lachemann spent 1955–1963 in the Dodgers' farm system. He then managed in the minors for 14 years, but he did finally make the majors as the Angels' bullpen coach under his brother Marcel in 1995. First baseman Jerry Siegret played for the University of Southern California, where he garnered All-American honors in 1958 when USC won the NCAA national championship. He logged three minor league seasons in the Red Sox's chain. Outfielder-pitcher Don Kenway spent six years in the Dodgers' chain. Pitching ace Frank Layana signed with the Chicago White Sox after graduation from Loyola High School, spending six years in the lower minors, mainly as an outfielder. Paul "Buzz" Schulte was elected school president at Loyola, but despite a good curveball decided against turning pro.[70]

After struggling in the state finals, Crenshaw sailed through the sectionals and regionals. Fortunately, the state finals were a best-of-three series against Sacramento. Crenshaw lost, 5–2, in the first game. Then Consolo batted in three runs to pace Crenshaw to a 10–9 victory in game two. In game three, Frank Layana was in control, pitching a four-hitter in Crenshaw's 3–2 win. Playing in a dust storm in Winslow, Arizona, they took four and one-half hours to beat Tucson's Morgan McDermott by the football score of 27–7. Farmington, Utah, fell 7–2 as Buzz Schulte threw a five-hitter. Tucson again went down, 11–0. On to the Regionals in Hastings, Nebraska, for Crenshaw. Omaha Post 1 provided the stiffest competition for Crenshaw. In their first meeting, Layana was in control the whole game, pitching a three-hitter in a 10–0 rout. After Schulte limited Billings, Montana, to three hits in a 6–0 Crenshaw win, the Los Angeles crew faced Omaha again. This time Crenshaw was happy to pull out a 3–2 win in 13 innings. Layana limited Omaha to four hits, and Consolo had two hits and two stolen bases. They entered the World Series with a 32–3 record.[71]

The Regional champions in 1951 were: Region one, Pittsfield, Massachusetts, Post 68; Region two, White Plains, New York, Post 135, featuring Grover Jones, a unanimous choice as Legion Player of the Year; Region three, Bunker Hill Post 31 of Washington, D.C.; Region four, Sandston, Virginia, Post 242; Region five, Edward DeSaussure Post 9 of Jacksonville, Florida; Region six, Travis Post 76 of Austin, Texas; Region seven, Robert E. Bentley Post 50, Cincinnati; Region eight, Thomas Hopkins Post 4, Wichita, Kansas; Region nine, Lenz-Gazecki Post 152, Menasha, Wisconsin; Region ten, Omaha, Nebraska, Post one; Region eleven, Yellowstone Post 4 of Billings, Montana; Region twelve, Crenshaw Post 715, Los Angeles, California.[72]

The Jacksonville Post 9 Generals beat the Austin, Texas Buddies, 9–4, and Sandston,

Virginia, 3–0 and 4–3, to gain the ALWS. Grover Jones' White Plains team beat Pittsfield, Bristol (5–2), and Bunker Hill of DC, 6–5, to gain the World Series. Cincinnati's Bentley Post 50 blew through Wichita, 5–2, before losing to Berwyn, 5–4, to end Bentley's 31-game winning streak. They then destroyed Berwyn, 17–1, as Russ Nixon collected five hits and five RBI.[73]

The final four who gathered at Briggs Stadium in Detroit consisted of Crenshaw Post 715 of Los Angeles, Bentley Post 50 of Cincinnati, DeSaussure Post 9 of Jacksonville, and White Plains Post 135. On opening day of the ALWS, Bentley beat White Plains, 6–1. Howard Whitson pitched a tidy five-hitter for his 13th win in a row. Left fielder Russ Nixon and shortstop Howard Sweet collected two hits each. In the other opening game, Crenshaw beat Jacksonville, 8–4. Shortstop George Anderson had three hits and two RBI, and Frank Layana struck out ten. Only 800 paid to see the game in 52,000-seat Briggs Stadium on a chilly and wet day.[74]

On day two, White Plains controlled the losers' bracket, beating Jacksonville, 6–0. Jack "Junior" Yvars pitched a three-hit shutout. Catcher Grover "Deacon" Jones, Jr. had two hits and a stolen base. White Plains now looked competitive, as they boasted a dominating battery in Yvars and Jones, Jr. Yvars was the younger brother of New York Giants catcher Sal Yvars. Jones would be selected the 1951 Legion Player of the Year and would win the Louisville Slugger award as the top hitter with a .408 average for the tournament. He signed with the Chicago White Sox in 1956 but lost a season to an arm injury and two to the military. He played three seasons in the majors and 11 in the minors, spent 14 years as coach with Houston, San Diego, and Baltimore, and spent 20 years as a scout for the Baltimore Orioles.[75]

Bentley Post 50 of Cincinnati was getting to be a perennial contender. Post 50 entered the regional with a 29-game winning streak. After knocking off Flint, Michigan, 6–4, and Berwyn, Illinois, 5–4, they were stunned by Berwyn, 5–4. In the rubber game, Bentley made clear they were the better team by destroying Berwyn, 17–1. Howard Whitson held Berwyn to four hits and Russ Nixon slammed out five hits and collected five runs-batted-in. In the key game of the Series, Crenshaw won a tight 1–0 game against Bentley, on John Siegert's single off the first baseman's glove in the bottom on the ninth. Paul Schutte pitched the shutout to improve his record to 13–1. The hard-luck loser was LA's Bill Barnes.[76]

Then White Plains made its move. They shut out Cincinnati, 6–0. George Raimo pitched the five-hit shutout, Jones had two hits and an RBI, and second baseman Sam Alston stole home. The following day, White Plains upset Los Angeles, 3–1, on a day when the Crenshaw lads came unglued, uncharacteristically committing three errors. Yvars struck out 12, and Jones walked three times, leading to two runs. Although all runs against him were unearned, Layana took the loss, his third against 20 wins. The White Plains win set up a final showdown between Crenshaw and White Plains for the 1951 Legion title. Neither team had its best pitcher available, and it showed. White Plains jumped on Schulte in the first inning. Jones' three-run homer gave White Plains the early lead. Crenshaw roared back with four runs in the bottom of the first. Outfielder Don Kenway and catcher Bill Lachemann each had two RBI for Los Angeles. Crenshaw stretched its lead with three more runs in the bottom of the second to give them a 7–3 lead. Jones later doubled home two more runs for White Plains, but it was not enough. Kenway also knocked in two more runs as Crenshaw Post 715 prevailed, 11–7. For the tournament, Billy Consolo led Crenshaw with a .390 batting average.[77]

The Crenshaw team arrived back in Los Angeles' Union Station on September 11. After posing for pictures, they paraded through downtown, winding up at Clampett's automobile dealership on Figueroa Street. Clampett himself gave each of the 16 team members an electric razor and team jacket. They were the seventh Legion national champions from the Golden State, which had clearly established itself as the center of Legion baseball.[78]

During World War II, and especially in the post-war years, American Legion baseball flourished as never before or after. By 1950 over 16,000 teams, with somewhere around two million players, donned uniforms of Legion posts. Two mini-dynasties had emerged. Oakland's 1949–1950 team, led by J. W. Porter and coached by George Powles, proved that it was possible to win batting titles and World Series championships back-to-back. No team had accomplished such a feat in the history of Legion ball. Cincinnati's Bentley Post 50 teams won national titles in 1944 and 1947, while finishing second in 1949 and third in 1951. On the national front, graduates of Legion baseball were beginning to dominate the rosters of major league teams. Without trying, Legion baseball had become the training ground for major league baseball. Finally, Legion baseball was increasingly seen as a force for good in American life. Los Angeles sportswriter Paul Zimmerman opined in 1947: "[The] Legion baseball program is the greatest single unified drive against juvenile delinquency in America today."[79]

4

The Fifties:
Lou Brissie, Cars,
Rock and Roll, and Cincinnati,
1952–1961

The American economy shifted into overdrive in the 1950s. After the post-war recession of 1946 and the inflation of 1947, the economy purred along at a 3.2 percent growth through the next decade. The automobile industry paced the American economy. Detroit churned out cars, new ones every year, and after 1953 with larger and larger fins, at least until 1958. Workers in all industries had more disposable income than ever before, as wages rose faster than inflation. The baby boom was well under way. Coupled with the baby boom was the move from cities to suburbs. After Dwight Eisenhower's election as president in 1952, he brokered the armistice which ended the Korean War. Although the Cold War continued, the remainder of the decade was one of peace and prosperity.

For baseball below the major leagues, the 1950s were uneven times. The minor leagues had prospered in the late 1940s. No other era, except the first decade of the 20th century, saw as many minor leagues. Then, rather quickly, the bottom fell out of minor league baseball. Some historians blamed the advent of commercial television in 1947 for the minors' decline in attendance. It was not just television, rather the minors were hit by the perfect storm that included the move to the suburbs, television, and the baby boom. The minors would not bounce back until the late 1980s. Kids, however, had every opportunity to play baseball on organized teams with uniforms and an organizational structure as never before. The creation of Little League baseball in 1951 provided opportunities for kids aged 8 to 12. Played on a smaller field, 60 feet between bases with its own World Series in Williamsport, Pennsylvania, Little League exploded in the 1950s. The Babe Ruth League, for boys 13–16, started in Hamilton Township, New Jersey, in 1951 and increased steadily for the next decade. American Legion baseball continued to grow and prosper through the decade, although at a lesser pace than in the late-1940s.

Legion baseball administrator Dale Miller hoped for a memorable year in 1952, knowing it would be his last at the helm of the Legion baseball program. A California team had won each of the past three World Series. Los Angeles' Crenshaw Post won in 1951, and Oakland's Bill Erwin Post 337 had become the first team to repeat winning back-to-back seasons which they did in 1949 and 1950. If a California team were to win in 1952, it would likely again be Fighting Bob Evans Post 364 of San Diego.

Challenging San Diego for national prominence would likely be Bentley Post 50 from Cincinnati. They had won the ALWS in 1944 and 1947. More importantly, they returned eight players from the third-place team of 1951. Coach Joe Hawk and his assistant, George Scholl, had developed an established system at Bentley. They had been to the American Legion World Series six of the past nine years, so they knew their system worked. Hawk said "hard work" was the only system he had, but that was only partly true. First baseman Jim Frey remembered, "We practiced a lot. We would practice or play almost every day all summer." Not just practice, but "we practiced defense a lot.... We were well-trained." Hawk had over 20 adults coaching in the Bridgetown Baseball Association. In addition to the "big" team, they had three teams in Knothole Leagues, for ages 9–11, 12–13, and 14–15-year-old boys. That farm system kept churning out experienced, well-coached players. Most of those players attended Western Hills High School, so they had been bound together for years. When summer vacation started, they played four evenings a week. Monday evenings were reserved for team meetings, movies, speakers, and just talking baseball. There was no time in this schedule for family vacations, and little time for girls and cars.[1]

Hawk tweaked his 1951 lineup only slightly for the 1952 season. Roy Nixon and Roger Sigler, pitchers in 1951, moved to first base and center field respectively. Dick Drott and Ed Schneider took their spots in the pitching rotation. Drott made the majors (1957–1963), and Schneider logged six minor league seasons, so the move worked out. Roy Nixon played five years (1953–1957) in the Indians' farm system. Batterymates Howard Whitson and Russ Nixon were the mainstays of Bentley's 1952 squad. Whitson, a skinny, 5-foot-10-inch, 160-pound pitcher, went 15–0, undefeated for the regular season. Following the Legion season, he signed with the hometown Reds. As an 18-year-old, he acquitted himself well in Class D ball, but it all came apart in his second professional year. Whitson ended his pro career with a 16–17 record in the minors. Nixon, a product of Western Hills High School, batted .500 in tournament play and was selected as American Legion Player of the Year for 1952. He signed with Cleveland in 1954 and won the Florida State League batting title to secure his reputation as a major prospect. He fashioned a nice, 12-year career in the majors with Cleveland, the Boston Red Sox, and the Minnesota Twins, compiling a .268 batting average in 906 games. He began managing in the Reds' farm system in 1970, moving up to Cincinnati as a coach in 1976. In 1988 he was given the helm in Atlanta, but he could not stop the Braves' slide to last place. He spent the remainder of his career, until 2008, as a minor league manager and a roving instructor for Houston and the Texan Rangers.[2]

Over 16,000 teams started on the tournament trail to determine the four finalists in the ALWS. The 12 regional champions were as follows: Region one, Sgt. John W. Powers, Post 59 of Milford, Massachusetts; Region 2, Trenton, Post 93; Region 3, Laurence Roberts Post 21, Wilmington, Delaware; Region 4, Memphis, Tennessee, Post 1; Region 5, Sumter, South Carolina, Post 15; Region 6, Travis Post 76, Austin, Texas;Region 7, Robert E. Bentley Post 50, Cincinnati, Ohio; Region 8, Louis K. Juden, Post 63, Cape Girardeau, Missouri; Region 9, North End Post 474, St. Paul, Minnesota; Region 10, Leyden-Chiles-Wickersham Post 1, Denver, Colorado; Region 11, Capital Post 9, Salem, Oregon; and Region 12, Fighting Bob Evans, Post 364, San Diego, California.[3]

Bentley had a surprisingly tough time getting through its Sectional in Bloomington, Illinois. They sailed past St. Paul, 4–0, in their opener. Cape Girardeau did likewise, beating St. Paul by a 6–0 score. Then Cincinnati creamed Cape Girardeau, 11–1, as Dick Drott struck out 14. The Cape lads then surprised Cincinnati, handing Bentley its only loss of the tournament, 9–8. Bentley came back to take the deciding game, scoring two runs in the ninth to win, 4–3. In that game, Russ Nixon collected three hits. San Diego came through its Regional in Hastings, Nebraska. The Fighting Bobs, behind Bob Thorpe, beat Salem, Oregon, 7–1. Salem came back to beat Denver, 2–2. Denver then surprised San Diego, 5–0. San Diego stayed alive by beating Salem, 9–0. In the final, San Diego's Thorpe carried a no-hitter into the ninth inning before losing the no-no, but he held Denver to two hits in 11 innings. The Fighting Bobs of San Diego overcame a 4–0 deficit by scoring five runs in the bottom of the 11th inning. Thorpe scored the winning run.[4]

Travis Post of Austin took the title at the Southeast Regional in Charleston, South Carolina. Travis loss to Memphis, 3–2, in a 12-inning contest.Memphis got outstanding pitching from Frank Roland, who won his 14th game. Austin, however, turned the tables on Memphis, coming back to win a doubleheader from Memphis, 4–2 and 8–2, to take the regional title and win a place in the ALWS. Clever left-hander Terry Whitworth (12–2) and Louis Bradshaw (7–0) led the way for Memphis. Milford, Massachusetts, with a 20–1 record, rounded out the competition. They beat Trenton, New Jersey, 6–0, behind the one-hit pitching of their staff ace, Bob Stoico, in the Eastern title game.[5]

The 1952 World Series was played at Bear Stadium in Denver. Later renamed Mile High Stadium and expanded, it was built in 1948 with a huge expanse and baseball dimensions of 348 feet to left, 420 feet to dead center, and 366 to right. There would be few home runs here. Mile High seated 19,000. Legion organizers expected to pack in record attendance. Unfortunately, Denver experienced terrible weather in the first week in September. Game time temperatures hovered around 40 degrees and sank from there. The four finalists carried impressive records. Cincinnati, with a 30–1 record and looking for its record third ALWS title, loomed as the favorite. New England teams had not threatened since the 1930s, but Milford's 20–1 record commanded some attention. Austin posted a 20–3 record, and San Diego had recorded 25 wins against only four losses.[6]

The Legion World Series turned on the two games between Bentley and San Diego. They met first on day two in the winners' bracket after Bentley beat Austin, Texas, 3–0, and San Diego's 7–2 win over Milford. Bentley road Whitson's three-hit, 12-strikeout effort and Roger Sigler's three hits against Austin. San Diego's win pinned the season's first loss on Milford's Stoico. Before the Bentley-San Diego match, Austin sent Milford home, 9–6. It took Bentley 11 innings to prevail, 9–6, over San Diego. Down three runs in the ninth inning, Bentley tied the game on Russ Nixon's RBI single and Carl Beiler's homer. In the 11th inning, San Diego's Bob Thorpe, who had pitched the entire game, walked Roy Nixon with the bases loaded to give Cincinnati the win.[7]

A disappointing crowd of 4,435 braved the unseasonable cold on the final day of the 1952 Legion World Series. Before the Bentley–San Diego rematch, San Diego dispatched Austin, 6–3, in 10 innings. In the final, after picking up a run in the second inning, Cincinnati scored four runs in the third inning. The big blow was Russ Nixon's two-run triple. Hawk turned the game over to Whitson, who kept San Diego at bay the remainder of the contest. San Diego got a run in the eighth inning and loaded the bases in the ninth, but a double play limited them to only one run. Whitson got credit for the win, his 15th straight, a 5–2 win for Bentley and the national Legion title.[8]

Russ Nixon's heroics in the final game led to his being selected the American Legion Player of the Year. Horace Tucker, Jr., San Diego outfielder, won the Hillerich & Bradsby trophy for the highest batting average, a .452 mark. Whitson signed with the home-town Reds for a "sizable bonus" right after the Series. Some 2,000 fans celebrated Bentley becoming the first team to win three national titles at the train station when the team reached Cincinnati. Coach Hawk called this team "the greatest champions in the world."[9]

The *Denver Post* selected an all-star team for the 1952 American Legion World Series. It consisted of Howard Whitson (Cincinnati), Bob Thorpe (San Diego), and Terry Whitworth (Austin), pitchers; Russ Nixon (Cincinnati) and Paul Petrosky (Milford), catchers; Joe Berardi (Milford) first base; Joe Alves (Milford) second base; Tony Agaro (San Diego) third base; Dick Johnson (San Diego) shortstop; Doyle Greeson (Austin) utility; Roger Sigler (Cincinnati), Ervin Symank (Austin), and Horace Tucker (San Diego) outfielders; Carl Beiler (Cincinnati) utility.

In American Legion baseball and in the United States too, the world changed in 1953. In December 1952 Dale Miller announced that he would retire as administrator of American Legion Baseball at the end of the calendar year. His six years as head had proved quietly productive ones. His assistant for the past two years, Bill Jarvis, was poised to assume the duties of administrator. Second, there was no California team in the 1953 American Legion World Series. For another, there was no team from Cincinnati. In the 13 years since 1941, eight of the world champions of Legion ball had been either from Cincinnati or California. In the larger world of baseball, a new day was beginning to take shape. Jackie Robinson had integrated the major leagues in 1947, although to assert that required people to forget Moses Fleetwood Walker's 1887 season. By 1953, African American stars were dotting most major league rosters. Only Roy Campanella of the Brooklyn Dodgers made *The Sporting News* all-star team in 1953, but before the decade ended, every team roster included black players, and no all-star team would omit Willie Mays, Hank Aaron, Frank Robinson, Ernie Banks, Orlando Cepeda, Minnie Minoso, or Don Newcombe. Despite these changes, on the field, the Yankees won their fifth straight world championship in 1953.

The Yankees were the epitome of stability, so few people remembered that they had been the last franchise to shift cities, when in 1903, as the Baltimore Orioles, they moved to New York. In an ironic twist, it was the desire of Bill Veeck, owner of the St. Louis Browns, to move his franchise to Baltimore that touched off a new round of franchise moves. At the same time, the National League Boston Braves wished to move to Milwaukee. Unlike the American League, the National League quickly agreed to the Boston-Milwaukee move, and the Braves found instant success, drawing a National League-record 1,826,397 fans to brand-new County Stadium. As was common, the American League lagged several steps behind the "senior circuit" in foresight and turned down Veeck's request to move his Browns out of St. Louis. The Junior Circuit also dragged its heels when it came to signing African American players, allowing the National League to load up on them for a generation.

America had to learn how to deal with a Republican in the White House for the first time in 20 years. "We Like Ike" had been the rallying cry that swept General Dwight Eisenhower into the presidency in the 1952 election. Domestically, Ike swiftly calmed fears that he would sweep away the still-popular New Deal. In foreign policy, he had promised "to go to Korea" if elected, either to win or end the Police Action that began in 1950. He chose to end the war, an overwhelmingly popular choice. Once out of wars, Eisenhower let his Secretary of State, John Foster Dulles, do some saber-rattling for the remainder of the decade, but he kept the country at peace for his two terms in office.

With the country at peace, prosperity continued. The most visible signs of that prosperity were the cars—big, eight-cylinder, 300 horse-powered, gas-guzzling automobiles.

Cars grew fins on the back. Boats, as it were. Those fins continued to grow during the late 1950s. Nothing symbolized the prosperous 1950s like its cars, unless it was rock and roll music. Bill Haley and His Comets blended music and car culture when they cut "Rocket 88." Haley's 1954 "Rock Around the Clock" gave the country a rock and roll blockbuster commercial success. Chuck Berry's 1955 classic, "Maybellene," added a hard-driving electronic guitar style brought from rhythm and blues. Rock and roll music had arrived full-blast. In 1956, Elvis Presley arrived as the "King of Rock and Roll" with his first number one hit, "Heartbreak Hotel." He followed that with a string of hits that made him the biggest selling recording star of all time. A distinct teenage culture had emerged in the mid–1950s centered around rock and roll music, 45 rpm records, fads in hair styles—duck tails for both boys and girls, ponytails, crew cuts, and pompadours—and cars. Beginning in 1956, Dick Clark brought the latest styles in music, dance fads, and clothing into teens' homes through television's *American Bandstand*.

Legion baseball, still officially "Junior" Baseball, had a new boss. On January 1, 1953, Bill Jarvis took over for Dale Miller after six years, but Miller stayed on as "adviser." There appeared to be new parity in Legion baseball. None of the four finalists who qualified for the 1953 American Legion World Series in Miami were familiar faces. True, Sgt. John W. Powers Post of Milford, Massachusetts, had made an ALWS appearance in 1952, but almost no one expected the New England sectional winner to make many sparks in tournament play. The dominant teams in recent years came from big cities: Cincinnati, Oakland, and Los Angeles.

In 1953, the final four teams came from decidedly not big cities: Cherryville, North Carolina; Yakima, Washington; Milford, Massachusetts; and Winnetka, Illinois. Logan Wheeler Post 36 of Yakima had been building its team since John Zaepfel, athletic director of the Yakima school system, took the coaching reins of the team 12 years before. As athletic director, he established a city system of pee-wee teams, each with its own uniform, played on 16 diamonds around the city. Yakima had made the sectionals twice before, only to fall to a powerhouse team from California. Winnetka was a town of 12,000 residents on Lake Michigan, 16 miles north of Chicago. The 1953 team advertised its coming of age by knocking off defending champion Bentley Post 50 of Cincinnati in the sectional. Cherryville, a town of just 5.000 in central North Carolina, had never won anything before 1953, but Post 100, the team of coach Norm Harris, caught the town's fancy and set attendance records at Cherryville Memorial Stadium that will never be broken. They also captured the post's first state title. Their ace pitcher, Hugh "Buzz" Peeler, who won three games in the sectionals, remained the toast of the town until his death in 2012.[10]

The 1953 American Legion World Series games was played September 1–5 in Miami Stadium. Built in 1949, the Stadium was a state-of-the-art park of 9,500 seats with a cantilever roof needing no posts, which obstruct sight-lines. It served as home of the Florida International League Miami Sun Sox. Its dimensions were a standard 330 feet down the left and right field lines, and 400 feet to dead center field. The outfield allowed for temporary bleachers to be set up to accommodate overflow crowds. The grandstand had a distinctive high, rounded roof.[11]

Yakima, Winnetka, Milford, and Cherryville came through the Regional round to advance to the ALWS. At Hastings, Nebraska, Logan-Wheeler Post 36 of Yakima beat Denver, 3–2, and Richmond, California, twice, 5–2 and 5–4. The first of the two snapped Richmond's 18-game winning streak. Third baseman Eddie Zander's mammoth 377-foot double provided the big blow for Yakima in that game. Winnetka, owner of a huge win over Cincinnati Bentley in the previous round, won over Topeka, 11–9, thanks to shortstop Dick Selinger's five hits. At Pittsfield, Massachusetts, Milford beat Elizabeth, New Jersey, 7–4, and Bunker Hill of Washington, D.C., 4–1. At Sumter, South Carolina, Cherryville beat Greenwood, South Carolina, and Monroe, Louisiana, 5–2 and 6–5. Lefty "Buzz" Peeler got the win in the second game.[12]

Yakima and Winnetka established their dominance on Opening Day of the 1953 Series. Yakima squeezed past Milford, 2–0. Ed Pleasant, the only African American player in the tournament, who faced segregation in Miami, scored the first run in the second inning on Ed Zander's RBI. Yakima's number two pitcher, "Big Dave" Dexter, threw a four-hit shutout. Winnetka's Chuck Lindstrom, son of ex–New York Giant Fred Lindstrom, locked up in a pitching duel with Cherryville's Peeler. Winnetka shortstop Dick Selinger doubled and scored the winning run in the ninth on Bill Poggensee's single to center, giving Winnetka a 2–1 win and breaking Peeler's 14-game win streak. Yakima had held its pitching ace, Tom Gibson, out for the second game. The strategy paid off as Gibson held Winnetka to five hits in a 6–1 Yakima win, snapping Winnetka's 28-game win streak. In the losers' bracket, Milford dispatched Cherryville, 3–2. Yakima, as the only undefeated team in the tourney, drew a bye into the final game. Winnetka came back in its next game to dispose of Milford, 8–6, behind Lindstrom's four-hitter. The decisive two runs scored in the seventh inning on singles by Mike Layden, son of the Notre Dame football great, and Ted Herbert, two errors, and a sacrifice fly.[13]

That left only Yakima and Winnetka alive in the 1953 ALWS. The Illinois club surprised everyone by pitching little-used lefty George Thompson. He went the distance and outdueled Dave Dexter, who carried a 10–0 record into the game, 5–2. That allowed Winnetka to pitch well-rested Lindstrom against Yakima's Gibson in the deciding game. On this day, Gibson was the better pitcher and hitter. He went the distance, allowing only three hits. As a batter, he scored Yakima's first run in the second inning, and he drove in Yakima's other three runs with a bases-loaded double in the fourth inning. Yakima's 4–1 victory was the first championship for a team from the Pacific Northwest.[14]

For reasons that remain unclear, the selection committee picked Winnetka's Chuck Lindstrom as the American Legion Player of the Year instead of Gibson, who had bested Lindstrom in the final game. Gibson had won three games, including a three-hitter in the decisive final game, a game in which he drove in three runs to beat Lindstrom. After baseball, Lindstrom tried his hand at teaching geography, coaching at Lincoln Junior College in his hometown, and being a parks and recreation director, before hitting it big as an entrepreneur with his Universal Sports Lighting company. His teammate at Winnetaka, shortstop Dick Selinger, won the Louisville Slugger trophy for batting .457 in 11 games. At sparkling new Miami Stadium, 19,650 fans attended World Series games, including 4,004 for the final contest.[15]

Before the 1954 season started, American Legion baseball got another new leader, one who seemed just the right fit for the job. On March 26, National Legion commander Arthur J. Connell announced the appointment of army Purple Heart veteran and former major league pitcher Leland Victor "Lou" Brissie as commissioner of American Legion Junior Baseball. The announcement was met with overwhelming acclaim. Even the title, "commissioner," signaled a new approach. His predecessor as chief operating officer of Legion baseball, Bill Jarvis, had the title of "administrator." There was no mistaking the level of authority. Brissie arrived with credibility no one in the leadership position of

Legion ball had ever had. He had actually played in the major leagues for eight years and played at an All-Star level. Physically imposing at 6-feet-4 inches and well over 200 pounds, the handsome Brissie cut an imposing figure. Boys in the American Legion program loved having Brissie in the commissioner's chair. Brissie, of course, was not just a major league player, he was a hero. Brissie started in the Legion job at a salary of $10,000.[16]

Brissie's narrative was widely known; if there was a kid who did not already know of the former pitcher, their fellows quickly filled him in. A South Carolina native, he had attended Presbyterian College before enlisting in the Army. He was a corporal with the U.S. 88th Infantry Division, working its way up the boot of Italy, when on December 2, 1944, a German artillery shell shattered his left leg. Brissie had to crawl for cover through mud; that left bacteria lodged in the wound. Medics were prepared to amputate his leg, but Brissie protested. Doctors acceded to his request, but it took 23 operations in numerous hospitals to save his leg. When he returned to playing in 1947, he walked stiff-legged and with a pronounced limp because of a metal brace on his leg. He was the most visible wounded warrior in baseball. Still, he enjoyed a highly successful season in 1948, recording a 14–10 record. His moving fastball, sharp curve, and deceptive change-up worked well enough to make him fourth in strikeouts among American League pitchers that season. His Philadelphia Ath-

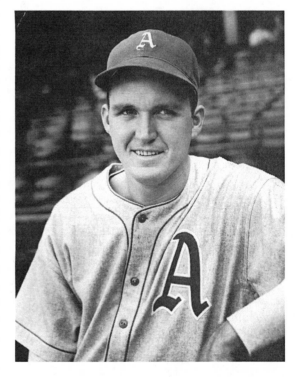

letics enjoyed their last winning season. They had a run at the pennant, owner-manager Connie Mack's last hurrah. In 1949 Brissie was selected for the American League All-Star team and pitched the middle three innings of the All-Star Game. The A's and Brissie fell apart in 1950. Both Brissie and Mr. Mack were gone in 1951, Mack to retirement, Brissie traded to Cleveland. The Indians relegated Brissie to the bullpen. By 1953, he appeared in just 16 games, all in relief. Nonetheless, his American Legion appointment, as Art Morrow wrote in *The Sporting News,* "struck a popular note with war veterans, baseball men and kids alike." Brissie threw himself into his new job, touring the country, checking facilities, and meeting people.[17]

Brissie's travels in the late summer of 1954 ended in the Pacific Northwest at Yakima, Washington, site of the American Legion World Series, September 1–5, 1954. The Regional champions were anxious to put on a show for Brissie. The 12 champs were: Region one, Brockton,

Lou Brissie served as Commissioner of American Legion Baseball from 1954 to 1961. His background as a much decorated and seriously wounded war hero and a major league all-star, who pitched for the Philadelphia A's and Cleveland Indians, made him Legion baseball's most popular and respected leader (courtesy Ernie Harwell Sports Collection, Detroit Public Library).

Massachusetts; Region two, Stamford, Connecticut; Region 3, Westport Post 33 of Baltimore, Maryland; Region 4, Gaston Post 23, Gastonia, North Carolina; Region 5, North Charleston, South Carolina, Post 241; Region 6, New Orleans, Post 307; Region 7, Lafayette, Indiana, Post 11; Region 8, Maplewood, Missouri, Post 103; Region 9, Cook-Fuller Post 70 of Oshkosh, Wisconsin; Region 10, Omaha, Nebraska, Post 1; Region 11, Billings, Montana, Post 4 Royals; Region 12, San Diego Downtown Post 492 Guardians. The ALWS was played at Parker Field in Yakima, constructed in 1937 as home for the Yakima Pippins of the Western International League.

In Yakima, Brissie saw the Guardians of San Diego Post 492 come through the losers' bracket to snatch the ALWS title from Gastonia, North Carolina, Maplewood, Missouri, and Westport Post 33 of Baltimore, Maryland. Baltimore, led by shortstop Barry Shetrone and pitchers Danny Welsh and Frank Brown, had the easiest time getting to Yakima. They beat Bunker Hill of Washington, D.C., 8–0, and Wilmington, Delaware, 8–3 and 15–2. Gastonia lost its first game in the Southeast Regional to New Orleans, 5–4, but came back to beat North Charleston twice, 12–2 and 14–3, after North Charleston had hammered New Orleans by a 9–4 score. San Diego Post 492 was a tiny Legion Post with only 35 members. They lacked money to buy uniforms, so the parents chipped in to purchase one set of uniforms. Uniforms or not, they got outstanding pitching from Ronnie Wilkins and Larry Elliott and sailed through Billings (14–8) and Omaha (1–0 and 5–3) in the Western Regional. Maplewood hammered Oshkosh, 8–0, and controlled Lafayette with pitching. Maplewood won the first game, 8–0, on a three-hit shutout by Bob Cooper, then cruised, 4–3, as Wayne Thompson struck out 16 Lafayette batters.[18]

Brissie saw some wild play and close games at the Series. In the opener, Gastonia beat Baltimore by a 4–2 score. Gastonia had won the Legion title back in 1935 with the aid of its outstanding shortstop, Lawrence "Crash" Davis. In 1954, their coach was the same Crash Davis. They got all their runs in the fourth inning. Roger Martin drove in two of the four runs. The second game of the opening night was as wild as a game could be. Maplewood pitcher Wayne Thompson struck out 15 San Diego hitters, but he also walked a record 12 batters and hit three more. Before the Series ended, Thompson set a tournament record with 84 strikeouts. Bob Sadowski's bases-loaded triple was the big hit in Maplewood's 8–2 victory. San Diego came back with a barrage of its own, surging past Baltimore, 10–8, to eliminate the Westport boys. The Guardians banged out 15 hits. Outfielder Jim Galasso had four runs batted in, and shortstop Billy Capps had three hits and put on a show in the field. Gastonia beat Maplewood, 5–3, in the other second-day game. Gastonia's Ken Sheppard took a one-hit shutout into the ninth inning, but he gave way to Harold Stowe when he faltered.

On day three, the two one-loss teams, San Diego and Maplewood, hooked up. Maplewood's Thompson suffered his first loss of the season by a 5–3 score. As ever, Thompson suffered from control problems, walking 17 batters, another record.[19] Gastonia, the fan favorite, needed just one win to take the 1954 title, but San Diego prevented the Piedmont team from taking the crown. San Diego managed a close, 3–2 victory in 11 innings. Third baseman Jim Galasso tripled to score Capps with the winning run. Lefty Joel Magy earned the win to necessitate a final game. In the 1954 title game, San Diego scored all seven of its runs in the first three innings, winning 7–2. Larry Elliott and Magy each drove in two runs to lead the assault by San Diego Downtown Post 492. Ron Wilkins earned the win as he held Gastonia to three hits. California had the 1954 championship, its eighth in 28 years.[20]

San Diego shortstop and co-captain Billy Capps was selected Player of the Year. Capps reminded spectators and sportswriters of St. Louis Cardinals shortstop Marty Marion. Capps, who stood six feet tall and weighed 145 pounds, resembled Marion in stature. Capps hit a solid but not spectacular .300, but he was scintillating in the field. San Diego third baseman Jim Galasso and Gastonia outfielder Bill Hopper tied for the Louisville Slugger award, both with a .375 batting average. Maplewood's Wayne Thompson struck out 84 batters to establish a record.

Only one of the 1954 Guardians made the majors, but several others took a shot. Outfielder and co-captain Larry Elliott turned pro; he played six major league seasons with Pittsburgh, Philadelphia, and the New York Mets. Pitcher Ronnie Wilkins signed after the Series and spent six years in the minors as an outfielder. Capps played a couple of years before serving time in the Air Force. He joined the San Diego police force at age 23, but he continued to play competitive softball into his 60s.[21]

Again in 1955, Cincinnati's west side produced a powerhouse team, but it was not sponsored by Bentley Post 50. This time they wore the uniform of Acme Glass-Postal Employees Post 216. All but one of the players came from Elder High School, the Catholic prep school that captured back-to-back state baseball titles in 1955 and 1956, so the Legion nine had plenty of talent. Coach Bob Kenney remembered, "they had such a positive attitude. They never thought they could lose." Pitching ace, lefty Ron Moeller led the mound staff. He did not lose in the summer of 1955. Later he played parts of four seasons in the majors with Baltimore, the Los Angeles Angels, and Washington. Third baseman Frank Birri and catcher Joe Cupito, who had played for rival Bentley in 1954, provided explosive bats. Birri was selected American Legion Player of the Year. Birri, Cupito, pitcher Tom Flynn, infielder Tom Prout, and pitcher Bill Beck went on to play minor league ball, but none rose to the level of a major league prospect. The Postal Employees crew had beaten Bentley, 4–1, in the local tournament and went on to the American Legion World Series at St. Paul, Minnesota, where they were established as pre-tournament favorites.[22]

The Cincinnati club (37–4) was joined in the 1955 Series by Bunker Hill Post 31 of Washington, D.C., Lincoln, Nebraska Post 3 Optimists, and Samuel C. Hart Post 14 of Salisbury, North Carolina (33–3). Along the road to St. Paul, teams from Billings, Montana, and Lewiston, Idaho, locked up in a 19-inning pitchers' duel that ended in a 1–0 victory for Billings. Pitcher Bob Bolingbroke of Billings struck out 25 batters in 17 innings before being removed. That established a Legion record for strikeouts in a game, but just barely, because Sammy Canner of Lewiston, who pitched a complete game, struck out 24. The total of 54 strikeouts in a game remains a record unlikely ever to be broken.[23]

The 1955 regional champions were: Region 1, Everett, Massachusetts; Region 2, Stamford, Connecticut; Region 3, Bunker Hill Post 31, Washington, D.C.; Region 4, Samuel C. Hart Post 14, Salisbury, North Carolina; Region 5, North Charleston, South Carolina; Region 6, New Orleans, Louisiana; Region 7, U.S. Postal Employees Post 216 of Cincinnati; Region 8, Oklahoma City, Oklahoma; Region 9, Oshkosh, Wisconsin; Region 10, Lincoln, Nebraska Optimists, Post 3; Region 11, The Dalles, Oregon; Region 12, Tucson, Arizona. In the Regional tournaments, all former national champs still in the tournament were ousted. At Bismarck, North Dakota, Cincinnati clocked Cook-Fuller Post of Oshkosh, 8–0, and Owens Furniture of Oklahoma City, 4–1. At Hastings, Nebraska, the Lincoln Optimists Post 3, led by second baseman Yogi Hergenrader's bat, emerged as winners over The Dalles, Des Moines, and Tucson. At Sumter, South Carolina, Salisbury beat out North Charleston and came back from a 6–5 loss to New Orleans to take the series, 15–4 and 18–2. Bunker Hill Post 31 beat Everett, Massachusetts, and Stamford, Connecticut, to punch its ticket to St. Paul.[24]

The Series did not begin Cincinnati's way. Washington's Bunker Hill upset Cincinnati, 6–5. The Postals now had to win four straight games or go home. Salisbury, North Carolina, which arrived after a three-day train ride only hours before game time, led off with a 6–3 victory over Lincoln. Pitching ace Tom Eaton (15–2) got credit for the win, but he experienced muscle cramps in his chest and was lost for the remainder of the World Series. Coach Joe Ferebee, who had 677 victories between Pfeiffer College (NC) and the Legion team, was closing in on 700 wins in a storied career. In Cincinnati's first game after their loss, the Postals locked up in a pitchers' duel between Moeller and Lincoln's Rudy Stoehr. Cincinnati scored the only run of the game without benefit of a hit. Catcher Joe Cupito walked, stole second, went to third on an infield out, and scored on a wild pitch. Moeller allowed just two Lincoln hits. Bunker Hill of Washington also won. An unearned run in the 9th inning gave them a 7–6 victory over Salisbury. The final three games belonged to Cincinnati. First, they beat Salisbury, 6–5, in 10 innings. After Salisbury scored three runs in the top of the 10th inning, the Postals scored four runs to win it. In a revenge game, Cincinnati took out Washington, 10–5, as Moeller, pitching in relief, struck out nine in the final three innings. In the championship game, Cincinnati's Bill Beck, who had lost the first game of the ALWS, pitched a five-hitter and struck out 15 batters in a 10–4 victory over Bunker Hill. First baseman Gary Haverkamp smacked four hits, shortstop Bob Birri homered, and backup catcher Mike Honold drove in four runs. Cincinnati finished the 1955 season with a record of 36 wins, four losses, and the national championship.[25]

The title, the fourth by a Cincinnati team, moved the Queen City ahead of San Diego and Oakland, each with three championships. The Postals' third baseman, Frank Birri, was selected the Legion's Player of the Year for 1955. Other Cincinnati players established records for most at-bats in a series. Outfielder Tom Prout got to the plate 60 times, first baseman Gary Haverkamp had 57 at-bats, and shortstop Frank Birri with 56, all broke the old record. Lincoln's second baseman/pitcher, Richard Hergenrader, won the Louisville Slugger Award with a .389 batting average for the tournament.[26]

Off the diamond, Commissioner Brissie was making changes. A native of Greenville, South Carolina, and a strong supporter of segregationist Dixiecrat Strom Thurmond's run for the Senate, Brissie was anything but a political radical; nevertheless, he changed Legion baseball's policy on race. The year before he took office, Yakima's Ed Pleasant was forced to stay with a black family in Miami because of the hotel's segregation policy. In Brissie's first year in office, he opined, "I thought that a team ought to stay together," and before assigning the championship series to a town or city, "I let it be known that blacks and whites had to stay together. If there was a problem, I just wouldn't go there." Brissie did not set out to change the world or even the South, but he believed that team came first. So, under Brissie's leadership, the Piedmont mill towns of the Carolinas did not get the contracts to host the World Series. Instead, the Series went to Yakima, Washington, St. Paul, Minnesota, Bismarck, North Dakota, Billings, Montana, Colorado Springs, Colorado, and Hastings, Nebraska.[27]

As a former pitcher, Brissie was concerned about youngsters throwing their arms out from overuse at a young age. For the first time in Legion history, he placed limits on the number of innings a pitcher could work in back-to-back days. Pitchers would not be allowed to pitch more than 12 innings or make three appearances in a 48-hour period. Brissie did not hide his political conservatism, but unlike many of his predecessors, he did not get involved in anti-communist activities. He left the hard-right activities to others in the Legion. Brissie did accept an appointment to President Eisenhower's Citizens Advisory Committee on Fitness of American Youth in 1957. He annually took Legion all-star teams to Central and Latin America, and for two years he conducted baseball clinics in Australia under the sponsorship of the U.S. State Department. Under Brissie's leadership, Legion baseball continued to grow, in both the number of participating teams and the number of players in the major leagues who came through Legion ball. Brissie estimated that over 1,500 major league players were graduates of the Legion system.

Still, not all was well with Legion ball; U.S. Postal Employees Post of Cincinnati, the defending national champions, did not field a team in 1956. On a more positive note, teams from different regions were making noise. Roseburg, Oregon, became the second team from the Pacific Northwest and the first from Oregon to make the World Series. Yonkers, New York, had captured the very first championship back in 1926 but had been unsuccessful in finding a way to return to the Series ever since.[28]

The 1956 season started with 16,500 teams before state and regional play winnowed the number down to 12. These were: Region 1, Everett, Massachusetts, the lone team to repeat from 1955; Region 2, Bodenstab-Thomas Post 884 of Yonkers, New York, returning for the first time since winning in 1926; Region 3, Gas Light Post of Washington, D.C.; Region 4, Wilmington, North Carolina; Region 5, Conway, South Carolina; Region 6, Fellowship Post 341 of New Orleans, Louisiana; Region 7, Maywood, Illinois; Region 8, Fred W. Stockham Post 245 of St. Louis, Missouri; Region 9, St. Paul, Minnesota North Post 39; Region 10, Hastings, Nebraska; Region 11, Umpqua Post 16, Roseburg, Oregon; and Region 12, Phoenix, Arizona.[29]

Brissie moved the sites about, giving an opportunity for different locations to experience hosting. Section A, for example, was played in Togus, Maine. Yonkers beat Washington's Gas Light Post and struggled to get past Everett, Massachusetts. Everett captured one game, 3–0, but Yonkers came back to win, 9–4 and 10–0. Gene Alberigi pitched a five-hitter in the deciding game. In Section B at Gastonia, South Carolina, LaRocca Post of New Orleans scored 10 runs in the ninth inning to hammer Conway, 16–4, in the final, after beating them 6–2 earlier. They also beat Wilmington, 6–5. New Orleans pitcher Jimmy Harwell was selected outstanding pitcher in the series. In the Section C tourney, Stockham appeared to have a clear road to the ALWS when it hammered Maywood, Illinois, 16–1, in the opening game. Then St. Paul North End upset the St. Louis club by a 16–4 score. Stockham stayed alive by beating Maywood again, 9–4. In the final, Stockham left little doubt which team was better, hammering St. Paul, 26–4. In Section D, Roseburg's Umpqua Post, sponsored by Lockwood Motors, lost 11–10 to Hastings, but came back to even things with an 8–7 win. Roseburg then beat Phoenix behind Dick Smith's three-hit pitching. The final against Hastings took 15 innings before Mack McClellan's squeeze bunt won it for Roseburg.[30]

Through the years, Stockham Post 245 of St. Louis had fielded strong teams but they had been trying unsuccessfully since 1926 to produce a championship club. This year they had a team capable of winning it all. Stockham's coach, Al Grosch, drew his players from both Central High and Beaumont High. Beaumont was coming off a state title; Central had won three state high school titles. First baseman and captain Larry Goudy proved he was the best hitter in the tournament; left fielder Rogers "Robbie" Robinson provided speed, and Bob Miller gave them pitching that alternated between unhittable and out of control.

In the 1956 Series, Bob Miller won another three games to give him a 6–0 record in national competition. He shut out Roseburg, 10–0. in the opening game as no runner got beyond first base. New Orleans' Jimmy Harwell, who had won three games in the sectional, was even better. He turned in a 2–0 one-hitter against Yonkers, striking out 13. The only hit was a bunt single in the third inning. Roseburg then eliminated Yonkers, 8–5. Winning pitcher Bill Oeding led Roseburg hitters with three hits for the day. Stockham, however, defeated New Orleans in their first meeting by a 7–3 score. Miller got credit for the win. New Orleans came back the next day to eliminate Roseburg, 15–2, as Jim Harwell struck out 11 batters.[31]

New Orleans refused to die. They scored 11 runs in the first inning against St. Louis. Stockham manager Al Grosch had chosen to rest Bob Miller, while Jimmy Harwell started for New Orleans. In that first inning, the leadoff batter for New Orleans walked, followed by a single, another walk, a single, a triple, and a double. After a pitching change, there was a single, pop fly out, a walk, a single, a walk, a fielders' choice, a walk, and a double. That was an 11–0 hole for St. Louis. The final score was 14–6. New Orleans shortstop Brian Petri had three hits, two RBI, and three runs scored.[32]

Harwell's appearance left him ineligible to pitch the 1956 final game. He closed out his Legion career with a record of 19–1. Pitching rival Bob Miller and St. Louis won the 1955 championship game, 8–3. This time, Stockham started hot, scoring four runs in the first inning. Rogers Robinson walked, as did Bob Hardcastle and Jerry Nauret. After a strikeout, Larry Goudy grounded to the third baseman, who threw the ball over the first baseman's head. Two runs scored, but Nauret was nailed at home. A protest followed, leading to the umpires reversing the call and sending Nauret back to third. Miller banged a triple, scoring two more runs. Miller was not his sharpest; he walked eight and gave up nine hits, but he was good enough. In 1956, Fred W. Stockham Post of St. Louis had its first national title.[33]

Harwell, who played shortstop when not pitching, won American Legion Player of the Year honors. Bob Miller signed with the hometown Cardinals in 1957 and played 17 years with ten different major league teams. His bumpy career brought him a 69–81 major league record with a 3.37 earned run average, but he did play in five World Series and was on three world champion teams: the 1963 and 1965 Dodgers, and the 1971 Pittsburgh Pirates. St. Louis first baseman and captain Larry Goudy took home the Louisville Slugger Award with a .449 batting average.[34]

Following the ALWS, Lou Brissie took 16 Legion players, each 17 years old, on a month-long goodwill tour of seven Latin American countries. The tour began September 26 and lasted until October 23, 1956. They played 23 games in seven countries. The stops included El Salvador; Managua, Nicaragua; Panama City, Panama; Barranquilla, Colombia; Cartagena, Colombia; Caracas, Venezuela; San Juan, Puerto Rico; and Havana, Cuba. The following spring, he went to Australia with a Department of State group to conduct baseball clinics.[35]

Legion ball was bigger than ever in 1957, when a record 23,000 teams started the season, which for the Legion meant participation in the tournament that led to the World Series. The trend of World Series teams coming from big cities continued. The finalists included teams from Washington, D.C., Cincinnati, and Portland, Oregon. The Cinderella team of the finalists was from Greer, South Carolina, a mill town of 5,050.[36]

The 12 regional championships had come to be seen as the demarcation that separated successful teams from the pack. In 1957 the regional winners were: Region 1, Post 68 Pittsfield, Massachusetts; Region 2, Post 2 West Warwick, Rhode Island; Region 3. Gas Light Post 44, Washington, D.C.; Region 4, Tim McCarver's Memphis, Tennessee Post 1 team; Region 5, John Ratteree Post 115 of Greer (SC) Community; Region 6, Post 1 Jackson, Mississippi; Region 7, Robert E. Bentley Post 50 of Cincinnati; Region 8, Oklahoma City, Oklahoma, Post 218; Region 9, Post 11 Mankato, Minnesota; Region 10, Leyden-Chiles-Wickersham Post 1 Denver, Colorado; Region 11, Willamette Heights Post 102 of Portland, Oregon; Region 12, Luke-Greenway, Phoenix, Arizona Post 1.

In Region 1, Pittsfield had to beat Bath, Maine, Barre, Vermont, and Manchester, New Hampshire, to capture the title. In Region 2, West Warwick beat Trenton, Stamford, Connecticut, and Staten Island. Gas Light of DC first lost to Frederick. Maryland, which featured Charlie Keller's son, then beat Wilmington and Whitefield, West Virginia, before taking two from Frederick for the Region 3 crown. Memphis had to win over Front Royal, Virginia, Owensboro, Kentucky, and Shelby, North Carolina, in Region 4. In Region 5, Greer got two wins from pitching ace Donnie Dill in beating Tuscaloosa, Savannah, and Miami. In Region 6, Jackson took out Little Rock, Monroe, Louisiana, and Lufkin, Texas. Bentley Post 50 beat Terre Haute twice, Chicago Heights, and Benton Harbor, Michigan, to take Region 7. Pitcher Scott Seger, who won two games, was selected most valuable player in the Region tournament. Oklahoma City captured three straight in Region 8 against Bancroft, Iowa, Topeka, Kansas, and Washington, Missouri. The most exciting game in Region 8 was Jerry Walschmidt of Washington no-hitting Topeka. In Region 9, Mankato won over Oshkosh, Bismarck, North Dakota, and Sioux Falls, South Dakota, to capture the title. Denver had little trouble with Omaha, Albuquerque, and Rock Springs, Wyoming. Lefty Jim Martin won two of those games with a one-hitter and a three-hitter. In Region 11, Portland lost to Seattle, but beat Anchorage, Lewiston, Idaho, and Billings, Montana. Their lefty, Mickey Lolich, won the final two games to deliver the Region 11 title. In Region 12, Phoenix, one of two repeats along with Gas Light Post, beat Reno, Ogden, and Oakland. Against Oakland, Phoenix managed just one hit but won a 4–2 game, thanks to three walks and an error.[37]

The final round of the tournament before the World Series, the Sectionals, was played at four locations: Sumter, South Carolina, Elkton, Maryland, Oshkosh, Wisconsin, and Hastings, Nebraska. The boys that Greer coach Paul Edwards selected for the Post 115 team came from five different high schools in Greenville County, South Carolina. The most, six, came from Greer High School: third baseman Steve Brown, shortstop Dan Harvey, outfielder Ted Holtzclaw, outfielder Don Lister, outfielder Jimmy Howell, and catcher Ralph Smith. Five attended Taylor High: outfielder Mickey Strickland, Larry "Goat" Johnson, infielder Dickie Lanford, catcher Larry Johnson, and Jimmy Ayers. Pitching ace Donnie Dill, pitcher Billy Cooper, Carl Leonard, and Gene Davis studied at Byrnes High. First baseman Lee Burns came from Travelers Rest, and Morris Mason hailed from Blue Ridge High. They relied on the bat of Larry "Goat" Johnson, a catcher and second baseman, and the curve ball of Donnie Dill, who was MVP in the Sectional when they beat Tim McCarver's heavily favored Memphis team, two games to one. Both Memphis and Greer beat Jackson to put them out of the tourney.[38]

At Oshkosh, Bentley and Oklahoma City each beat Mankato, knocking them out of the tournament. Bentley then took out Oklahoma City by a 5–3 score. At Elkton, Maryland, Gas Light won over West Warwick, 1–0, and Pittsfield, Massachusetts, 4–1. In the

Hastings, Nebraska, tourney, Portland beat Denver, 11–1, and Phoenix twice, 6–1 and 4–3. Mickey Lolich, Portland's left-handed pitcher and center fielder and future Detroit Tigers great, led the team sponsored by Bradford Clothiers.[39]

At Billings' Cobb Field, Bentley's dominance became apparent in the first game of the tourney. Greer Post 115, along with Willamette Post 102 of Portland, Oregon, and the Gas Light Post 44 from Washington, D.C., got a taste of the best of American Legion baseball in 1957 from Bentley Post 50 of Cincinnati. Cobb Field, located just north of downtown Billings, opened in 1948. Bentley won three straight games to take the title. It was Bentley's unprecedented fourth crown and the fifth for Cincinnati. On September 5, 1957, which happened to be the first televised baseball game in Montana, Bentley's ace left-hander, Scott Seger, defeated the Gas Lighters and in doing so put up strange numbers: he walked 10, hit one batter, and balked once, but he gave up just three hits, struck out 19 batters, and won with ease. Portland took down Greer, 4–2, in the other opening day game. Karl Haag's two-run double in the ninth was the difference. Jerry Drew pitched and won Bentley's second game, 8–6, over Portland. Portland's leading hitter and pitcher, Mickey Lolich, played little and ineffectively because of a virus infection.[40]

In the final game of 1957, Bentley again beat Portland, this time by a 10–6 score. The highlight of the final game, indeed of the Series, came in the seventh inning when Portland, trailing 6–4, loaded the bases. Portland pitcher George Spenser smashed a low line drive which shortstop Gerald Drew stabbed moving toward second base. He touched second to double up the runner well on his way to third, and then had the wits to pivot and throw to third base before the runner could get back. That was the third out of the triple play. In the eighth inning, Bentley put icing on the cake as first baseman Tom Weber doubled down the right field line to bring in three more runs.[41]

Bentley's third baseman Fred Fox finished the day leading all hitters with a .412 batting average in the ALWS. He was selected Player of the Year. A mere 5-foot-eight and 155 pounds, he batted a hefty .412 in national play. First baseman Tom Weber was right behind Fox with a .410 average. Coach Joe Hawk enjoyed his fourth title with Bentley. The bespectacled principal of Bridgetown Elementary School did not have the appearance of a grizzled baseball man, but he had a deft coaching touch. He began coaching legion ball in 1937, and had developed a system that produced players on the West Side of Cincinnati. A biographer of Pete Rose, who grew up on the West Side, wrote, "Being a baseball player has always been one way to have success on the West Side. I wouldn't say it's a way of getting out … because I don't think many of us really thought that way. We liked it there."[42]

Bentley surprised the American Legion baseball world when it won back-to-back titles by again taking the World Series crown in 1958, this time at Colorado Springs, Colorado. In so doing, they matched the feat of Oakland's 1949–1950 teams as the only teams to win successive crowns. No other team had won the Series title more than three times; this was Bentley's fifth national championship and the sixth for Cincinnati. Coach Joe Hawk and his long-time assistant coach, George "Pop" Scholl, returned two ace pitchers—lefty Scott Seger and Tom Tiettmeyer—from the 1957 championship team, but they pieced together the rest of the club. Hawk was not alone in thinking it was their best coaching job. The source of players shifted from Western Hills High School to Elder High School, holder of the Ohio state title for 1958.[43]

Bentley was anchored by its pitching and its infield of Tom Weber, a holdover from 1957, Ken Peters, Eddie Brinkman, and Jerry Marx. Seger, who won the tournament's Sportsmanship award, won two ALWS games. Peters batted .420 to win the Hillerich &

Bradsby trophy as the leading hitter of the tournament. Marx signed with the Cardinals and played four years in their system. Brinkman's greatest moment in the Series came as a pitcher, but his fame in pro ball came as a shortstop. Against Greenwood, in the ninth inning Brinkman took over mound duties with the bases loaded and struck out the one batter he faced to preserve the victory. Peters went on to play at Ohio State before signing with the Reds. He quit after three mediocre minor league years. Brinkman, however, played shortstop for 15 years at Washington and Detroit, winning a Gold Glove Award in 1972 and All-Star recognition in 1973. His high school coach at Western Hills saw Brinkman, rather than Pete Rose, as the future superstar.[44]

There were new faces in the 1958 tournament. Everett, Massachusetts Post 176 finally made the Show after making a habit of losing in the Sectionals. In fact, they finished second in the ALWS, beating Yellowstone Post 4 of Billings, Montana, as well as Greenwood, South Carolina Post 20 in World Series play. Greenwood boasted the Legion Player of the Year in pitcher-shortstop Kiebler James. Although it had lost to Everett in Sectional play, Brooklawn, New Jersey, gave notice it would be heard from in the future when it arrived undefeated and upended favorite Albany, New York, winner of 25 straight games, by the humiliating scores of 15–0 and 11–0.[45]

The 12 regional champions in 1958 included Everett Post 176 in Region 1, which had appeared in 1956. They beat Saco, Maine, Barre, Vermont, and Keene, New Hampshire. Region 2 champ Brooklawn, New Jersey, made its first appearance at this level, but it would not be their last. In Region 3, Gas Light Post of Washington, D.C. was making its fourth appearance as regional champion. They lost to Greenbelt, Maryland, in the opener. The outstanding individual performance came from Wierton, West Virginia's Mike Tomasozich, who struck out 19 Wilmington batters. Gas Light came on to beat Wierton and take two from Greenbelt, 13–11 in 14 innings and 5–0. In Region 4, Memphis, a repeat from 1957, pounded Louisville, 10–0, and slipped past Shelby, North Carolina, before losing to Shelby, 2–1. Memphis came back to beat Shelby, 13–12, in 11 innings, and 4–0 on Joel Porter's five-hitter. In Region 5, Greenwood, South Carolina, lost its first game to Shades Valley, Alabama, 6–5, on a passed ball with two outs in the ninth, but came back through the losers' bracket. Greenwood then won two from Shades Valley, coached by former major league manager Ben Chapman, 14–4 and 10–0. Kieber James pitched the shutout. In Region 6, New Orleans beat North Little Rock, Fort Wayne, Indiana, and Jackson, Mississippi. Floyd Fourroux threw a three-hitter in the final against Little Rock.[46]

West of the Mississippi, fans saw even more new teams making noise. Bentley Post 50 sailed through Region 7. In Region 8, Maplewood, Missouri, beat Enid, Oklahoma, Salina, Kansas, and Bancroft, Iowa. Maplewood's Jim Card struck out 22 Enid batters. In Region 9, tiny Drayton, North Dakota, population 900, lost to Sioux Falls, but came back to beat them, 4–3. Drayton also beat Fond de Lac, Wisconsin. In Region 10, Denver beat Hastings, Nebraska, Roswell, New Mexico, and Sheridan, Wyoming. Billings, Montana, won Region 11, beating Centralia, Washington, in 11 innings, Lewiston, Idaho, Fairbanks, Alaska, and Bend, Oregon. Finally, Ontario, California. Post 112 beat Holladay, Utah, Tucson, Reno, and Sheridan, Wyoming, to take Region 12.[47]

The final four shook down from the 12 Regional champs. In "A section," Brooklawn upset Gas Light Post. Everett then knocked Gas Light out of the tourney behind the slugging of Dick DePari. They followed that by knocking off Brooklawn on DePari's 10th-inning home run. In Section B, New Orleans beat Memphis and Greenwood, but

Greenwood toppled New Orleans thanks to four errors by the Louisiana lads to earn a trip to Colorado Springs. In Section C, Drayton's Cinderella run came to an end when they lost to Bentley and Maplewood. Then Cincinnati beat Maplewood and Jim Card, 9–5, before Card threw a one-hitter at Cincinnati for an 11–2 Maplewood win. In the rubber game, Cincinnati punched its ticket to the final four by winning a close 6–5 game. Tall Tom Tiettmeyer got credit for the win. Hitting star Jerry Walters of Billings led his Yellowstone Post 4 team to victories over Ontario, California, and Denver.[48]

At the American Legion World Series, players from all teams stayed at the Broadmoor Hotel, the grand old railroad hotel in Colorado Springs. Brissie spotted the Greenwood, South Carolina, boys preparing to go into the dining room dressed in jeans. Brissie told them, "you can't go to dinner in blue jeans." When told by the boys that was all they had, Brissie dug into his pocket and gave them money to buy dress pants. He did not want his homeboys looking like hicks.[49]

Bentley won the ALWS in 1958, its fifth national championship, by beating each of the other three in the Finals. Scott Seger threw a four-hit, complete-game 5–2 win over Yellowstone Post on the first day. Greenwood struggled past Everett, 12–11, in ten innings. In the losers' bracket, Everett knocked Billings out of the tournament, 7–0. The two first-day winners, Bentley and Greenwood, hooked up in a close game, but Bentley prevailed, 6–5. Eddie Brinkman pitched the final out with the bases loaded, getting a strikeout to save the victory. In a rematch between Greenwood and Everett, the Massachusetts lads prevailed by an 8–7 score. The final game was not even close, as Cincinnati locked up its fifth national title in a 12–1 blowout of Everett.[50]

The most disappointing news from the Colorado Springs World Series was that attendance was a mere 4,200. Brissie was looking to make changes in the World Series format, but he would need at least a year to implement his alterations. One option that he floated was to have a centrally located, permanent site for the Series. The College World Series was doing quite well with regional playoffs that fed winners into Omaha, which was always the location for the Series. Little League baseball had always held its playoffs at Williamsport, Pennsylvania. Brissie let it be known that Hastings, Nebraska, was a likely site, if they could prove they could handle the job. So he named Hastings as the site for the 1959 Legion World Series. Duncan Field in Hastings, the home of the Hastings Giants of the Nebraska State League, was a huge field with dimensions that invited inside-the-park home runs, measuring 353 feet down the foul line to left field, 377 to right field, and an impossible 448 to dead center. The stands were particularly unattractive. Bleachers down third and first and covered bleachers behind home plate lacked backs or other amenities. The local organizing committees, however, did their jobs well, and the attendance of 23,615, while not record-setting, was deemed quite satisfactory.[51]

Before any games were played in the 1959 Series, Detroit's Thomas A. Edison Post 187—with Ready Kilowatt displayed on the back of their uniform—was deemed the odds-on favorite. They had played far more games than any other team, posting a 49–10 record, much of that in an under-19 league that hardened the Edisons. Their pitchers benefited from coach Art Kohn's nephew, Billy Pierce, an All-Star lefty for the Chicago White Sox, who tutored the Edison mound staff. Fred Fleming, in noting Pierce's contribution, said, "I was learning to be a pitcher, not just a thrower." Players came from the west side of Detroit—Catholic Central, Benedictine Catholic, and Western High Schools.[52]

Edison lost in the Sectional to West Allis, Wisconsin, but came back to put a 20–8 whipping on their opponent, thanks to a record 22 walks issued by West Allis pitchers.

Edison prided themselves on being a team. In the Sectional, their African American center fielder, Richard Miller, had five hits but took racist abuse from fans, who kept calling Miller a "watermelon eater." Miller took the abuse, but big first baseman Ron Balatero threatened to jerk the tormentor through the fence and turn him "into liquid watermelon." Edison's tiny shortstop, Fred Bowen, Jr., was selected as the Legion Player of the Year. Bowen stood just 5-foot-6 and weighed all of 145 pounds. He was not the best hitter; that honor went to Phoenix left fielder Lou Webb, who batted .478. Bowen hit just .307, but, by all accounts. he was the slickest fielder at the Series since Ed Brinkman.[53]

The Legion again put the number of teams at 18,000. The regional winners reduced the field to 12. Only New Orleans returned from 1958. Others in the elite 12 included: Riders Post 59 of Milford, Massachusetts, from Region 1; Region 2, Hayes-Velhage Post 96 of West Hartford, Connecticut; Region 3, Greenbelt, Maryland Post 136; Region 4, Fuller-Urick Post 48 of Hampton, Virginia; Region 5, West Palm Beach Post 12; Region 6, New Orleans Post 125; Region 7, Edison Post 187 of Detroit; Region 8, Enid, Oklahoma; Region 9, West Allis, Wisconsin; Region 10, Las Cruces, New Mexico, Post 10; Region 11, Earle B. Stewart, Post 16 of Roseburg, Oregon; and Region 12, Luke-Greenway Post 1, Phoenix, Arizona.[54]

The lineup of teams in the 1959 World Series contained new faces. It had always been a struggle for New England to place a team in the Series. Now, Hayes-Velhage Post 96 of West Hartford made the Series, the first team from Connecticut to do so. They were joined by Luke Greenway Post 1 of Phoenix, and Detroit Edison Post 187. The biggest surprise was seeing Fuller-Urick Post 48 of Hampton, Virginia. Two years before, in 1957, the team did not even exist, but here they were, thanks largely to their coach Bill Ball, his son Bobby Ball, the team's best player, and outstanding pitching which held opponents to 2.57 runs per game. Most of their players came from Phoebus High School, so "Phoebus" was the name the Legion team took. In the Sectional, they had hooked up with New Orleans. Freckle-faced George Jones won the first meeting for Phoebus. New Orleans dominated the second game, winning 15–2. It took 12 innings in the rubber match before Hampton prevailed, 2–1, when first baseman Brink Miller scored the winning run on an error.[55]

In the ALWS, Edison stumbled coming out of the gate. In the opening game, Detroit lost, 4–3, to West Hartford in a huge upset. Hampton's George Jones pitched a 5–0, two-hit shutout over Phoenix. The Arizona lads lost their next game to Detroit, 14–6, which eliminated them. Hampton's Bobby Ball allowed just three hits and shut out West Hartford 5–0. That was the first time West Hartford had been shut out this season. Hartford came back on day two to beat Phoenix, 14–6, a loss that eliminated the Arizona team. In the rematch between West Hartford and Edison, the Connecticut boys ran wild on the bases in the first two innings against starter Arnie Jent. Edison coach Art Kohn brought in Fred Fleming, who shut things down, allowing only one hit in 6⅔ innings and striking out 10. Still, West Hartford racked up a record 19 stolen bases in the game. Detroit prevailed, 7–6. Phoebus had the opportunity to take home the title with a win over Detroit. In the crucial meeting between Edison and Hampton, Mark Esper threw a three-hitter to give Edison the 5–3 win.[56]

In the 1959 championship game, Terry Barden pitched a strong game for Edison, but in reality the Hampton team suddenly felt the pressure. They became inept, committing 10 errors. That assured Detroit a 5–0 victory. Edison's pitching had been strong throughout the Series, allowing a mere 2.27 earned runs per game. The win gave Edison the national championship and a 46–5 record for the season. When Edison arrived back in Detroit, they were welcomed by an enthusiastic crowd of over 2,000 on hand to greet Michigan's first American Legion champions.[57]

Before the 1959 Series ended, Lou Brissie let it be known that Hastings would again host the Series in 1960. Hastings had drawn an acceptable 23,615 to the 1959 series, but Brissie believed they could do better. There would, in all likelihood, be additional changes for the next year. First, there would be an eight-team tournament instead of the traditional four. Also, the age limit might be raised to 18, and the roster size might be increased. Finally, requiring players to wear protective helmets was under discussion.[58]

An eight-team World Series did become a reality in 1960. Brissie devoted two weeks of traveling and speaking across Nebraska and parts of Kansas, drumming up business for the tournament. Brissie believed the eight-team format would give a greater opportunity for different regions of the country to gain access to the Series. Teams would now reach the Series through eight regional tournaments, each with six teams. Roster sizes remained at 20, but teams could still dress only 16 players. Mandatory helmets had been discussed but not approved, though South Dakota made helmets required for Legion games in that state.[59]

In the East, favorites emerged as winners in Regions 1, 2, and 3. Pittsfield needed 14 innings to beat West Hartford, 2–1. The winning run scored on an RBI by its flashy shortstop, Mark Belanger, who went on to win eight Gold Glove Awards while with Baltimore between 1969 and 1978. Brooklawn, New Jersey, lost its first game to Gas Light Post of Washington, but worked its way back to a final game against the same Gas Lighters. The Brooks prevailed, 10–4, behind the four-hit pitching of Rick Phalines. Pan American Post 140 of Miami, like Brooklawn, lost its first game but still won over Wilmington, North Carolina.[60]

In Region 4, Crescent City Post 125 of New Orleans continued the pattern of a strong team losing its first game. New Orleans' loss was to Nacogdoches, Texas, 5–4, despite Dick Roniger's grand-slam home run. The team was referred to both as the "Blue Jays," the nickname of Jesuit High School where they attended, or "Tulane Shirts," the team sponsor whose name adorned the back of their uniform shirt. New Orleans also came back to take the Regional. In the final game, Roniger and hard-hitting first baseman Dan "Rusty" Staub homered. Defending champion Detroit Edison was in Region 5, the Mid-west, but it went out quickly. Owensboro, Kentucky, was in position to take the title, but it lost two games in a row to Berwyn, Illinois, which happily traveled to Hastings. In Region 6, the hometown Hastings team, Post 11, led by Allen Curtis, reeled off four straight victories to advance through the Regional.[61]

Region 7 was the home of the Billings Yellowstone Post 4 Royals. They had won three straight state titles, and in Dave McNally they had one of American Legion's all-time pitching greats. How good was McNally? In the state tournament, he pitched back-to-back no-hitters. New Orleans coach Kevin Trower referred to him as "the best high school pitcher I ever saw … no one comes close." He commanded "a completely overwhelming fast ball and an un-hittable curve." Against Seattle, he struck out 19 batters, allowed just two hits, and won, 2–0. He went into the World Series with a 16–0 record.[62]

Roswell, New Mexico, Phoenix, Arizona, and Klamath Falls, Oregon, battled it out for the right to advance to Hastings from Region 8. Roswell's Butch Thompson slugged two grand-slam home runs in a 25–1 demolition of Las Vegas After Roswell beat Klamath

Falls, 11–0, the Falls came back to win the finals, 9–6, over Roswell on outfielder John Bisnchi's grand-slam.[63]

Billings was loaded. With a record of 47–5, they were by far the most experienced team in the 1960 ALWS. They had been to the ALWS in 1958, and they lost in the Regionals in 1959. They had the best kid pitcher on the planet in Dave McNally, plus three outstanding hitters. Center fielder Bob Fry would capture the Louisville Slugger Award as the top hitter in the World Series with a .417 average. Second baseman Kenneth "Pete" Cochran finished second with a .389 average, and left fielder Dick Letwak, with a .371 average, was not far behind. Right fielder Gary Coatsworth was good enough to sign with the Angels. They had a second pitcher, Steve Huntsberry, who was no slouch. But it was McNally whom all the scouts came to watch. He was later selected as the best Montana Athlete of the 20th Century. Following the ALWS he would sign with the Baltimore Orioles for an $80,000 bonus. He pitched in 14 major league seasons, winning 20 games four times.[64]

New Orleans (29–3) countered with American Legion Player of the Year Dick "Swifty" Roniger, a 6-foot-6-inch, dominating pitcher-outfielder. He brought a record of 14–3 to the Series. Backing up Roniger in the rotation were two future lawyers, Richie Hammel and Bill Bassett. Their leading hitter was third baseman Harry Morel, a .333 hitter for the tournament. Power came from first baseman and cleanup hitter, left-handed-hitting Daniel "Rusty" Staub, out of Jesuit High School, who would soon sign with the Houston Astros for a hefty $100,000 bonus and go on to an outstanding 23-year career with the Astros, Detroit Tigers, Montreal Expos, New York Mets, and Texas Rangers. His older brother, Chuck Staub, patrolled one outfield position. Rusty and outfielder Louie Triche served as co-captains of the Blue Jays.[65]

The first eight-team World Series began with Pittsfield, Massachusetts Post 68 (21–4); Brooklawn, New Jersey Post 71 (38–10); Miami's Pan-American Post 140 (16–5); New Orleans' Crescent City Post 125 (24–2); Berwyn, Illinois Commodore Barry Post 256 (25–4); Hastings, Nebraska Post 11 (39–8); Billings, Montana Royals of Yellowstone Post 4 (47–5): and Klamath Falls, Oregon Post 8 (26–5). Hastings hoped to ride the hot bat of Allen Curtis, who posted a .460 batting average and 81 RBI. New Orleans and Billings, however, were the pre-tournament favorites at the start of the 1960 Series.

Great pitching dominated the opening round. Hard-throwing Dave McNally struck out 19 Brooklawn batters in a 3–0 Billings win. New Orleans' Roniger threw a two-hitter at Klamath Falls in a 2–0 win for the Crescent City club. Hastings upset Miami, 8–0, behind Bob Fish's one-hitter. The exception to the fine pitching in the opening round was sloppy work by the Berwyn mound staff, in the form of 10 walks which contributed to Pittsfield's 9–6 victory.[66]

In the second round, Pittsfield took on the role of favorite. Taking advantage of 12 bases on balls by Billings pitchers as well as two errors, Pittsfield upset Billings, 9–5. Mark Belanger got the only extra-base hit of the game. In the double elimination format of the tournament, Brooklawn's 7–5 triumph sent Berwyn home. Miami's tiny Roberto Rodriquez, weighing only 128 pounds, pitched a shutout to sideline Klamath Falls. New Orleans got all four of its runs in the eighth inning to nip Hastings, 4–1.[67]

In the third round, Brooklawn got another shot at McNally, but the results were little different from their first meeting. McNally struck out 17, gave up only three hits, and Billings won 5–3, sending Brooklawn back to Jersey. Miami, behind Julian Peeples's three-hit shutout, topped Hastings, 8–0, to eliminate the host team. Pittsfield, behind Joe

Costanzo's four-hit complete game, established its dominance by beating New Orleans, 4–1, thanks to three unearned runs. The win made Pittsfield the only unbeaten team in the Series.[68]

Pittsfield's advantage was not long-lived. They lost their next game, 8–2, to Billings. Huntsberry set Pittsfield down on three hits and struck out 14 batters. New Orleans got back in the championship hunt by knocking Miami out of the Series in a 6–5 game that took 11 innings. New Orleans' Rusty Staub launched a mammoth triple followed by co-captain Louie Triche's RBI single to give the Blue Jays the win. That left New Orleans, Pittsfield, and Billings to battle for the title. Billings got the bye into the finals. In the semi-final game, New Orleans prevailed, 6–1, over Pittsfield. Henry "Bubby" Winters pitched a three-hit game, and third baseman Harry Morel, catcher Joe McMahon, and outfielder Dick Roniger each drove in two runs.[69]

The 1960 championship game belonged to New Orleans. Billings jumped out to a 3–0 lead. McNally's ball "hopped," as Blue Jays coach Trower described it. "We could hardly make contact," he explained. On the New Orleans bench, backup catcher Dale Boudreaux picked up the Billings catcher's signs. That was the breakthrough for New Orleans. The New Orleans bench jockeys began to call all the pitches as McNally delivered. McNally, understandably, believed he was tipping off his pitches. The Blue Jays pushed across one run in the fifth inning thanks to two Billings errors. In the sixth, McNally became unglued and walked four batters to give the Blue Jays a run. New Orleans did not stop until seven runs had crossed the plate, McNally had given up 10 walks, and he had been chased from the mound. McNally would later be selected as Montana's Athlete of the 20th Century, but he was not that on this day. Final score: New Orleans 9, Billings 3.[70]

It was 26-year-old coach Kevin Trower's first title. The national title was the second for New Orleans Crescent Post. The first had come in 1946 with Eddie Toribio, another first-year coach. The tournament drew 29,144 paying spectators for the Series. With the new format, the World Series included 15 games, more than double the number for previous years. Bob Fry, Billings center fielder and sometime pitcher, captured the Louisville Slugger trophy with a .417 batting average. He also won the Sportsmanship Award. Dick Roniger, pitcher-outfielder of New Orleans, was voted Legion Player of the Year.

In March of the 1960–1961 off-season, the American Legion and, indeed, the entire baseball world, experienced a seismic event. The National Commander of the American Legion, William R. Burke, announced the firing of Lou Brissie as commissioner of Legion baseball. In some statements from the Legion, the term favored was "released," in others "dismissed," "dropped," or "discharged." Brissie knew he was without a job. Fired was the appropriate term. Reasons were never clearly stated. C. A. Tesch, director of the National Americanism Commission of the Legion, who took over Brissie's duties on an interim basis, identified "streamlining" as the reason for firing the commissioner. Since Brissie's bureaucratic empire consisted of himself and a secretary, it is hard to imagine a more streamlined organizational chart. Some in the Legion thought they needed the head of the baseball program to do other things in the Americanism Commission. That had been the way before Brissie's appointment, but baseball people within the Legion and without had been pleased that he had stuck to baseball.[71]

There were concerns inside the Headquarters in Indianapolis about rising costs of the baseball operation, and a desire in some quarters to reduce operating costs. Brissie's decision to take the American Legion World Series from four to eight teams did increase the costs of running the tournament, as did his decision to center the World Series at

Hastings, Nebraska. The 1960 budget of $105,000 included $65,000 for tournament travel expenses. The net gate receipts at Hastings amounted to only $19,000. Major league baseball's grant of $60,000 provided the largest outside income. Ford Motor Company, City Service, and Coke made up the remainder needed to cover the cost of the World Series. Costs were a cause for concern, but hardly a strong reason for firing the chief operating officer.[72]

The Legion brass refused to elaborate on Brissie's termination. Brissie immediately retreated to Greenville, South Carolina, where he had maintained a home. A week after his return, W. B. "Monk" Mulligan, head of the Greenville YMCA, announced Brissie's appointment to the YMCA staff to work with boys and adults. He did not stay long with the YMCA, but he did live out his life in the Greenville area. He later worked in employee relations for United Merchants, an important player in the garment industry, and then became associated with the South Carolina Board of Technical Education as a manager of technical training for new industries. A lifelong Legion member, he died in 2013. He had brought stability to Legion baseball and given it greater visibility and awareness among the general public.[73]

The Legion continued to grow the number of former players in the majors. Although the Legion never recognized that producing stars of the future was a goal, even a byproduct of its baseball program, still, as the decade of the 1950s closed, the Legion could look with pride at the major league stars who cut their teeth on dusty fields playing for Legion teams. The greatest of the ex-Legion players, those who ultimately were selected to Baseball's Hall of Fame, included Bob Feller (1962) and Ted Williams (1966), who started their major league careers before World War II. Other Hall of Famers from the 1940s and 1950s were Stan "the Man" Musial (1969), Roy Campanella (1969), Lou Boudreau (1970), Yogi Berra (1972), Early Wynn (1972), Warren Spahn (1973), Ralph Kiner (1973), Bob Lemon (1976), Robin Roberts (1976), Eddie Mathews (1978), Al Kaline (1980), Frank Robinson (1982), George Kell (1983), Harmon Killebrew (1984), Pee Wee Reese (1984), Hoyt Wilhelm (1985), Bobby Doerr (1986), "Prince Hal" Newhouser (1992), Richie Ashburn (1995), and Nelson Fox (1997). The 1950s, indeed, have a strong claim to being the Golden Age of baseball.

5

The Rulon Years,
1961–1975

In early May 1961, the Legion's National Commander, William Burke, introduced George W. Rulon as "director of Junior Baseball." Rulon brought some baseball credentials to the job, but without the name recognition of Lou Brissie. A native of Jamestown, North Dakota, where he was born in 1921, he had played Legion baseball there as a youth. After serving in World War II, he attended North Dakota State University, graduating in 1946. He became a sportswriter for the *Fargo Forum* and then public relations director for the Fargo-Morehead Twins of the independent Northern League. In 1958, he joined the Legion administration as director of membership and post activities. After three years, Rulon moved to the baseball side of the organization. He proved to be a good choice for the Legion, lasting from 1961 to 1987 as director of Legion baseball.[1]

Soon after his appointment, Rulon and his wife Corene met with Commissioner Ford Frick. Major league baseball now contributed $60,000 annually to the Legion operation. Whether connected with that meeting or not, Rulon soon announced that the Legion was dropping the appellation "Junior" from its formal title. From now on, the program would officially be American Legion Baseball. In reality, that decision caught the official wording up with the common usage.[2]

The country, too, entered a new era. The election of John F. Kennedy as president in November 1960 brought optimism and hope to the vast majority of Americans. To Catholics, JFK's election symbolized their arrival as full-fledged Americans. Long had American boys been told they could be anything they wanted, but Catholic boys understood that did not include the head of the state; now that ceiling was busted. As the first president born in the 20th century, Kennedy brought hope for a better future. He promised to "get the country moving again." Young people could identify with this president of their century. At his inauguration, his "Ask not what your country can do for you, ask what you can do for your country" ushered in a new "come-outer spirit." This dovetailed with Martin Luther King, Jr.'s, drive to achieve civil rights for African Americans. Kennedy was a World War II hero and also a cold warrior determined to resist Communism everywhere, including the jungles of Vietnam.

That year, 1961, in the Northeast Regional tourney, fans saw Chicopee Post 452 pitcher Al Stanek strike out a Legion-record 22 batters. The game, played at Keene, New Hampshire, pitted Chicopee, Massachusetts, against Sweeney Post of Manchester, New Hampshire. The only hit he gave up was a dribbler down the third-base line. Stanek had fanned 25 for Chicopee high school against Amherst earlier in the year. San Francisco signed the lad to a healthy bonus at the end of his high school career, but he never made the major leagues. Neither of those teams made the ALWS, as Hayes-Velhage Post 96 of West Hartford, Connecticut, won the Northeast Regional. They were not newcomers, having last appeared in the Series in 1959.[3]

Lou Brissie had arranged for the American Legion World Series of 1961 to be played at his favorite spot, Hastings, Nebraska, from August 26–September 5. The Yellowstone Post 4 Governors of Billings, Montana, were picked by many as the favorite. They had finished second the year before, and while they no longer had Dave McNally, they had several solid holdovers, including center fielder Bob Fry, the reigning Legion Player of the Year, second baseman Pete Cochran, who would sign a $50,000 bonus contract with the Los Angeles Dodgers, pitcher-outfielder John Huntsberry, and promising newcomers, including fleet African American outfielder Richard Lucero.[4]

Other teams in the World Series had fought through Regionals and Sectionals. They included Brooklawn, New Jersey Post 72, back for a second straight year. The Brookers beat Clifton in the state final, their fourth New Jersey title, having also won in 1954, 1958, and 1960. They roared through the Regional in College Park, Maryland. Others in the ALWS were Colonial Heights, Virginia Post 284; Graves Post 7 Gassers of Jackson, Mississippi; Cincinnati, Gehlert Post 554, loaded with players from Western Hills High; Omaha Post 1 Storz; and Phoenix's Luke-Greenway Post 1, aka Kerr Sporting Goods. At the banquet before the ALWS got underway, Brissie attended as a "special guest."[5]

In the opening round, Phoenix made it clear they should be taken seriously by ending Billings' 27-game winning streak, beating the Yellowstone boys, 5–3. After Phoenix scored four runs in the first inning, Phoenix lefty Larry "Buck" Staley was in control the whole game. In other games on the first day, Brooklawn survived a pitching duel against West Hartford by a 2–1 score. Dick Laxton pitched five-hit ball for the Brooks to get the win. Colonial Heights of Petersburg, Virginia, won its first-ever World Series game, 6–4 over Omaha. Petersburg came back from a 4–2 deficit in the eighth inning on hits by Hugh Powell, Ollie Jarvis, Billy Horrell, and Tom Kidd, and a big Omaha error. Jarvis had two hits and picked up the save by pitching the ninth inning. Cincinnati's Gehlert Post 554, not to be confused with previous winners from the Queen City, either Post 50 or U.S. Postal Workers Post 216, continued the city's tradition of strong teams. Their coach, Dick Hauck, had been a member of the 1944 Bentley team. They pounded out 20 hits, four by third baseman Larry Stahl, and coasted to a 11–3 win over mismatched Jackson.[6]

Before the second round of play, attention shifted from baseball to the issue of race. Jackson was scheduled against Billings, who had a player of mixed African American and Native-American parents. Jackson's coaches, Bob Berry and Willis Steenhuis, had asked not to play Billings because the Montana team used a "colored player." When that request was denied, Berry first announced that Jackson would forfeit rather than play Billings, but then the two Jackson coaches turned tail and returned to Mississippi, leaving their team and its players to fend for themselves. Fortunately, the commander of the Jackson post, Frank Chambers, dropped everything and rushed to Hastings to manage the post team. Appropriately, Jackson lost a close game when the African American player, Rick Lucero, doubled in the winning run in the ninth inning to win a 4–3 game. Jackson's loss meant the entire team returned to Mississippi.[7]

In other second-day games, Omaha's Ed Melo threw a three-hitter and struck out 11 in a 5–1 win that sent West Hartford home. Brooklawn handed Colonial Heights its first loss, 6–4, behind Jim Megee's pitching and shortstop Denny O'Brien's two hits and two

RBI. Finally, Cincinnati got the best of Phoenix, 5–3. Despite the loss, the Phoenix lads still believed they could win it all. In elimination games, the dreams of Colonial Heights and Billings came crashing down. Colonial Heights had themselves to blame by committing 11 errors in a 6–3 loss to Omaha. Bob Churchich struck out 11 Colonial Heights batters. Cincinnati knocked Brooklawn from the undefeated ranks by a 7–3 score. First baseman Larry Stahl and shortstop Jim Gruber provided the fire power behind the win. In the opening round, Phoenix had upset Billings, 5–3, but in the rematch, the two went to 11 innings before Phoenix scored the winning run on a squeeze bunt by Greg Sorensen. The upset loss knocked favorite Billings completely out of the tournament.[8]

Now Phoenix was the team to beat. Phoenix and Cincinnati remained undefeated. Brooklawn and Omaha were left with one loss. The undefeated teams took care of business. Phoenix did in Brooklawn, 4–3, as John Hill collected three RBI, and Cincinnati knocked out Omaha with a 10–7 win. That set up the two best teams in the 1961 final. Phoenix won the first game, 2–0, behind the pitching of Buck Staley, who limited Cincinnati to four hits. It was the only shutout of the entire Series. Phoenix scored an unearned run in the fourth inning and the other run on a double by co-captain and second baseman Tim Meyers in the seventh. Phoenix captured the 1961 ALWS title by winning, 4–1, in the final game. Cincinnati scored first on John Nebel's triple and Walt Lambert's sacrifice fly. Phoenix went ahead in the eighth inning when Gary Wolf tripled and third baseman Larry Martin added a two-run triple. In the ninth inning, four walks and a Wolf single posted two more runs. Phoenix hurler Dan Swingle got stronger as the game progressed and finished with 10 strikeouts.[9]

Phoenix's Kerr Sporting Goods team dominated the 1961 all-tournament selections. Jim Brock was selected coach of the year. Fred Combs was a unanimous picked as catcher even though he batted a mere .212; he threw out 13 baserunners in six games. Joe Swingle, who batted .351, was selected at first base. Other Phoenix selections were third baseman Larry Martin, who hit the only home run of the Series, and pitchers Buck Staley, who finished with a 1.14 earned run average, and Dan Swingle, who had four wins and six saves in regionals and World Series play. Others picked for the all-star team were Bobby Lombardo, Brooklawn outfielder, pitchers Ken McEwen and Bob Churchich of Omaha, outfielder Steve Huntsberry of Billings, Cincinnati shortstop Jim Gruber, outfielder John Nebel, and pitchers Jerry Storm and Russ Feth. Gruber was selected Player of the Year.[10]

Rulon's effort to put the World Series on solid financial footing seemed to pay off. He traveled over 75,000 miles and visited 25 states in his first year as head of Legion baseball. Rulon's first tournament was a modest success. Attendance for the 1961 World Series was 26,140, down from 29,144 in Brissie's last year. Nonetheless, that brought in a profit of $35,000 from the gate. The three-year commitment to Hastings hosting the World Series ended, and few were interested in extending the relationship. Rulon believed he could cut transportation costs even more in 1962, although he had not counted on a team from Honolulu making the tournament. The biggest change in Rulon's first year was to raise the age limit from 17 to 18; more specifically, players could not turn 19 before September 1. This had been on the agenda for the past several years but lacked the momentum to get approved until December 1961. Rulon thought the change would benefit state champions, but only the first year. The number of players leveled off at around 225,000. The Legion took pride in the recognition that 286 major league players had come through Legion ball.[11]

The 1962 World Series moved from Hastings, Nebraska, to Bismarck, North Dakota.

Bismarck Municipal Ballpark, site of the games, was a traditional wooden minor league park. Built in 1928, it seated 2,000 fans under roof and 3,000 more in bleachers down the foul lines. It had hosted the North Dakota state tournament in 1945 and the American Legion World Series in 1956. Currently, it was the home of Bismarck-Mandan Partners of the Class C Northern League, as well as the Yellowstone Post Governors American Legion team. Its most famous occupant had been a semi-pro team, the Bismarck Churchills (aka Giants), who had won the National Semi-Professional Baseball Championship back in 1935. Team owner Neill Churchill, a local car dealer, put together an integrated team that included great African American players Satchel Paige, Quincy Troupe, Ted "Double-Duty" Radcliffe, and Hilton Smith.[12]

When Rulon managed to get the age limit raised to under 19, there was fear among some that raising the age limit would merely strengthen the best teams. This concern failed to materialize. Of the eight World Series participants in 1961, only Billings repeated in 1962. The real surprise to make the elite eight was Kau Tom Post 11 of Honolulu, Hawaii (14–0). They took great pride in being the first team from Hawaii to qualify for the World Series. The "Hammering Hawaiians," out of Farrington High School, were a multi-racial collection of Japanese, Chinese, Puerto Rican, and German players. They featured the smallest player in uniform for the Series in outfielder Jim Nakada, who stood only 5-foot-3. They also featured left-handed first baseman-pitcher John Matias, who would win the Sportsmanship trophy. Left fielder Ron Ramie emerged as a star of the Regional, where he hit a cool .500.

Other teams that qualified for the 1962 World Series were Somerville Post 19 of Somerville, Massachusetts (28–4); Adam Plewacki Post 799 of Buffalo, New York (20–2), sponsored by Federal Credit Union; Hampton Roads Post 31 Bears of Hampton Roads, Virginia (28–6); Crescent City Post 125 of New Orleans (28–5); Anheuser-Busch Post 299 of St. Louis, Missouri (21–7); and Tanner Paull Post 123 of West Allis, Wisconsin (22–3). The Billings Governors (47–6) were slight favorites going into the Series.

Somerville entered with high hopes based on their star pitcher, Bobby Taylor, who had pitched five no-hitters in his three years of Legion ball. Hampton, coached by Nelson Catlet, also had a tiny player, pitcher-shortstop David O'Beirne (5-foot-5, 130 pounds), and a big bopper in first baseman Fred Balmer. Still, they were just happy to have made the Series. St. Louis hoped to repeat the success of Stockham Post's 1956 World Series triumph on the same field. Catcher Bill Mahan, at 6-foot-4, 220 pounds, was the star. He had three RBI in Anheuser-Busch's 5–3 win over Owensboro, Kentucky, in the Section 5 finals. He played linebacker at the University of Missouri and for the New York football Giants. Based on their play in Regionals, Billings looked to be favorites. They sailed through Region 7 in five straight games. Pitching ace, veteran Steve Huntsberry, threw a two-hitter against Aurora, a game in which he struck out 21 batters, a record for a nine-inning game in the World Series. First baseman Rick McLaughlin had eight runs batted in against Casper. West Allis featured pitcher Jim Peters, who had struck out 20 Bancroft, Iowa, batters in the Regionals. In the Regional final, they defeated St. Paul 12–5.[13]

Based on their success the previous year and their domination in the Regional and Sectional, Billings deserved its billing as the 1962 favorite, just as they had been the previous year. Billings had rolled through the Regionals, winning five straight from Lawrence, Kansas, Lewiston, Idaho, Casper, Wyoming, Aurora, Colorado, and Anadarko, Oklahoma. First baseman Rick McLaughlin, who drove in a record eight runs against

Casper in the Regional, headed a lineup of strong batters. Pitcher Steve Huntsberry, who struck out a near record 21 batters in the Regional, led a deep mound staff. In the opening game of the tournament, Billings came from behind to score nine runs in the final three innings to defeat Hampton.[14]

In other first-round games, St. Louis and Honolulu got off to strong starts. Starting pitcher Dan Rudanovich doubled in the winning run in the ninth inning to give St. Louis a 6–5 win over Somerville. Kan-Tom Post of Ferrington, Hawaii, scored six runs in the eighth inning to beat New Orleans, 8–3. West Allis' pitcher, Jim Peters, won his 19th game of the season, 5–4 over Buffalo. In the second round, St. Louis pulled off a key win, taking out Billings by a 7–4 score. Mahan and shortstop Bob Robben each had two hits, and Rudanovich's two RBI paced Anheuser-Busch. Terry L'Ange threw a five-hitter, struck out 12 batters, and homered. Honolulu kept pace with a devastating 22–6 win over West Allis. First baseman Kohn Mathas homered twice for the Hawaiians. Hampton Roads had little trouble in eliminating Somerville with a 10–0 whitewashing. New Orleans kept its hopes alive with a 6–4 win over Buffalo. Gerald Landry and John Stephens each had a single and double to pace the Crescent City bunch. The loss sent Buffalo home with two straight losses.[15]

Billings' loss to St. Louis apparently destroyed the Montana boys' confidence. The next day they lost again, to New Orleans, 4–1, which eliminated them after only three games. St. Louis now took on the favorite's role. The key match between St. Louis and Honolulu went to Anheuser-Busch, 6–3. Terry L'Ange allowed only five hits and struck out 13 batters. The loss ended Honolulu's 16-game win streak, but it did not knock them out of the Series. Hampton Roads sent West Allis home with a 3–1 loss. Pitcher Butch Wheeler threw a tidy five-hitter, and first baseman Fred Balmer had three hits. Honolulu and St. Louis continued winning. Honolulu ended Hampton's dream, sending them back to Virginia with a 10–9 win in ten innings. St. Louis continued to roll, hammering New Orleans, 8–0, on Dan Rudanovich's three-hitter. The St. Louis win set up a rematch between Anheuser-Busch and Honolulu for the 1962 title.[16]

In the final game of 1962, St. Louis gave the pitching assignment to its regular third baseman, Jerry Mueller. He gave Anheuser-Busch seven strong innings, allowing just two hits. Rudanovich came on to finish the game. St. Louis got seven runs in the seventh inning, highlighted by a triple by third baseman Charles Dyn on a chilly wind-swept field. Honolulu came back to score five runs in the eighth inning, but the inning ended on a strikeout with the bases loaded. St. Louis outfielder Denny Horton homered, and shortstop Bob Robben had three hits.[17] Anheuser-Busch's seven-run seventh held up, giving them the 9–6 victory over Honolulu in the 1962 Legion title.

St. Louis' Bill Matan, the huge, six-foot-4-inch, 220-pound catcher who caught every game, displayed a powerful arm, and batted .389, was selected Player of the Year. He later played for the New York football Giants. Fred Balmer, Hampton's first baseman, captured the Louisville Slugger Award for highest batting average at .553. Honolulu slugger John Matias, who belted three home runs in the Series, was awarded the recently minted James F. McDaniel, Jr. Sportsmanship Award. The Anheuser-Busch Brewing team had been underestimated before the tournament. They sailed through, winning five straight games. Besides Matan, outfielder-pitcher Dan Rudanovich had a great Series. Strong-armed shortstop Bob Robben led the team with a .405 batting average.[18]

Shortly after the 1962 World Series, much to the delight of the American Legion from top to bottom, Bob Feller, a Legion member and former player, was selected for membership in the National Baseball Hall of Fame. He became the first graduate of American Legion baseball to be enshrined in the Hall. It was, of course, a tremendous honor for Feller, but the Legion basked in the reflected glory. As Feller described his baseball career: "I cut my eye teeth on American Legion Junior baseball." He remembered, "it was the Legion program that gave me the opportunity to play organized ball." At age 12 in 1931, he had joined the Legion team in Adel, Iowa, ten miles from his home in Van Meter. The local mail carrier, Lester Chance, coached the team and gave Robert a lift to practice. Chance made him a pitcher in his second year of Legion ball. "Rapid Robert" was on his way. He remembered being shy, but "competitive sports are an ideal way to bring a boy out of his shell." His battery mate was Nile Kinnick, who gained fame in football and won the Heisman Trophy at Iowa in 1939. In 1933 Feller switched teams, moving from Adel, whose team folded, to Highland Park in Des Moines. That team made the state finals in 1934, and scouts took notice of the hard-throwing youngster. The following year he switched again, to a semi-pro team, and signed a contract with Cleveland. In 1936, at age 17, he started pitching for the Cleveland Indians, and by 1939 he became the best and most-feared pitcher in baseball. The Navy took four prime years out of his career. When he retired in 1956 after 18 years in the majors, he had won 266 games and had led the league in strikeouts seven times. After returning home from World War II, he joined the American Legion and became a huge supporter, always available to speak at Legion events.[19]

Bob Feller had the honor of becoming the first former American Legion player to be elected to the Baseball Hall of Fame, which occurred five years after his last major league game in 1956. Despite losing three wartime years to the navy, he led the league in wins six times and strikeouts seven times. He was the fastest pitcher of his era and many think he was the hardest thrower of all-time (National Baseball Hall of Fame Library, Cooperstown, N.Y.).

In 1963, the American Legion World Series shifted to Keene, New Hampshire, on the campus of Keene State Teachers College, from August 25–30. Players were housed in college dormitories. The school's Alumni Field, constructed in 1948, was small and disjointed. Covered stands along the first base line contained 1,000 permanent seats. Large, uncovered bleachers extended down the third base line. Additional bleachers were located behind home plate. In all, the stands could accommodate 5,000 for the World Series. Before the start of the Series, George Rulon, national director of American Legion baseball, reminded the media that the age limit had been changed the year before, allowing 18-year-olds who were college freshmen to play Legion ball.[20]

Memphis, Tennessee, Post 1 entered the ALWS as the strong favorite to take the 1963 championship. When the World Series started, Memphis had recorded 32 consecutive wins. They had romped through the Regionals with seven straight wins in impressive fashion, beating Baton Rouge, Louisiana, Blytheville, Arkansas, Jackson, San Antonio, and a team from the Canal Zone. Pitcher John Schroeppel won three of those seven games. Center fielder Mark Uhlman led the team with a .428 batting average. They appeared to be unbeatable.[21]

Several of the qualifying teams for the 1963 ALWS were familiar faces. Somerville Post 19, with stronger pitching than usual, believed they had a chance to go deep in the tournament. They were undefeated in the Regionals. John Mountain notched two wins, and Chuck Paglierani and Ronnie Amenkowitz pitched shutouts. Gas Light Post 44 of Washington, D.C. was prone to sloppy fielding, but lefty Jim Jenkins posted two wins and a save in the Regional at College Park, Maryland. They lost only once, to Wheeling, West Virginia, a game in which Gas Light committed seven errors. Cone Post 386 of Greensboro, North Carolina, pulled off a triple play in their Regional final against West Palm Beach, a 1–0 win in 12 innings. They had taken 17 innings and five hours to get past Orangeburg, South Carolina. Nonetheless, they lacked the firepower to carry them far in the ALWS. Funkhouser Post 8 of Evansville, Indiana, bragged about a future Hall of Fame player, but pitcher Bob Griese's destination was Canton, not Cooperstown. The quarterback great had thrown for two wins in the Sectionals. Their leading hitter, Jerry Mattingly, was an older brother of Don, who became the better known of the Mattingly boys. Riders Omaha Post 1 was a perennial at the Series, having been there four of the previous five years. After losing the opening game to Cedar Rapids, they ran off five straight wins to take the Section 6 title at Salina, Kansas. Umpqua Post 16 of Roseburg, Oregon, battled it out with Billings before a 4–1 win gave them the trip to the ALWS. They boasted pitcher Dick Williams, who struck out 20 Billings batters in the Regional final, and power-hitting catcher Jim Beamer.[22]

The final team, representing California, came from Arthur L. Peterson Post 27 of Long Beach. Drawing on boys from Long Beach Polytechnic High School, they came in with a 29–4 record. They possessed two strong pitchers in Terry Roe and Bob Wiswell, and five other all-city players scattered through their lineup—catcher Bob von Eps; first baseman Jerry Martin; second baseman Dick Dash; shortstop Ike McCraw; and outfielder Oscar Brown. California had enjoyed a nice run in World Series play, winning championships clustered in 1949, 1950, 1951 and 1954, and five other titles before that mini-dynasty concluded. A California team had won often enough to cause some to believe the longer playing season gave California an unfair advantage. Previous California winners were from Oakland (1928, 1949, 1950), San Diego (1938, 1941, and 1954), and Los Angeles (1942 and 1951). Since 1954, however, the state had neither won nor had a runner-up. Long Beach's run took them through the California state title at Yountville and the Western Regional, where they beat teams from Salt Lake City, Las Vegas, Hawaii, and Tucson. Their run through the Regional culminated in a 10–0 blowout of Roswell, New Mexico. In the Regional final, Wiswell struck out 21 batters. Still, the California team was not expected to win in 1963 even though Long Beach had a strong, well-balanced team.[23]

The first round of the 1963 World Series brought no upsets. Omaha destroyed Roseburg, 23–9, despite Jim Beamer's two homers and seven RBI. Omaha's 23 runs tied the record set in the very first World Series by Yonkers. The combined score of 32 runs tied the record for most runs in a game by both teams, also set in 1926. Hapless Roseburg committed 24 errors in the game. Memphis had little trouble with Greensboro, winning 8–3. Charlie Shimerdla led Memphis with a home run and six RBI. Long Beach topped Somerville, 4–2, behind shortstop Ike McCraw's home run and two RBI. In the only tight game, Evansville's lefty Jim Jenkins pitched a no-hitter into the ninth inning before losing, 2–1. A walk, a bloop single, and a double steal preceded Mike Milton's two-run double. Hard-luck Jenkins had driven in his team's only run and struck out 16 batters. In the second round, Greensboro eliminated Washington, D.C., 6–1, and Somerville sent Roseburg back to Oregon, beating them, 4–3. Long Beach hammered Omaha, 8–1, a game in which Wiswell pitched a five-hitter and drove in four runs himself. Memphis looked stronger than ever, pounding Evansville, 13–0. Next, the undefeated teams, Memphis and Long Beach, were scheduled to face off.[24]

In the pivotal ALWS 1963 game between the remaining undefeated teams, to the surprise of most, Long Beach showed it had the most firepower by pounding out 13 hits and destroying previously undefeated Memphis (34–0) in a 12–3 victory. Left fielder Oscar Brown contributed four RBI, and second baseman Dick Dash homered, scored four times, and drove in three runs. Center fielder Jerry Flynn had two runs batted in and a homer. Suddenly, Long Beach was the team to beat.[25]

Memphis did not let the thrashing destroy them as they stayed alive, beating Omaha, 6–4. Catcher Tom Mitchell's home run provided the big blow, along with shortstop Ralph Gagliano's two RBI. Long Beach eliminated Evansville, 5–2, behind the three-hit pitching of Jerry Flynn. That set up a return match between Long Beach (28–4) and Memphis (35–1) for the 1963 title. In a close, seesaw game, Long Beach used a running game to take the lead. In the first inning, speedy shortstop Ike McCraw stole home. Oscar Brown duplicated that feat in the fourth on a double steal. Pitcher Bob Wiswell cruised along until the eighth inning, when Memphis' Mark Uhlman homered. In the ninth, Long Beach appeared to break the game open by scoring three runs to take a 5–1 lead. Third baseman Larry Lauriha's homer was the big blow. But Memphis refused to quit. Two singles, two walks, and a hit batter brought Terry Roe from the bullpen to try to choke off the rally. A ground out and a sacrifice fly made the score 5–4, but Steve Betzelberger was out trying to reach third base on a sacrifice fly.[26]

Long Beach was the 1963 national championship. They continued a tradition that had brought them state titles in 1930, 1937, 1944, and 1945. Five members of the 1963 Long Beach team went pro—Bob Wiswell, Bob von Eps, Ike McCraw, Oscar Brown, and Jerry Flynn. Only Brown, who led Long Beach with a .410 batting average, made it to the Big Time, spending five years with the Atlanta Braves.

The Legion organization had to be pleased with the 1963 ALWS. The games at Keene drew a respectable 45,757 fans. Evansville's Jerry Mattingly, who batted .413, won the Louisville Slugger Award for the highest batting average. Mattingly did not choose to continue his baseball career, instead accepting a basketball scholarship to Evansville College. His younger brother Don, however, had a long career with the New York Yankees. Dick Dash, Long Beach's fleet second baseman, batted only .343, but nonetheless gained a unanimous selection as Player of the Year. Teammate Oscar Brown was selected for the Sportsmanship Award.[27]

Shortly after the Legion World Series, in late August 1963, the March on Washington demonstrated the appeal of the civil rights movement and provided the occasion for Martin Luther King's "I Have a Dream" speech. That same autumn, on November 22, 1963, President Kennedy's assassination in Dallas, Texas, traumatized a generation. Hope and idealism gave way to despair and anger. Soon teenage boys were growing their hair long, protesting the Vietnam War, doing dope, dropping out, and turning on. Not all fell into this slough of despair, but it dominated a generation.

The 1964 American Legion World Series should be called the "Rollie Fingers Series." The lanky (6-foot-4, 190 pounds) pitcher/left fielder for Upland, California, dominated both on the mound and at the plate. His performance reminded people of Dave McNally's 1960 performance. Fingers' effort earned him the Player of the Year Award and the Louisville Slugger Award for highest batting average, a lofty .450 mark. He also earned two wins as a pitcher. He went on to capture the American League's Most Valuable Player Award in 1981. That made Fingers the only player to win the highest award in American Legion baseball and in Major League Baseball.

Although Fingers lived in Rancho Cucamonga, he attended neighboring Upland High School. Both were located 40 miles east of Los Angeles in the foothills of the San Gabriel Mountains. For Upland American Legion, Fingers' 1964 pitching record was 11 wins and only two losses, with a minuscule earned run average of 0.67. He notched 102 strikeouts in 81 innings. *The Sporting News* termed his pitching "completely dominating." Upland Post 73 had three other players who had brief professional careers: pitcher Steve Koker toiled in the White Sox's and Giants' systems from 1966–1972; catcher Dean Harmon played in the California Angels' farm system one season; and lefty Mike Price had two seasons, 1970–1971, in the St. Louis Cardinals' organization. Otherwise, Post 13 fielded several nice Legion players, including second baseman Dan Wilcox, a .400 hitter, shortstop Dave Shoji, who batted .394, and first baseman Ed Holland, a .333 hitter. Fingers, Price and Koker gave Upland a strong rotation. In the Regional, they lost their opening game to Aica, Hawaii, then rolled through Greeley, Colorado, 16–5, Clearfield, Utah, 22–1, Aica, 7–1, and Clearfield, 3–2. That put Upland in the World Series, played at Travelers Field in Little Rock, Arkansas.

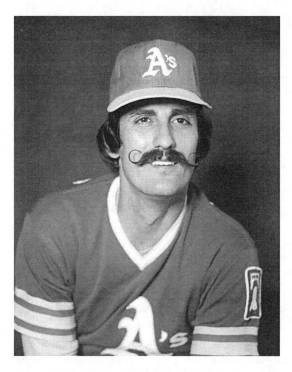

Rollie Fingers won both the Legion's Player of the Year Award and the Louisville Slugger Award for highest batting average in 1964 when he led Upland, California to the Legion title. In 1981 he was selected the American League Most Valuable Player to become the only player to win the highest awards in MLB and Legion baseball. He was inducted into the Baseball Hall of Fame in 1992 (National Baseball Hall of Fame Library, Cooperstown, N.Y.).

Other clubs to make the 1964 American Legion World Series were: Sweeney Post 2 of Manchester, New Hampshire; Huttner-Pasqualini Post 1367 of Staten Island, New York; Hornets Post 9 of Charlotte, North Carolina; Broadmoor Post 1215 of New Orleans; Thomas Edison Post 187 of

Detroit; and Lewis-Clark Post 13 of Lewiston, Idaho. The team from Detroit had won the title in in 1959. Manchester, Hornets' Post of Charlotte, and Lewis-Clark Post had experienced the Series before. Huttner-Pasqualini Post 1367 of Staten Island, New York, Broadmoor Post 1215 of New Orleans, and Beckner-Chapman Post 138 of Waterloo, Iowa, were making their first appearance in the ALWS. Charlotte appeared most confident based on previous success in younger leagues. They had won the Babe Ruth World Series in 1962 and the Colt League World Series in 1963. Lewiston, with the most wins (42–4), attracted attention on the field because of their spiffy summer uniforms of knee-length shorts, long socks, and blue tee-shirts. Waterloo's hopes rested on its bespectacled pitcher, Rick Folkers, who would toil in the majors from 1970 to 1977.

In 1964, games were played at Travelers Field in Little Rock, Arkansas. Constructed in 1925, the traditional minor league park had a seating capacity of 7,500 with dimensions of 325 to left field, 405 to center, and a short 300 feet to right field. Pitching dominated the Series. Two opening-round shutouts foreshadowed the record-setting five whitewashes in the 15 games of the tournament. Lewiston's John Hamilton pitched a tidy, three-hit shutout (3–0) of Manchester to open the tournament. Waterloo's Folkers, who entered the Series with a record of 17–0, struck out 12, and Roger Thompson contributed the game-winning hit as Waterloo nosed out New Orleans, 3–2. Charlotte, with Gary Hill on the mound, breezed past Staten Island, 8–3. Ron Lemonds paced Charlotte with four hits. Upland lefty Mike Price held Detroit Edison scoreless while his teammates posted seven runs for the easy victory. Fingers collected three hits.[28]

Upland pilot Ted Miller had saved Fingers, so he was fresh to face Charlotte. Fingers responded with a three-hitter that gave Upland a 3–1 win. In the game that followed, Folkers struck out 14 without issuing a base on balls, but his Waterloo teammates gave up two unearned runs in a 2–0 loss to Lewiston. Bill Grogan of Lewiston yielded only two hits. Detroit eliminated Staten Island, 3–2, thanks to Mike Jamulu's two RBI in the ninth inning. Manchester committed six errors to contribute to their elimination via a 14–4 loss to New Orleans. Winning pitcher George Ditta extended his record to 14–1. In their next game, Waterloo committed seven errors to hand Detroit an easy 11–2 win. Charlotte regrouped from its loss to Upland and eliminated New Orleans, 6–1, as Garry Hill pitched his second successive three-hitter. Upland continued to roll, blasting Lewiston, 5–0. The loss knocked Lewiston from the undefeated ranks. Steve Koker struck out 11 to notch the win, and Fingers collected three hits again.[29]

After Detroit eliminated Lewiston, the Series concluded with a three-team battle for the title between Upland, Detroit, and Charlotte. Upland and Charlotte faced off first. Charlotte's Bob Boyd and Upland's Mike Price squared off in a pitching duel. Price struck out 16 Charlotte batters, but Boyd was even better, shutting out Upland while allowing only one hit, a single by Fingers. Charlotte scored twice on catcher Joe Moody's double to gain the 2–0 victory. Upland won the coin flip that gave them a bye into the final game. Rain delayed the start of the Detroit-Charlotte game for 40 minutes. When play resumed, it was all Charlotte, as they coasted to a 10–2 win.[30]

Fingers was available for the final game of 1964 against Charlotte. The big right-hander was never in trouble as he struck out 11, allowed just two hits, and won, 3–1. Upland got one run in the third when outfielder Fred Wilding tripled and shortstop Dave Shoji knocked him in. In the sixth, with first baseman Ed Holland and outfielder Mike Balboni on base, catcher Dean Harmon doubled to score both runners and give Upland a 3–1 lead that held up. For Upland's manager of 15 years, Ted Miller, the victory justified a shaky season where his team coalesced into a well-balanced club that now claimed the championship.[31]

For the season, Fingers clearly posted the best numbers. As a pitcher, he went 11–2 with an almost invisible ERA of 0.67. In 81 innings, he struck out 102 batters. As an outfielder, he batted the World Series-best .450. He went on to pitch in the majors from 1968 to 1985, gaining fame as the outstanding relief pitcher of his era, picking up 341 saves. He was on three world champion teams. In 1992 he was elected to the National Baseball Hall of Fame. Other Upland hitters compiled heady numbers. Second baseman Dan Wilcox finished with an even .400 batting average. His double-play mate, Dave Shoji, was just behind with a .394 average. First baseman Ed Holland finished with a .333 average. Lefty Mike Price and right-hander Steve Koker were good enough to be signed by St. Louis and the Chicago White Sox, respectively.

Fingers took home the coveted Player of the Year Award for 1964 and won the Louisville Slugger Award with a .450 batting average. He signed a pro contract with Kansas City for a modest $13,000 bonus. When he won the American League Most Valuable Player and the Cy Young awards in 1981, he became the first player to win major awards in both American Legion and the big leagues. Joe Moody, Charlotte's scrappy catcher, was voted the Sportsmanship Award. Unfortunately, rainy weather kept attendance for the Series down to a mere 12,064, a far cry from the 45,757 for the 1963 ALWS in Keene.

The civil rights movement reached its peak in 1963–1964. The long summer in Birmingham and the March on Washington in 1963 had shown the national spotlight on racial segregation and intolerance. Congressional passage of the Civil Rights Act of 1964 legally opened doors to integration in public places. In the American Legion, one of the more significant developments in 1964 was integration on the ball fields of North Carolina. Gastonia Post 23 broke the North Carolina Legion color line by playing two African Americans. Willie "Jet" Gillispie and Elmore "Moe" Hill took verbal abuse, and their team could never get past Charlotte Post 9. Hill became a baseball lifer, playing in the minor leagues for 15 years and coaching in the minors for another 32 years. Gillispie attended Shaw University, played for teams in independent leagues, tutored in baseball academies, and worked for the Veterans Administration until retirement. Both were inducted into the North Carolina Sports Hall of Fame in 2015. Thanks to them, the most degrading racism to tarnish American Legion baseball appeared to be a thing of the past.[32]

In November 1964, Lyndon Johnson swept to a landslide victory in the presidential election. Johnson's 61 percent of the popular vote was the greatest margin of victory ever recorded. He brought Democratic control of both houses of Congress along with him. Johnson's Great Society program promised to increase opportunity and protection for all Americans. Medicare, Medicaid, and the Appalachian Regional Development Act helped cut the proportion of poor people in the United States from 22 percent to 11.1 percent by 1973; it would never be lower. On the other hand, Johnston escalated the war in Vietnam, committing American combat troops in 1965. Anti-war protests quickly dominated the political agenda. The American Legion stood behind the president and did its best for the next decade to keep Legion baseball on the sidelines or supporting the war effort.

Aberdeen, South Dakota, hosted the World Series in 1965 for the first and only time. The city in the northeast corner of the state had gone through a growth spurt of 23.8 per cent in the 1940s, leveling off at 21,000. Municipal Ball Park there was a WPA project completed in 1936, but an all-consuming fire had burned it to the ground in 1951. A new grandstand had been constructed for the 1952 season after a $65,000 bond issue got approved. The Class C Aberdeen Pheasants played there from 1946 to 1971. Locals remembered Earl Weaver, who managed there in 1959, and his star pitcher, Steve Dalkowski, who in one game pitched a no-hitter while striking out 23 batters, but also walked 16.[33]

Unfortunately, the weather failed to cooperate with the Legion. Instead of sunshine, late August produced clouds, drizzle, cold, and rain which kept crowds down, Officially, attendance registered 15,549, not as low as the previous year, but the second-lowest since 1958 in Colorado Springs. On the other hand, the banquet that preceded play got rave reviews. Featured speakers included former Legion players Bob Feller, recently inducted into the Hall of Fame, and Ted Williams, who would be elected to the Hall the next year.

After finishing second in the 1964 World Series, Charlotte had to be one of the favorites in 1965. California had produced champions the past two years, so it was reasonable to assume they would challenge again, even though there was not an obvious candidate. In a surprise, Ontario Post 112, a neighbor of 1964 winner Upland, captured the California state title. Ontario possessed power and worked its way through Region 8 thanks to the bats of Garry Ovitt, John Hix, Ron Shotts, and Greg Gayborg. In the Sectional final, a 10–9 victory over Phoenix, Gayborg collected four hits, including a ninth-inning homer. One challenger was Allied Post 150 of Portland, Oregon, which came out of Section 7 by beating Yakima, 2–1. Pitcher Terry Ley starred in key wins over Lewiston and Yakima. Omaha Post 1, sponsored by Pepsi Cola, had appeared in the 1953 ALWS and had reloaded with strong pitching. They won the Region 6 tourney with a record of 34–12. They looked to an outstanding left-handed pitcher in Ken Fila, who brought a 0.46 ERA to the Series. Scammon Post 36 of Arlington Heights, Illinois, upset powerful Detroit Edison, 7–6, in 11 innings to reach the World Series. They had a stellar pitcher-outfielder in Paul Splittorff, who would play for 15 seasons in the major leagues. Memphis Post 1 always seemed to send a solid team to the tournament, one that was almost always in contention for the title. Charlotte's Hornets' Nest Post 9 finished second the previous year and returned most of their team. They arrived with a 35–8 record. Garry Hill pitched them into the Series with a 1–0 victory over Colonial Heights, Virginia. The Barringer-Walker Post 139 of Lyndhurst, New Jersey, made its first appearance in the ALWS. Completing the eight-team field was Ryan-Scammon Post 36 of Berlin, New Hampshire. They reached the Series by beating Middletown, Connecticut, 8–5, thanks to the hitting of left-handed outfielder Roger Goulet.[34]

The favorites won their opening-round games. Charlotte appeared unbeatable in a 16–1 laugher over Berlin. Memphis defeated Portland, 4–1. Ontario had little trouble with Lyndhurst, winning by an 8–3 score. The game of the day was a pitching duel between left-handers Ken Fila of Omaha and Tom Lundgren of Arlington Heights. Fila struck out 11 and allowed just two hits, winning a 1–0 decision. Berlin and Lyndhurst went quickly, eliminated by Portland and Arlington Heights. Portland's Steve Chamberlain pitched a one-hitter in a 3–0 victory against poor Berlin. Lyndhurst fell to Arlington Heights, 7–1. Omaha had little trouble in an 8–4 showing against Ontario. The surprise in the second round came when Memphis took advantage of control problems by Charlotte's Garry Hill and beat the Hornets, 9–3. Omaha followed with an 8–4 victory over Ontario.[35]

In elimination games, Ontario refused to die and knocked Portland out of the tournament, 12–4. In another win or go home game, Charlotte returned to form by sending Arlington Heights back to the Chicago area and out of the competition, 9–4. Bill Sellers got the win for the Hornets. With pitching ace Ken Fila throwing his second shutout of the Series, Omaha beat Memphis, 5–0. Memphis rebounded by dropping Ontario, 8–1, thanks to Frank Olita's four-hit pitching, a loss that eliminated Ontario. When Charlotte squared off against unbeaten Omaha, their pitcher, Dave Lemonds, turned in a powerful, 19-strikeout performance. He allowed just five hits in a 6–0 victory. Charlotte, Memphis, and Omaha were dead-locked with one loss each. A coin toss gave Charlotte the bye to the final game. In the first game of the final day, Omaha sent Memphis home, winning 6–3. For the victors, lefty George Stilen notched victory number 12 of the season without a loss.[36]

In the 1965 championship game, Charlotte did not let cold weather and rain showers stand in their way. Charlotte got a major break when neither of Omaha's pitching aces, Stilen nor Fila, was available to start; instead Bill Nosek started against Charlotte's ace, Garry Hill. Charlotte got a run in the first inning when Ron Lemonds walked, stole second, and scored on Gary Hill's single. Charlotte picked up another run in the sixth inning when outfielder John Daurity reached on bunt single and scored on catcher Skip Hull's double. Omaha then inserted Fila into the game. He had three innings left before his eligibility ran out. In the bottom of the sixth, Omaha outfielder Larry Gomez walked, went to second on a sacrifice, moved to third on a scratch single, and scored on a sacrifice fly. Hill closed the door no Omaha the rest of the game. Charlotte had the World Series title by a 2–1 score. Hill, a 6-foot-2, 175-pounder, matched the earlier 19-strikeout performance of Dave Lemonds and the 1960 effort of Dave McNally.[37]

Omaha's Ken Fila, who pitched 21 innings of scoreless ball in the national finals, was named American Legion Player of the Year. Fila a 5-foot-11 lefty out of Archbishop Ryan High School, was selected by San Francisco in the 1965 draft. After two minor league seasons, he left professional baseball with a disappointing 4–4 record. Rollie Goulet, Berlin first baseman-pitcher, batted .542 to take home the Hillerich & Bradsby Louisville Slugger Award. The champions' Lemonds brothers, Ron and Dave, contended for the batting title with .419 and .417 seasons. Gary Hill (Atlanta) and Dave Lemonds (Chicago Cubs and White Sox) both had a cup of coffee in the majors. Cold and wet weather kept attendance down to 15,549 for the tournament and just 1,204 for the final day.

None of the eight participants in the 1965 World Series made it back for 1966. Orangeburg, South Carolina, hosted the ALWS. Its Mirmow Field had a concrete grandstand build in 1948 with a covered roof. The Bill Erwin Post 337 of Oakland, the first back-to-back winners back in the J. W. Porter World Series of 1949–1950, returned in the role of favorite. They entered with a record of 31 wins and only two losses. Their coach, Bill Cox, believed their strength came from both "discipline and ability." Other teams in the World Series were Manchester, New Hampshire Post 79; Adelphia Post 38 of Washington, D.C.; Farley M. Moody Post 34 of Tuscaloosa, Alabama; Inglewood Post 82, Nashville, Tennessee; George W. Benjamin Post 791 of Northbrook, Illinois; and Lewis-Clark Post 13 of Lewiston, Idaho.

None of the other teams seemed capable of challenging Oakland. In Region one, Coach Nick Gabardino's running game carried Manchester to three straight victories and a 4–3 win over Bristol, Connecticut, in the final. Washington D. C.'s Tom "Ice Man" Fisher won three games in Region two. Tuscaloosa ran off four straight wins in Region three, finishing with a 4–3 win over Miami in 11 innings. In Region four, Nashville's Dave Speck won three games, including a one-hit, 20-strikeout performance against Balboa of the Canal Zone, and the final in relief over South San Antonio. In Region five, Northbrook lost game two, but came back behind lefty Bob Moody to beat Adrian, Michigan. Catcher Doug Karns led Enid over Bismarck for the Region six title. Lewiston ran off four straight wins to capture Region seven. Finally, Oakland went undefeated through the Region eight tourney. They beat Hawaii, 10–4, in the final thanks to Bernie Williams' three RBI.[38]

Tuscaloosa and Oakland faced each other in the opening round of the 1966 ALWS. Oakland rammed through eight runs in the seventh inning, and Joaquin "Butch" Vargas struck out ten in Oakland's 8–2 victory. Bob Moody of Northbrook threw a two-hit shutout in his team's 1–0 win over Lewiston. Washington's Joe Stover pitched a four-hit, 5–0 shutout against Nashville. Enid's little Terry Meyer outdueled Manchester, 1–0. That made three shutouts on the first day of the Series. On day two, Tuscaloosa eliminated Lewiston, 7–1, as Mike Innes allowed only three hits and struck out 12. Outfielder Bill Parker had three hits and four RBI. Oakland benefited from 12 Northbrook errors to win a sloppy 12–8 game. Manchester eliminated Nashville by a 9–8 score. Enid scored twice in the ninth inning to slip by Washington, 6–4.[39]

On the third day of the ALWS, Tuscaloosa eliminated Washington by a convincing 7–1 score. Enid turned a triple play but still lost to Oakland, 10–5. Manchester's Steve Saunders stole second, stole third, and scored on an error to give the New Hampshire club a 3–2, ninth-inning win over Northbrook. The heart-breaking loss eliminated Northbrook. Tuscaloosa beat Enid, 6–2, to send Enid back to Oklahoma. Bill Parker had a single, double, and triple and knocked in three runs. Oakland scored five runs in the first inning to knock out Manchester, 6–2. The final two games of the World Series matched Oakland and Tuscaloosa. After losing the opening game to Oakland, Tuscaloosa had run off three straight wins and became the crowd favorite. In their rematch against Oakland, hard-throwing lefty Mike Innes was superb, striking out 13 Oakland batters and allowing only a single by Bernie Williams. Tuscaloosa got an unearned run in the first inning, three in the second, and single scores in the fourth and seventh. In the big third inning, Innes and Marvin Herring were safe on bunt singles, Larry Norris brought one run home with a single, and the other two scored on an error and a wild pitch. In the seventh, shortstop Elton Reese blasted a solo home run to make the final score 6–2.[40]

Oakland had saved their pitching ace, chunky (5-foot-8, 185 pounds) Joaquin "Butch" Vargas for the championship game of 1966 at Mirmow Field, and he was up to the task. Oakland got all the scoring it needed in the fourth inning when shortstop Albert Strane tripled, Steve Byre singled in front of the plate, and Bernie Williams tripled to score two. Albert Strane homered in the eighth. Oakland plated the final run in the ninth when Paul Brown scored on a wild pitch. In the bottom of the ninth, Vargas walked in a run, but he managed to get the final out with the bases loaded. Vargas posted his third win of the Series and his sixth in national competition, without suffering a loss. He walked four to gift Tuscaloosa its only run, but he regained his poise to finish the game and notch the 4–1 win.[41]

Oakland failed to win any of the individual awards, but they did have three players who played pro ball and two who made the major leagues. Shortstop Albert Strane chose to attend Santa Clara University after Legion ball, but he was drafted from there and played a season in the minors. Third baseman Steve Byre had more success; he played nine years in the majors with Minnesota, Milwaukee, and Pittsburgh, but never became a regular. He compiled a career .258 batting average. Outfielder Bernie Williams was drafted by San Francisco and signed after the American Legion World Series. He reached the majors in 1970 and played through 1974 with the Giants and Padres.

Tuscaloosa's left fielder Bill Parker, who batted .325 for the tournament, took home the Legion's Player of the Year award. Curiously, he became the first outfielder to win the award. Ron Harris, Washington, D.C.'s first baseman, captured the Louisville Slugger award by compiling a .406 batting average for the tournament. Buddy Plummer of Enid, Oklahoma, earned the Sportsmanship Award. The final attendance numbers were 19,248, more than at frigid Aberdeen, South Dakota, the previous year, or in Little Rock the year before that, but less than Bismarck (1962) or Hastings (1959, 1961).[42]

One of the significant off-field events of 1966 came when Pennsylvania decided to return to the American Legion World Series tournament after a 30-year absence. The Keystone state had withdrawn back in 1936 over a dispute in Middletown, Ohio. The issue that touched off Pennsylvania's decision revolved around Reading, Pennsylvania, protesting Middletown's alleged use of an ineligible player. When the Americanism Commission refused the protest, George E. Bellis, Athletic Director of the Pennsylvania Legion, pulled his 707 teams, the largest of any state, out of the competition. Bellis maintained that the absence of the tournament allowed more time for its boys actually to play ball. Over the years, the Keystone state developed a series of all-star games culminating in an East-West game in Harrisburg that turned out more than its fair share of major league players, including Hall of Famers Stan Musial and Roy Campanella. As long as Bellis retained the title of state American Legion Executive Director of Activities, there was no revisiting the decision to pull out of the tournament. Over the years, Pennsylvania continued to field Legion teams, but remained outside the Legion's playoffs. During its 30 years outside the national play, the Lehigh Valley village of Coplay (ca. 3,000) won six state titles, while Reading captured four. After Bellis retired, that position eventually fell to Charlie Gangaware in 1965. He took the position that Pennsylvania youth should have the opportunity to compete for a national championship. As part of the agreement that brought Pennsylvania back into the Legion fold, teams would be allowed to carry 18 players, and Pennsylvania would have two teams in the 1969 Regionals. Pennsylvania was home to over 400 Legion teams, still the largest of any state, so its return was welcomed.[43]

Charlotte in 1965 and Oakland in 1966 had won after finishing second the previous year. Logic would make Farley W. Moody Post 34 of Tuscaloosa the favorite for 1967. That, in fact, was the case, and like Charlotte and Oakland before them, Tuscaloosa emerged from the tournament as American Legion champions. Coach Jerry Belk's crew lost 1966 Legion Player of the Year Bill Parker and its shortstop, Elton Reese, but it returned the rest of the team, especially pitchers Mike Innes, Marlin Homan, Carl Wright, and Johnny Rushing, and catcher Randy Ryan. Tuscaloosa's pitching carried the team. In the state and regional tournaments, lefty Marlin Homan won three games and saved another. In 22-plus tournament innings, he gave up only one run.

Other teams to make the 1967 World Series in Memphis were: George William Benjamin Post 791 of Northbrook, Illinois; Post 1 of Memphis, Tennessee; Post 79 of Manchester, New Hampshire; Joseph B. Stahl Post of Wilmington Manor, Delaware; Post 6 from Grand Forks, North Dakota; Post 8 of Klamath Falls, Oregon; and Leyden-Childs-Wickersham Post 1, Denver, Colorado. Northbrook boasted about its catcher, Ray Larsen, and pitcher Hank Hyde, who struck out 24 batters in 18 innings in the Regional. Memphis got power from giant (6-foot-7, 240 pound) first baseman and pitcher Ken Kauerz, who pitched two wins in the Regionals. Manchester lacked hitting, but pitcher Grant McRenars earned MVP honors in the Regional after collecting three wins. Wilmington Manor gained the Series berth by beating Cheverly, Maryland, behind Doug Hooper, who struck out 17 Cheverly batters. In addition, Steve Nepa boasted four no-hitters to his credit. North Dakota teams were strangers to the World Series; Grand Falls would be the first to make an appearance after beating Hastings, 13–3. Klamath Falls, Oregon, rode home runs by Ken Pound to victory in Region 7. Denver reached the Series when third baseman Rick Corbin came through with a bases-loaded single in the tenth inning against Las Vegas.[44]

Memphis lacked a proper field for the Series. Storied Russwood Park, which dated from 1921, had burned to the ground in 1960. The Southern Association Memphis Chicks tried playing in a high school football facility where the right field foul line measured only 204 feet. A 40-foot-high wall did little to keep balls in the park. Next the team moved to Tobey Park, a neighborhood playground. When that move failed to work, the team gave up the ghost after the 1960 and did not return to organized baseball until 1968. Unfortunately, the new Chicks Stadium (aka Tim McCarver Stadium) was not yet available. Tony Gagliano, coach of Memphis' American Legion team, spearheaded construction of a diamond in the Mid–South Fairgrounds which seated 2,000 under a roof and another 3,000 in bleachers. Almost singlehanded, he landed the 1967 ALWS.

Tuscaloosa drew a tough opening assignment in Northbrook but managed to eke out a tough, 3–0 win. Johnny Rushing's double scored two of the runs. Mike Innis got credit for the win, but Coach Belk called on Rushing to save it. In other first-round games, Grand Forks shut out Denver behind Gary Schuler's three-hitter. Klamath Falls beat Stahl of Delaware, 3–2. Memphis ran wild, swiping 10 bases in a 6–1 win over Manchester. In the second round, Tuscaloosa trounced Grand Fork, 6–2. Marlin Homan pitched seven perfect innings to get credit for the win, and second baseman Danny Morrison accounted for three runs. Delaware pulled off a triple play in the first inning on its way to crushing Manchester, 8–0. The triple play went 6–3–2–5, an unusual play. With two on, a sharp grounder went to shortstop Joe Cherico, who threw to first for the first out. First baseman Fred Blome threw to catcher Bob Scott to nail the runner trying to score; Scott fired to Ray Justison at third, who put the tag on the runner for the third out. The loss eliminated Manchester. Northbrook benefited from eight unearned runs to beat Denver, 9–1, a loss that eliminated the loser. Klamath Falls beat Memphis, 3–1, to conclude the second round.[45]

The Alabama boys went 3–0 by beating Klamath Falls. Rushing notched the win by a 3–1 score. Northbrook, with only a first-day loss to Tuscaloosa, gained confidence by winning a hotly contested elimination game against Memphis by a 2–1 score. In another elimination game, Delaware had little trouble with Grand Forks, winning 7–1. Stahl post of Delaware, a team that had achieved more than expected, took on Tuscaloosa. The Alabama boys scored in the first inning on Innes's double. That lead held up until the eighth, when Stahl tied the game. Stahl loaded the bases in the ninth, but Marlin Homan put out the fire. The two teams fought it out in the only extra-inning game of the Series. Finally, in the 12th, Wilmington Manor ran out of pitchers, forcing them to turn to Vince McMahon, who had not pitched in the Series. With the bases loaded, Homan, a light-hitting (.143) pitcher, singled home two runs. The game, however, was not over. Stahl loaded the bases with one out when Tuscaloosa's right fielder, David Elmore, went to the wall to pull in a long fly, turned and threw out a runner at home to end the game.[46]

That left Northbrook and Tuscaloosa as the only two teams remaining in the 1967 Series. Tuscaloosa's hometown newspaper allowed in retrospect that after the hard-fought Delaware game, Tuscaloosa was "a completely drained team." They lacked the spark they had shown in earlier games, and they ran into a hot pitcher in Northbrook's Paul

Brubaker, who struck out 14 and allowed only two hits in Northbrook's 5–0 victory. First baseman Dave Thake had three hits and turned in several sparkling plays in the field. In the 1967 championship game, Rushing proved superb, pitching a three-hit shutout in a 1–0 Tuscaloosa win. Alabama's only run came in the seventh inning. After shortstop Bo Baughman doubled and moved to third on a wild pitch, Coach Belk called upon little-used Woody Sexton as a pinch-hitter. He sent an RBI single up the middle to score the deciding run of the game. Alabama had earned its only American Legion championship and finished with a record of 40–5.[47]

For the 1967 tournament, Wilmington Stahl Post 30 shortstop Joe Cherico took the Louisville Slugger Award with a .514 batting average. Northbrook catcher Ray Larsen was named Legion Player of the Year. Tuscaloosa catcher Randy Ryan was honored with the Sportsmanship Award. Attendance at Memphis was 22,821, higher than any of the past three years. Given the less than adequate facilities at Memphis, the Series had to be judged a success.[48]

No year in the 20th century had been as tumultuous as was 1968 for the U.S. The year began with the Tet offensive in Vietnam. After being reassured by President Johnson and Secretary of Defense Robert McNamara over and over that the U.S. was winning the war, the North Vietnam army and the Viet Cong overran almost all cities in South Vietnam. Although American troops eventually recaptured all the cities, Tet shattered the myth of American invincibility, proved that the American government had lied, and shifted public opinion against the war. Public opposition led to the move by Democrats to dump President Johnson and the rise of support for Eugene McCarthy and Robert Kennedy entering the presidential race. Johnson renounced his candidacy at the end of March. The next week, Martin Luther King, Jr., was gunned down in Memphis. The flickering flame of optimism was extinguished; the civil rights movement and the symbol of peaceful change was dead. Riots by African Americans erupted in over 100 American cities. Washington, where anger led to setting ghetto neighborhoods on fire within sight of the capitol, symbolized the anger in black ghettos. That spring the student New Left turned on the campuses from which it sprang, pushing for confrontation and demanding black studies and African American dorms, student power, and, rhetorically at least, revolution. In June, the senseless assassination of Bobby Kennedy by Sirhan Sirhan further disillusioned and alienated students in particular. The August Democratic convention in Chicago became the site for massive demonstrations by the new left, broken up by a "Police Riot," as identified in the Kerner Report, shown for all the world to see on national television.

The 1968 American Legion World Series tournament came on the heels of the Democratic Convention. The tournament seemed strangely unaffected by events of the year. The Legion tournament and World Series went off without any protests. Manchester's Gill Stadium, renamed from Athletic Field the previous year after Parks and Recreation Director Ignace J. Gill, could have been a world apart. Photographs of participating teams show that the era of crew cuts was over, but these Legion boys had not yet adopted long hair as an act of protest.

Under the leadership of Tony Gagliano, who had taken over as coach of Post 1 in 1956, Memphis developed a deep system of teams that produced strong clubs for the post teams. He had led teams capable of winning it all to the American Legion World Series on three previous occasions in the 1960s, including 1963, when they finished second, 1965 in third place, and 1967, when his team finished fourth. The "soft spoken, whisp [sic] of a man" had won the Tennessee state title 11 times. His teams won 369 games while losing

65. Gagliano was known around Legion circles for his use of the bunt, especially squeeze plays. Memphis enjoyed strong sponsorship from former star athlete turned auto dealer Bill Speros. Gagliano's 1968 club was his strongest. He was armed with two outstanding pitcher-hitters. Donnie Castle, a left-handed pitcher-first baseman-outfielder, went 17–1 on the mound and struck out 20 New Orleans batters in a Regional game. He also batted .351. He was the number one pick in the major league draft by Washington for his hitting. Castle spent ten years in the minors before getting a cup of coffee with Texas in 1973. Ross Grimsley, another lefty, played second fiddle to Castle in Legion ball, but he came into his own after they turned professional. Grimsley pitched 1 years in the majors for Cincinnati, Baltimore, Montreal, and Cleveland, winning 124 games. In his most productive season, 1978, he won 20 games for the Montreal Expos. Memphis entered the World Series with a 32-game winning streak. No wonder they were favorites going into Series play.[49]

Winners of other Regionals were: East Springfield, Massachusetts Post 420; Staten Island's James J. Tappen Post 125; J. Arthur Wild Post of Timmonsville, South Carolina; Bendix Aviation Post 284 of South Bend, Indiana; Post 1 of Omaha, Nebraska; and Morgan McDermott Post 7 of Tucson, Arizona. Klamath Post 1 Falcons from Klamath Falls, Oregon, was the only other team to return from the 1967 Series.

East Springfield rode the shoulders of batting star Hosea Kelly, who was MVP of the Region One tourney, to gain a spot in the World Series. Unfortunately, Staten Island could not start pitcher Jack Donovan every day. He won his 24th straight game, beating Lyndhurst, New Jersey, in the final of Region Two. Pennsylvania was back into the ALWS after an absence of 30 years but could not notch a win in Region play. Mike Andrews won the MVP award for Timmonsville in Region 3, batting .368 and pitching two winning games, including the final against Athens, Georgia. In that Regional, Rick Pipan of Greensboro, North Carolina, pitched a no-hitter against Sumter. Memphis's Don Castle struck out 20 New Orleans batters, then got the save and game-winning RBI in the 7–6 win over San Antonio in the championship game. South Bend Bendix scored four times in the bottom of the ninth inning to slip past Owensboro, Kentucky, and into the ALWS. Ed Teshack batted .555 to lead Omaha Post 1 Vikings out of Region Six. Mike Kech, 12–1 as a pitcher and .489 as a batter, led the Klamath Falls Falcons past Lewiston, Idaho, in Region seven. The eighth and final spot in the World Series went to Tucson, Arizona. They held off Hawaii to gain a 9–7 victory.[50]

The highlight of the opening round at Gill Stadium occurred when Gene Guerriero of Staten Island pitched a no-hit game against Springfield in a 2–0 win. He allowed just one baserunner, a walk in the seventh inning, and struck out just three. His mound opponent, Dan Murphy, whiffed 14. In another pitching gem, Don Castle threw a two-hitter to lead Memphis' 3–0 win over South Bend. Timmonsville had little trouble beating Omaha, 7–1. Klamath Falls walloped Tucson, 9–2. In the second round, Memphis' Ross Grimsley duplicated Castle's effort by pitching a two-hit, 1–0 shutout over Klamath Falls. Second baseman Lynn Alford drove in the only Memphis run. In other second-round games, Staten Island stayed unbeaten, knocking off Timmonsville, 6–2, as Jack Donovan struck out 16 and allowed just five hits. On the losers' side, South Bend ousted Tucson, 4–3, and Springfield took out Omaha, although it took 14 innings to complete the 3–1 victory. South Bend and Springfield were the next to exit the tournament, losing to Timmonsville (5–4) and Klamath Falls (1–0) respectively. In a battle of the final two unbeatens, Staten Island proved they were not ready for elite play as they committed eight errors. All the Memphis runs were unearned as they coasted to an easy 8–3 win over the New York boys.

Third baseman Charley Blanchard provided the bog blow in the seventh inning to break a 3–3 tie. Staten Island's woes continued, as they went down in their next game, eliminated by Klamath Falls by the same 8–3 score.[51]

Memphis' last two games of the 1968 Series proved to be nail-biters. Against Timmonsville, Memphis resorted to Gagliano's "little ball." Castle singled, went to third on an error, and scored on Charley Blanchard's single. Blanchard came around to score on catcher Al Andre's single. Timmonsville tied the game in the top of the eighth inning on Walt Braddock double followed by Howie Barfield and Glenn Wall singles. With the score tied in the bottom of the eighth, second baseman Lynn Alford scored on Duane Donaho's single to give Memphis a 3–2 win. In the final against Klamath, Memphis was again the beneficiary of sloppy fielding as they picked up two unearned runs to tie the game in the third inning. With the score deadlocked, 3–3, in the ninth inning, Blanchard singled. He moved to second on a sacrifice bunt and to third on another sacrifice bunt. Outfielder Terry Dan laid down the third consecutive bunt, a perfect one down the third base line to score Blanchard with the winning run. Grimsley got credit for the win, while Castle, who pitched the bottom of the ninth, got the save.[52]

Castle's all-around play won him the 1968 Player of the Year Award. As a pitcher, he had a 17–1 record in Legion play, and as a batter he hit .351. After the World Series, Castle signed a professional contract with the Washington Senators, who had drafted him in the first round of the first amateur draft. Andy Dominguez, a switch-hitting shortstop for San Antonio, Texas, took the Louisville Slugger Award with a .409 batting average. Mike Young, Timmonsville pitcher, won the Sportsmanship Award.[53]

While 1968 was the most dramatic year of the decade, 1969 brought deep changes in the culture of protest. The political New Left was dealt a serious defeat by the election of Richard Nixon at the end of 1968. If political protest failed to bring systematic change, perhaps, the argument went, young America could change themselves to actuate profound change. Millions of alienated young people turned to drugs, sex, and rock and roll. "Hippies" they were initially dubbed. The "counterculture movement" culminated at Woodstock in upstate New York in August 1969. The guru of the movement, Harvard professor Timothy Leary, claimed that hallucinogenic drugs like LSD would "open the doors of perception." In an overlapping movement, thousands would drop out and hope to find a utopia in communal life.

None of the elite eight ALWS finalists of 1968 made the World Series in 1969. East Springfield, Staten Island, Timmonsville, South Bend, and Omaha Post 1 failed even to make it out of their state tournament. Memphis, the defending champion, lost a heartbreaker in Region Four to Bartlesville, Oklahoma, 2–1 in 16 innings, then suffered a second loss to Lake Charles by the same 2–1 score. Klamath Falls and Tucson went down early in their respective Regionals. Only one of the eight teams that made it to Hastings, Nebraska, for the 1969 World Series had been to the Series before, Budde Post of Cincinnati. Naugatuck, Connecticut's Jim Hankey earned the MVP award of Region One; he got four hits himself and allowed only four hits in pitching an 11–2 win over Lynn, Massachusetts. Pennsylvania's efforts finally to place a team in the Series rested on the Boyertown Bears, but they were eliminated by Towson, Maryland. In that Region Two tournament, Brooklawn, New Jersey, had become the favorite when their lefty, Joe Neal, no-hit Northampton, but in the final, Towson scored four runs in the eighth inning to beat Brooklawn, 4–2. West Palm Beach won Region Three thanks to shortstop John Adeimy's hitting and the pitching of Penny Holmes, who threw two shutouts. Cincinnati always seemed to have a team capable of making trouble if not winning everything. Budde Post 507 got hitting from third baseman Steve Gray, who batted a resounding .687 in the Region Five tournament, and pitcher Wes Moore, who allowed only two earned runs in 20 innings. The Gilbert C. Grafton Post 2 from Fargo, North Dakota, was led by left fielder Mickey Anderson, who batted .429 in the Regionals. Colorado Springs Post 5 captured Region Six thanks to MVP Ray Zaremba, who won two games, saved another, and powered two home runs. Portland, Oregon's, Hollywood Post 105 took the Region eight title. Shortstop-pitcher Tom Wise batted .500 for the regional.[54]

The dimensions of Duncan Field in Hastings and the weather combined to limit the offensive production. Distances down the lines were a hefty 370 and 367 feet, and dead center was 408 feet from home plate. If those figures were not enough, over six inches of rain fell on Saturday during the World Series. Local officials tried to dry the field by pouring gasoline on it and setting the gas on fire. The advantage clearly went to the pitchers. No home runs were hit during the Series, and four of the 15 games were shutouts.[55]

The park and weather conditions favored Portland, coached by Dick McClain and sponsored by Leo Wynans, a general contractor. The boys from Madison High School had won their first state title before the 1969 Legion season began. They possessed the deepest pitching staff. Jim Officer, a 6-foot-2 left-hander with a 12–1 record, headed the mound corps. Tom Wise (12–2), younger brother of major league pitcher Rick Wise, doubled as the shortstop. Officer would sign with the Angles, and Wise signed with Houston. Lefty Doug Oja and Dale Danger rounded out the deep mound staff.

Bartlesville, having knocked off defending champion Memphis, had high expectations before they faced Officer in the first game. However, the Portland lefty struck out 13 and coasted to an easy 4–1 victory. In other first-round games, catcher Bruce Maxwell's theft of home in the fifth inning was the highlight for the Contractors. West Palm Beach's Steve Baumiller won his 13th game in a 2–1 victory over Colorado Springs. Russ Bryant won his 13th straight in Towson's 4–3 win over Fargo. Cincinnati's Bill Rutham allowed only four hits, but he also hit four batters and issued seven walks; nevertheless, he got the win over Naugatuck in the only opening-round game that was not a pitcher's duel. On the first day, pitching proved strong, but fielding proved as sloppy as the rain-soaked field; there were 22 errors on the day, thanks in large part to the weather. In day two action, Portland topped West Palm Beach behind the pitching of Tom Wise (6–4) and three hits by third baseman Bill McCord. Naugatuck got an ALWS win for New England, a 1–0 victory over Fargo. Bartlesville sent Colorado Springs home with a 4–0 win.[56]

Portland next faced a surprisingly tough team from Towson, Maryland. It took 12 innings for Portland to establish itself. In the crucial 12th inning, Towson pitchers gave up four bases-on-balls before third baseman Bill McCord cleared the bases with a double to give the Contractors a 5–2 win. Dale Danger pitched a complete game for Portland to gain credit for the win. Bartlesville got five runs in the seventh inning to knock Cincinnati out of the competition. Fred Anyzeski of West Palm Beach held Naugatuck to three hits while striking out 11 in a 4–2 win that sent the Connecticut team home. Through six inches of rain, wind and mud, West Palm managed to knock Bartlesville out of the tournament by the slim margin of 2–1 in a game that lasted until 1:00 Monday morning.[57]

After Towson beat West Palm Beach, 6–3, only Portland and Towson remained standing in the 1969 ALWS. In the first meeting of undefeated teams, Portland pitched its ace, Jim Officer, and Towson threw its ace, Rick Foelber, owner of an 18–1 record. Foelber allowed only two hits to shut Portland out for the first time in 54 games, winning 3–0.

On the penultimate day of the Series, Portland handed Townson its first defeat, 5–2, in 12 innings. Four walks, a double by Bill McCord and a fielder's choice gave Portland the win. The two teams with one loss, Towson and Portland, squared off in a winner-take-all game for the 1969 title. Portland coach Dick McClain had two fine pitchers, Wise and Oja, ready to go; he chose to start Oja. Portland got three runs in the third inning on outfielder Jack Flitcraft's run-scoring triple and Wise's two-run single. The Contractors scored another run in the fourth on Bill McCord's sacrifice fly. Towson loaded the bases with two outs in the sixth inning. McClain brought Wise in to put out the fire, which he did by inducing a pop-up to end the threat. Wise shut Towson down without a hit for the final three innings. Portland took the 1969 crown by a 4–0 score. The Pacific Northwest proudly claimed the title.[58]

West Palm Beach had locked up third place. Their shortstop, John Adeimy, was named Player of the Year, and he also captured the batting title with a .513 average. Only J. W. Porter in 1950 and Rollie Fingers in 1964 had won both awards. The sportsmanship award, now named the James F. Daniel Award, went to Portland's third baseman, Bill McCord. Attendance at the 15 games was 20,908.[59]

Across the country, cities continued to experience long, hot summers with their black ghettos exploding in riots. While the 1969 Legion World Series was going on, Portland experienced a riot in the Albina neighborhood in the northeast section of the city. Officials feared more to come the following summer when the American Legion would hold its national convention there, bringing an estimated 25,000 revelers into the city. President Richard Nixon was expected to speak at the convention, assuring a huge increase in anti-war protestors, expected to number 50,000. Republican Governor Tom McCall was prepared to try a radical approach to undercut protests. Instead of calling out the national guard, he proposed something called the "Biodegradable Festival of Life" or "Vortex 1" at Milo McIver State Park, a kind of West Coast Woodstock.[60]

The 1970 World Series moved to Klamath Falls, Oregon, a city of 15,000 in the high desert region, just 25 miles north of the California border. The city had produced strong Legion teams that did well in American Legion World Series, often coming close to the title while always falling just short. The local Legion team's games and the World Series were played in cozy Kiger Stadium, with hitter-friendly dimensions of 315 feet down both foul lines and 385 feet to center. The park, which dated to 1948, seated only 2,878 in wooden stands with roof overhang. Klamath Falls played host to the following teams: Henry J. Sweeney Post 2 of Manchester, New Hampshire; Levittown-Western Post 960, just the second Pennsylvania team to appear in the World Series since 1937; Joseph Stahl Post 30 of Wilmington Manor, Delaware; Post 10 of Wilmington, North Carolina; Post 1 Riders of Omaha, Nebraska; Carson-Wilson Post 1 of Tulsa, Oklahoma; Post 790 of West Covina, California; and Luke Greenway Post 1, Phoenix, Arizona.[61]

Despite the short fences of Kiger Stadium, West Covina pitchers logged three shut-outs, giving up only three runs in four games. Before the Series, Corvallis sportswriter Roy Gault said: "West Covina is big and quick and has three starting pitchers who are nearly untouchable."[62] His analysis was bang-on. The opening game against Manchester went to the 14th inning before either team scored. West Covina's Coleman "Corey" Smith worked 12 shutout innings, striking out 18, before giving way to Greg Terlecky. West Covina outfielder Mike McManus worked his way around to third base. Jesus Mendoza squared around to bunt, but the catcher could not handle the pitch; the passed ball allowed McManus to score and gave West Covina a 1–0 victory. In other first-round games, Levittown slipped past Stahl, 5–4. The Delaware team took a 4–3 lead into the ninth inning, but Levittown shortstop Dale Forchetti singled home two runs to cap the win. Omaha struggled but got past Phoenix, 2–1. Wilmington, North Carolina, beat Tulsa, 11–2, to complete first-round play. In the second round, facing Wilmington, Ter-lecky struck out 17 to pace West Covina to a 6–3 victory. It proved to be the only game in which West Covina allowed a run. Levittown won its second game in the winners' bracket by thumping Omaha, 6–2, behind the four-hit pitching of Mike Kirkpatrick. At that point, both West Covina and Levittown were unbeaten. Tulsa enjoyed a laugher, a 19–0 win that eliminated Manchester. Carroll Watts picked up four hits to pace Tulsa. The Chris-Town team of Phoenix took out Stahl, 5–0, a loss which eliminated the Delaware club.[63]

West Covina coach Don Sealy chose to start his number three pitcher, Frank O'Con-nor, against Levittown. O'Connor rose to the occasion, struck out 12, and threw a two-hit shutout. Manny Estrada's three-run homer provided the big blow for the victors in a 7–0 win. Wilmington built an 8–0 lead over Phoenix only to see it slip away. Wayne Luton's three-run homer proved the big blow as Chris-Town managed a 10–9 come-from-behind win, although the winning run came on a Wilmington error. Steve Bolling's homer was the key hit in Tulsa's 10–8 win over Omaha; the loss sent Omaha home. The three one-loss teams—Tulsa, Chris-Town of Phoenix, and Levittown—had at it to pick a finalist to take on West Covina. Tulsa ousted Phoenix, 6–2. Levittown then took out Tulsa in a tight, 3–2 game.[64]

In the final 1970 game, facing Levittown, Smith returned to the mound for West Covina. He struck out 11 in a 10–0 romp. That gave him 21 scoreless innings in the World Series. Third baseman Doug Lyons banged a three-run homer as part of a six-run explo-sion in the third inning. Outfielder Mike McManus collected four hits. Coleman Smith, who had thrown 12 innings of shutout ball earlier against Manchester, struck out 11 and scattered four hits. West Covina had sailed through the World Series undefeated, giving up runs in just one game. The state of California had its 12th ALWS title.[65]

For their work, Smith and Terlecky of West Covina were selected as pitchers on the first official all-star team. Joining them were first baseman Ron Beaurivage of Manches-ter; second baseman Ira Willis, Tulsa; third baseman Greg Dalton, Wilmington, North Carolina; shortstop Manny Estrada, West Covina; outfielders Steve Bowling, Tulsa, Mike McManus, West Covina, and Ron Brown, Phoenix; catcher Rick Messner, Phoenix; util-ity Carroll Watts, Tulsa, and Howard Edgerton, Wilmington, North Carolina. The Player of the Year Award went to Carroll Watts of Tulsa, a .412 batter and a flawless fielder. Ron Brown, Phoenix leadoff hitter, reigned as batting champion with an average of .429. The RBI Award went to Greg Dalton of Wilmington, who knocked in 12 runs. Phoenix short-stop Gil Stafford nailed down the Sportsmanship Award. Attendance for 14 games was 22,379.[66]

Since the 1967 Summer of Love, and Woodstock in fall of 1969, kids began to grow long hair, shout revolutionary slogans, and proclaim their independence. Pundits talked of a "generation gap." The American Legion was having none of this. They ruled against long hair and facial hair, beards and mustaches. By long hair, the boys at Klamath were told the rule meant that no hair should touch a boy's ears. The boys from Delaware had the most trouble with that rule, but they abided by it. Before the first games in Klamath Falls, there was a great deal of collective haircutting.[67]

Outside the San Gabriel Valley, no one expected West Covina to repeat in 1971. A repeat was almost unprecedented; only the J. W. Porter-led Oakland team of 1949–1950 and Cincinnati Bentley in 1957–1958 had won back-to-back titles. Besides, only two players from West Covina's championship team returned for 1971, outfielders Randy Haas and Jesse Mendoza. Coach Dan Sealy had to put together a whole new team. Fortunately, he had a strong group of youngsters who had played together for three years and captured the Colt championship in 1970. The key members were catchers Ed Putnam and Steve Monke, second baseman Rob Wilfong, third baseman Steve Twigg, outfielder David Skidmore, and pitchers Jeff Migdal and Max Schneider. Shortstop Ron Zakoor started the season playing in a Connie Mack League but joined Sealy's team before playoffs started. Sealy found first baseman Bruce Mulligan and pitchers Ernie Sanchez and tiny (110-pound) Mike Shippe. As usual Sealy had to worry about "girls, cars, and beaches." The 1971 team was not even good enough to win their district title, finishing second to Glendora. Nevertheless, when the playoffs began, Post 790 came to play.[68]

In the West Regional at Medford, Oregon, West Covina lost a heartbreaker, 2–1, to Lewiston, Idaho, but beat Roseburg, Oregon, 4–1, by scoring four runs in the ninth inning. They got their mojo, beating Honolulu, 12–0, a game in which Hass collected four hits. Then they beat Lewiston twice by scores of 2–1 and 18–7. In the championship game, Zakoor drove in six runs and Mendoza plated four. West Covina placed six boys on the Regional all-star team: pitcher Jeff Migdal, catcher Ed Putnam, second baseman Rob Wilfong, shortstop Rob Zakoor, and outfielders Jesse Mendoza and Randy Haas.[69]

From 3,086 Legion teams, eight made it to Hi Corbett Field in Tucson, Arizona. Hanford Post 5 of Cedar Rapids, Iowa, 11-time Iowa champion, was the favorite going into the World Series. The winner from the New England Region almost never made noise in the Series, and Shields Post 43 of Warwick, Rhode Island, did not scare anyone. From Region 2, Lyndhurst, New Jersey, Barringer-Walker-Lopinto Post 139 could win a game or two. Post 90 from Congaree, South Carolina, represented Region Three. Winning was not a habit for Beppo-Arnold-Knowles Post 32 of Greenville, Mississippi. Their Eagles' state title was the very first for Greenville. Lincoln Park, Michigan Post 67 was primed to go deep in the Series. Phoenix's Chris-Town John C. Greenway Post 1971 filled out the tournament.[70]

Doubts about West Covina escalated after they blew the opening game to Lincoln Park. West Covina held a 2–0 lead with two out in the ninth inning. Then Max Schneider, who had relinquished only two weak hits until the ninth, got a flyout, then gave up a single, but that batter was erased by a force-out at second. Then the wheels came off as Schneider hit a batter and walked the next. They then brought Ernie Sanchez into the game to close the door. Instead he walked two batters, the second bringing in Lincoln Park's first run. Sealy brought in Jeff Migdal to save the game, but he walked Tom Geragosian, who brought in the winning run. In other first-round games, Cedar Rapids looked strong in beating Greenville, 8–6. Mike Curran got three hits for Cedar Rapids. Phoenix had no trouble with Warwick, winning 12–2; Warwick committed ten errors. Rob Walton picked up three hits and drove in three Phoenix runs. Congaree beat Lyndhurst, 4–2, in 10 innings. On the second day, two teams were eliminated, Greenville and Warwick. Warwick lost to West Covina by a 10–2 score. Migdal pitched a solid game, outfielder Pat Cocoran had three hits, and Haas had two RBI. Lyndhurst had little trouble with Greenville, winning 5–1. Outfielder Dick Carter led Lyndhurst's attack with two RBI. Phoenix lost to Lincoln Park, 7–4. Cedar Rapids continued to cruise, beating Congaree, 8–2. Blake DeMaria led with three hits and three runs batted in.[71]

To the disappointment of the local fans, Phoenix went out the next day, Saturday, losing to Lyndhurst, 8–5. In a battle of the remaining undefeated teams, Cedar Rapids took out Lincoln Park, 9–7. Curran had four hits and three RBI. West Covina avoided elimination by beating Congaree, 11–0, a game in which Putnam picked up three hits and drove in four runs, while Haas knocked in three teammates. Mike Shippe pitched the shutout. West Covina was now on a roll. They continued their winning ways by eliminating Lyndhurst, 4–2. Mendoza and Rob Zakoor paced West Covina, Mendoza with three hits and Zakoor with two RBI. Next West Covina took out Lincoln Park, 8–3, as Putnam had four hits and outfielder Bob Bloomer contributed three.[72]

That left Cedar Rapids and West Covina to fight for the 1971 title. Cedar Rapids needed just one win to take the Series. West Covina, however, was getting production throughout the lineup. In the first meeting, West Covina got eight runs in the fourth inning to take a commanding lead in a 16–4 romp. Putnam, Wilfong, and Steve Monka each plated three runs. The championship game proved to be a laugher with West Covina coasting to a 16–1 victory. Putnam and Zakoor each had three RBI to pace the attack. West Covina, the "Prune Pickers," joined Oakland (1949–1950) and Cincinnati Bentley (1957–1958) as the only back-to-back winners. Putnam, with a .439 average and 15 RBI, and Haas, whose .429 average was not shabby, were the two stars. Second baseman Rob Wilfong, however, turned out to have the greatest longevity of any on the team, playing 11 years in the major leagues with Minnesota and California.[73]

West Covina's Randy Haas won the Most Valuable Player award. A strong case could be made for Ed Putnam whose .439 average and 15 RBI exceeded Haas' numbers. Phoenix catcher Rod Walton won the Louisville Slugger Award with a .538 average for all post-season games. Walton also captured the newly named Dr. Irvin Coger Award for most RBI by bringing home 20 teammates. Cedar Rapids third baseman Mike Curran, who ranked second in batting with a .474 average, was awarded the James Daniel Memorial Sportsmanship Award.[74]

Attendance at the 1971 World Series proved to be a major disappointment. Only 12,502 paid their way into Tucson's Hi Corbett Field, nearly 50 percent less than the past few years. Jack Williams, the local chairman, conceded that the Series "was a financial bomb." The local Legion had paid $25,000 to the national to get the Series. The city of Tucson guaranteed $20,000 of that. The local organizers expected to draw 25,000–30,000 fans. George Rulon had an explanation. "Metropolitan areas are not interested" in Legion baseball. "We do much better in smaller cities."[75]

Having said that, for the 1972 World Series, the Legion nevertheless selected Memphis, Tennessee. With a population of 623,000, Memphis hardly met the definition of a "smaller city." Memphis had hosted the Series in 1930 and 1967. Games would be played at Blues Stadium, home of the Texas League Memphis Blues. The park, with a seating capacity of 6,900, opened in 1968 at the State Fairgrounds. It was initially intended for high school baseball, so its dimensions were relatively small, 322 feet to left field, 324 to right field, and 400 to center field. Memphis, of course, continued to have a prominent music tradition. Blues clubs on Beale Street gave birth to the unique Memphis blues, while in the 1950s, Sun Records produced Elvis Presley, Johnny Cash, and the rockabilly sound.[76]

The greatest surprise in the 1972 World Series was that West Covina failed to appear among the eight finalists. After winning back-to-back national titles, West Covina did not even win the California title. The Golden State was instead represented by Louis

Hagan Post 340 of El Cerrito, a community of 25,000 on the shore of San Francisco Bay adjacent to Berkeley. They won the state title for the first time, and beat Tucson, 7–2, in the Region 8 finals, boosting their record to 41–9. Lewis-Clark Post 13 of Lewiston, Idaho, had been to the Series twice in the 1960s. They arrived with 46 wins against 12 losses. Bill Speros' Memphis Post 1 (64–9) team came in with the most wins. Findley, Ohio's Ralph D. Cole Post 3 came to the Series with a lofty record of 41–4. Findley also boasted the best pitcher, 6-foot-5 Charles Rogers, who struck out 21 Arlington Heights, Illinois, batters in the Regional final. Dalton-Cartier Post 204 of Norfolk, Virginia, came in with a record of 21–3. North Haven, Connecticut, bragged of its lofty 27–2 record, but they garnered little respect. Monte Carlo Post 146 from Rio Piedras, Puerto Rico (33–3), came through the Southeast Regional. They brought a young club whose peak seemed a year or so away.[77]

Memphis and Ballwin, Missouri, shared favorite status before the 1972 Series began. Ballwin, Missouri Memorial Post 611 was located in the far western suburbs of St. Louis in a town of 10,000. Appropriately, the summer of 1972 saw St. Louis' native son and former Legion player Yogi Berra inducted into the Hall of Fame. Ballwin believed that was a good omen. Most of Ballwin's players came from Lafayette High School, the Missouri state prep school champions. Ballwin came through the Central Plains Regional in Hastings, Nebraska, outscoring their opponents, 44–3. Ballwin beat Rapid City twice to take the Regional title. In the first game, little-used lefty Dave Tuttle pitched a no-hitter in a 7–0 Ballwin win. Then they defeated Rapid City, South Dakota, 13–2. In that game, shortstop Steve Viefhaus smashed a 377-foot homer out of the park. It was only the second ball hit out of Duncan Field in 30 years of Legion competition. They entered the ALWS with a 39–7 record. Since the mid–1950s, Memphis Post 1 coach Tony Gagliano had developed a strong program. His teams had captured the Tennessee state title 15 of the last 16 years. They finished second nationally in 1963, third in 1965, and fourth in 1967 before bringing home the national title in 1968. In 1972. they relied on the left-handed hitting of right fielder Keith Kauerz.[78]

George W. Rulon was the longest serving leader of American Legion baseball, holding that position from 1961 to 1987. He presided over a long period of steady growth. The Player of the Year award is named for him (courtesy American Legion).

Ballwin struggled in its opening game against Findlay's Charles Rogers, who shut them out, 7–0. That was Ballwin's only shutout of the season. Other than that game, Ballwin and Memphis sailed through the tournament. Ballwin's Mike Murphy threw a two-hit shutout at Lewiston in a 6–0 game. Dan Ingram, who had taken the loss against Findlay in the opener, came back strong in a 7–2 win over North Haven. Lefty Dave Tuttle was at his best in a rematch against Findlay. He allowed only two hits, struck out 12, and drove in two runs. With Murphy on the mound, Ballwin won another pitchers' duel, 2–1 against El Cerrito. That set up the Ballwin-Memphis finals. Memphis had slipped past Lewiston, 4–2, beat Findley, 7–4, and took a close game, 3–1, from El Cerrito.[79]

Before Ballwin and Memphis, the two best teams, met in a two-of-three finals for the 1972 national title, Ballwin caught a break. Rain washed out a day's schedule, giving Ballwin's weary pitchers an extra day of rest. In the first game, Ingram returned to the mound for Ballwin, winning 7–4. In the final game of 1972, Tuttle held Memphis to four hits and two runs. The winning run came in the eighth inning when center fielder Charles Kick doubled, went to third on a ground out, and scored on first baseman Jeff Haferkamp's perfect and unexpected squeeze bunt. Tuttle pitched a complete-game four-hitter to get the win.[80]

For winning that national championship, the team was inducted into the St. Louis Sports Hall of Fame. Third baseman Mike Umfleet led Post 611 in batting with a .378 average, but their pitching carried them to the title. Mike Murphy finished with an 11–1 record, Dan Ingram closed with a 15–2 record, lefty Dave Tuttle was 5–3, and Charlie Kick was 6–1. Metro Memphis drew well for the ALWS, attracting 24,817 paying customers for the 15 games, even though Legion officials blasted local officials for poor upkeep of the stadium. That was the highest attendance since 1961. Ballwin's little (5-foot-9, 160 pounds) pitcher, Mike Murphy, was selected Most Valuable Player for the Series. Memphis' Keith Kauerz, a 6-foot-3, 190-pound, left-handed hitter, won the Louisville Slugger Award as batting champion of the playoffs with a .583 average. Ballwin's third baseman, Mike Umfleet, became only the second winner of the now-named James Daniel Sportsmanship Award. In Memphis, John "J. J." Guinozzo began a career as national Legion official scorer that lasted five decades.[81]

In 1973, the Puerto Rico club, Rio Piedras, returned to the World Series with essentially the same cast as they brought in 1972. The team had a new coach in Alfredo Carlo Toro, a San Juan lawyer, who had coached a Babe Ruth League team, Puerto Nuevo, to the national championship in 1971. Rio Piedras' Monte Carlo Post 141 had only started playing Legion ball in 1968. Only five other Legion teams competed in Puerto Rico, so the opportunity for games remained limited. Unlike in the previous year, they had a hard-hitting team. Three starters, infielder Guillermo "Juan" Bonilla, outfielder Carlos Lezcano, and catcher Jose Lugo, already had baseball scholarships to play for Florida State. The team came into the tournament through the Southeast Region, where they beat Rocky Mount, North Carolina, in the finals to qualify for the World Series. If they needed any more incentive, the death on January 1 of Roberto Clemente, Puerto Rico's greatest player, provided that spark. They dedicated every game to Roberto's memory. To commemorate their support to Clemente's memory, the team wore arm patches with Clemente's number 21 in a circle on their right sleeve. They started at a disadvantage because their uniforms and equipment managed to get lost between Salisbury, North Carolina, and Lewiston, Idaho, arriving just in time for their first game.[82]

The 1973 Series took place in Lewiston, Idaho, for the first time, some 6,000 miles from San Juan. Bengal Field dated to 1938, when the WPA provided funds for a high school football/baseball field. An early version of multi-purpose fields, it had football stands down the right field foul line which gave it a seating capacity of 3,500.

Dimensions were 335 feet to left field, 411 to center field, and only 308 to the right field fence.[83]

The eight teams in the 1973 American Legion World Series included some familiar names. Hayes-Velhage Post 96 (27–3) of West Hartford, Connecticut, and Region One had been there before. Richmond's James Waters Westenders Post 361 (34–11) did not appear to represent a danger to big-time teams. Monte Carlo Post 146 of Rio Piedras (20–6) returned almost all players from its 1972 team that had gone home quickly, and they now appeared to be a collection of heavy hitters. Post 1 of Memphis (62–10) had finished second the previous two years and rated the favorite's role again in 1973. Bentley Post 50 of Cincinnati (41–6) remembered its glory years of the 1940s. The Richfield, Minnesota Reds' Post 435 (36–5) was a past champion. Watco Electric, Post 52 of Portland, Oregon (52–6) hoped to replicate the 1969 feat of the Portland Contractors. San Fernando, California, Sylmer Post 176 (28–2) lost their best player, Pete Redfern, to a dislocated shoulder in Region 8 play. Redfern would later become the number one choice of Minnesota in the 1976 draft.[84]

Rio Piedras needed only four games to wrap up the 1973 Series. In the opening round, the Puerto Rico boys took out poor San Fernando, 7–0. Catcher Jose Lugo tripled and drove in three runs, and Ramond Rosario pitched shutout ball. West Hartford gave New England a surprise win, beating Richfield, 5–1. Memphis needed 11 innings to beat Richmond thanks to John Lee's game-winning hit. Portland's Watco Electric slipped past Cincinnati, 5–4, in 10 innings. In the second round, San Fernando ousted Richfield, 4–2, and Cincinnati sent Richmond home behind the pitching of Bill Earley. Puerto Rico's heavy hitting was on display in their 10–3 victory over West Hartford. After Portland beat Memphis, 5–3, on Steve Randolph's two RBI, Rio Piedras became the favorite.[85]

Memphis rebounded by beating San Fernando, 6–4. Cincinnati eliminated West Hartford, 3–1. In a battle of undefeated teams, Rio Piedras slammed Portland, 8–4. Memphis looked hot beating Cincinnati, 5–2, in 10 innings, and Portland, 3–2, to set up the 1973 final. The 1973 title game between Rio Piedras and Memphis, two strong, evenly matched teams. It took the Islanders ten innings to put away Memphis, but they did so in convincing fashion, winning 10–6. In the bottom of the ninth, Memphis shortstop Tucker Ashford singled home the tying run. In the tenth inning, Carlos Rodriquez doubled home one run to make the score 7–6. Shortstop Luis Ferrer lofted what appeared to be a routine fly ball, but the Memphis center fielder misplayed the ball, allowing a three-run, inside-the-park home run. Rio Piedras had a 10–6 win and the American Legion title. This Puerto Rico group was irrepressible, never giving up and playing with heart and mental toughness. They knew how to win, how to close out games. In their four Series games, Rio Piedras collectively batted a resounding .361 with 17 extra-base hits.[86]

Rio Piedras second baseman Carlos Rodriguez captured the Louisville Slugger Award with a .435 batting average. Third baseman Guillermo "Juan" Bonilla led all players with 13 runs batted in. Catcher and cleanup hitter Jose Lugo took home the James F. Daniel, Jr., Sportsmanship Award. The one award Rio Piedras did not win was the Most Valuable Player Award, which went to Memphis' slick-fielding, hard-hitting shortstop, Tucker Ashford, who batted .478 for the Series. Ashford went on to play parts of seven seasons in the majors with San Diego, Texas, the Yankees, the Mets, and Kansas City.[87]

In the 1973–1974 off-season, major league baseball agreed to increase its appropriation to the American Legion for 1974 from $50,000 to $75,000. The 1974 Series was scheduled for Roseburg, Oregon, a small city of 14,461 located in the Umpqua River Valley in southern Oregon. Roseburg branded itself as the "Timber Capital of the Nation." Legion Memorial Field, where Legion teams would play August 22–27, 1974, boasted a new concrete grandstand installed in 1970, but that did not alter the normal seating capacity of 3,125. Using seating from the Douglas County Fairgrounds, the local organizers expanded seating capacity to 5,000 for the Series.[88]

The women's movement reached its peak in the early 1970s. Congress approved Title IX of the Education Amendments to the Civil Rights Act in 1972, prohibiting discrimination by sex in any education program that received federal aid. In the same year, Congress sent the Equal Rights Amendment (ERA) to the states for ratification. For the next several years, lawsuits plastered newspapers, including the sports pages. In 1974, Little League Baseball agreed to admit girls, but also set up a softball league for girls. American Legion baseball, after plenty of debate, followed suit, allowing girls to participate. Legion play opened with 3,457 teams, the largest since 1950.[89]

Except for defending champion Rio Piedras Post 146, teams in the 1974 World Series were not familiar to Legion baseball fans. Seicheprey Post 2 of Bristol, Connecticut, had been playing Legion baseball since 1928, but 1974 was their first trip to the World Series. Charles H. Johnson Post 108 of Cheverly, Maryland, won the Mid–Atlantic Regional at Lyndhurst, New Jersey. Rio Piedras took the Southeast Regional at St. Petersburg, Florida. After a long run, Memphis failed to make the tournament, even though the Mid–South Regional was held in their hometown. Instead, Post 175 from Metairie, Louisiana, and

Bill Gray Stadium dates to its origin as Legion Memorial Field in 1958. It seats 3,125, but portable bleachers raised the seating to 5,000 for Legion World Series games. It hosted the Series in 1974, 1993 and 1996 when it was one of three locations considered to be the permanent home for the Series (courtesy of *Rosemont News-Review*).

Rummel High School, the AAAA Louisiana state champion, sponsored by Schaffe Brothers Construction, prevailed. Jenkins Post 5 of Rockport, Indiana, also won its first trip to the World Series with a 6–4 victory over Bowling Green, Kentucky, at the Great Lakes Regional in Stevens Point, Wisconsin. Cedar Rapids, Iowa Post 5, the Hanford Post, beat Gardenville, Missouri, 5–1, to punch its ticket to Roseburg. Lake Oswego, Oregon Post 92 beat Yakima, 3–1, at Klamath Falls, Oregon, to make the tournament. Down to 12 active players, they would be known as "The Dirty Dozen." Campbell Post 99 of Campbell-San Jose, California, beat Hawaii to punch their ticket to the World Series.[90]

In the opening round, Rio Piedras pushed Rockport to the losers' bracket with an 11–5 win. Weak Rockport defense gave Puerto Rico six unearned runs, five in the first inning. Shortstop Alexis Firri drove in two runs, and Abner Ortiz collected three hits. Also in the first round, Campbell shut out Cedar Rapids, 2–0, behind the pitching of Eric Bauer and the hitting of Jim Guardino; Metairie bested Bristol, 7–4, and Lake Oswego topped Cheverly, 4–2. In the second round, Rio Piedras had an even easier time against Campbell, California, whose pitchers walked ten batters. Rodriquez had four hits, and Oscar Negron pitched a shutout. Rockport eliminated Cedar Rapids by a 3–1 score, and Cheverly send Bristol home with a 5–4 win powered by Bill Foley's three-run homer. Metairie scored three runs in the eighth inning to hand Lake Oswego the 3–0 loss. Rick Zibilich tossed the shutout. After two games, Rio Piedras and Metairie remained the only unbeaten teams.[91]

Rio Piedras and Metairie met in the next round. This was a tougher game for Puerto Rico than the first two, but they prevailed, 6–3. Metairie lost not only the game, but also their catcher and the glue that held them together, Dom Giambrone, for the remainder of the Series. Cheverly knocked Campbell out with a 10–5 victory. Metairie lost their second straight to Cheverly by the lopsided score of 13–1 and were eliminated from the tournament. Next the Puerto Rico boys faced fan favorite Lake Oswego, "The Dirty Dozen," and, as the only Oregon team, were treated as the home team. Right fielder Glenn Heard led the Cinderella team in the 9–3 upset of Rio Piedras with three RBI. Hard-throwing Scott Anderson struck out ten and kept Monte Carlo batters off stride. Heard then pitched Lake Oswego over Cheverly by a 6–1 score to gain a rematch with Rio Piedras.[92]

In the 1974 World Series championship game, before a standing room only crowd of 5,194, the "Dirty Dozen" of Lake Oswego took a 3–0 lead in the first inning. Scott Anderson singled in two runs, and Dennis Paterson plated the other. Then Rio Piedras' tiny left-handed pitcher, Arnutto Comacho, settled down, allowing only one hit for the rest of the game. Jesus Vega homered in the second inning to put Rio Piedras on the scoreboard. In the third, Carlos Rodriquez drove in Edwin Lopez, who had doubled. In the seventh, Rio Piedras tied the score on sloppy fielding. Rene Rivera struck out but gained first when the catcher could not hold the ball. He stole second and went to third on another passed ball by the catcher. Abner Ortiz singled in the tying run. The winning run came in the eighth inning when Ernesto Cruz doubled and scored on Alexis Firpi's single to give Puerto Rico the win, 4–3. Rio Piedras became the fourth team to win back-to-back championships.[93]

Edwin Lopez, a muscular, 5-foot-6, 145-pound outfielder for Rio Piedras, won the award as the tournament's Most Valuable Player. He also got the Louisville Slugger for the highest batting average for the tournament, .433. The Rawlings Big Stick Award for total bases went to Greg Tooley of Rockport. The Dr. Irvin L. "Click" Cowger RBI Award went to Charles Johnson of Cheverly. Finally, the James F. Daniel, Jr., Sportsmanship Award was awarded to Glenn Heard of Lake Oswego. Some 30,102 fans attended the Series, the most since 1954, when Yakima drew 40,000.[94]

American Legion baseball celebrated its 50th anniversary in 1975. In its 50 years, at least 3,400,000 boys had played on an estimated 200,000 teams. It all began in Milbank, South Dakota, so it was appropriate that the 1975 American Legion World Series would be played in South Dakota. Rapid City was picked to host the event, August 28–September 1. Games were played at Sioux Park Stadium (later renamed Floyd Fitzgerald Stadium), which seated 1,272 in reserved seats and 3,000 in general admission seats. It had been constructed in 1957 for the Western International League team.[95]

In 1974, there were 3,457 certified Legion teams in all 50 states plus the District of Columbia, Puerto Rico, and the Canal Zone (Panama). Some 469 of those teams were newly returned Pennsylvania clubs. Eight of those 3,000-plus teams participating in the World Series gathered at Sioux Park Stadium on August 28, 1975. Teams from Cheverly, Maryland, and Cedar Rapids, Iowa, returned from the 1974 Series. The Puerto Rico team, Nievas Carrillo Post 113, was from San Juan, not Rio Piedras, but five members of Post 113 had played for Rio Piedras, the champions in 1973 and 1974. Some people grumbled that the weather in Puerto Rico gave its teams an unfair advantage. Of course, the same thing had been heard when California teams dominated. In Region One, the Cyril P. Morrisette Post 29 of West Quincy, Massachusetts (31–4) captured the New England Regional by beating Old Town, Maine, 4–2 in 11 innings. Cheverly, Maryland, Post 108 (29–3) had won its spot in Petersburg, Virginia, with a 4–3 victory over Newport News in the Region Two final. Nieves Carrillo Post 113 of San Juan (19–6) came through the Southeast Regional (Region Three) in Anderson, South Carolina. Harvey H. Graves Post 1, Bombers of Jackson, Mississippi (34–13) came out of the losers' bracket to beat Greenville, Mississippi, 11–0 and 7–5. Worthington, Ohio's Leasure-Blackston Post 239 (35–5) took out Belleville, Illinois, by scores of 4–1 and 15–9 to win Region Five. Hanford Post 5, Cedar Rapids, Iowa (33–10) was a long-time Legion power. This year they prided themselves on Mike Boddicker, a great pitcher and hitter. Yakima's Logan-Wheeler Post 36 Beetles (48–21) won the Pacific Northwest title with a new coach, Bob Garretson, Jr., who had taken over from his father. The Beetles beat Portland, 9–7, for the title. Fullerton, California (35–6) Post 142 captured their sectional with a 22–0 slaughter of Las Vegas, Nevada.[96]

After the first eight games, West Quincy and Jackson were gone. West Quincy proved to be the hard-luck team, losing by one run in each of their first two games. In the opening round, they lost to Cheverly, 12–11, in 12 innings thanks to Bill Foley's four hits, the last of which was a two-out RBI for the win. Then they lost to Yakima, 4–3, as first baseman Don Crow singled in the winning run in the ninth inning. Jackson lost to Worthington, 6–4, and Cedar Rapids, 11–10, in ten innings as Bill Wilson had four hits and scored the winning run. In other early-round games, San Juan slipped by Cedar Rapids, 9–8, as Arnulfo Camacho and Ernesto Cruz each knocked in three runs. Dickie Thon starred as San Juan beat Worthington, 5–2.[97]

On day three, Yakima send Worthington back to Ohio, beating them, 14–9. In that game, second baseman Jamie Allen pounded out four hits, including a home run, and left fielder Dave Edler homered and drove in four runs. Cedar Rapids eliminated Cheverly, 13–7. Bill Wilson had three hits and three RBI. At that point in the Series, Fullerton and Puerto Rico were undefeated, while Yakima and Cedar Rapids each had one loss. As Yakima, Fullerton and Cedar Rapids got hot, and the undefeated had to fall by the wayside. Fullerton knocked San Juan from the unbeaten ranks with an 8–5 win as Jerry Gunderman drove in three runs. Undefeated Fullerton ran into Cedar Rapids' buzz-saw pitcher, Mike Boddicker. The Norway, Iowa, lad struck out 16 and had three hits of his own. Yakima continued its hot hitting in a 14–11 elimination of San Juan. Dave Edler pitched a complete game and had three hits including a homer, and shortstop Greg McDonald contributed a home run of his own. Cedar Rapids' Wilson continued hitting, banging out three hits with three RBI in Cedar Rapids' elimination of Cheverly. That left three one-loss teams: Fullerton, Cedar Rapids, and Yakima. Yakima won the toss to determine who got the bye. Cedar Rapids beat Fullerton, 6–2, as Mike Boddicker struck out 16 batters. Cedar Rapids continued its hot hand, beating Fullerton, 8–1. Bruce Barber pitched a nifty five-hitter.[98]

In the 1975 title game between Yakima and Cedar Rapids, Dave Edler scattered eight hits and clobbered a home run as Yakima defeated Cedar Rapids, 8–4. After Cedar Rapids got on the scoreboard first with a score in the first inning, Yakima's outfielder Jim Potter tripled home two runs in the second. The Beetles picked up another run in the third inning when shortstop Greg McDonald unloaded his sixth homer of the season. Mike Boddacker's two-run homer for Cedar Rapids in the third inning made it a close game. Yakima added three more runs in the fifth. Dave Elder opened the inning with a homer to left field. A single by Don Crow, followed by Mike Moore's double, set up a squeeze by Ron Gregson to score Crow. Moore came home on a wild pitch. Dave Elder pitched the complete game for the win. Final score: Yakima 8, Cedar Rapids 4.[99]

Dave Edler, Yakima pitcher/outfielder, headed the official awards as Player of the Year. During the World Series, he batted a robust .611 and drove in 15 runs to win the Irvin L. "Click" Cowger Award for RBI. He earned two wins in the ALWS to finish the year with a 15–1 mound record and a 2.30 ERA. He collected 34 total bases to tie Dennis Duncanson of Fullerton for the Rawlings Big Stick Award. For the season, Elder batted .448 with 77 RBI and 13 home runs. Edler went on to play college ball at Washington State and then had a brief stint with the Seattle Mariners, 1980–1983. Following his playing career, he served on the Yakima City Council and as Mayor. Despite Edler's great hitting in the World Series, Armulfo Camacho of San Juan won the Louisville Slugger Award for batting .545 during the entire post-season. Finally, the Jack Williams Award for Leadership went to Curt Becker, coach of Cedar Rapids.[100]

Journalists at the Series selected a 1975 All-Tournament Team for the *Cedar Rapids Journal*. It included: first baseman Jim Leicht (Fullerton); second baseman Ron Gregson (Yakima); third baseman Jamie Allen (Yakima); shortstop Dickie Thon (San Juan); outfielders Dave Edler (Yakima), Dennis Duncanson (Fullerton), and Bill Wilson (Cedar Rapids); utility Bill Foley (Cheverly); left-handed pitcher Juan Quinonez (San Juan); right-handed pitcher Mike Boddicker (Cedar Rapids). Thon played 15 seasons in the majors with the Angels, Astros, Padres, Phillies, Rangers, and Brewers. Mike Boddicker pitched in the majors for 14 years, nine with Baltimore followed by Boston, Kansas City, and Milwaukee. He would be selected as the Most Valuable Player in the 1983 American League Championship Series.[101]

American Legion baseball had reached its Golden Anniversary in 1975. It had survived issues of sexism, racism in the 1920s, and a desperate shortage of money during the Great Depression. It continued to grow during World War II, although trapped by Southern racism. It took off in the post-war years, when graduates of Legion ball poured into the Major Leagues, coming to dominate the rosters of big-league teams and All-Star teams. Since 1961, under the steady leadership of George Rulon, Legion ball managed to survive the culture wars of the 1960s. It brought on-field excitement from Rollie Fingers, one of the greatest Legion players, perhaps the greatest of all time. Two mini-dynasties—West Covina in 1970–1971 and Rio Piedras in 1973–1974—dominated team play. Legion baseball had become a fixture in America's summers.

6

Mid–Atlantic Dominance, 1976–1986

The 1976 American Legion World Series came on the heels of the Legion convention in late July 1976. Philadelphia had been chosen as the convention site to coincide with the 200th anniversary of the signing of the Declaration of Independence. That convention will always be remembered for the first known outbreak of what came to be known as "Legionnaires' disease." At the Bellevue-Stratford Hotel, where most of the convention goers stayed, there appeared the first occasion of a cluster of a particular type of pneumonia cases caused by Legionella bacteria. A total of 182 cases were identified. Of those, 29 died. As bad as that crisis was for the Legion, it made surprisingly little impact on the ALWS.

Although teams from the Golden State had dominated American Legion baseball in the 1940s and 1950s, and they had won the American Legion World Series five times in the past 13 seasons, the tide was shifting. In the next 25 years (1976–2000), California would win only twice. However, here was Santa Monica Post 123 not just winning the championship in 1976, but also making it to the World Series three consecutive years—1976, 1977, and 1978. Rio Piedras, Puerto Rico, had made the ALWS three straight years in 1972, 1973 and 1974, but prior to that, the last team to make three straight World Series was Dave McNally's Billings team in 1960, 1961, and 1962. Making the Series three consecutive years was no small feat.

Santa Monica built its 1976 team around the immense talents of its pitching duo of Tim Leary and Rick Schroeder. Leary compiled a regular season record of 12–2, and Schroeder was undefeated at 10–0. Leary won Most Valuable Player honors at the California state tournament and also at the Regional tournament in Murray, Utah, where Santa Monica beat Glendale, Arizona, 13–3 in the final. In that game, Leary also collected six hits, including two home runs. At 6-foot-4 inches, 205 pounds, he dominated Legion ball. After the New York Mets made him the second pick in the draft, he spent 13 seasons in the major leagues with the Mets, Reds, New York Yankees, Seattle, Texas, Milwaukee, and the Los Angeles Dodgers. In addition to Schroeder and Leary, Santa Monica had outfielder Rod Allen, who would play three seasons in the majors with Seattle, Detroit, and Cleveland. In addition, second baseman David Montanari, outfielder Stan Younger, and catcher Tony Diaz went on to play professional ball short of the majors.

Santa Monica faced stiff competition from two returning teams. Defending champion Yakima Beetles and the second-place club, Cedar Rapids, Iowa, had well-established programs. Yakima created the model Legion program in the 1970s. In 1976 they played

88 games, all of them broadcast live on radio. They lacked money problems. Cedar Rapids was the favorite in 1976, mainly because they returned most of their players from 1975, including pitcher/second baseman Mike Boddicker, seen as the premier Legion player, both pitcher and hitter. In addition to those two teams, coach Lloyd Meyer brought a strong team out of the Midwest, whether called Arlington Heights or Des Plaines. Confusion reigned regarding the name of the team. The team uniform read "Arlington Heights," their caps sported a clear "AH," and the Arlington Heights Boosters ran the program, raised money, and paid the bills. But Des Plaines, Illinois, Post 36 was the sponsoring Legion post. The back of the team uniforms read Bill Cook Buick, a team sponsor.[1]

Manchester, New Hampshire, hosted the 1976 World Series. Games were played at Gill Stadium, a concrete and steel structure built in 1913 with a seating capacity listed as 3,700. Participating teams were: Region one, Warwick, Rhode Island, Post 43; Region two from Wilmington Manor, Delaware, Stahl Post 30, a team that had slipped past Newport News, Virginia, 1–0 in ten innings in the Region final; Region 3, Southeast, Manati, Puerto Rico Post 39, the fourth team from the island to make the ALWS in as many years; Region 4, Metairie, Louisiana, Post 175; Region 5, Des Plaines, Illinois, Post 36/Arlington Heights; Region 6, Hansford Post 5, Cedar Rapids, Iowa; Region 7, Yakima, Washington, Post 36; Region 8, Santa Monica Bay Cities, California, Post 123. Games got underway on September 2.

On the opening day of the ALWS, there was only one true upset. New England teams almost never managed a win, but Warwick, Rhode Island, behind lefty Craig Ricci's one-hit pitching, burly cleanup hitter Jim Kilborn's three-run home run, and third baseman Bunny Johnson's bases-loaded double, upset Des Plains/Arlington Heights 6–1. In other opening games, Manati upset defending champion Yakima, 3–2; Cedar Rapids slipped past Wilmington Manor, 2–1, behind Steve Rooks' pitching and catcher Kem Kraimer's game-winning double. Santa Monica had an easy time (8–1) with Metairie.[2]

The highlight of day two was a pitching duel between Santa Monica's Rich Schroeder and Cedar Rapids' Mike Boddicker. Schroeder won with a ten-inning no-hitter, while Boddicker allowed only three hits and struck out nine. Both pitchers walked four. Outfielder Stan Younger drove in Ron Allen with the winning run to secure the 1–0 victory. Metairie had little trouble knocking out Wilmington Stahl post, 8–4. A towering two-run homer by outfielder Gus Malespin was the big blow. Defending champ Yakima ended its run on the second day, losing 8–1 to Des Plaines. Yakima stranded 12 runners and committed six errors.[3]

Last year's second-place finisher, Cedar Rapids, bit the dust on day three. Des Plaines/Arlington Heights took out Mike Boddicker's club, 1–0, behind Dennis Drolet's five-hit shutout which bested Cedar Rapids' Chuck Johnson. The winning run scored on a triple and an error in the third inning. Metairie eliminated Manati, 5–3. Warwick's win streak ended with a 4–2 loss to Santa Monica. Lee Wentzel got the win, but Leary picked up the save. The win put Santa Monica in the final.[4]

Des Plaines/Arlington Heights had become the giant-killer, knocking out Yakima and Cedar Rapids. On day five, they faced two more teams in elimination games. They took care of business by beating Metairie, 4–2, in the first game. Catcher Tony Spinelli's three-run homer provided the win. They needed 13 innings to beat Warwick, 5–4. Kevin McBride, who came on in relief, collected the win, which came on a walk.[5]

On the final day of play in 1976, Arlington Heights needed to win both games against Santa Monica. They took the afternoon game, 4–3. McBride was, again, the winning pitcher, but Bobby Huber entered to save the game. Jerry DiSimone's two-run double in the seventh inning put Des Plaines/Arlington Heights ahead. It would be understandable if the boys from Des Plaines/Arlington were tired, playing their fourth game in two days, but they showed no signs of fatigue. They failed, however, to keep up the pressure in the finale. Stan Younger gave Santa Monica the lead with a two-run double in the fourth inning. In Des Plaines/Arlington's seventh inning, two walks, an infield hit off the third base bag, a Mike Mayerick single, and another hit by John Vuckovich tied the score. Santa Monica put the game away in the top of the eighth when second baseman Dave Montanari singled and came home on third baseman Tom Colburn's double. Rick Schroeder went the distance on the mound for Santa Monica in their 4–3 win.[6]

Hard-luck Mike Boddicker, who lost a no-hitter to Rick Schroeder, and who was appearing in his third American Legion World Series, was presented with the Sportsmanship Award. Santa Monica pitching tandem, Rick Schroeder and Tim Leary, both possessed strong claims to Player of the Year honors. Leary had been the Most Valuable Player in both the California state tournament and the Regional. The award for the ALWS, however, went to Gus Malespin of Metairie instead. Tim Leary, who finished with a 12–2 Legion record before attending UCLA, had a 13-year major league career. Schroeder played one year in the low minors before turning to scouting in 1982 for the Texas Rangers and Kansas City Royals

In November 1976, America put the Nixon era to rest when it elected Jimmy Carter president. A Washington outsider, Carter was a devout Baptist who attempted to govern as a preacher and an engineer, which he also was, rather than a politician. Carter was refreshingly low-key, but his lack of political skills and his religious principles made it difficult to govern a fractious country. Unfortunately for Carter, jumps in OPEC oil prices made 1979 and 1980 the worst years for inflation in the post–World War II era.

Legion baseball offered its own surprise. Teams seldom come out of nowhere to become champions. Charlotte had finished second in 1964 before winning the championship in 1965. Tuscaloosa, likewise, placed second in 1966 and won everything in 1967. Memphis Post 1 announced its arrival with a second-place finish in 1963, but could not win it all until 1968, followed by second-place finishes in 1972 and 1973. Santa Monica seemingly came out of nowhere to take the title in 1976, but they were a California team and they were loaded. In 1977, Santa Monica returned seven starters from the 1976 club; that made them virtually a prohibitive favorite to repeat.

Instead of back-to-back Santa Monica wins, South Bend, Indiana, and Hattiesburg, Mississippi, caught lightning in a bottle. Neither had come close before. No team from either state had ever won a national title before or since. South Bend had won the state title in 1976, but they did not get out of the Regional. Nor did they ever get to the World Series again. Hattiesburg Post 78 had only been playing for four years, not enough time for those who followed Legion ball even to know they played baseball down there. South Bend possessed only modest talent. None of their players made the major leagues or even the high minors.[7]

South Bend Post 50 manager Mel Machuca seemed to have an unlimited supply of pixie dust to spread about; August and the first week of September was a magic time for Machuca and his team. Post 50 won the Indiana title by beating Elkhart, 6–4, in a game that ended in a fight and forfeit. Elkhart held a 4–2 lead, and Jim Heeg had a no-hitter going when he developed arm trouble and had to be removed. Post 50 quickly ended the no-hitter and took the lead on third baseman Jeff Coker's monster homer. Second baseman Gary Vargyas tripled and attempted to score on a ground ball. In the collision at the plate, the ball came loose, as did tempers. Elkhart's coach pulled his team in protest, and the forfeit followed. Next, Post 50 beat cross-town rival Post 357 of South Bend on another Crocker home run. They then beat Lafayette twice, 4–3 and 7–5. Pitcher Dave Haskins won the first game. First baseman Jim Andert drove in the tying run, and second baseman Will Shepherd drove in the winning one. In the second game, Shepherd knocked in the go-ahead run. In the Regional, Haskins and Greg Heyde took care of the pitching. Coker, Shepherd, and shortstop Bill Schell provided the offense. They beat Arlington Heights, 6–5, Morehead, Kentucky, 1–0, and Blissfield, Minnesota, 3–0 and 3–2.[8]

For the second straight year, Manchester, New Hampshire, hosted the World Series at Gill Stadium. The New England representative, Trumbull, Connecticut Post 141, brought a stronger club (32–7) than usual. Their hopes rested on two 6-foot-4-inch pitching twins, Mark and Mike Dacko, who carried Trumbull through the Regional at Augusta, Maine. Charles B. Yerger Post 471 of Boyertown, Pennsylvania, representing Region 2, brought the best record (45–2) to the Series. West Palm Beach Post 12 (29–2) enjoyed good fortune in the Region 3 final. College Park, Georgia, handed West Palm Beach five unearned runs in the ninth inning to send the Floridians off to Manchester. The Hattiesburg Rocks of Francis L. Miller Post 78 had to beat Pine Bluffs, Arkansas, 5–3, in the final of Region 4. The Rocks brought a 41–13 record to the Series after beating Fenton, Missouri, in the Regional final. Rapid City, South Dakota, Post 22, a long-standing Legion power, beat St. Cloud, Minnesota, 7–0, to gain its 61st win against nine losses, and to punch its ticket to New Hampshire as the representative from Region 6. Lewis-Clark Post 13 of Lewiston, Idaho, the Region 7 winner, played the most games and won the most, 63–16. Santa Monica (41–3), ALWS defending champions, sailed through the Region 8 tournament, beating Las Vegas 8–1 in the final.

Santa Monica started off the Series like a champion. Tim Leary pitched a two-hitter, striking out 14 in an easy win, 6–2, over Trumbull. Rapid City, behind Jeff Andrews' pitching (18–0) and Tony Remer's successful suicide squeeze in the 10th frame, bested Lewiston, 3–2. South Bend took out Boyertown, 5–1, thanks to Greg Heyde's pitching and Bill Schell's four hits. Hattiesburg won Mississippi's first Series game, 9–6 over West Palm Beach. Unusual things began to happen on day two of the Series. The big surprise came in South Bend's upset of Santa Monica. Dave Hankins took care of the Santa Monica bats by pitching a complete-game four-hitter, allowing just one run. Schell again hammered out four hits to lead the offense, and he made spectacular plays in the field. The Benders seemed to never stop making plays in the field, running, taking the extra base, always putting pressure on Santa Monica to make perfect plays in the field. The final 8–1 score left little doubt about the better team, at least on this day. In other second-day games, Hattiesburg stayed unbeaten and announced that they needed to be taken seriously by beating Rapid City, 5–2. Lefty Jeff Eure pitched and batted Hattiesburg to the win, his ninth against one loss. Third baseman Roger Wirtz cleared the bases with a triple. Trumbull got a run in the second inning on Talley Noble's double, and Mark Dacko silenced Boyertown's bats with a three-hit shutout. The loss sent Boyertown home. West Palm Beach eliminated Lewiston by a 7–5 score.[9]

In the third day of play, favorites continued to drop. Trumbull beat Rapid City, 8–2, the second loss eliminating Rapid City. Greg Meyers pitched and hit well for Trumbull. He threw a sharp four-hitter and drove in two runs on three hits. Three Rapid City miscues in the eighth inning spelled doom for the South Dakota club. Santa Monica also fell for the second time, losing 4–2 to West Palm Beach in a listless game. Ted Adkins picked up the win, and Doug Robertson homered and drove in two runs for West Palm Beach. Hattiesburg gave South Bend little trouble in an 8–1 win. South Bend's number three pitcher, Dennis Janiszewski, never faced trouble in picking up the complete-game victory. That left Trumbull, West Palm Beach, and Hattiesburg in the semi-finals, playing for the right to take on South Bend. Trumbull had gone further than any New England team in memory, but their dream came to an end against West Palm Beach. Doug Robertson, who had led the West Palm Beach hitting attack the entire Series, pounded a home run, the big blow in an 10–5 victory. Hattiesburg awaited West Palm Beach, the winner of the first game. West Palm Beach appeared to have the game wrapped up as they took a 6–0 lead into the eighth inning. Hattiesburg, however, came back with five runs in the eighth and three more in the ninth to gain the right to play South Bend for the title. The Rocks' runs in the eighth came on two base hits, two costly West Palm Beach errors, and two walks. In the ninth, base hits by catcher Randy Pickering, his third hit of the day, and outfielder Howard Thomley brought the winning run to the plate. Left-handed-hitting Stan Massengale responded with a walk-off hit that put the Rocks in the final against South Bend.[10]

Manager Mel Machuca had his South Bend club ready for the 1977 final against Hattiesburg. Greg Heyde pitched as sharp as ever, spreading seven Hattiesburg hits and allowing just one run. For South Bend, Schell went two-for-four, including a triple, to bring his final batting average to .441. He scored the first run on an error by the Hattiesburg third baseman. A moment later, Coker scored on a double steal. As they had done throughout the tournament, South Bend played flawless ball in the field. South Bend's 3–1 victory in the final gave them a 41–6 record and the first national title won by a team from the state of Indiana. Schell was the offensive leader in the final game as he had been all season. He led the team with a .429 batting average, 33 hits, and 17 stolen bases.[11]

Thirty years after his greatest triumph, Machuca reflected back and tried to explain the outcome. Somehow, in the course of the summer of 1977, "a relatively ordinary team … was able to accomplish the extraordinary." He believed the answer to the how question was commitment. Because of their unyielding work ethic, they were not the same team at the end of the season as they were at the beginning. "It is difficult [now] to find the same level of commitment…. It seems that nobody wants to work for the prize anymore," as his boys had done in 1977, he said. His players, of course, had much to do with winning the title. Jeff Coker, who signed with the Phillies, was second among regulars in almost every offensive category. Will Shepherd led in RBI. Pitching workhorses Greg Heyde and Dave Hankins each posted a 15–1 record.[12]

South Bend shortstop Bill Schell dominated the awards. He was selected Player of the Year and won the Louisville Slugger Award for the highest batting average in the national tournament, .441. The Rawlings Big Stick Award for most total bases (30) went to Doug Robertson of West Palm Beach. The newly created Dr. Irwin Cowger RBI Award went to Clifford Wenzel of Santa Monica. The James F. Daniel Sportsmanship Award was given to Scott Benedict, catcher of West Palm Beach.[13]

The *Berkshire Eagle* selected an All-Series team. It included: first base, Kevin Korve, Rapid City; second base, Dave Montanari (Santa Monica); third base, Craig Gero, West Palm Beach; shortstop, Bill Schell, South Bend; outfielder Doug Robertson, West Palm Beach; outfielder Randy Thomley, Hattiesburg; outfielder Jay Polydys, Trumbull; catcher

Gary Pickering, Hattiesburg; pitchers Tim Leary, Santa Monica; Greg Heyde, South Bend; Dave Hankins, South Bend; Greg Myers, Turnbull; and Jeff Andrews, Rapid City.[14]

In the late 1970s, parity overtook the American Legion World Series. In 1976, Santa Monica and Arlington Heights/Des Plaines were surprise one and two finishers. The following year, South Bend, in not just winning but dominating, did what no Indiana team had come close to accomplishing. Second-place Hattiesburg had existed only four years, and the Rocks would be a "one hit wonder," never again approaching what they accomplished in 1977. That trend of teams catching lightning in a bottle continued in 1978 when a team from Hialeah, Florida, that had never been to the World Series before, took home the trophy after going undefeated in tournament play. Sullivan-Babcock Post 32 of Hialeah arrived at Yakima, Washington, for the Series with an eye-opening record of 43 wins against a mere three losses. That commanded attention. Manager Louis Reilly, a detective on the Miami police force, had strong pitching, but he built his team around a running game. The year before, South Bend had demonstrated the advantage of putting stress on the opposition through a running game. Reilly took that practice to an extreme. Hialeah loved to steal and to take an extra base. To get to the ALWS in Yakima, they beat defending state champ West Palm Beach, the third-place finisher in the 1977 World Series, and then beat St. Petersburg, 7–1 and 12–2, to take the state title. They crushed St. Petersburg again, 15–0, in the Regional tourney. They stole 26 bases in the five-game Regional.[15]

Parker Field in Yakima, Washington, hosted the 1978 American Legion World Series. The field on the campus of Yakama Valley Community College dated to 1937. Since then, it had been home to the Pippins (1937–1941), Stars (1946–1947), Packers (1948), and Bears (1949–1966) of the Western International League. Hialeah quickly became the fan favorite. Eight of Hialeah's 15 players were Cuban-Americans. In some places, that would be reason to root against them, but in Yakima they were seen as exotics. Other teams in the ALWS included East Springfield, Massachusetts, Post 420, who boasted a big bopper in Pete Kumiega. He set an RBI record at the University of North Carolina but failed to get to the majors after five minor league seasons. James Caldwell Post 185 of Caldwell, New Jersey, reached the World Series for the first time. Dobie/South Houston Post 490 also appeared in the ALWS for the first time. Allen Park, Michigan Post 409 brought a 30–7 record to Yakima. They were led by shortstop David Boomer. New Ulm, Minnesota (22–6), had long been a hotbed of town teams, but they too had not experienced the World Series before. They did have two big-time hitters in Terry Steinbach, who would spend 13 seasons as a major league catcher, and Doug Palmer, who would set an American Legion record for the highest batting average in the tournament. Richey's Market, the Marketmen, of Corvallis, Oregon, representing Post 11, had knocked the Yakima Beetles out in the Regional finals. That was reason for local fans to root against them. Santa Monica, California, Post 123 (41–3), came with the most World Series experience. This was their fourth straight appearance in the World Series, having been national champions in 1976. They and Hialeah were pre-tournament favorites.[16]

Hialeah jumped into the Series running. They raced past Caldwell, New Jersey, in their opening game by a 6–3 score. Roberto Estrada pitched a strong game, and first baseman Ross Jones blasted a three-run homer. Allen Park upset Santa Monica, 9–6, in the opener thanks to Gene Vacca's homer and five RBI. East Springfield first baseman Pete Kumiega homered and drove home four runs in an 8–3 win over Corvallis. South Houston held off New Ulm, 7–5. The winning hit was pitcher Markus Brogdon's ninth-inning homer. In the second round, Hialeah ran all over Allen Park, winning 15–3. Third baseman Ivan Mesa and outfielder Orlando Fernandez each drove in four runs. One of the pre-tournament favorites, Santa Monica, went home, eliminated by Caldwell, 6–2. Despite Terry Steinbach's two homers and five runs batted in, Corvallis managed to eliminate New Ulm, 9–8. Shortstop Tim Atkinson belted a three-run homer in the eighth inning to tie the game. Richey's Market won it on pitcher Dave Opoien's ninth-inning RBI. East Springfield won its second straight, beating South Houston, 8–5.[17]

In the battle of unbeatens, Hialeah knocked off East Springfield by a 6–1 score. Corvallis held on to win over Allen Park, 12–9, thanks to John Pinion's grand slam. The loss eliminated the Michigan team. Caldwell followed by eliminating South Houston, 7–4. Despite its earlier loss to Hialeah, East Springfield came back to beat Caldwell, 8–4, to earn another shot at Hialeah. Hialeah then eliminated Corvallis, 15–4. Ross Jones padded his resume by gaining the win as pitcher and raised his batting average to .381 for the tournament. He also tripled in the seven-run third inning. Corvallis was hurt when its star, Harold Reynolds, left the game in the third inning with a shoulder separation.[18]

The 1978 championship game between Hialeah and East Springfield was the Series in miniature. Hialeah jumped out to a 6–0 lead on the way to a 7–4 victory. They stole nine bases in the win. Ivan Mesa homered in the seventh inning, one of his three hits. Ross Jones also had three hits and three runs batted in. Outfielder Tomas "Tommy" Gil set a Series record by stealing six bases. Hialeah went through the Series undefeated, averaging ten runs per game. Coach Lou Reilly believed his champions were the best team "I've ever had." None would argue that. They finished the season with a 43–3 record.[19]

Hialeah first baseman Ross Jones was named the 1978 Player of the Year. The 6-foot-2, 180-pounder was drafted in the first round of the MLB free agent draft, but he elected to attend the University of Miami before turning professional. After Miami, he spent three years in the majors with the New York Mets, Seattle, and Kansas City. Cuban-born teammate Ivan Mesa, who batted .520 and drove in 19 runs, captured the Big Stick Award for most total bases. Hialeah coach Lou Reilly was tabbed for the Leadership Award. Glenn Roe of Caldwell received the Bob Feller Award for outstanding pitching. Pete Kumiega of East Springfield won the award for most runs batted in, while teammate John Maner was named the recipient of the Sportsmanship Award. Doug Palmer of New Ulm set the World Series record, still standing, with his .659 batting average.[20]

If the previous three years, 1976–1978, spotlighted unlikely, surprise, or one-shot wonders in the World Series, 1979 saw an old, established team reign supreme, but in a new and different location. The 1979 ALWS location was Greenville, Mississippi, a dusty county seat town of 40,000 in the heart of the Mississippi Delta. In late July and early August, the delta could be counted on to be stifling, hot and humid. In 1979 the weather did not disappoint, hovering around 100 degrees and 80 per cent humidity. Games were commonly halted to allow umpires to hydrate and cool down. Back in the 1930s and 1940s, the American Legion World Series were commonly played in mill towns of North and South Carolina; too often they ended in a racial incident. This was the first and only time the World Series was played in Mississippi, but in 1979 there were no such incidents, a sign of how far America had come in a generation.[21]

Two of the eight clubs that gathered for the World Series were comfortable to be there. Rapid City, South Dakota, Post 22, under long-time coach Dave Ploof, had last appeared in the Series in 1977 and had hosted it in 1975. Ploof had captured ten South Dakota state titles. Yakima's Logan-Wheeler Post 36 had won the national title in 1953 and 1975. They hosted the Series in 1954 and 1978. Known as the Pepsi Beetles, they possessed a long tradition of quality baseball. In the 1950s, they won five consecutive state titles, but then had an 11-year gap before picking up another in 1965. Bob Garretson took over the reins of the club from his father in 1975 and promptly won a World Series. His team had also appeared in the Series in 1976. If there was any doubt about Yakima, the Beetles erased it with a 28–0 spanking of Coeur d'Alene in the 1979 Regional before beating Milton-Freewater, Oregon, 8–3, in the final. So both Rapid City and Yakima knew the process.[22]

The other six teams in the ALWS expressed varying degrees of confidence as the tournament began. Barrington, Rhode Island Post 158, a middle-class suburb of East Providence (25–7), hoped to win a game or two; they turned out to be stronger than anticipated. Shaler Township Post 785 (36–9), from western Pennsylvania, drew players from the towns of Shaler, Millvale, and Etna, north of Pittsburgh. Coach Walt Banze felt he suffered from lack of funds. "I'm tired from hassling over where the money's coming from," he moaned.[23] Gainesville, Georgia, Post 7 (34–8) made its first appearance in the Series. They had beaten Orangeburg, South Carolina, Orlando, Florida, and Hamlet, North Carolina, in the Southeast Regional at Greer, South Carolina. Tulsa, Oklahoma, Post 1 (54–14) and Barrington, Illinois, Post 158 (34–16) were happy to be there. Rapid City Post 12 (58–12) looked good on paper. They beat Springfield, Missouri, 12–1, in the Regional final. Shortstop Steve Wolff was the MVP of the Regional. They looked like a favorite in the World Series. The Logan-Wheeler Post 36 Beetles of Yakima remained co-favorites at the start of play. They brought a 61–18 record to the ALWS. Norwalk, California Post 359 (29–3) looked as if they could be the surprise team.[24]

In the big opening day surprise, Rapid City lost to Barrington, Illinois, 9–2. Steve Peterson blasted two homers for the winners, and Bill Prosksa also homered and drove in three runs. Favorite Yakima rolled over Tulsa, 5–3, thanks to shortstop John Cruz's homer and Bruce Dunn's pitching. Barrington, Rhode Island, took out Gainesville, 7–2. Norwalk had an easy time beating Shaler, 9–2. On the next day, the temperature cranked up to 94 degrees, and the humidity reached 80 per cent. Against Rapid City, another first-round loser, Tulsa Post 1 scored two runs in the ninth inning to win, 5–4. The loss knocked Rapid City out of the competition. Gainesville eliminated Shaler in 10 innings by a 5–3 score. Dewayne Williams homered in the ninth, and a double by Jim Edwards broke the game open. Norwalk beat Barrington, Rhode Island, 5–3, as Brian Reams and Mark Friedly homered. Center fielder Dave Trimble homered, and Bill Rice pitched a solid game to lead the Yakima Beetles to an 8–2 triumph over Barrington, Illinois.[25]

The tournament's two remaining undefeated teams, Yakima and Norwalk, California, met next. Yakima prevailed by a 6–4 score. The two Barringtons won on day three. Barrington, Rhode Island's, Ernest Pacheco limited Tulsa to four hits in winning, 5–0. Barrington, Illinois, needed Thomas Talashek's ninth-inning RBI to carry them to a 3–2 win, thereby ending Gainesville's chances. Against Barrington, Rhode Island, the Beetles stumbled, losing 6–3. Barrington, Rhode Island, next beat Barrington, Illinois, 3–2, in 11 innings to set up the championship game against Yakima. Scott Vierra drove home Roger Vierra in the 11th inning for the win.[26]

The 1979 final between Yakima and Barrington, Rhode Island, the second game of the day for Barrington, was played in 100-degree temperature and heavy humidity. Yakima jumped ahead with a five-run first inning to set the tone. Yakima shortstop Juan Cruz popped a three-run homer, while Doug Greefe collected four hits, including a homer, and scored four times. Pitcher Bruce Dunn gave up 10 hits to Barrington, but he kept them well spaced; he got credit for the win. Yakima rolled to the championship, 13–6. It was Yakima's third title, having won in 1953 and 1975.[27]

In selecting the Player of the Year, voters looked past Juan Cruz, Yakima's power-hitting shortstop, who set a record for the most runs batted in during national play with 30, to pick his teammate, second baseman Pat Allen. Cruz did receive the Dr. Irwin L. "Click" Cowger RBI Award and the Rawlings Big Stick Award for the most total bases. The Bob Feller Award went to Brian Keith Reams of Norwalk, California. (The award, named after the first Legion graduate to be inducted into the National Baseball Hall of Fame, went to the pitcher who compiled the most strikeouts in the regional and national competition.) The Louisville Slugger Award for highest batting average went to Steve Wolf of Rapid City, who compiled a .423 average. Stephen Michael Peterson of Barrington, Illinois, received the Sportsmanship Award.[28]

When the calendar turned to 1980, it not only marked the beginning of a new decade, it also marked a decade-long dominance by the Mid–Atlantic Region. Over the next 11 years, a team from Region 2 either won the World Series or finished second in ten of those years. Tiny Boyertown, a village of under 4,000 in rural southeastern Pennsylvania, set the standard. They won the Series twice, in 1982 and 1987, and finished second three times, in 1980, 1983, and 1988. The Boyertown community loved and supported their Bears. No better evidence of that support could be found than in the shining new stadium the community built for its team. By the end of the Mid–Atlantic era, Brooklawn, New Jersey, emerged as challenger to Boyertown's dominance. Along the way, teams from Virginia and Maryland also took national titles.

In politics, 1980 brought a decisive victory for the Republicans. With Ronald Reagan, the "Teflon president," in office for eight years, followed by four years of George H. W. Bush, political conservatives were free to make sweeping changes. At the beginning of the decade, the American electorate worried about inflation without growth at home and reduced influence abroad. Tough individuals like movie heroes "Dirty Harry" Callahan and John Rambo took care of the bad guys. The implied message was that neither government bureaucracies nor well-meaning elitist politicians could solve society's problems. Politically, the Republican answer lay in cutting taxes and reducing regulation. These policies greatly benefited the rich and hurt working-class people; the lowest one-fifth of income earners got poorer, and the wealthiest one-fifth benefited greatly.

After winning the 1979 ALWS title in convincing fashion, Yakima seemed poised to take back-to-back titles, until a lightly regarded team from Honolulu ambushed them. The team from Moiliili, a neighborhood in Honolulu, brought only 13 players because several opted for high school football practice. Their star was a hefty, some labeled him "chubby," left-handed pitcher named Sid Fernandez, who blew batters away with a sneaky 94 mile per hour fastball and a wicked slider. In Region 7 tournament play, he caught the eye of scouts when he struck out 19 Casper, Wyoming, batters. His mates struggled against Roseburg, Oregon, before winning, 9–8, in 12 innings. Then they surprised Yakima, 11–5. In the Regional final, Fernandez shut Yakima down without a hit while striking out 18 batters in Honolulu's 1–0 victory.[29]

The Honolulu team had several strikes against them. Their small roster limited what moves the coach, Clyde Hayashida, could make. Fernandez came down with a sore arm after the Regional but continued to pitch. A majority of the players bore Japanese names, including first baseman Howard Kapuinai, second baseman Wade Okuma, third baseman Ross Hayaski, shortstop David Nakama, outfielder Corey Okemura, catcher Keith Komeioji, and pitcher Gary Nishikawa. The dominance of Japanese names on the roster could have turned fans in isolated Ely, Minnesota, against them. So could their practice, common in Japanese baseball but not in American, of all the team gathering outside the foul lines after each half-inning to congratulate and encourage each other. *Minneapolis Star* sports columnist Bill Hengen believed the Hawaiians "seldom received a 'break' on possible strikes," and "their batters occasionally found that the strike zone had become elastic and stretched high, wide, inside and outside." Nor did the early fall weather favor the boys from Honolulu; temperatures dipped into the 30s in the evening. On the other hand, they did not beat themselves. Second-place Boyertown committed 22 errors and had several mental mistakes in the five games, while Honolulu was charged with just five errors. Local fans adopted the Hawaiians and rooted for them throughout the World Series.[30]

The 1980 World Series was played at Veterans Memorial Stadium in Ely, Minnesota, August 28 through September 1, on a field maintained by the local high school. Ely, a town of 4,800 in northeast Minnesota, prided itself on being a sportsmen's center for fishing, hiking, canoeing, and hunting, but the limited road system made it difficult to reach, assuring a small attendance at the Series. The roster of teams began with Section One champion West Warwick, Rhode Island, Post 2, sponsored by Penalty Box Sports. The Boyertown Bears, Post 471, Pennsylvania state champs the past three years, and a 1977 ALWS team (50–10), were developing a powerhouse program. Hialeah, Florida Post 32 (47–9) brought a team with a majority of its players Cuban-born. New Orleans, Post 125, composed of players from Jesuit High School, sponsored by Odeco Drillers, were led by Will Clark, who would spend 15 years in the major leagues. Waukegan, Illinois, Post 281 (32–8) depended on the arm of Ed Sedar, who posted a 17–0 record during the regular season. Crestwood, Missouri (35–13), from the greater St. Louis area, gained the ALWS by narrowly beating Independence, 11–10. They had little expectation of going deep in the Series. Moiliili, Honolulu, Hawaii (25–5) in its Regional championship defeated defending national champion Yakima, 1–0, behind Sid Fernandez's no-hitter. Finally, Palo Alto, California Post 375 brought lower expectations than most California teams.[31]

Only Honolulu and Boyertown survived the first two days without a loss. On the opening day, Honolulu slipped past Waukegan, 3–2, behind Fernandez's gutty performance. Pete Kameiji drove in the winning run. Boyertown's John Babel threw a nifty three-hitter in recording his 17th win against just one loss, in the Bears' 2–1 opening victory. Crestwood beat Warwick behind the pitching of lefty Brad Macko. He held Warwick to four hits and struck out 11. Bob Melvin of Palo Alto garnered five RBI in the Californians' 8–4 win over Hialeah. The Hawaiians had an easier time with Palo Alto, winning 6–1. Pitcher Ross Hayaski banged a home run, drove in three runs, and got the win, while Howard Kapuinai drove in two runs. Boyertown won its second straight game, beating Crestwood by a 7–5 score. Hialeah eliminated Waukegan, 4–2, on Thomas Gil's home run. Despite a four-hour rain delay, New Orleans had enough to eliminate Warwick. Dick Wentz struck out 14 in the 6–3 victory.[32]

Atop the winners' bracket, Boyertown took down Honolulu, 6–3, in ten innings. Boyertown pitcher John Bael held Moiliili in check. He allowed just three hits. Randy Moyer drove in three runs. A tired Sid Fernandez was removed in the tenth inning with the game tied, 3—3. Hialeah remained alive. It had absorbed an opening loss to Palo Alto, but went on to beat Waukegan, 4–2, a game in which Thomas Gil hit the decisive home run, and Crestwood, 5–4, in 11 innings behind Gil's double, home run, and two RBI. New Orleans stayed alive by beating Palo Alto, 10–3. New Orleans, however, failed to keep its streak going, losing to Hawaii, 15–3. Hawaii's giant (6-foot-1, 240 pounds) Howard Kapuinai collected four hits.[33]

Continuing on its run, Hialeah upset Boyertown, 5–1. With three teams having one loss—Boyertown, Hialeah, and Honolulu—Boyertown got the bye by virtue of being the last to lose. Honolulu then put an end to Hialeah's run with a 7–4 win. Moiliili got four runs in the fourth inning on three singles, a two-run error, and Vince Bedoya's two-run double. Second baseman Wade Okuma's triple keyed a sixth-inning uprising, aided by another Hialeah error.[34]

The 1980 championship game between Boyertown and Honolulu, a first for both teams, was played before a tiny crowd of 1,986 chilly fans. They witnessed a back-and-forth thriller. Boyertown's Neil Fox brought home a run in the first inning. Moiliili tied it in the second when Ross Hayashi doubled, took third on an error, and scored on a wild pitch. Ron Moyer singled home a run in the third inning, but Hawaii got that run back with an unearned run in the bottom of the inning. Boyertown went up, 4–2, in the fifth inning on RBI singles by Neil Fox and Tim Koch against lefty Gary Nishikawa. Hawaii got one run back when Vince Bedoya walked, advanced to third on a hit-and-run, and scored on yet another Boyertown error. With Dave Nakama on board, Lance Belen crushed a 390-foot home run in the fifth to erase the Bears' lead. Marlin "Fish" Van Fleet shut Boyertown down in the eighth and ninth innings to preserve the win. Moiliili survived playing four games in 30 hours to claim the championship. They finished the season with a 25–5 record.[35]

Sid Fernandez, who won two games in the ALWS and struck out 55 in national play, made a strong case for Player of the Year Award, but had to settle for the Bob Feller Award. Tomas "Tommy" Gil, the Cuban-born outfielder for Hialeah, took home the Player of the Year Award and the Rawlings' Big Stick Award for most total bases. He batted .409 with two homers and five RBI in five games. Cedric Gray of Palo Alto won the Louisville Slugger Award for his .567 batting average. Howard Kapuinai, Honolulu first baseman, collected 17 RBI to capture the Cowger RBI Award. Finally, Bob Melvin, Palo Alto pitcher, was voted the Sportsmanship Award. Of course, the best prospects do not always merit awards. Had there been a best prospect award, it would have gone either to "El Sid" or to Will Clark of the Odeco Drillers and New Orleans Jesuit High School. Clark played in the majors from 1985–2000 for San Francisco and Texas. He played in six All-Star Games and seven World Series.[36]

Attendance at the ALWS in cold and wet Ely disappointed. At 18,962, it was more than the Series had drawn the previous year in the hot and humid Mississippi Delta town of Greenville, where only 14, 661 attended. Both were dwarfed by the 24,605 that attended at Yakima in 1978 and Manchester, New Hampshire, in 1977. With those numbers in mind, the Legion reverted to the small Carolina mill towns that had been its bread-and-butter in the 1930s by selecting Sumter, South Carolina, to host the World Series for 1981. Games were played at Riley Park, a tidy little facility built in 1934 with only 2,000 seats under roof, and another 2,000 in bleachers. It was home to the University of South Carolina–Sumter, Morris College, Sumter American Legion P-15s, and the Sumter Braves. Its dimensions were rather standard: 337 feet, 372 feet, and 338 feet.[37]

Several of the eight teams in the 1981 ALWS sported gaudy records. Tulsa, Oklahoma Carson-Wilson Post 1 Contractors had lost just one game, but played only 24 contests, so it was easy for people to think their record suspect. Sacramento, California, sponsored by Kennedy Baseball Boosters, came in with a record of 40 wins against four losses. R. C. Winters Construction team from Bellevue, Washington, had posted a 40–5 record. Omaha, Nebraska Post 1, always seemed to have a contender; this year they had the most experience, having played 69 games, winning 62 of them. Composed of boys from perennial high school power Creighton Prep, they reached the Series by beating Rapid City, another perennial power, 6–0, in the Central Plains Regional. The winning pitcher was lefty Tim Daze, who brought a record of 19–0 to the Series. The Omaha team, sponsored by Nebraska Credit Union, was one of the favorites to take home the championship trophy. West Tampa caught people's attention when they pounded Greer, South Carolina, by a 25–2 score in the Southeast Regional final. They entered the Series with a 35–4 record. Richmond, Virginia's James Waters Post 361 won the Mid–Atlantic Regional with a 38–5 record Their victories over 1980's second-place club, Boyertown, Pennsylvania, and then Brooklawn. New Jersey, garnered them support among the press. Meriden, Connecticut, sported a 41–5 record. They slipped into the ALWS by beating Westbrook, Maine, 6–5, on Fred Parcesepe's RBI in the ninth inning, but the New England Regional winners never got much credit. The final team, the Owensboro, Kentucky, Bombers of James L. Yates Post 9, almost failed to make the Series. After winning the Great Lakes Regional by beating Indianapolis, 11–6, their team manager let it be known that they could not get even 13 players to go to South Carolina. Players, he moaned, either had college, or football or college baseball tryouts, or just did not want to travel to the South. Finally, they got a 13th player to agree to play in the Series, but their modest 38–16 record scared no one.[38]

West Tampa and Meriden came through the first two rounds as the only undefeated teams. Meriden, behind the pitching of George Purcell, got past Tulsa, 2–1, and then, with John Boomber on the mound, beat Bellevue by the same score. West Tampa shut out Owensboro, 9–0 with Lou Armado on the hill, and then beat Omaha, 6–3, behind the pitching of Dave Magadan and the hitting of Greg Burgner, who drove in three runs. Bellevue got home runs from Brent Blum and Billy Moore to beat Richmond, 10–3. Omaha beat Sacramento with ease by a 10–2 score, before falling to West Tampa. Richmond, after losing to Bellevue, pounded Tulsa, 17–1, to send the Contractors home. Mike Hoggs had four of Richmond's 16 hits. In the winners' bracket, West Tampa became the only undefeated team when Noel Alphonso singled Magadan home in the eighth inning for a 9–8 win over Owensboro.[39]

Bellevue, with a win and a loss, upset West Tampa, 3–2, as Noel Alphonso walked in the winning run. Despite the loss, West Tampa got the bye into the championship game, leaving Richmond and Bellevue to contest the other final slot. Richmond took a 6–2 lead by scoring six runs in the bottom of the sixth. Kevin Sickinger's double was the only extra-base hit in the offensive explosion. Bellevue refused to fold and came back to tie the game, 6–6. In the bottom of the ninth, Mike Hogge banged a run-scoring double for the 7–6 Richmond win.[40]

The 1981 championship game between West Tampa and Richmond went down to the final pitch before being decided. West Tampa came back twice and needed great relief pitching from Magadan to seal the victory. Tampa overcame a 4–0 deficit with four runs in the fifth inning. A second-inning double by Richmond's Oscar Talley, which had netted two runs, had given Richmond the early lead. Hits by Magadan and second baseman Brian Hubbard, plus two Richmond errors, netted the tying runs. Richmond retook the lead with a run in the seventh inning thanks to two West Tampa errors. Doubles by

Magadan and first baseman George Hornik tied the game again in the seventh. Hornik appeared to ice the game with an RBI single in the eighth. With two Richmond runners on base in the ninth, coach Frank Permuy brought Magadan to the mound to record the final two outs and give West Tampa a 6–5 victory, and the 1981 title.[41]

Dave Magadan, a sophomore at the University of Alabama, was named Player of the Year. He went on to play 16 seasons in the majors, mostly for the New York Mets, before finishing with six other clubs (San Diego, Oakland, Florida, Chicago Cubs, Seattle, and Houston). Following his playing career, he served as hitting coach for the Red Sox, Diamondbacks, and Padres. Victor Garcia, catcher for West Tampa, won the Dr. Irvin "Click" Cowger RBI Award. Kevin Sickinger of Richmond took home the Big Stick Award for extra-base hits. Keith Eric Peterson of Bellevue was awarded the Sportsmanship Award. Tulsa first baseman Roger Hulse took the Louisville Slugger Award by compiling a .478 average. Scott Anderson of Bellevue took the Bob Feller Pitching Award with 44 strikeouts.[42]

Sumter, South Carolina, had been a questionable site for the World Series, coming after disappointing attendance the previous two years at Greenville, Mississippi, and Ely, Minnesota, where attendance had been 14,661 and 18,962. Sumter's Riley Park proved the naysayers correct; the 1981 Series drew only 16,371 spectators for 15 games. By contrast, the Little League World Series drew far more to their championship game alone.

The 1982 season belonged to Boyertown, Pennsylvania. Not only did the Bears win the ALWS, but brand-new Bears Stadium drew 34,023 fans, the most since the ALWS went to an eight-team format. Post 471 of Boyertown had been developing a powerhouse program through the 1970s. In 1969, long-time coach Melvin "Buck" Rhoads brought on Dick Ludy, who had led the high school team to a 24–1 record, as assistant coach. Boyertown was poised to raise their play to another level. That year the Bears won their first state championship. Since Pennsylvania, with 462 teams, had more Legion teams than any state, constituting 11 per cent of all Legion teams, winning the state title was no small feat. They continued to win, taking state titles in 1971, 1976, 1977, and 1978. In the 1980s, they won the state title seven times. Rhoads installed a strategy that featured bunting and running, taking pitches, and putting the ball in play. To that basic formula, Ludy added outstanding pitching and confidence; his teams started talking about the World Series on day one of practice. His Bears knew they were good, but they played to win one game at a time. They had won the state title in 1976, 1977, and 1978 and their first Mid–Atlantic title in 1977. They were back in the World Series in 1980, when they finished second to Sid Fernandez's Honolulu team.[43]

The Boyertown Baseball Committee, the brainchild of Clarence "Bud" Garber, owner of a local well-drilling company, began in the late 1970s to plan for hosting the ALWS. Don Specht, a real estate and insurance man, became involved when his son David was a catcher on the 1969–1971 teams. Ken Ellis, a local contractor, served as treasurer of the group. To get the attention of George Rulon, they arranged to host the 1979 Mid–Atlantic Regional Tournament. The only problem was that they lacked an appropriate field. The Legion team played on a field behind the high school where most fans sat in lawn chairs down the foul lines. So Boyertown's first foray into American Legion turf was played at Reading's Memorial Stadium, 33 miles from Boyertown. Based on the success of the Mid–Atlantic Tournament and the promise of a brand-new stadium in Boyertown, the Boyertown Baseball Committee made its proposal to host the 1982 World Series. Rulon was convinced by the proposal and gave his support to Boyertown.

Specht was the driving force behind the drive to build a stadium. The school board agreed to donate land for the field if the Army Corps of Engineers would undertake site preparation. The Corps, however, turned down the proposal. The School Board then agreed to sell a tract of land near the high school to the Legion group. Ken Ellis offered to design and build the stadium for cost, but nothing had happened by spring 1981, when ground-breaking took place. Actually, opposition had developed, especially from the local newspaper, the *Boyertown Times*. Specht, chairman of the stadium project, began to implore and berate his colleagues, and he met with success. The organizers aimed for a roofed brick park, seating 3,500, with high-quality turf and lights. The construction took place between March 1981 and the stadium dedication in August 1982. The stadium cost at $75,000 but was mortgaged for $600,000. Most of the work was done by volunteers, while Specht and Garber raised money. They raised enough to pay off the mortgage before the stadium opened. "Fanaticism, pure and simple," one observer described Boyertown's effort.[44]

Even with a brand spanking new stadium, Boyertown faced obstacles. With a population of 3,800, it was the smallest town ever to host an American Legion World Series. Not only was it small, it was also isolated. Transportation to Boyertown was not easy. Planes needed to fly into either Philadelphia or Lehigh Valley Airport near Allentown. Visitors could find lodging in the Pottstown area, home of the *Pottstown Mercury,* the nearest daily newspaper. The local population, however, was crazy for its Bears, both the high school, which went 24–1 in the spring of 1982, and the Legion team. Home teams

Bear's Stadium, Boyertown, Pennsylvania built for the Legion team by local volunteers, opened in 1982 for the American Legion World Series, which the Bears won. Boyertown reigned as the dominant team of the 1980s. Boyertown was on of the places considered to be the permanent home for the Legion World Series (courtesy of Dave Sherman).

had not fared well in the ALWS which they hosted. It was thought by many that the host team had *never* won a Series; in fact, the host had not won since 1941. Besides, although Pennsylvania had the largest number of Legion teams, it had never won a World Series.[45]

The Generals of Lafayette, California Post 517 and Edina, Minnesota Post 471 looked to be the strongest challengers to Boyertown. The team from Lafayette (32–16) depended on the power hitting of Ron DeLucchi. The Generals beat Medford, Oregon, twice by scores of 3–2 and 7–6 to make the World Series. Edina came in with an impressive 43–5 record. In Rob Wassenaar, Edina boasted the most dominant pitcher in the field. His 13–1 record and ERA of 0.92 were eye-popping. Shortstop Steve Blietz had hit .471 for Edina. They had won five straight games in the Regional, beating Fenton, Missouri, 1–0, Bismarck, North Dakota, 3–1, Des Moines, Iowa, 5–4, Rapid City, South Dakota, 8–3, and Fenton again by another 1–0 score. Other teams believed they stood a chance in the World Series. Grand Junction, Colorado's Robbins-McCullen Post 37 compiled a 50–10 record, which included a win over Fullerton, California, 13–2. to make the Series. Manchester, New Hampshire, Henry Sweeney Post 2 beat Utica, New York, for the Region One title and a seat in the Series. Starkville, Mississippi's Oktibbeba Post 13 (33–11) beat the tough Hamlet, North Carolina, team, 6–2, in the championship of Region Three. Richmond, Kentucky's Jesse M. Dykes Post 12 (45–14) nosed out Lafayette, Louisiana, 9–8, to take the Region Four title. Kokomo, Indiana, Post 6 came in with a 44–9 record which included a 5–1 defeat of Allen Park, Michigan.[46]

Based on its 54–3 record, Boyertown appeared to be one of the Opening Day favorites. They had beaten Claymont, Delaware, 7–1, in the Mid–Atlantic finals. Coach Dick Ludy took over in 1971 and ran off a string of state titles in 1971, 1976, 1977, 1978, 1981, and 1982. The Bears always had strong pitching, and 1982 was no exception. John Ludy, the coach's nephew, compiled a record of 18 wins and no losses, with a 1.30 ERA. Evan Snyder had a 12–1 pitching record, but his strength as an outfielder made him the team MVP. He batted .565 at the Regional. Lefty Durrell Schoenly compiled a tidy 7–0 record. The Kokomo manager said of him, "If he's their number 3 [pitcher], we are in deep trouble." Snyder and Ludy were the strongest batters, but infielder Tim Koch batted .401 during the season. Catcher Andy Ruppert earned Most Valuable Player recognition at the Region 2 tournament.[47]

In the opening round, Boyertown and Edina had little trouble with Manchester (4–1) and Starkville (14–8) respectively. Lafayette and Kokomo struggled to get one-run victories over Grand Junction (7–6) and Richmond (6–5). In elimination games on day two, Grand Junction rolled to an easy victory to oust Richmond by a 12–2 score, but Starkville barely managed to beat Manchester, 4–3. Boyertown controlled Edina, 4–1, behind Snyder's three-hitter. Kokomo won its second game, 9–8, over Lafayette. The California lads then had little trouble in closing down Starkville, 8–0, as Doug Robbins homered and drove in four runs. Carl Schoelkopf allowed just five hits. Boyertown's Schoenly pitched a four-hitter, striking out 12 Kokomo batters in an 8–3 win, but Kokomo hurt their own cause by committing seven errors. The win left Boyertown as the only undefeated team after 11 games.[48]

Kokomo, Grand Junction, and Lafayette battled it out for the right to take on Boyertown. Against Grand Junction, Kokomo scored seven runs in the first inning, then watched as Grand Junction chipped away and exploded for seven runs in the eighth inning for a 12–7 win that sent Kokomo home. Lafayette pulled off the upset of the Series beating Boyertown, 7–2. Kevin Roullier limited the Bears to three hits, and Ron Delucchi drove in three runs for Lafayette. Suddenly, it looked as if Lafayette could roll to the title. They had little trouble putting away Grand Junction, winning 5–1.[49]

In the 1982 championship game, 6,563 fans, far more than Boyertown's population, packed Bears Stadium for the Boyertown-Lafayette Generals final, most of those fans, of course, rooting for the Bears. Boyertown came up with seven runs in the second inning to take a commanding lead. Ivan Snyder had four hits and three RBI in the game. Boyertown first baseman Scott Gilbert chipped in with two doubles and a triple and scored four runs. By the seventh inning, Boyertown had a comfortable 14–0 lead, but Lafayette picked up three runs in the seventh and five in the eighth to scare the Bears, though the final score remained 14–8.[50]

Worthy of note, Gilbert scored 19 runs in the tourney, just one shy of J. W. Porter's 1949 record. Snyder's four hits in the championship game gave him an even .600 batting average for the national games. For the Series, tiny Boyertown drew 34,023 fans to the 15 games. That was the highest attendance since Omaha in 1950. The victory gave coach Dick Ludy a record of 460 wins against 74 losses since becoming head coach in 1971, a winning percentage of .861. His 1982 Legion record closed out at 54–3. Not surprisingly, Ludy said, "This was the best *team* I ever had."[51]

Snyder's robust batting average of .600 earned him the Louisville Slugger Award. His 27 hits for the Series tied him with J. W. Porter, who accomplished the record in 1949. Snyder received the Player of the Year Award as well. Lafayette slugger Ron DeLucchi earned both the Irvin L. Cowger RBI Award and the Big Stick Award. Edina's Rob Wassenaar took home the Bob Feller Award with 34 strikeouts. The Sportsmanship Award went to Michael David Hufhand of Kokomo.

George Rulon, the director of American Legion baseball, was from the Dakotas and preferred to locate the Legion World Series there, but he also needed to turn a profit as they had done in 1982 in Boyertown. So the 1983 Series went to Fargo, North Dakota, where Rulon had started his career. Its Jack Williams Stadium was, like Boyertown, Legion-owned and operated. It was not large, seating only 2,291 in permanent seats, but bleacher seats and standing room could bring crowds of 5,000 or more. Floods from the Red River of the North ravaged the field almost every spring. The facility was dedicated in 1966 after construction of the lighting system. The stadium was named after former North Dakota Legion Adjutant Jack Williams, one of the originators and supporters of Legion baseball, who died in 1967. The Stadium served as home to the Fargo Post 2 Governors.[52]

Boyertown appeared primed to repeat as national champions in 1983. They returned pitcher John Ludy, who would be the 1983 Bob Feller Award winner. He had a record of 19–0 in 1982, and this year posted an 18–0 record with a minuscule earned run average of 0.11. Crafty lefty Durrell Schoenly again lent support. The Bears got to the ALWS by beating Denbigh, Virginia, in the Mid–Atlantic finals, 7–3. Edina, Minnesota, a team that finished fifth in 1982 but showed flashes of brilliance, was set to challenge Boyertown. In hard-throwing Bob Wassenaar, who entered with a 12–0 record, they matched Ludy. Edina compiled a record of 41 wins against six losses. They had battled to the wire with New Ulm in the state tourney to win their second consecutive title. After losing the first contest, Edina won, 1–0 and 2–1. Wassenaar won both games, and Brian Martinson got credit for saves in both games. Coach Bruce Barron remembered thinking, "A championship team aspires to that championship before the season even starts."[53] Other teams with a good chance of winning the World Series included San Mateo, California, New Orleans

Jack Williams Stadium, Fargo, North Dakota, like Bear's Stadium, was built exclusively for Legion baseball and commonly hosted the American Legion World Series. The neighboring Red River of the North floods the field almost every spring (courtesy www.post2baseball.com).

East Post 367, and the Leasurer-Blackton Post 239 of Worthington, Ohio (45–0). The San Mateo, California, Post 82 Shockers, from a Peninsula community near San Francisco, won the California title with 61–8–3 record. Greg Jefferies led San Mateo with a .550 batting average. New Orleans featured the hitting of Reynaldo "Chito" Martinez, who won the Regional MVP award for batting .676. Worthington, a suburb of Columbus, also featured offense. The team posted a batting average of .310. Others in the tournament were from Natick, Massachusetts, Hamlet, North Carolina, and Chico, California. The Edward P. Clark Post 107 of Natick came in with a 38–4 record, having beaten Bristol, Connecticut, 10–2, to reach the ALWS. Hamlet Post 49 (36–14) had to beat North Charleston, South Carolina, which they did, 9–4. Hamlet was just happy to be in the Series for the first time. Chico, California, Post 17, the Blackhawks (46–10), were also making their first World Series appearance. The Blackhawks only made it because California, along with Pennsylvania, got to send two teams to Regionals. They beat Medford, Oregon, 8–7, in Region 7 in Caspar, Wyoming.[54]

Edina drew Boyertown in the first-round feature game. Bob Wassenaar pitched like a pro, shutting Boyertown down with just four hits and no runs, striking out 10 in a 4–0 victory. Edina took a 1–0 led in the first inning on Pat Donohue's RBI double. Catcher Mike Holloran led the attack with two triples; his second scored Wassenaar with Edina's final run. San Mateo, Chico, and Worthington also won first-round games. San Mateo beat New Orleans on two homers. Their leading hitter, Greg Jefferies, crushed one of them, Scott DeLucchi the other. Chico managed to just slip past Hamlet, 2–1, in ten innings. Worthington had little trouble with Natick, winning 4–1. Mark Hertel's RBI and

Jay Hammond's homer led the way. On the second day, Edina slaughtered Chico, 17–0, as they pounded out 22 hits, five by first baseman Pat Donohue. They got their second shutout, this one from Pat Egan. Boyertown eliminated Hamlet by a 12–4 score. Pitcher Durrell Schoenly upped his record to 15–2. Natick jumped out to a 7–0 lead, but New Orleans scored four runs in the ninth inning to send Natick packing, winning 11–7. Chito Martinez drove in three runs to key New Orleans' comeback. Worthington took out San Mateo, 8–2, as Kevin Ubert rapped out three hits, driving in two runs. After two days, Edina and Worthington remained undefeated.[55]

Boyertown and New Orleans looked to be strong contenders to come through the losers' bracket. Boyertown knocked San Mateo out of the Series, 9–7. Schoenly picked up his second win and drove in three runs himself. New Orleans had little trouble with Chico as they banged out a record 28 hits and scored a 16–6 victory. Chito Martinez homered and added to his record 28 hits in the tournament. That eliminated Chico.

In a battle of the last undefeated teams, Edina displayed its domination, topping Worthington, 3–0. Run-scoring hits came from Pat Donohue, Dan Carroll, and Mike Halloran. Worthington loaded the bases in the ninth inning, but Pat Egan came on to close out the game. In the next game, it was Boyertown beating Worthington by a 6–2 score. Ludy got the win. In the upset of the Series, the final undefeated team, Edina, fell to New Orleans, 15–6. Edina, however, had already qualified for the championship game. Then Boyertown punished New Orleans with a 10–6 elimination win, guaranteeing at least a third-place finish.[56]

In the championship game of 1983, Boyertown appeared destined to win back-to-back titles when it jumped out to an early 4–0 lead. After a 34-minute rain delay in the first inning, John Ludy drove in two runs, while shortstop Greg Gilbert and first baseman Scott Gilbert had one each. Edina, however, refused to quit. They scored three runs in the eighth inning. Two walks set the table for Edina. Donahue drove them in. Ludy took the mound for Boyertown and induced a doubleplay ball, but Boyertown failed to turn the double play, allowing the third run to score. In the ninth inning, with one out, Mark Hoffman singled. Boyertown again failed to turn the double play. Edina second baseman Carl Ramsth punched a bloop "Texas Leaguer" to short left for what appeared to be the second out. Left fielder Tony Shade got his glove on the ball, but a collision with shortstop Greg Gilbert knocked the ball loose, allowing the tying run to score. Pat Dono-hue drove in the run that finally gave Edina the lead, 5–4. In the bottom of the ninth, Boy-ertown got runners on first and third with no outs, but they failed to score. Appropriately, Wassenaar got the final out on a strikeout.[57]

The 1983 Player of the Year Award went to Edina catcher Mike Holloran. New Orle-ans' Reynaldo "Chito" Martinez, a native of Belize and graduate of Brother Martin High School, was the hitting powerhouse of the Series. He won the Triple Crown of hitting, taking the Louisville Slugger Award fwith a .566 average, the Big Stick Award with 44 total bases, and the RBI Award with 17. In addition, he set a record for hits with 30, break-ing the mark of 27 set in 1982 by Ivan Snyder of Boyertown. A second New Orleans hitter, David Ward, set a record with 23 runs scored, breaking the previous record set by J. W. Porter in 1949. The Bob Feller Award went to Boyertown's John Ludy, who also collected the Sportsmanship Award. The Jack Williams Leadership Awards went to Edina coach Bruce Barron and manager Clifton Olsen.[58]

The decision to hold the 1984 Legion World Series in New Orleans proved to be an unfortunate one. The Crescent City had hosted the Series twice before, in 1933 and

1937, without incident. In those years, the Series was held at the home of the New Orleans Pelicans of the Southern Association. In 1984, the site was Privateer Field, home of the University of New Orleans. There was really nothing wrong with the spacious field (330–400–330), but attendance was a minuscule 7,765 total for all 15 games. That figure was not the lowest ever, but it was the lowest in 25 years, since 1958 when Colorado Springs hosted the Series. The greatest problem seemed to have been scheduling the American Legion World Series against the Louisiana World Exposition (World's Fair). Gaylord Sheline, who orchestrated the 1985 Series in Kokomo, Indiana, characterized the 1984 Series as "pathetic." Too bad because the teams put on an exciting Series, won by a team from Guaynabo, Puerto Rico, who had to win two games on the last day, and did so in a one-run final.[59]

Teams from Puerto Rico were not uncommon in the World Series. A decade earlier, in 1973–1974, a team from Rio Piedras, joined West Covina, California, Cincinnati Bentley Post 50, and Oakland's 1949–1950 teams in winning back-to-back championships. This Puerto Rico-based team, Jesus Bruno Post 134, hailed from Guaynabo (34–7), a city of 90,000 on the north coast of the island. The path for Puerto Rican teams has proven more difficult than for most U.S. teams. There were only 18 American Legion teams on the island, so the competition was limited. To make the Series, they had to come through the Southeast Region. In the past decade, half of the ALWS winners came out of that region. DeLand, Florida, hosted the 1984 Regional. The Jets of Guaynabo Post 134 had to beat the likes of Tuscaloosa, 8–6, West Tampa, the 1981 champions, 9–7, and Salisbury, North Carolina, 8–0. In the championship game, ace Livo Rivera pitched the shutout. In addition to Rivera, their best players were slick shortstop Jorge Robles and slugging outfielder Jose Marzan.[60]

The strongest challenge to Guaynabo in the ALWS came from Brooklawn, New Jersey (32–8). Coach Joe Barth, an accountant, had started the program in 1952. By the 1980s, he had relinquished much of the day-to-day managerial responsibilities to son Joe, Jr., but he retained ultimate control of the team. He understood that his players might not be the most gifted athletes or baseball prospects, but he maintained: "We have been successful because we work harder. We play or practice six days a week." He had been to Regionals before, but getting to the Series was a harder nut to crack. John McGettigan and Steve Mondile were fine Legion pitchers, and pitcher/outfielder Wil Vespe had some power. In the Regional at Hampton, Virginia, they beat former champion Midlothian, Virginia, and Boyertown, 6–4, behind a Vespe home run.[61]

On paper, 1984 did not stack up as the strongest field of teams. Memphis, Tennessee Post 1 arrived with the best record (59–6). Rapid City, South Dakota Post 22, coached by long-timer Dave Ploof, came in with a record of 53–12. They always seemed to be contenders. Others in the mix were Bristol, Connecticut's Seicheprey Post 2 with a 37–10 record; Rockport, Indiana, Jenkins Post 254 (38–15), had to win two games against Mt. Prospect, Illinois, on the final day of the Regional to get to New Orleans; Roseburg, Oregon, Umpqua Post 16 (46–21); and Las Vegas, Nevada Post 8 (43–17).[62]

In the first round, the favorites won. Rapid City had the easiest time, beating Roseburg, 11–1. Pete Torgerson's three-hit pitching and three RBI each from Kevin Carter and shortstop Jason Wolff paced Rapid City. Brooklawn cruised past Rockport, 14–10, thanks to shortstop Bob Rivell's grand slam in the seventh inning. Guaynabo beat Millington, 6–3, as pitcher Lino Rivera won his tenth game in 11 starts. Las Vegas slipped past Bristol, 7–5. Gary Corbin hit a pair of homers for Vegas. On the second day, Roseburg eliminated

Bristol, 7–5, behind Ryland Summers' four-hitter. Rockport ousted Millington, 8–2, in the losers' bracket. Rapid City needed 11 innings to beat Las Vegas, 2–1. In the 11th, Derrick Bren was hit by a pitch, Wolff walked, and Brett Boushele's run-scoring single was the difference in the game. In the featured game, Brooklawn took the measure of Guaynabo, 13–7.[63]

In the battle of the remaining undefeated teams, the Brooks took the measure of Rapid City, 13–7, in a game where Rapid City beat themselves, committing seven errors, allowing 11 walks, and throwing two wild pitches. Wil Vespe added a home run for the Brooks. For the losers, Kevin Carter had four hits, including a homer. First-round losers Roseburg and Rockport were eliminated. Rockport lost to Las Vegas, 10–9. Tom Griffin struck out the last batter with the bases loaded. Roseburg fell to Guaynabo, 10–6. The big story from that game was Guaynabo's shortstop Jorge Robles setting an ALWS record by getting six hits in six at-bats. He hit three singles, a double, and two triples. The loss eliminated Roseburg. Guaynabo eliminated Rapid City behind Fernando Rodriquez's four hits, including a triple, a home run, and three RBI, in a 9–5 game. Then Brooklawn took the measure of Las Vegas, 17–4. That left undefeated Brooklawn and once-defeated Guaynabo.[64]

Brooklawn had defeated Puerto Rico earlier; now they needed to win one of the two remaining games for the 1984 title. Guaynabo, however, won the first game, 5–2. Lino Rivera pitched a five-hitter. That set up the title game between the same two clubs. In the bottom of the ninth inning of the title game, Brooklawn clung to a one-run lead. Outfielder Jose Marzan singled to center and moved the third when pitcher Carlos Hermina singled. Outfielder Javier Gonzales singled up the middle, sending Marzan home to tie the game. Following a Carlos Morales sacrifice, Brooklawn's pitcher, Steve Mondile, intentionally walked first baseman Jorge del Toro to load the bases and set up a force play at any base. Second baseman Jorge Hernandez then worked Mondile to a full count before taking ball four. The winning run crossed the plate as Guaynabo capped off a brilliant comeback, winning 7–6 to take their World Series title.[65]

Jorge Robles earned the 1984 American Legion Player of the Year Award. Robles, a 5-foot-7-inch, 150-pounder, went on to play for the University of Miami and had two minor league seasons. The Big Stick Award for total bases went to Jose Marzan of Guaynabo with 32. The Louisville Slugger Award went to Jon Bradley of Millington, who hit .461. The Dr. Irwin L. "Click" Cowger RBI Award was won by Will Vespe of Brooklawn. The Bob Feller Award for strikeouts was awarded to Lino Rivera of Guaynabo. Finally, the Sportsmanship Award went to John McGettigan, pitcher for Brooklawn.[66]

Plans to get the 1985 American Legion World Series played in Kokomo, Indiana, had begun at the 1982 Series in Boyertown, Pennsylvania, where Kokomo Post 6 made the World Series. Gaylord Sheline agreed to be the point man for the project. George Rulon told him that the Series had been promised to Rapid City, South Dakota, but as he was fond of repeating, he did not have final decision. The Americanism Commission held the final decision. Sheline set up a hospitality room to help convince members of the Commission to look with favor on Kokomo. Sheline committed Kokomo to massive improvements to Highland Park Stadium, the town's old Midwest League park that had served the Kokomo Giants and Dodgers from 1955–1961. Its playing field was small (dimensions of 294 feet, 340 feet, and 270 feet), as were the stands (under 3,000 seats). No improvements had been made in 25 years. Sheline, however, promised major improvements including new fencing, a new scoreboard, four new restrooms, dressing rooms and showers, and

1,000 new seats. He failed to mention the inadequate parking, and that proved to be an insurmountable problem during the Series. Sheline estimated the cost at $250,000. The commission was impressed and voted 5–1 to award the series to Kokomo.[67]

The defending champion Guaynabo Jets (31–7) returned, looking for back-to-back titles. They had lost Player of the Year Jorge Robles but replaced him at shortstop with 16-year-old sensation Carlos Baerga, who the *Kokomo Tribune* called the "most talked about player at the Legion World Series." Two California teams seemed capable of winning the title. West Covina Post 170 (45–6) did not have the powerhouse that had won back-to-back titles in 1970–1971, but they had won the California state title. In Larry Gonzales, their stopper and power hitter, they had a player who looked to be the second coming of Rollie Fingers. A team from Sacramento, the Carmichael Elks (38–4), was loaded with prospects. First baseman Ned Heitz, third baseman Dave Hajek, outfielders Bobby Jones and Deryk Gross, catcher Mike Musolino, and pitcher Clyde Keller would make the tournament all-star team. The Omaha Post 1 Gladiators came with the prospect closest to being major league ready in pitcher/outfielder Gregg Olson. Finally, the Midlothian, Virginia Post 186 Mules arrived with a tidy 40–5 record; it had established its creds by beating 1984 runner-up Brooklawn in the Mid–Atlantic regional. Remaining teams were the John Coleman Prince Post 9 of New London, Connecticut (53–18); Woodward, Oklahoma Post 19, which arrived with a .353 team batting average; and New Ulm, Minnesota Post 132.[68]

The opening game between Midlothian and Guaynabo demonstrated the band-box effect of Highland Park, which was quickly named "the launching pad." Balls were flying out, as Midlothian got a record six home runs in their 13–9 victory. Two homers each went off the bats of Mark Chambers and Mark Wroniewicz. Sacramento doubled the score on New London, 10–5, as Dave Hajek drove in two runs, including the go-ahead marker, and both Bob Russell and Dave Piela homered. Omaha's Greg Olson dominated with a homer, two RBI, and a save as Omaha banged out 14 hits in a 7–3 win over Woodward. Rett Smith had a three-run homer for Omaha. Larry Gonzales threw a three-hitter with 15 strikeouts in West Covina's 4–2 win over New Ulm. Sacramento, victor over New London in their opening game, slipped past Midlothian, 1–0, as Clyde Keller pitched a one-hitter, running his record to 16–0. He recorded 14 strikeouts. Sacramento's run came on Hajek's double followed by a Bobby Jones single. It was the only shutout of the Series. Guaynabo eliminated New London, 7–4, on Jose Pagan's homer in the seventh inning. Adrian Pabon and Jose Ramos also homered. New Ulm eliminated Woodward, 4–3, as Brian Raabe collected four hits. Omaha beat West Covina by a 4–2 score behind Gregg Olson's complete-game five-hitter.[69]

In the third round, defending champion Guaynabo fell to West Covina, 5–4, in ten innings. The loss eliminated the Jets. Vince Aguilar ripped a homer in the tenth to give West Covina the win. Ray Hopson and Larry Gonzales also homered for the California team. Midlothian eliminated New Ulm, 5–2. Second baseman Tris Lipscomb gave Midlothian a 3–0 lead in the fourth inning and picked up his tenth save of the season, pitching the last three innings. In the battle of unbeatens, Sacramento destroyed Omaha, 15–3. Dave Hajek and Mike Musolino homered for Sacramento. Next, Sacramento eliminated West Covina by the football score of 17–14. First baseman Ned Heitz and outfielder Deryk Gross contributed four RBI each. Gross' came on a grand slam. Midlothian kept pace by knocking Omaha out by a 3–2 score. Tris Lipscomb moved to the pitching mound in the fifth inning and got the win.[70]

All was set for the showdown between Midlothian and Sacramento to decide the 1985 title. Midlothian was an upstart. This was their first time in the World Series. Their coach, Dave George, was in his first year in that position. Midlothian had originally been a coal mining community a dozen miles west of Richmond on highway U.S. 60, but was now a suburban community. Winning required the Midlothian Mules to win two games on the same day. That they did, 8–4 and 3–2. In the first game, starting pitcher Rick Jarvis slammed a homer in the fifth inning. Lipscomb took the mound in the sixth and picked up the victory. Outfielder Dick Barrett slammed a two-out single in the ninth inning of the championship game to provide the margin of victory for the Mules. Sacramento's lineup included three players who made the major leagues and five more who played pro ball. Midlothian stars Tris Lipscomb and Mark Chambers turned pro but did not come close to tasting the majors. Midlothian, however, played within themselves, getting key hits, playing air-tight defense, hitting the cut-off man, and not beating themselves.[71]

Although they did not capture the championship, Sacramento dominated the 1985 all-tournament team as selected by a five-man committee. Sacramento's all-stars included: Ned Hietz, first base; Dave Hajek, third base; Bobby Jones, outfielder; Deryk Gross, outfielder; Mike Musolino, catcher; Clyde Keller, pitcher. Other selections were Brian Raabe, New Ulm, second base; Carlos Baerga, Guaynabo, shortstop; outfielders Larry Gonzales, West Covina; Greg Olson, Omaha; and Bobby Jones of Sacramento. Tris Lipscomb of Midlothian, a sophomore at Furman University, was selected as pitcher and as the Player of the Year. The Bob Feller Award was shared by Olson and Larry Gonzalez of West Covina. Olson also shared the Louisville Slugger Award with teammate Steve Nelson. Mike Musolino of Sacramento won the RBI Award and the Big Stick Award. Sacramento's Bobby Jones won the Sportsmanship Award. Midlothian coach David George won the leadership award with Maurice Beck, manager of Midlothian. Carlos Bearga of Puerto Rico went on to a 14-year major league career with six teams, playing in three All-Star Games. Pitcher Greg Olson went from Omaha to Auburn University and then to the Baltimore Orioles, where he stayed for 14 seasons.

The 60th anniversary edition of the World Series was awarded to Rapid City, South Dakota. The choice was appropriate because American Legion baseball dated its origins to South Dakota. Rapid City had planned to host the 1985 Series, but they were outhustled by Kokomo. The choice of Rapid City became even more appropriate when Legion headquarters announced that 1986 would be the last year for Legion baseball's *major domo*, George Rulon. A native of Fargo, North Dakota, he had served as head of Legion baseball for 26 years, and he estimated that during his reign he had visited 126 cities for regional and Series games. Organizers of the Rapid City World Series announced that they would throw him a retirement party on the Sunday of the Series. Rulon enjoyed talking about his good luck "yellow shoes," actually mustard-color. Rulon wore them during World Series play as a good luck charm to keep rain away. He also used the occasion to preach against having the ALWS in big cities; "we shouldn't take American Legion World Series to big cities" he repeated. Attendance had bottomed out at the New Orleans Series in 1984, when only 7,765 attended the 15 games and a mere 524 were in the stands for the final game. Compare that to the 34,023 at Boyertown in 1982 and 27,433 at Fargo in 1983.[72]

Rulon fielded a question about the most significant change or changes that had occurred during his tenure as head of Legion ball. In the past, he had replied, "not much." Now he was clear that the answer was, "the coaching is more refined." When he took over, a parent or Legionnaire agreed to coach a squad, and he generally "threw out the ball" and left the boys alone. Now coaches knew what they were doing and stressed fundamentals of baseball. To recognize Rulon's long service, the Player of the Year award was renamed the George W. Rulon Player of the Year Award.[73]

Rapid City's games were held at Floyd Fitzgerald Stadium. Formerly named Sioux Park Stadium, it had been changed in 1972 when a major flood of the Red River forced significant repairs and renovations. For the 1986 Series, 13 sections of bleachers were moved in from the fairgrounds to increase the seating capacity to 5,000. Half of the teams in the 1986 World Series were there for the first time. This group included Jensen Beach, Florida Post 126 (47–12); Lake Charles, Louisiana W. B. Williamson Post 1 Coco-Colas (40–8) batted .350 as a team; Maynard, Ohio's, Community Post 66 (46–8); and El Segundo, California (37–7). Only one team returned from the previous year, New London. Connecticut Post 9 (48–14–1). Others with ALWS experience were the Bears from Post 471 in Boyertown, Pennsylvania (50–6); Hansford Post 5 of Cedar Rapids, Iowa (17–18); and Las Vegas, Nevada, Post 8 (58–9). El Segundo was the outlier of the group. Woodland Hills, California (38–8) had captured the California state title and the Northwest Regional in Corvallis, Oregon. El Segundo appealed on the grounds that Woodland Hills engaged in recruiting violations. After a lengthy appeals process, the American Legion National Appeals Board ruled in favor of El Segundo in early August.[74]

Jensen Beach looked like the most well-rounded and balanced of the teams, even though it was their first visit to the ALWS. Their second baseman, Jon Anderson, hit .497 at the regional tournament and won MVP honors. First baseman Doug Rogalski, who batted .450, was not far behind. Pitchers Rusty Meacham (11–1) and Joe Grahe (14–3) had "prospect" on every scout's card. Boyertown had been to the Series five times in the past decade, having won in 1982. They came in with a gaudy 50–6 record, a team batting average of .350, and a large group of boisterous followers. Cedar Rapids had been to the ALWS five times, including a second-place finish in 1975, but this year they sneaked in with a losing record of 17–18. Finally, Las Vegas, Post 8, with a 58–9 record, looked to challenge for the title.[75]

In the first round, Jensen Beach, El Segundo, Las Vegas, and Maynard gave notice that they were the powers by posting big wins. Jensen Beach pitcher Joe Grahe held New London to two hits and struck out 18 batters in a 9–2 victory. Center fielder and leadoff hitter Brian Reimsnyder homered and drove in three runs. El Segundo rolled to a 16–5 win over Lake Charles, thanks to 10 errors by the Coco-Colas and shortstop Willie Parsons' four hits. Las Vegas not only upset Boyertown, they embarrassed the Bears, 11–4. Third baseman Dan Opperman collected four hits, including a home run. Maynard destroyed Cedar Rapids, 19–2. In that game, Mitch Hannahs of Maynard tied the record by scoring five times. In the losers' bracket, Boyertown and New London stayed alive by eliminating Cedar Rapids and Lake Charles. Boyertown mauled Cedar Rapids, 15–7. With their running offense, the Bears stole nine bases and forced the Iowa team into eight errors. New London had a field day, downing Lake Charles, 14–0. Catcher Bobby Russell finished with three hits and three RBI. In the winners' bracket, Jensen Beach bested El Segundo, 6–0, as Randy Mecham threw a five-hitter and struck out 12. Third baseman Jon Anderson homered. Las Vegas had a harder time, but it beat Maynard, 3–1. Pitcher Sam Calarusso controlled the game. That left Jensen Beach and Las Vegas as the unbeaten teams.[76]

In the battle of undefeated, Jensen Beach survived an uncharacteristic five errors, three by third baseman Joe Russo, to beat Las Vegas, 4–3, thanks to Joe Grahe's save. Catcher Chris Hirsch drove in the game-winning run, causing coach Bob Shaw to say to his team, "Gentlemen, Chris Hirsch is a hell of a ballplayer." El Segundo and Maynard eliminated Boyertown and New London. El Segundo rolled over Boyertown, 18–6, on a rainy day. Maynard got two crucial RBI from Bill Hagey to win a close 6–5 game over New London. In its next game, Las Vegas knocked El Segundo out of the series, 14–9.[77]

Jensen Beach closed out the 1986 Series in dominating fashion, beating Maynard, 6–2, and Las Vegas, 8–2. In beating Maynard, second baseman Jon Anderson, clubbed two home runs. In the final against Las Vegas, they had to wait four hours for the field to dry out from an overnight storm. For Jensen Beach, third baseman Joe Russo homered, catcher Chris Hirsch collected four hits, Reimsnyder was 3-for-5, and pitcher Joe Grahe struck out 13 batters. Jensen Beach coach Bob Shaw could only say, "It's incredible. They absolutely do everything any manager could ever want them to. Every player contributed."[78]

Grahe won not only the newly named George W. Rulon Player of the Year award, but also captured the Bob Feller Award with 52 strikeouts in 35 innings. Mitch Hannahs of Maynard took home the Louisville Slugger Award with a .486 average. Las Vegas' Dan Opperman won the Rawlings Big Stick Award for total bases and tied with Mike Tonucci of New London for the Dr. Irwin Cowger RBI Award with 19. Las Vegas outfielder Tom Griffin won the Sportsmanship Award. Jensen Beach's coach Bob Shaw, who had pitched in the majors for 11 years, won the Leadership Award along with his assistant coach, Floyd Wilkes. Attendance at the Rapid City series was 16,949, well shy of the 27,054 the city drew in 1976.

Jensen Beach had won 20 of its 21 games in the post-season tournaments. Their two pitching aces, Joe Grahe and Rusty Meacham, both made the major leagues. Grahe, who had a 16–3 record for the championship season, pitched in the majors from 1990 to 1999 with California, Colorado and Philadelphia. Meacham, who was 11–1 for the 1986 Legion season, played in the majors from 1991 to 2001 for Detroit, Kansas City, Seattle, Houston, and Tampa Bay.

Rulon officially retired on January 1. He could look back on his time as head of Legion baseball, 1961–1986, as one of stability in very unstable times in the country. Legion Commander Dale Renaud announced that the annual Legion Player of the Year Award would be named the George W. Rulon Player of the Year Award. Future Hall of Fame pitcher Rollie Fingers said at Rulon's retirement party: "He's put his heart into this program, and I love him dearly." Rulon, who retired to Florida, died in 1989.[79]

American Legion graduates continued to be inducted into the National Baseball Hall of Fame on a regular basis. For the period 1976–1986, the list included pitcher Bob Lemon (1976), pitcher Robin Roberts (1976), third baseman Eddie Mathews (1978), outfielder Al Kaline (1980), pitcher Bob Gibson (1981), outfielder Frank Robinson (1982), third baseman George Kell (1983), third baseman Brooks Robinson (1983), pitcher Don Drysdale (1984), infielder Harmon Killebrew (1984), shortstop Pee Wee Reese (1984), pitcher Hoyt Wilhelm (1985), and second baseman Bobby Doerr (1986).

7

Toward Parity,
1987–2000

For 1987, American Legion baseball had a new leader in Jim Quinlan. A former Marine and native of West Branch, Iowa, and a graduate of the University of Iowa, Quinlan earned his credibility as an assistant to George Rulon. His appointment carried a less prestigious title than Rulon; Quinlan's title was Assistant Director of Americanism and Children and Youth Divisions. That was a long way from Lou Brissie's "commissioner" title, but Quinlan preferred using the term "American Legion Baseball Director." Whatever his title, Quinlan had become the face of American Legion baseball.

One of Quinlan's first tasks was the selection of Stevens Point, Wisconsin, as the site for the 1987 American Legion World Series. Stevens Point, a small city of 10,647, had never hosted a World Series before, but neither had any city or town in Wisconsin. The city had committed $200,000 to improvements to Leo "Cub" Mancheski Field in Bukolt Park, a 56-acre park located on the Wisconsin River. The field and stands, built in 1963, had hosted the Great Lakes Regionals in 1974, 1978, and 1983.[1]

It was becoming apparent that the 1980s belonged to Boyertown Post 471. By reaching the ALWS in 1987, the Bears made their fifth Series in the decade. They had won it all in 1982, and according to assistant coach Rick Moatz, "from day one of practice Stevens Point was on their mind." Dave Specht, the 34-year-old coach in his final year at the helm, remembered his 1987 team as having "mental discipline and [they] believed in themselves." Boyertown (55–12) featured the left side of its infield, third baseman M. J. Weller, who hit .434, and shortstop Tom Szilli, a .414 hitter with a team-leading 44 RBI. Catcher Willie Stout batted .347 and ran the pitching staff led by Scott Mutter (15–2, 2.78). The team demonstrated resiliency by its ability to come from behind. In the state tourney, the Bears lost their first game to Mike Mussina's undefeated Montoursville, but they came back to win, 14–2 and 17–4, to capture their tenth state title. In the Mid–Atlantic Regional at Frederick, Maryland, they lost the opener to Williamsport, Maryland, by the narrowest of scores, 2–1. But the Bears came back to beat Kingston, New York, Wilmington, Delaware, Hamilton Township, New Jersey, and Frederick twice by 8–1 and 9–2 scores. In the opening game of the 1987 Legion World Series, Boyertown went down at the hands of Midwest City, Oklahoma, 3–2, on a chilly, rainy day that quickly rained out the other three scheduled games.[2]

Before the ALWS began, West Tampa, Florida Memorial Post 248 (54–8) was the favorite to take the national title. West Tampa, in winning the Southeast Regional, demonstrated "one of the most potent attacks in Series history." They were labeled "the team to beat." Unfortunately, they lost their best player, Regional MVP Steve Mauldin, who broke a collarbone in their final tune-up for the Series. A .431 hitter, he had led West Tampa in batting average, hits, RBI, and runs. Even without Mauldin, they were left with three outstanding pitchers. Sam Militello, a future major leaguer, posted an 8–1 record with a 1.43 ERA. Kevin Skelly was 10–1/2.00, and Omar Brito was 12–1/1.33 with 128 strikeouts in 98 innings.[3]

The rest of the Elite Eight included three-time state champion Norwood, Massachusetts, Post 70 (42–7); Clark Tinker Post 170 (55–15) of Midwest City, Oklahoma; the George Budde Post 507 of Cincinnati (45–12); Fairview Knights Post 10 of Boulder, Colorado (37–18); Quincy, Illinois, Logan Post 37 (60–16); and Salmon Creek Heights Cardinals Post 176 (48–23) of Vancouver, Washington. Norwood boasted the best pitcher in the Series, Rob Baxter, who played for Harvard and posted all-Ivy League credentials, with a minuscule 1.45 ERA in Legion play. Norwood, however, was tired, from having played four games in two days the previous weekend. Quincy, Illinois's, Post 37, with a 60–16 record, had played more games than any ALWS team. They featured first baseman/pitcher Mike Kirkpatrick, the MVP of the Great Plains Regional. Cincinnati attracted a following because their third baseman, Pete "Petey" Rose, Jr., was the son of all-time hit leader Pete Rose. They also had strong pitching in Jamie Birkofer (9–0, 2.14) and Jason Shire (12–3, 2.40), and hitting in Brad Mills (.438) and Scott Hughes (.401). Midwest City, featuring shortstop Mitch Simons, a .450 hitter with 80 RBI, and catcher Greg Blevins, who hit .400 with 17 home runs, presented a balanced team. They also possessed an outstanding pitcher in Stan Spencer, who sported a perfect 11–0 record. Spencer went on to play college ball at Stanford and, briefly, for the San Diego Padres.[4]

After Boyertown's opening-day loss to Midwest City, rain washed out the remaining three games and forced seven games to be crammed in on day two. Boulder did not belong, losing 11–0 to West Tampa and 22–3 to Boyertown on day two. That score tied the largest margin of victory in Series history. Shortstop Tom Szilli, catcher Willy Stout, and outfielder Jeff Seymour each banged out three hits for the Bears, and Stout drove in four runs. Norwood lost twice, 4–2 to Quincy and 4–0 to Cincinnati, so their Series lasted just one day. Vancouver picked up two wins, 4–3 over Cincinnati and 7–2 over Quincy. In the Quincy game, Aaron Dorlarque struck out 16 batters. Midwest City upset West Tampa, 4–2, behind the three-hit pitching of Gary Haught.[5]

On day three, West Tampa hammered Cincinnati, 14–0, highlighted by Paul Russo's homer, and Boyertown knocked out Quincy, 10–0. The winning teams emerged as new favorites. The Bears avenged their opening-day loss to Midwest City by beating them, 6–2, thanks to Chris Ludy, the winning pitcher, who drove in three runs, and Chris Mackey's go-ahead RBI. Vancouver also beat Midwest City, 3–1, knocking the Oklahoma team out of the Series. West Tampa continued its heavy hitting in a 17–3 trouncing of Vancouver. That left three teams—Vancouver, Boyertown, and West Tampa—each with just one loss in the tournament.[6]

Vancouver got the bye into the final game. West Tampa pitched its ace, Sam Militto, but the team was flat according to coach Emeterio "Pop" Cuesta. Boyertown outfielder Dave Willman drove in two runs in the fifth inning and homered in the eighth to lead the Bears to a 5–2 victory. Cuesta lamented, "We had the best team, but the best team doesn't always win." In the 1987 championship game, after a one-hour rain delay, Boyertown scored five runs in the fourth inning and went on to defeat Vancouver, 12–6. The win came against Vancouver's well-rested pitching ace, Stan Spencer. Outfielder Chris

Macky's two-run double provided the big blow in the fourth-inning uprising. Scott Eidle also drove in two runs in the fourth, and later drove in two more. Boyertown became the first team to lose its opening game and come back to win the title. The win gave Boyertown its second national title in the 1980s, the only team to accomplish that feat.[7]

Boyertown's 1987 championship team was a solid group without a player who went on to achieve major league greatness. Catcher Willie Stout was a leader who knew how to handle pitchers. Apparently, he knew how to handle kids too; he became the principal of Hempfield High School. Pitchers Scott Mutter and Chris Ludy headed a strong pitching staff. M. J. Weller led the team with a .434 batting average for the season. Outfielder Dave Willman led with 46 RBI. Shortstop Tom Szsilli, a .414 hitter with 44 RBIs, led the club with 35 stolen bases. They were solid throughout and had strong mental discipline.

Boyertown catcher and leader Wilber "Willie" Stout won Player of the Year honors. The Louisville Slugger Award for highest batting average went to Brad Dolejsi of Midwest City. There was a tie for the Rawlings Big Stick Award between Boyertown's Jeff Seymour, known for his defense more than his hitting, and Tad Thompson of Vancouver. Stan Spencer, also from Vancouver, captured the Bob Feller Award, and his catcher, Brett Blechschmidt, took home the Sportsmanship Award.[8]

Boyertown's triumph in the 1987 World Series stamped the Bears' dominance in American Legion ball. If more were needed, they opened the 1988 season as the favorites to repeat even before the first game was played. They returned seven starters from the 1987 championship team. They raced through the regular season with an impressive 61–8 record. The Bears, however, ran into trouble in the regional, played on their home turf. They lost to up-and-coming Brooklawn, New Jersey, 11–4. The Brooks, in turn, were knocked out by Mayo, Maryland, 13–11. Boyertown, however, came back to beat Mayo, 12–5, in the regional final to assure their spot in the ALWS at Middletown, Connecticut. Several Bears standouts—catcher Dave Willman, shortstop Tom Szilli, second baseman Marty Bauer, and outfielders Chris Mackey and Jeff Seymour—would be playing in their third ALWS. At the ALWS, they faced teams anxious to knock the Bears from the top seat.[9]

Yakima, Washington's, Logan-Wheeler Post 36 (61–26) and Cincinnati's George Budde Post 507 (51–12) appeared the strongest challengers to Boyertown preeminence in 1988. Yakima, like Boyertown, had the most experience; they were proud of their 61–26 record and of catcher Scott Hatteberg, whom scouts labeled the top prospect in the tournament. Indeed, he would spend 14 seasons in the major leagues with Boston, Oakland, and Cincinnati. For the 1988 season, Hatteberg batted .476 with 24 home runs and 116 runs batted in. Those were big-time numbers in any league. The Yakima Pepsis also boasted an outstanding Legion pitcher in Craig Miller, who sported a 15–1 record.[10]

Cincinnati teams had been part of the Legion's old guard since Bentley Post 50 dominated in the 1940s and 1950s. Budde had appeared in the 1987 Series, and given their 51–12 record, they looked forward winning more than one game in 1988, especially after Oak Hills High School, which all the Budde players attended, won the city title in 1988. Cincinnati's best-known player, Pete Rose, Jr., held down shortstop and served as captain for his Legion team. After his Legion playing days ended, he played in 1,918 minor league games from 1989 to 2002, and 11 games for the Cincinnati Reds in 1997. He then caught on with independent league clubs from 2002 through 2009. Other teams in the 1988 World Series were Post 150 from Kingston, New York (31–5); Post 12 of West Palm Beach Florida (44–12); Gautreau-Williams Post 81 of Gonzales, Louisiana (43–12); Melvin E. Hearl Post

21 of Moorhead, Minnesota (48–16); and Boulder, Colorado, Post 10 (40–24). Kingston featured pitcher Mike Juhl, who posted a perfect 11–0 record during the regular season. West Palm shortstop Luke Martinez had earned Most Valuable Player status in the Southeast Regional with a .444 batting average. Gonzales, self-proclaimed jambalaya capital of Louisiana, featured pitcher-outfielder Ryan Ricci, 11–4/.460, and third-baseman Bubba LeBlanc, a .430 hitter. Moorhead had two fine high school pitchers in Phil Lier (14–0) and lefty Tony Kunka (12–3). Boulder came to the Series with the worst record (40–24) of any of the eight finalists. Their pitching ace, Jeff Seales, had been the number two selection of the New York Mets in the June draft. Overall, the number of Legion teams went up slightly to 3,915, but Houston Astros scout Ed Buckie allowed that there was a lack of top prospects in this year's World Series.[11]

The 1988 ALWS returned to the east at Middletown, Connecticut's Palmer Field. Local Post 75 used it as home field, as did Xavier High School. Wesleyan University used it when hosting NCAA Division III tournaments. A tidy and clean park, it seated 3,500. Organizers could do nothing about the rain that fell on Palmer Field August 24, forcing the postponement of the first day of play. Five games were scheduled for the next day beginning at eight in the morning, and six the following day.[12]

Yakima and Cincinnati got off to a flying start. Yakima destroyed Boyertown, 11–0, aided by four Boyertown errors and Pat Leahy's four-hit pitching. Leahy (6-foot-6, 225 pounds), who struck out 12, was the grandson of Notre Dame coaching legend Frank Leahy. Kingston sneaked by West Palm Beach, 3–2, as Mike Bailey had three hits. Gabe Duross doubled to drive in the winning run in the 11th inning. Boulder pitchers had trouble finding the plate, issuing ten walks to help Moorehead to an 8–6 victory. Cincinnati got a game-winning home run from Pete Rose, Jr., and outstanding pitching from Scott Klingenbeck to beat Gonzales, 4–3.

Games began to pile up in the second round. Boulder lost to Boyertown, 14–4, and Gonzales was nipped by West Palm Beach, 3–2. The two losers went home. Yakima, however, lost in an upset to Moorhead, 7–4. Jay Ceruse tripled in two runs in the seventh inning to give Moorhead a 5–4 lead which held up. Scott Hughes homered twice as Cincinnati beat Kingston, 19–4, in "a dreadful" game. Budde scored 13 runs in the third inning, when 17 players batted, to put the game away.[13]

On the third day, the number of pro scouts went from 31 to three, a clear indication of the lack of top prospects. Yakima, Boyertown, and Cincinnati returned to their winning ways. Yakima knocked Palm Beach out of the Series, 6–5. Boyertown bounced Kingston, 8–7, which eliminated the New Yorkers. Cincinnati had little trouble with Moorhead, winning 11–3. Boyertown then knocked Moorhead out of the competition by an 8–6 score. Cincinnati beat Yakima, 6–3, thanks to Rose's three hits and three RBI. Yakima committed six errors to contribute to their demise.[14]

In the 1988 championship game between Cincinnati's George W. Budde Post and Boyertown, Cincinnati got on the board in the first inning when Scott Hughes singled, stole second, and came around on Mike Kessler's RBI. Later Jamie Birkhofer contributed a double and a two-run home run. Scott Klingenbeck kept Boyertown at bay and off the scoreboard, while his mates coasted to a 7–0 victory. Coach John McMichen, a teacher at Oak Hills High School, summed up the title by saying, "we live by being aggressive, and that's what got us here." The championship was the first for a Cincinnati club since Bentley Post 50's last title in 1958.[15]

The Player of the Year Award went to Cincinnati first baseman/pitcher Mike Kessler.

He batted .361 for the Series and pitched two winning games. A strong case could have been made for giving that award to Cincinnati's hitting star, outfielder Scott Hughes, who won the Louisville Slugger Award by batting .455, the Rawlings Big Stick Award for his 36 total bases, and the Dr. Irwin L. Cowger RBI Award with 17. He also led the Series in stolen bases with 13. Pete Rose, Jr., picked up the Sportsmanship Award. Scott Klingenbeck received the Bob Feller Pitching Award after striking out 34 batters in 34 innings and earning two victories. The attendance of 19,423 was the highest in five years.[16]

Although the decade of the 1980s was Boyertown's time to shine, the final two years of the decade were throwbacks to earlier eras. Cincinnati teams had won more World Series titles than any other city, but until 1988 their last title had come at the end of Bentley Post 50's run of five titles between 1944 and 1958. Thirty years after Bentley's run, Cincinnati's Budde Post 507 regained the title by beating Boyertown in the 1988 finals. Although the Golden State had accumulated more championships than any other state, they had failed to win a title since Santa Monica took the crown in 1976 and West Covina captured back-to-back titles in 1970–1971. In 1989, a California team, Woodland Hills West Post 826, returned to the World Series and reclaimed the ALWS title for a California team.

Woodland Hills needed supernatural help to get on the winning track. In the state tourney, the usually hard-hitting group found themselves in a slump. They did not win the state title, losing to Fullerton. First baseman Ryan McGuire called a team meeting at the ballpark in Yountville, California, where the state tourney was being played. His ploy was right out of the 1988 movie *Bull Durham*. The boys gathered in a circle, placed their bats on the ground in front of them, and held hands. McGuire, with a dog bone purchased at a local store, began tapping and rubbing each bat to take the hex out of the bats. Catcher Bobby Kim, of Korean extraction, burst forth in a Korean prayer to rid the team of "evil hitting spirits." Outfielder Jeff Marks followed with a similarly unexpected Jewish prayer. Jason Cohen insisted, "It really worked." In the three games following the ritual, Woodland Hills scored 40 runs on 47 hits. The team was on its way.

California, along with Pennsylvania and Minnesota, had an advantage in that they were able to place two teams in the sectional tournaments, because of the disproportionate number of teams in those states. The Fullerton Post 142 Angels stayed in Section 8 (Western Regional), while Woodland Hills West went to the Section 7 (the Pacific Northwest) tournament. Fullerton beat Las Vegas, 4–3, in its regional final. Woodland Hills West Post 826 struggled through their tourney, including a 14-inning game against Alaska's representative before beating Lewis-Clark, 9–4, thanks to second baseman Carl McFadden's grand slam.[17]

The eight teams that made the 1989 ALWS included: Braintree, Massachusetts, Post 86; Glen Allen, Virginia Post 244, aka Richmond, winner by 10–5 over Stahl Post of Wilmington; Jesus Bruno Post 134 of Guaynabo, Puerto Rico; Gonzales, Louisiana, sponsored by All-Star Ford of Baton Rouge; Richard Ellis Post 205 of Janesville, Wisconsin, winners over Steubenville, 7–4, in Sectional finals; and Fargo, North Dakota Post 2. Janesville featured pitcher Jeff Thelen, who entered the ALWS with a 14–0 record. Fargo's ace, Rick Helling, the MVP of Region 6, was even more impressive with a 15–0 record. Helling proved to be the real thing, pitching 12 years in the big leagues with Texas, Florida, Arizona, Baltimore, and Milwaukee.

Millington, Tennessee, hosted the 1989 American Legion World Series. Some ten miles north/northeast of Memphis, the city of 17,866 was the site of the Naval Support

Activity, Mid–South. The field where the World Series would be played went by the names Legion Field and USA Stadium, because it became home of the United States Olympic team in 1986, the year the stadium opened. The facility featured an enormously steep roof behind home plate, with aluminum bleachers down the first and third base lines, the stadium seating 5,000 plus. The turnout, however, remained disappointing. Tournament organizer Babe Howard lobbied Legion officials to make the Millington site the permanent home for the ALWS. However, his appeals fell flat when only 6,585 fans paid to watch the 15 Legion Series games; that was the fewest to attend a Series since 1958 at Colorado Springs, when a low of 4,200 attended the ALWS.[18]

Before the Legion Series began, no clear-cut favorite emerged. Overall, it appeared that parity prevailed. There seemed to be agreement that, as usual, the New England Regional winner, Braintree, Massachusetts, Post 86, had little chance. Mid–Atlantic had been a strong region in the 1980s, but Glen Allen Post 244 of Richmond, despite coming through the regional at Boyertown, Pennsylvania, where it beat Stahl Post of Delaware, appeared to lack the skills to make a run at the title. Jesus Bruno Post 134 of Guaynabo, Puerto Rico had won in 1984 and in 1974, so they had a history of playing well under pressure. Gonzales, Louisiana's All-Star Ford of Baton Rouge possessed the ability to make trouble, but few scouts expected them to win it all. Janesville, Wisconsin, Richard Ellis Post 205 beat Steubenville, Ohio, 7–4, to make the Series. They boasted one of the best prospects in pitcher Jeff Thelen, he of the 13–0 record. Fargo, North Dakota Post 2 had a long history of strength, and they had pitcher Rick Helling, MVP of the Sectional which included a 7–4 victory over Sioux Falls in the final game. Woodlawn Hills West Post 826 of Woodlawn Hills, California, had to qualify through the Pacific Northwest Sectional, having lost to Fullerton in the California state tourney. Fullerton Post 142 Angels of Orange County made a strong case for being the favorite. They had scored a 4–3 win over Las Vegas to reach the Series. Their pitching ace, Steve Trachsel (12–1), matured over the summer.[19]

In the opening round of play Guaynabo, Fargo, and Fullerton met with surprise losses. Guaynabo beat itself, giving up nine walks in a 6–5 loss to Woodland Hills. Fullerton fell to Gonzales, 8–4. Fargo beat Richmond, 6–2, behind the pitching of Rick Helling. Janesville topped Braintree, 11–7, thanks to Jerry Wellnitz's three-run homer. On day two, Braintree and Richmond suffered their second losses. Guaynabo beat Braintree, 6–0. Fullerton's Steve Trachsel pitched his Angels to a 6–2 win over Richmond, as Steve Borowski homered and doubled. Todd Landry pitched a three-hitter and slugged three hits with three RBI to power Gonzales over Fargo, 9–6. Woodland Hills West also got outstanding pitching from Lance Gibson, who held Janesville to five hits while striking out 13 batters. Del Marine tripled in the winning run in a 3–1 Woodland Hills victory.[20]

Both Janesville and Guaynabo had lost to Woodland Hills, but they still had life. Janesville eliminated Fullerton, 9–2, as Mark Sievert spaced seven hits and picked up his 11th win without a loss. Guaynabo eliminated Fargo, 13–2. Gonzales took Woodland Hills West to the limit before losing in the bottom of the ninth, 8–7. For West, Del Marine singled, Jason Cohen doubled, and Carl McFadden tripled in two runs for the victory. Next, Janesville scored three runs in the first inning, and that would be enough to beat Gonzales, 3–2. RBI hits by Tom Drew and Kyle Anderson sandwiched a wild pitch to account for all of Janesville's runs. Woodland Hills then had the opportunity to knock Guaynabo out of the tournament, but they also knew they would have another opportunity to beat Guaynabo if they failed on the first effort. They failed, falling by a

12–6 score. Guaynabo and Janesville had to play to determine who would play for the title against Woodland Hills. Victor Negron unloaded a massive home run for Guaynabo in the sixth inning and pitched a five-hitter. Jose Mateo drove in the final run in the eighth as Guaynabo squeaked out a 3–2 win. Janesville was the first Wisconsin team to advance this far.[21]

In the championship game of 1989, Woodland Hills West earned the American Legion title by a 11–5 score. Outfielder Jason Cohen got West on the board in the first inning with an RBI double. Jeff Marks, also an outfielder, plated two runs in the third. The Island boys came back with four runs in the top of the fourth inning for a 5–3 lead. In the bottom of the fourth, however, catcher Bobby Kim knotted the score at 5–5. Pat Treend, who often had trouble throwing strikes, came on and shut the Guaynabo down on one hit the rest of the game, striking out three batters in the ninth inning. Woodland Hills broke the game open with six runs in the sixth inning. Marks, Treend, shortstop Ricky Banuelos, and Paul Geller all drove in runs. Treend got credit for the win.[22]

Woodland Hills had a nicely balanced, good, but not great team. They had two fine pitchers in Lance Gibson, the coach's son who won three games, and hard-throwing Pat Treend, just wild enough to keep batters on their toes and his teammates urging him to "just throw strikes." He won three World Series games and posted a 1.77 ERA. Second baseman Del Marine enjoyed a great Series. He won the George Rulon Legion Player of the Year Award and the Louisville Slugger Award for his .459 average in national play. He even caught a couple of games when regular backstop Bobby Kim was injured. First baseman Ryan McGuire, the alpha male of the group, kept his teammates loose and always seemed to come through in the clutch. The outfielders Jeff Marks, Jason Cohen, and Carl McFadden were solid batters and flawless fielders. McFadden captured the Big Stick Award for most runs batted in during national play. Aside from Woodland Hills, Janesville pitcher Jeff Thelen took home the Bob Feller Award by striking out 34 batters. Andy Sheets of Gonzales was selected for the Sportsmanship Award.[23]

The World Series had been showing parity for the past several years. That trend continued in 1990, when the World Series was absent any of the traditional powers—Yakima, Boyertown, Cincinnati, or Rapid City. Rather, the ALWS cast of 1990 included Rockland County, New York OTB Pirates aka Fred Eller Post 1447; Richey's Market, representing Post 11 of Corvallis, Oregon; and Windward Legion of Kailua, Hawaii. Windward had bested Woodland Hills, California, 7–4, in the Western Region. The players of Oscar A. Rolon Post 48 of Bayamon, Puerto Rico, were a loose bunch by the time they got to Corvallis. The Bud Dry Razorbacks from Texarkana, Arkansas Post 58 got to the ALWS by beating Paducah, Kentucky, 4–3, in the Region 4 championship, as Chad Cowling homered and drove in three runs. In Region 2 play, Mayo, Maryland Post 226 Wildcats beat Delaware, 11–2. Others in the Series were Olathe, Kansas Post 153, and Midland, Michigan Post 165.[24]

Mayo and Bayamon ranked as favorites out of 4,111 Legion teams before the Series opened. The Mayo Wildcats had captured the Maryland title in 1988, 1989, and 1990. Going into the ALWS, they had won 66 games, giving them plenty of experience and confidence. On the negative side, the Wildcats were without their manager, Bernie Walter, who was fulfilling a commitment to coach the U.S. Junior team in Cuba. Wilfredo Trinidad took the reins, assisted by Charles "Tut" O'Hara. Bayamon had the two best prospects of the tourney in catcher Benji Molina and outfielder Ricardo Otero. Molina spent 13 years in the majors with the Angels, Toronto, San Francisco, and Texas. He won two

Gold Glove Awards and played in two World Series. Little Otero had three major league seasons.[25]

The two favorites met on the second day, with Bayamon taking a convincing 9–3 win. Bayamon and Mayo would meet again in the finals. On the first day, Texarkana needed 12 innings to beat Rockland, which they did, 4–3. Shortstop Rod Wyatt's solo homer won it for Texarkana. Bayamon scored seven runs in the fourth inning and hammered Olathe, 11–4. Richey's Market scored an 8–3 win over Midland as pitcher Kevin Hooker threw an unheard-of 177 pitches. Mayo slipped by Hawaii, 5–4. On day two, Hawaii got back on track by pounding Olathe, Kansas, 12–4, thanks to sloppy fielding by Olathe. Midland eliminated Rockland OTB, shutting them down, 4–0. In Bayamon's 9–3 win, Otero collected three hits and Juan Garcia pitching four spotless relief innings to get the win. Bayamon manager Jorge Santiago predicted, "we are going to win in five games."[26]

On day three, Mayo eliminated Midland, 8–4, as Brent O'Dea led the way with four hits and three RBI. Hawaii eliminated the home team, Corvallis, 3–1. Dwayne McCoy drove in two runs, and Kala Kahura plated the final run. Pitcher Lee DeSota got the win. Otero keyed a four-run rally in the fourth inning to lead Bayamon to a 9–7 win over previously undefeated Texarkana. That left four teams standing—Mayo, Hawaii, Texarkana and Bayamon. Mayo then eliminated Texarkana, 10–6, thanks to Jerry Nicklow's three-run homer.[27]

On the final day of the 1990 ALWS, Mayo knocked out Kailua, Hawaii, 16–4, to set up the final against Bayamon. Mark Foster pitched the first two innings, but he retired after Mayo scored nine runs in the second inning to take an 11–0 lead. He went the distance in the second game, throwing 150 pitches for the day. The exciting final ended in a 7–6 victory for Mayo before a crowd of 3,626. Puerto Rico took a 4–3 lead in the third inning. Mayo regained the lead in the eighth on Chris Dinoto's RBI triple and Pat Kahl's run-scoring groundout. Mayo added another run in the top of the ninth when Jerry Nicklow singled, stole second, and scored on Jim McNally's single. In the bottom of the ninth, Nelson Padro, who had three hits on the day, singled with two outs. Otero brought him around on an opposite-field double to make the score 7–6. Foster walked a batter, and Otero took third to raise the tension level to a peak. Foster then induced Manuel Cora to lift a soft fly to right to end the game. For Mayo, Foster drove in three runs, as did outfielder Jerry Nicklow. Mayo finished its championship season with a record of 71 wins and seven losses. The 71 wins was an ALWS record. The championship was the third for Maryland in the 65-year history of Legion ball.[28]

Foster, a graduate of Old Mill High School, took his selection as Player of the Year and MVP of the Series in stride. He had to drive to the University of Richmond to begin classes the next day. Mayo's left-handed-hitting outfielder, Brett O'Dea, took Louisville Slugger honors with a .514 batting average in national play (regionals and ALWS). Bayamon's little (5-foot-7) Little Ricky Otero captured the Big Stick Award with 37 total bases. Bayamon first baseman Luis Rosario went home with the RBI Award with 16. Clifton Foster of Texarkana won the Bob Feller Award. Otero also took home the Sportsmanship Award.[29]

In the off-season, Jim Quinlan, Assistant Director of Americanism and Children and Youth Divisions, put out a call for proposals from towns to host the American Legion World Series for at least the next six years. He left open the possibility of a permanent home for the tournament. Eleven cities submitted proposals. Boyertown, Fargo, and Roseburg were selected to alternate, with Boyertown hosting 1991 and 1994, Fargo in 1992 and 1995, and Roseburg 1993 and 1996. All three had hosted the World Series before, and all had experience hosting Sectional tournaments. Each city had drawn reasonably well, all three were hotbeds of Legion baseball, and all had conducted smooth programs. Manchester, Yakima, and Rapid City presented good cases, but the three cities selected had the highest attendance records over the years. In announcing the six-year rotation, Quinlan made clear that this decision did not close the door on a permanent location. Bears Stadium in Boyertown, where the rotation would begin, now had the fourth-brightest lights in Pennsylvania behind the major league Phillies and Pirates, and Scranton-Wilkes-Barre, home of the Triple-A International League team. Built in 1982, it was the Legion's equivalent of Baltimore's Camden Yards, the sweetest park in its league.

Many thought the 1991 Legion title would be played out in the Mid–Atlantic sectional tournament. In the past nine years, four title holders came through that section, along with two runners-up. In 1991, that Section two's hopes rested on Brooklawn, the team that knocked Boyertown out in the regional by a 2–0 score, leaving the Bears at home with a gaudy 50–8 record. So 1991 saw the coming-out party for Brooklawn. The team's founder and manager since 1952, Joe Barth, had unapologetically modeled his program after Boyertown. He declared, "Boyertown's got the premier Legion baseball program in the country." The village of Brooklawn had sprung up during World War I as a dormitory town for workers in the shipyards of Gloucester City, New Jersey. It became incorporated in 1926, the same year that American Legion baseball began play. By 1990, its population numbered only 1,800 residents. That a town so small continued to field an American Legion power was a testament to Barth's dedication and inspiration. Barth's club entered the 1991 World Series with an impressive 50–9 record, almost identical to that of Boyertown. Barth, now 72, took pride in winning 16 state titles, but he longed for that elusive national title. The other club that generated a great deal of buzz was All-Star Ford of Gonzales, Louisiana (49–6). Although they had not won a national title, Wade Simoneaux's club had been in the ALWS three of the past four years. Reporters saw them as a spirited and talented team. One described them as "a snappy, fun-to-watch bunch of Cajuns managed by the engaging Wade Simoneaux." Escondido coach Tim Chatton picked them to win it all.[30]

None of the other teams that made it to Boyertown were familiar names in Legion baseball. East Hartford, Connecticut, Post 77 (46–4) had little chance of advancing deep in the tournament despite their gaudy record. Glen Peters Post 266 of Sarasota, Florida (39–8), hoped at least to get a win. Newark, Ohio's, Levi Phillips Post 85 (60–13) boasted an outstanding shortstop in Ryan Beeney, who many believed was the best player in the tournament. Wyandotte Post 83 of Kansas City, Kansas (53–10), entered with little chance of success. Fremont, California, Post 837 Colts (41–14) brought a two-way performer in slugger and flame-thrower Bob Pailthorpe, but little else. A second California team, Escondido Post 149 (29–5), beat Lodi, 11–0, to win the state title.[31]

Brooklawn started off by winning two tight, low-scoring games, beating Newark, Ohio, 3–1, and Escondido, 3–2. Scott Lavender won the opening game, and Brett Laxton the second. In other first round games, East Hartford got an unusual win for Region One, beating Kansas City, 5–3. Catcher Mick Cormier led the way. Union City, California, slipped by Gonzales, 1–0, on Aaron Arroy's game-winning RBI in the ninth inning. Escondido beat Sarasota, 6–1, behind the four-hit pitching of Mike Frank. On the second day, Gonzales eliminated Kansas City. 9–4. as Jason Williams got three hits. Newark had to go ten innings to eliminate Sarasota, 4–3, on a throwing error. East Hartford won its second game by slamming Union City, 14–2.[32]

Game three for Brooklawn provided a laugher with Brian McGettigan shutting out East Hartford, and batters having a field day in a 12–0 win. Pitching proved the strength of Brooklawn throughout the Series. The win assured them of a place in the Series final. Their pitchers compiled a 1.82 ERA. Newark eliminated Union City, 11–9. Gonzales continued its comeback, beating Escondido, 8–5, a loss that eliminated the California club. With little pressure left, pitching let Brooklawn down against Gonzales in a 12–7 loss. Jason Williams of Gonzales set an ALWS record with four doubles. Newark won a close, 7–6 victory over East Hartford to burst Hartford's bubble and send the East Hartford lads back home. Cleanup hitter Brian Cummings hit a two-run home run and later a two-run double to pace the winners. In a late game, Newark picked up a 10–7 win over Gonzales for the right to play Brooklawn in the finals. Chris O'Dell had four hits, and Beeney collected three for Newark.[33]

The Brooks faced Newark in the final game of the 1991 ALWS. Barth selected Brett Laxton to start on two days' rest, but his fastball was not with him, and Newark jumped out to a 2–0 lead on Ryan Beeney's home run. Lavender relieved Laxton, who moved to first base. Lavender pitched the rest of the way, giving up just two hits. Brooklawn took the lead in the sixth inning as Newark pitcher Troy Hupp came unraveled. Brooklawn third baseman Mike Harris was hit by a pitch; outfielder Kevin Cunane walked; Lavender was hit by a pitch to load the bases with one out. Right-fielder John Mader blooped a single to get Brooklawn on the board. Newark manager Dave Froelich brought in a relief pitcher who walked Laxton to force in another run. Outfielder Jeff Manuola walked to score yet another run. One more walk, this to catcher Derek Forchic, gave Brooklawn the 4–2 lead. Shortstop Mike Moriarty scored the final run in the seventh inning on a Newark error, and Newark picked up one more run to make the final score 5–3.[34]

Joe Barth, Sr., at age 72, "wept uncontrollably after the last out was recorded." In his 40 years of coaching, he always had a way of churning out pitchers, and his World Series triumph was the ultimate vindication of his approach. "This makes up for the last 40 years," he said. "This is unbelievable." Second baseman Brian Obemeire was the team's only .400 hitter for the season, but it was pitching that made Brooklawn a championship club. As a team, Brooklawn posted a 1.82 ERA. His mound corps went deep: Lavender (2–0, 1.81), Laxton (3–0, 1.84), who made it to the major leagues with Oakland and Kansas City, and McGettigan (2–1, 0.84) led the attack.[35]

Newark shortstop Ryan Beeney, who batted a tournament high .414 and tied for the most RBI, was named National Player of the Year. Bob Pailthorpe of Union City, who tied Beeney for the RBI lead, took home the Big Stick Award for most total bases with 36, and won both the Louisville Slugger Award as top hitter and the Bob Feller Award for top pitcher. Jason Williams of Gonzales received the Sportsmanship Award. The all-tournament team selected by writers consisted of:Brian Cummings, first baseman of East Hartford; David Gautreau, second baseman, Gonzales; Mike Harris, third baseman from Brooklawn; Beeney, shortstop, Newark; Brady Babin, outfielder of Gonzales; Chris O'Dell, outfielder, Newark; John Mader, outfielder, Brooklawn; Mike Cormier, catcher of East Hartford; and pitcher Scott Lavender, Brooklawn.[36]

Joe Barth believed his Brooklawn team would win back-to-back titles by repeating their 1991 run. But unlike 1991, the 1992 World Series field was filled with teams recognizable from previous tournaments. They included East Hartford, Connecticut's Brown,

Landers, Ratti Post 77 (49–8), back for a second year. Guaynabo Jets (30–7), the Puerto Rico team sponsored by a telephone company, who had won the title in 1984, were not as strong as previous teams from the island. All-Star Ford, representing Post 81 of Gonzales, Louisiana (48–9), was back from a third-place finish the year before. Arlington Heights, Illinois (41–15), Post 208 believed it could cause trouble. Fargo, North Dakota, Post 2 (64–10) had the most wins and was playing in its home park. Rounding out the field of eight were the Medford, Oregon, Riders (43–15) Post 15, and Newbury Park, California, Oaks (36–2), a team without post affiliation. If Brooklawn (43–7) Post 72 could be beaten, Newbury Park appeared most likely to do that. Newbury Park was only in its second year of baseball. Coaches Chuck Fick and Joel Silverstein put the team together, drawing from Thousand Oaks and Newbury Park High Schools. They prohibited college players who might qualify under the age limitation. Lacking post sponsorship, funding for the team came from the players, their families and coaches, and whatever outside sponsorship they could find, which was not much. Players were asked to pony up $150, putting the team in a pay-to-play situation. Limited funding was the reason they had played fewer games than any other team in the Series.[37]

The 1992 Legion World Series was played in Fargo, North Dakota, hosted by the Gilbert C. Grafton Post 2 at its Jack Williams Park. Like Boyertown's stadium, Jack Williams got a lot of use, and the local community supported American Legion baseball. The park had opened in 1966 and had hosted the ALWS in 1983. For the 1992 season, Fargo agreed to pump $100,000 into upgrading the facility. Williams Park had only 2,291 permanent seats, but bleachers and standing room could bring the capacity to 5,000. It lacked a roof, and seating continued down the first base line to the 300-foot sign on the right field wall. Just a block away, the Red River of the North guaranteed that the park was subject to frequent flooding, especially in spring time.

Newbury Park's hopes for a title appeared to come crashing down in the opening game. Their pitching ace, Tighe Curran, came into the Series undefeated (10–0), but he lacked his best stuff, and Arlington Heights smashed the Oaks, 8–5. Phil O'Grady had four RBI for the winners. In other opening round games, East Hartford hammered Medford, 14–6, getting home runs from pitcher Chris Sawyer, Harry Rivera, and first baseman Stu Perry. Brooklawn won a close contest over Guaynabo, 4–3, behind Scott Lavender. In the feature game for Fargo fans, 5,000 fans cheered the locals, but Gonzales got three runs in the ninth inning to beat Fargo by a 5–4 score. Newbury Park returned to form in its second game. Behind lefty Adam West's four-hit pitching and David Lamb's three RBI, the Oaks eliminated Guaynabo, 7–1. The otherwise dull game became chippy when Guaynabo's manager announced that they were protesting the game on the grounds that Newbury did not have a post number on their uniforms. Newbury coach Chuck Fick threatened bodily harm to his counterpart. Calm returned when it was discovered that such a rule existed in Puerto Rico but not elsewhere in the United States. To the delight of the home fans, Fargo also rose from its heartbreaking opening day loss to oust Medford, 5–2. East Hartford, in a mild upset, defeated Gonzales pitching ace Reggie Wheat (16–2) by a convincing 12–1 score. Arlington Heights pulled a major upset over Brookland in a 2–1 pitchers' duel.[38]

Brooklawn came right back to knock Fargo out of the Series, 6–2. Brett Laxton pitched a complete game and struck out 11. Scott Lavender drove in four runs. Newbury Park continued its winning ways, knocking out Gonzales in a close 6–5 game. Shortstop David Lamb led the way. In a battle of undefeated teams, Arlington Heights bested East

Hartford, 5–4. Newbury got the bye among three one-loss teams. Brooklawn had little trouble with East Hartford, eliminating the Connecticut team, 14–4, thanks to six Hartford errors. Third baseman Mike Harris' two-run homer started the rout.[39]

Newbury Park and Arlington Heights played the critical Game 13 in terrible weather, with the temperature registering 50 degrees in light rain and a 20 mile per hour wind. Arlington Heights had defeated Newbury in the opening game, 8–5, so they felt confident going into this game. Newbury Park, however, prevailed, 7–4. On the heels of that big win, Newbury faced defending champion Brooklawn. Lefty Adam West was at his best. He limited the Brooks to five hits in shutting them out, as Newbury sent last year's winners back to New Jersey, winning 3–0. Ryan Kritscher drove in the first run in the sixth inning with a triple and finished with four hits.[40]

In the 1992 championship game, Newbury Park displayed its dominance by hammering Arlington Heights, 10–0. The Oaks pounded out 17 hits to tie a record that had stood since the first ALWS in 1926. Jeff Nastor got the win on a five-hitter before 2,545 fans. Outfielder Trent Martin collected four hits. Shortstop David Lamb, third baseman Ryan Kritscher, outfielder Jim Chergey, and catcher Robert Frick each got three hits. The boys from Thousand Oaks and Newbury Park High Schools gave California its 16th Legion title.[41]

Newbury Park collected most honors for the Series. Shortstop David Lamb was named Player of the Year. He later played for Tampa Bay, the New York Mets, and the Minnesota Twins, without great distinction. Ryan Kritscher batted .448 in regional and Series games, as did Brandon Weigel of Fargo, so they tied for the Louisville Slugger Award. Trent Martin of Newberry Park drove in 17 runs to claim the RBI Award. Tighe Curran, the Newbury pitcher, won the Bob Feller Award by striking out 35 batters. Arlington Heights' John Klopp took home the Sportsmanship Award.[42]

In 1993, the Legion World Series shifted to Roseburg, Oregon's Legion Memorial Field. Like Fargo and Boyertown, Roseburg had established itself as a stronghold of Legion baseball. The Stadium seated 3,125, but bleachers from the Douglas County Fairgrounds brought capacity to over 5,000. Roseburg had to be pleased when the 1993 ALWS attracted 34,306 fans, the highest total since 1960.[43]

The Series, however, would prove to be about long-time coach Dave Ploof and his Rapid City Hardhats. Just as the 1991 Series featured Brooklawn's Joe Barth's ultimate quest for the elusive title, 1993 proved the culmination to Ploof's four-decade-long Legion coaching career. A native of Austin, Minnesota, and a Mankato State graduate, he began coaching Post 22 in 1965 and continued in that role until 2011. In that time. he won 2,483 games against 808 losses, a winning percentage of .755. His 1993 South Dakota state title, a 7–2 win over Pierre in the championship game, was number 34 for him. This was his eighth trip to the World Series. All had ended in disappointment. Mark Ellis, Ploof's 1993 star shortstop, who went on to a 12-year major league career, said of playing for Ploof: "You have to work harder than everybody else, and take pride in what you are doing." Mitch Messer, who succeeded Ploof as coach, described his mentor this way: "He was a hard guy. He expected nothing but the best and you either figured it out or you weren't back." There is a clear pattern here.[44]

Nothing was ever given to Dave Ploof, and 1993 was no different. Although his Hardhats came in with an amazing 66–4 record, the Nevada Youth Baseball Association team from Green Valley, Nevada, playing as Las Vegas Post 8 with a 52–10 record, came in as the favorites. New England teams were little respected. New Bedford,

Dave Ploof coached Rapid City's Post 22 Hardhats for 47 years. He retired with 2,483 wins, including 33 state titles, eight Legion World Series appearances and one national title in 1992 (courtesy *Rapid City Journal*).

Massachusetts, Post 1 (30–6) was no different. New York's Off-Track Betting (OTB)-Fred Eller Post 1447 of Rockland County, New York (55–23), boasted a 9–6 win over Boyertown, but they lost their star, John Esainko, when he broke a leg against Mayo. Miami Sound Barrier Post 346 (53–21) hoped to win a game. From the midlands, beside Rapid City, Norman, Oklahoma, Post 88 (57–15), was making its first ALWS appearance. Osseo, Minnesota (32–6), counted on its hitting; in the Regional, Nate Larson hit a resounding .778 and Bryan Mileski batted .625. The Far West was represented by Fairfield, California, Post 182 (61–16).[45]

The Series opened with a bang as Rockland and Norman teed off in one of the wildest games in years. The two combined for 36 hits to establish a new Legion Series record. Rockland managed to blow a seven-run lead but still won, 13–12, on Mike Rooney's walk-off RBI. Las Vegas had little trouble disposing of New Bedford, 6–4. Chad Stevenson hit a three-run homer for Las Vegas. Rapid City pounded out 20 hits in its 15–2 triumph over Osseo. In that game, Bill Freytag pitched a five-hitter, while Ryan Merritt and Ben Thomas collected four hits each. In the final first-round game, Fairfield edged Miami, 12–11.[46]

In the second round of play, Osseo and New Bedford were the first to be eliminated, losing to Norman, 10–7, and Miami, 9–5, respectively. Rapid City and Las Vegas continued their winning ways. Rapid City took out Rockland, 14–5, and Las Vegas beat Fairfield, 1–0. Against Rockland, Nate Barnes and Ben Thomas each banged out three hits.

Miami and Fairfield headed for the exit after losing to Rockland, 6–5, and Norman, 5–3, respectively.[47]

Rapid City and Las Vegas, the two favorites, stood apart from the pack as the only undefeated teams and seemingly on the track to the finals. When they squared off for the first time in Game 11, Dave Ploof's Hardhats were taking no prisoners, winning 16–0. Thomas limited Las Vegas to four hits, and he and Scott Dressler collected three bingles. The following day, Las Vegas returned to its winning ways, eliminating Rockland, 12–0, on Kevin Eberwein's one-hitter. Then the leaders surprisingly became even again as Norman upended Rapid City, 11–5 thanks to third baseman Allan Layman's three-hit performance which included a home run. Rapid City supporters said it was a meaningless game because win or lose, they would be in the finals. Las Vegas reclaimed its ranking and a place in the championship game by beating third-place Norman, 16–4. Torrey Walson led the 16-hit attack with three hits and three runs batted in.[48]

The 1993 championship game made clear that Rapid City deserved the title. Las Vegas committed four errors in Rapid City's 7–4 win. Pitcher Bill Freytag picked up his third win of the Series for Rapid City. Left-handed-hitting first baseman Ben Thomas put Rapid City in front with a two-run double. He and outfielder Brian Ogle both had two hits, including a double and two RBI. Ryan Merritt also contributed two hits and scored three runs. Ploof and South Dakota finally had a national title. The Series drew 34,306 fans, the best showing since the eight-team format began in 1960.[49]

Throughout the season, the Hardhats got outstanding play from their stars, Thomas, Merritt, and shortstop Mark Ellis. Thomas, a 6-foot-3 first baseman and pitcher, posted a .435 batting average for the tournament and an ERA of 0.65 with 27 strikeouts and three wins. He went on to Wichita State, followed by five years in the Atlanta farm system and three in independent leagues. Merritt, the leadoff hitter, batted .490 for the tournament to claim the batting title, following .441 for the regular season. He played six seasons in the minors, making it to the AAA level before retiring. Freytag tried his hand at pro ball, two years in the independent Heartland League. Shortstop Mark Ellis was not the biggest star in the ALWS, but he had already established his credentials by being selected South Dakota Player of the Year, after batting .361 for the Hardhats. He would attend the University of Florida on a baseball scholarship, followed by 12 years in the major leagues, 2002–2014, with Kansas City, Oakland, Colorado, and St. Louis.

Thomas was selected American Legion Player of the Year. He also won the Bob Feller Award for most strikeouts in regional and Series play. Ryan Merritt took the Louisville Slugger Award for his .490 batting average. Norman's Allen Layman went home with the Big Stick Award (total bases) and the Cowger RBI Award. Chad Stevenson of Las Vegas received the Sportsmanship Award. The Leadership Awards, of course, went to Dave Ploof and his assistant coach, Steve Wolf. Ploof was not yet ready to retire, but when he did in 2011, after 47 years of coaching with 2,483 wins, he was the winningest coach in Legion history.[50]

The 1994 World Series shifted back to Boyertown, where it had been in 1991. Little change was noticeable in Boyertown for the final five days of August. The change, rather, was to major league baseball. Relations between major league club owners and the Major League Baseball Players Association had continued to worsen after the owners forced Fay Vincent out as commissioner and refused to replace him, leaving Milwaukee Brewers owner Bud Selig in charge as acting commissioner. That decision polluted labor relations in baseball because Selig was the sworn enemy of Don Fehr, executive director of the Players Association. In January 1994, owners proposed a salary cap, which the players had made clear was not negotiable. Making matters worse, the owners hired Richard Ravitch, an aggressive anti-union lawyer, to negotiate a contract for them. It did not work. Fehr called the players out on strike on August 12. Hope of a settlement continued for a month before Selig announced the cancellation of the remainder of the season and, for the first time in history, the World Series itself. Although the players' strike had no direct bearing on Legion baseball, it cast a huge shadow over the American Legion World Series.

Brooklawn (42–11) became the fan favorite in Boyertown. They were the fan base closest to Boyertown and had become the main rivals of Boyertown in Mid–Atlantic play. The Brooks managed to lose the New Jersey state title to Atco, but advanced to the Region 1 tournament in Rhode Island. There they beat Bristol, Connecticut, 7–0, to gain a place in the ALWS. Coach Bob Barth, Sr.'s grandson and hard-hitting first baseman, also named Bob Barth (Jr.), led the Brooks' attack. Pitcher Fran Weikel pitched a shutout in the Regional final. Bedford, Virginia Post 54 (34–2) took Brooklawn's traditional place as champions of the Mid–Atlantic region. This was their first trip to the ALWS. Coach Jack Krause, who made it to the championship game as a player with Phoebus, Virginia, in 1959, admitted to "playing Boyertown ball," which included bunting, aggressive base running, and strong pitching. Former major leaguer Ken Clay took responsibility for Bedford's improved pitching. Bedford boasted an excellent infielder in Brandon Inge, who subsequently played 12 seasons for the Detroit Tigers. The Miami Post 346 team (31–6) had the experience of being the only team to return from the 1993 ALWS. That experience had lasted just three games, but it gave coach Carolos Hernandez and his boys a sense of what it took to win on the big stage. They brought a 36–7 record to Boyertown. Their Cuban fans were by far the most boisterous of the eight finalists. Tiny outfielder Esteban Barrios, pitcher Danny Alvarez, and first baseman Roy Muro would go in the free agent draft, although none made it to the majors.[51]

Three teams from the Midwest—Russellville, Arkansas, Post 20 (35–7), Blissfield, Michigan, Post 325 (48–12), and Omaha North Vikings Post 1 (58–2)—all appeared to have a chance. Russellville boasted flame-throwing pitcher Lance Franks, who would win the Bob Feller Awards for most strikeouts. Unfortunately, they had little else. Cooke Stationery, representing Post 136 of Salem, Oregon, was a crowd favorite, partly because they had traveled the furthest to get to the tournament. Their pin-striped uniforms with "COOKE'S" emblazoned on the front, gave them the most professional look. They drew players from five high schools and Western Oregon State University. The hard-hitting Chino Reds Post 299 came in with a modest 38–10 record, but they possessed a powerful offense led by Frank Hinojosa, who was the MVP of the regional, where he hit .520. They got to Boyertown by beating Upland in the state final and the Colorado champs in the regional. They would set ALWS records for hits (148), doubles (41), and batting average (.347). This was a team to take seriously.[52]

In the opening round, Chino proved its merit by whipping Omaha, 12–6. Erick Gomez went 5-for-5 and set an ALWS record when he drove in eight runs. In the feature game, Miami got the best of Brooklawn, 5–3, thanks to Esteban Barrios' two-run home run and Marc Suarez' two-run double. Cooke's Stationery bested Bedford, 4–1. Blissfield beat Russellville, 5–2. Pitcher Rob Redman pitched a complete game without giving up an earned run.

On day two, the weather became hazy, hot, and humid, not atypical for late August in southeastern Pennsylvania. Omaha eliminated Russellville, 1–0, on Drue Council's three-hitter. Chino defeated Blissville by a 5–2 score. In a record-tying contest, Brooklawn went 14 innings to beat Bedford, 5–4. Brooklawn had runners thrown out at home in the ninth, tenth, and 13th innings. The winning run scored when right fielder Jack Marcellus drew a bases-loaded walk to force in the run. The loss eliminated Bedford. This tied for the longest game in World Series history with Spartanburg–San Diego in 1938, Manchester-Nashville in 1966, and Springfield-Omaha in 1968.[53]

The 14-inning game appeared to take the starch out of Brooklawn. On Sunday, facing elimination, they lost to Blissfield, 7–6. The RBI double of the victors' catcher, Randy Pfeiffer, in the eighth inning provided the winning blow. Chino's vaunted attack exploded in the final Sunday game, hammering Miami, 19–9. Pitcher Jeff Bajenaru tied the record with eight RBIs, and battery mate Frank Hinojosa knocked in five runs to lead the Reds, which were now the only undefeated team remaining, and guaranteed a spot in the championship game. Despite the humiliating loss, Miami refused to die. They came back the next day in Game 12 to beat Blissfield, 4–1, in an elimination game. Barrios's seventh-inning homer was the big blow for Miami. Danny Alvarez did not give up an earned run. Cooke's took Chino out of the undefeated ranks, putting on their own batting show in a 15–1 win. They collected 19 hits, led by Jake Underwood's mammoth grand-slam homer. B. R. Cook got credit for the win. In a semi-final game, Miami had to face a Salem team that was confident after its thrashing of Chico. With Salem ahead, 3–1, in the seventh inning, Miami's Luis Cabral tied the game up with two-run single, before Esteban Barrios drove in the game-winner. Daniel Gomez posted the 6–3 victory.[54]

In the 1994 championship game, Miami avenged its earlier ten-run loss to Chino with a decisive 9–0 win to capture the title. Fernando Rodriquez hurled a five-hit complete game for his 15th win of the season against only one loss, his third win of the World Series, and his fourth in national play. He also contributed a home run. Roy Muro led Miami with three hits and two RBI, while Jose Zabala, Louis Cabral, and Rodriquez had two hits each. Chico had to be satisfied knowing it set records for most hits in the tournament (148) and the most doubles (41).[55]

Miami's Rodriquez won recognition as Player of the Year. Other award winners were Bob Barth, Jr., of Brooklawn, who took the Louisville Slugger Award with a .438 average. Esteban Barrios won the Big Stick Award with 35 total bases. Frank Hinojosa of Chino captured the RBI Award with 24. Lance Franks of Russellville received the Bob Feller Award with 30 strikeouts. Chino's Eric Gomez was voted the Sportsmanship Award.[56]

The 1995 Series returned to Fargo and Jack Williams Park on the Red River bounding South Dakota and Minnesota, where the ALWS was last held in 1992. Joe Parmer, known locally as "Mr. Baseball," had been the main shaker and mover, getting the Legion to select Fargo for the World Series. Parmer had become manager of the Fargo Municipal Airport in 1953, the same year he became chairman of the Post 2 baseball program. He was a power organizer who co-chaired three ALWS in 1983, 1992 and 1995. Unafraid of jobs others avoided, he had been the chief fundraiser for 40 years.[57]

In 1995 Portland, Maine, Post 17 (30–6) became the first team ever to make the World Series from the state of Maine, having surprised Middletown, Connecticut, in the Region One finals. New England teams were usually "one and done," but this club had high expectations. Waldorf, Maryland (54–11), also in its first appearance in the ALWS, was not as strong a team as the Mid–Atlantic Regional had sent to the Series in recent years. Columbia, Tennessee, Post 19 (37–17) was the third team making its first showing in the Series. Starkville, Mississippi, Post 17 (44–10) would also be surprised to get a victory. Osseo, Minnesota, Post 172 (37–4) beat Blue Springs, Missouri, 13–5, in the Great Lakes Regional to gain a spot in the ALWS. Rapid City Post 22 (65–8), the 1993 champions, had beaten Omaha to earn its spot in the Series. As long as Dave Ploof coached the team, it had a chance. The Lakeside Recovery Center of Bellevue, Washington (51–8), won the Northwest Regional by defeating Lodi, California. Aiea, Hawaii (30–4), emerged as a serious contender in the Regionals. Because they had played the fewest games of teams in the Series, and because they had the greatest distance to travel for the Series, they were an unknown entity. Key members of the team, pitcher/first baseman/outfielder Jason Adaro and first baseman/outfielder Kevin Bagoyo, had played on the 1988 Pearl City, Hawaii, Little League team that lost in the final to Taiwan. Adaro went 4–0 as a pitcher and batted .488. Lon Yamaguchi was selected MVP of the regional after batting .460. Assistant coach Garrett Nago summed up their advantages: "Defense was our biggest strength and also pitching."[58]

In the first round, Portland did, indeed, get its victory, 9–1, despite a three-hour rain delay, over Osseo. First baseman Kevin McDonald collected four hits to lead the attack. It was the first win by a New England team since 1991. Aiea's pitching strength was apparent in its 2–0 shutout of Waldorf. Shawn Nakamura got the win, and third baseman Davey Meguro homered. Columbia shortstop Bobby Morgan homered twice to lead his team over Starkville by an 8–7 score. The host team got its win, 4–3, over Bellevue. In the second-round losers' bracket, Osseo sent Starkville home, 3–0, as Matt Erickson struck out 10 in his complete game. Bellevue squeaked by Waldorf, 7–6, thanks to Mark Thomas' grand slam and Dom Crispo's bases-loaded single. Columbia's Bobby Morgan homered again, his third of the Series, and his team won, 6–2, over Portland. Aiea's pitching ace, Jason Adaro, threw a two-hitter to beat Rapid City, 3–0. Adaro and Mark Pevy accounted for the runs. Shortstop Lon Yamaguchi had three hits, including a triple.[59]

On the third day of the Series, Aiea and Osseo emerged the only undefeated teams. Bellevue sent Portland back to Maine by a convincing 11–1 score in a game shortened to six innings due to the mercy rule (a 10-run lead). Osseo eliminated Rapid City, 4–3, on Kyle Winberg's home run in the eighth inning. Dustin Carlson pitched a complete game and struck out the last batter with two men on base in the ninth. Aiea won a pitching duel between Delane Barley and Bobby Morgan of Columbia by a 3–2 score. The next day, Bellevue hammered Columbia, eliminating them, 16–9. Catcher Burke Eshorne homered and tied a record by scoring five runs. In the so-called "dumb-dumb" game, meaningless for Aiea because win or lose, they were guaranteed a place in the championship game, Kyle Winberg limited Aiea to six hits as Osseo coasted to a 10–0 win in a game called after seven innings because of the mercy rule. Catcher Bill Lockwood homered and drove in three runs. That left three teams with one loss. Bellevue played Osseo for the chance to play Aiea. Bellevue's Woody Heath pitched nine shutout innings and racked up enough strikeouts to win the Bob Feller Award, but he was removed from the game that remained scoreless until the 14th inning. Osseo got two runs, but Bellevue came back with three of its own, the last scoring on a sacrifice fly by Dom Crispo.[60]

In the 1995 championship game, Aiea coach Alan Higuchi chose to pitch his ace, Jason Adaro, despite a hamstring injury he suffered in an earlier game. He fired a 2–0, four-hit shutout to beat Bellevue, Washington. The only runs came in the bottom of the first inning. Jason Takamura led off with a single, stole second, and went to third on a groundout. Lon Yamaguchi walked. Then Takamura scored on a double steal. One out later, Yamaguchi scored on a wild pitch. For Adaro, it was his second shutout of the World Series and his fourth in regional and Series play. His ERA for sectional and Series games was a minuscule 0.90. Officially, 3,546 fans crowded into Jack Williams for the game, and millions more watched on ESPN.[61]

In past years, the selection of an all-tournament team had been a sometime thing, dependent on the journalists who showed up. In 1995, *Baseball America* took over the task and selected the mythical team thereafter. Jason Adaro headed the team as the first baseman. Others were Greg Anderson (Osseo) second base; David Meguro (Aiea) third base; Lon Yamaguchi (Aiea) shortstop; Dom Crispo (Bellevue) outfield; Larry Lockridge (Columbia) outfield; Mike Wirrick (Bellevue) outfield; Bobby Morgan (Columbia) utility; Bill Lockwood (Osseo) catcher; Matt Erickson (Osseo) pitcher; and Woody Heath (Bellevue) pitcher. In other awards, Adaro was named 1995 Player of the Year and captured both the Louisville Slugger Award with a .488 batting average, and the Big Stick Award for most total bases with 29. He also won a $2,000 Gatorade college scholarship. Bellevue's Dom Crispo took home the RBI Award with 15. Woody Heath of Bellevue won both the Bob Feller Award for most strikeouts and the Sportsmanship Award.[62]

The early to mid–1990s brought a new generation to political power. Generation X came with deep worries about their future and the future of the world. Bill Clinton, a baby-boomer, rode the generational change to the presidency in 1992. Even after losing control of Congress but before being impeached, he swept back into the presidency in 1996. Clinton worked to modernize the American economy and enjoyed an economic upturn that lasted the decade.

The 1996 World Series was full of surprises, first-evers, and upsets. A little-known team, Yardley Western Post 317, caught fire and got a ride on the magic carpet through the tournament. Yardley, a community in Bucks County, Pennsylvania, could not beat out Boyertown in the Pennsylvania tournament; in fact, Boyertown beat Yardley twice, 3–0 and 6–0, on its way to the Pennsylvania title. But by finishing second, Yardley was able to enter the New England sectional, which it won by beating Swampscott, Massachusetts, in the final, 5–4, on first baseman Brian Moyer's RBI in the 10th inning. Yardley had never been to a World Series before. Even so, the champion from Region one had never won a World Series title, and generally won few games. So entering the ALWS, little was expected from Yardley. On paper they were not close to being the best team. Its coach believed their 1995 team was better than the 1996 club. Yardley had only one player, outfielder Vic Hillaert, thought highly enough of by the major league teams to be drafted. They also had just one player who made the all-tournament team.[63]

Gonzales, Louisiana, also known as All-Star Ford, had the best team on paper with a 48–11 record. Gonzales was a familiar face in American Legion World Series, having been there four times in the past decade. According to Yardley's second baseman, Joe Ferrero, Gonzales had "better individual players; bigger, stronger, faster." Their pitching ace, Ben Sheets, was considered the outstanding prospect in the World Series. He would go on to pitch ten years in the majors, eight of those with Milwaukee. He appeared in four All-Star Games. Five of Gonzales' players from the 1996 team made the all-tournament team. Other teams in the 1996 World Series included: Fred Eller Rockland County, New York, Off-Track Betting Pirates, Post 1447 (52–38), which got there by beating Boyertown 2–1 in the Mid–Atlantic Regional final behind the pitching of Rob Richey; Rowan County, also known as Salisbury, North Carolina, Post 81; Berryhill Lightning of Post 22, Midland, Michigan, entered with an impressive 52–12 record; Dave Ploof's Rapid City, South

Dakota, Hardhats, Post 22 (67–22), a fixture in the ALWS they had won in 1993, featured Regional MVP Luke Wheeler; Salmon Creek Post 176 of Vancouver, Washington, was making its first appearance in the classic; Holladay Post 71 of Sandy, Utah, was not only making its first appearance, it was the first team from Utah ever to make the World Series. The ALWS would go without a team from California.[64]

On the opening day of the Series, Yardley served notice that they should be watched. Outfielder Vic Hillaert homered in the eighth inning to tie Gonzales, and second baseman Joe Ferraro homered in the ninth to give Yardley a 10–9 win. For Rapid City, Calvin Hofer's double scored two runs in the first inning, and the Hardhats were off to a 10–3 win over Rockland.Vancouver beat Sandy, 7–3, and Rowan County just slipped by Midland, 2–1.On day two, in the losers' bracket, Rockland pitched its ace, Pete Memeth, with a 14–0 record, but he could not hold Midland, losing 10–6 in ten innings. Pirates pitchers walked 15, four in the fateful 10th inning. The loss eliminated Rockland. The Utah team could not play with Gonzales, losing 7–0, so it went home without a win. One advantage of playing in the winner's bracket, said Dave Ploof, was that they played at night, thus avoiding the 100-degree heat. That advantage failed to help Rapid City, which lost to Rowan County, 5–2. Yardley beat Vancouver, 12–6.[65]

In elimination games, Sparky Anderson lent his support to Dave Ploof's club, but to no avail as Gonzales sent Rapid City home by a 7–3 score. James Jarreau went 4-for-4 with a home run and three RBI. Midland knocked Vancouver out of the tournament by a 9–8 score. In the battle of previously unbeaten teams in the crucial Game 11, Yardley beat Rowan County, 9–8, to assure itself of a place in the championship game. In Game 12, Gonzales handed Rowan County its second straight loss, 7–4, eliminating the North Carolinians. In the meaningless Game 13, Yardley rested as many starters as possible and lost, 13–1, to Midland.[66]

On the final day of the 1996 ALWS, a crowd of 4,089 showed up despite the 102-degree temperature. Gonzales had little trouble beating Midland, 11–3, to reach the final game. In the championship game, Gonzales took a 3–2 lead into the seventh inning. Then Yardley struck. Shortstop Keith Balent walked, followed by singles by Brian Moyer and Nelson Rednate, scoring Balent. Joe Ferrero reached on an error which scored Moyer. Vic Hillaert drove in the final run of the inning. Balent drove in an insurance run in the eighth to make the final score 6–3. Ed Soley, the winning pitcher, gave up ten hits, but kept Gonzales off the scoreboard over the final three innings.[67]

Yardley, with a final record of 48 wins against 11 losses, had no shortage of heroes. Outfielder John Wakely batted .429 in the Series, second baseman Joe Ferrero collected 12 RBI, and first baseman Brian Moyer, the MVP of the Regional, who batted .341 with 20 total bases, were big contributors to Yardley's success. Their number two pitcher, Bob Krout, had two ALWS wins and a 0.87 ERA. Coach Meade Tenaglia, who operated his family's 7-Eleven store in Bensalem when not on the coaching lines, would bask in an unexpected championship.[68]

The George W. Rulon Player of the Year for 1996 went to Christian Bourgeois of Gonzales. He also took home the RBI award with 15. Bryce Gehlen of Vancouver earned the Slugger Award with a .514 batting average. James Jarreau of Gonzales took the Rawlings Big Stick Award with 34 total bases. The Bob Feller Award went to Ben Sheets of Gonzales, with 37 strikeouts. Andy Hoffman of Midland took home the Sportsmanship Award. Yardley coach Meade Tenaglia received the Leadership Award, which automatically goes to the coach of the championship team.[69]

Baseball America's all-tournament team did not include even one member from Yardley. It consisted of catcher Andy Fontenot, Gonzales; first baseman Christian Bourgeois, Gonzales; second baseman Casey Lambert, Gonzales; third baseman Bryce Gehlen, Vancouver; shortstop Kevin Quinn, Midland; left field Matt Madison, Vancouver; center field John Wakely, Yardley; right field Kip Harris, Midland; designated hitter James Jarreau, Gonzales; utility Travis Goins, Rowan County; pitcher Ben Sheets, Gonzales; and pitcher Andy Hoffman, Midland.

Jim Quinlan and the rest of the Legion hierarchy had to be satisfied with the 1996 Series. The weather remained clear and dry, although hot. Roseburg's Legion Field at Stewart Park drew 38,836 fans for the 15-game Series. Roseburg had drawn 34,306 when it hosted in 1993. Those were the highest attendance totals since Yakima drew 40,269 in 1954.

The following year, 1997, the ALWS returned to the upper Midwest, where it had been in 1992 and 1995, except it moved from Fargo, North Dakota, to Rapid City, South Dakota. It was like returning to the wild-wild West to view a shoot-out in hitter-friendly Floyd Fitzgerald Stadium. Never had a Series witnessed such an offensive explosion. The Series set records for the most runs scored (273), a whopping 18 runs per game. It also had the most doubles (187). Conversely, with no shutouts, it tied the record for the fewest shutouts recorded in a Series, tying the ALWS of 1978, 1980, and 1984. Only one of the 15 games saw fewer than 12 runs scored.

Although half the teams were newcomers, powerful teams abounded. Rock Island, Illinois, Post 200 appeared to be the offensive juggernaut of the tournament. Few teams had ever arrived at the ALWS with such a gaudy record as Rock Island's 47–1 mark. In the Regionals, they batted nearly .500, winning five straight games and outscoring opponents 72–20. The Rock's final game was a convincing win over Midland, Michigan, the defending Great Lakes Regional champion. Other contenders were the Medford, Oregon, Mustangs and Sanford, Florida, Post 53. Medford Post 15, known as "The Bomb Squad," came in with a 53–9 record and loaded with prospects. They beat San Fernando, California, 9–6, in Region 7. Those prospects included outfielder Nate Philo, third baseman Brian Fachet, catcher Rick Dorman, and pitchers Stan Spencer and Steve Becher. Medford had appeared in the 1992 ALWS but went home disappointed. Sanford, with a 43–12 record, seemed to be meshing at the right time. They defeated Gallatin, Tennessee, 14–1, in the Region 3 final. Sanford had its own set of prospects, led by second baseman Tim Raines, Jr., son of the future Hall of Fame star of the Montreal Expos. They featured a fine pitcher in Ryan Mau, the MVP of the Southeast Regional, as well as first baseman Clyde Williams, third baseman Chris Louwsma, and shortstop Andy Neufeld.[70]

Other teams seemed to have flaws. Bristol, Connecticut, Post 2 (42–9) had beaten Spring City, Pennsylvania, 3–2, in the Northeastern Regional, but except for last year when Yardley, an outlier from Region Two, came out of Region One to win the title, no New England team had gone beyond three games in decades. Severna Park, Maryland Post 175 (56–13) beat Brooklawn on Mark Teixeira's two homers to take the Region Two title. Teixeira would go on to a 14-year big-league career in which he hit 409 home runs, but he was just one guy and not a pitcher. Tulsa, Oklahoma Post 1 (39–5), a 4–2 winner over West Point, Mississippi, in the Region 4 final, was in its fourth ALWS, hoping to get one win in the Series. New Brighton, Minnesota, Post 513 (47–7) beat Excelsior, Minnesota, 2–0, in Region 6 and was just happy to be in the Series. The Fairfield, California, Expos (54–14) filled out the eighth spot. They had defeated Aiea, Hawaii, 7–4, in Region 8.[71]

The shootout began on opening day. Bristol surprised everyone by smashing Severna Park, 18–4. Catcher Matt Herbert had four hits, three runs, and four RBI, as did battery mate Adam Platt. Rock Island failed to live up to its lofty credentials, losing to Medford, 14–4. Medford hammered out 20 hits, including back-to-back mammoth home runs by third baseman Brian Fochet and left fielder Kevin Follett. Tulsa beat Fairfield, 10–9, thanks to six Fairfield fielding errors and several mental errors. Sanford topped New Brighton, 10–7.

In day two play, Fairfield eliminated Mark Teixeira's Severna Park team, 10–7, as designated hitter Danny Bivian drove in five runs. Rock Island pounded out 19 hits in its 15–7 thrashing of New Brighton. The loss eliminated the Minnesota team. In the only low-scoring game of the entire Series, Bristol slipped by Tulsa, 3–2. In the defensive play of the series, Bristol outfielder Mike Rose made a spectacular diving catch while crashing onto the right field wall to preserve Bristol's victory. Workhorse Adam Platt got the save. In what proved to be a crucial game, Sanford overcame a 6–2 Medford lead to explode for a record-tying 12 runs in the seventh inning on their way to a 17–7 win. A combined 13 doubles—nine by Sanford—was also a new record. Shortstop Andy Neufeld had four RBI.[72]

In elimination games, Rock Island sent Tulsa home by a 10–8 score, and Medford outlasted Fairfield, 16–14, after rain suspended the game overnight. For Medford, first baseman Shawn Walker and outfielder Ryan Peterson hit homers, and Nate Philo collected four hits. Sanford continued its winning ways, beating Bristol by a 11–1 score, guaranteeing Florida a spot in the final game. Aaron Black pitched a masterpiece. Medford sent Bristol home, 14–4. Philo again got four hits. Undefeated Sanford went to the bottom of the ninth before it eliminated Rock Island on Clyde Williams' walk-off home run to give the Florida club a 10–8 victory. Raines and Neufeld had homered earlier for Sanford.[73]

On the final day of the 1997 Series, Sanford and Medford, clearly the two best teams, were left to determine the championship. Medford had everything working in the first game, while Sanford knew it could afford to lose. Philo, Fachet, and Peterson homered as Medford ran away with a 12–2 victory. In the championship game, rain troubled play from the first pitch. After five innings, Medford held an 8–2 lead, powered by two home runs and three RBI by Shawn Walker. In the sixth inning, however, Medford collapsed, allowing seven Sanford runs. After two singles, one of which could have been ruled an error, Chris Louwsma's three-run homer put Sanford ahead. Raines contributed two homers and four RBI in the game. Sanford had a championship in its first ALWS.[74]

Only Tim Raines, Jr., made the major leagues from the Sanford championship club. He spent three years with the Orioles, but he was not the second coming of his father. Several others gave pro ball a shot. Clyde Williams played seven minor league seasons. Chaz Lytle played five seasons and Chris Louwsma played four seasons, as did Andy Neufeld. Pitcher Ryan Mau played two years in the minors before turning to coaching.

Sanford dominated the all-tournament team. The entire infield was there—first baseman Williams, second baseman Raines, and shortstop Neufeld were selected at their positions. Third baseman Louwsma was picked as the utility player. Outfielder Paulo Silvo and pitcher Jeff Monaco rounded out the Sanford members. Others selected for the team were Nate Philo, outfielder of Medford, whose 11 doubles for the tourney set a record; Bob Vanhoorbeck, outfielder from Rock Island; Rick Dorman, Medford's catcher; Shawn Walker of Medford was the designated hitter; and Steve Becher, Medford pitcher.

Nate Philo of Medford won the Louisville Slugger for his .520 batting average, the Rawlings Big Stick Award with 44 total bases, and was selected the George W. Rulon Player of the Year. Brian Fachet of Medford took home the Irvin "Click" Cowger RBI Award. Stan Spenser of Medford won the Bob Feller Award with 37 strikeouts. Finally, Sanford manager Rod Ferguson received the Jack Williams Memorial Leadership Award. Attendance at the Rapid City Series was 24,525, disappointing organizers and Legion management.[75]

Even though experience had taught the Legion powers to stay away from large cities and big venues, they selected Cashman Field, home of Las Vegas' AAA Pacific Coast League team, to host the 1998 World Series. Initially, the Series had been awarded to Milardo-Wilcox Post 75 of Middletown, Connecticut, but when TV crews looked at the facility, they said the lighting was below par for television cameras. Since nothing needed to be done to Cashman, it got the nod. The facility was owned and operated by the city's Convention Bureau. Constructed in 1983, it was a state-of-the-art facility when built, but by the turn of the century it showed shop-wear. Players complained especially about the rock-hard turf that was hard on the legs. Cashman Field officially seated 9,934 in permanent seats, but it had held 12,500. Its spacious dimensions were 328 to left field, 433 to center, and 328 to right field.[76]

The major change in the ALWS for 1998 was a significant change in the format of the Series. Since the American Legion World Series had gone to its current eight-team format, it had always been a double-elimination tournament. That is, a team that lost twice was eliminated and went home. The same format pertained to regional and state tournaments. Teams that went "two and done," losing their first two games, always complained that being sent home after only two games prevented slow starters from having a second chance. In part to address that complaint, the rules committee adopted a new format of "pool play" or "Olympic play." The pattern had been used in the Olympics for baseball and in World Cup soccer. Eight teams still would make the World Series. Then they were divided into two four-team pools or divisions, called American and National. Each pool played a round-robin of games in their own pool. That assured that all teams would play at least three games. The top team in each pool would then play the number two-ranked team in the other pool in two "semifinal" games. The winners of the semifinal games would square off in a championship game for the national title. That game would be televised nationally on ESPN, as had been the case since 1988.

For the 1998 Series, two teams—Brooklawn Post 72 (48–1) and Jefferson City, Missouri, Post 5 (50–1)—arrived with just one loss each. Brooklawn had become a Series regular in the past decade. They were making their seventh appearance, and fourth in the 1990s, having made the ALWS in 1991, 1992, 1994, and 1998. In their last game to qualify for the ALWS, the Brooks beat Frederick, Maryland, 12–11, in the Mid–Atlantic Regional finals. Jefferson City, on the other hand, was the first Missouri team to appear in the World Series since 1980. Despite the credentials of Brooklawn and Jefferson City, the favorite before the Series began was Edwardsville, Illinois, Post 199 Tigers. They compiled a 41–7 record in Legion ball, but the team had just sailed through the Great Lakes Regional, where they recorded a .452 team batting average, culminating in a convincing 15–2 win over Anderson, Indiana, the team they had lost to, 7–6, in the first game of the Regional. They had played together since they were 10 years old. Before the Legion season, playing on the Edwardsville high school team, they won the Illinois state title with a perfect 40–0 record, and they were named the mythical national champion by *Collegiate Baseball Magazine*. Coach Ken Schaake believed the team's attitude was as important to the team's success as its talent. "They were a gritty group of players that gave a great effort the whole time." Schaake later explained. Shortstop Chad Opel was the Tigers' star, along with pitchers Justin Hampson, a lefty, and brothers Jim and Ben Hutton, both right-handers.[77]

Other teams that appeared to be contenders were State College, Pennsylvania (52–9); Cherryville, North Carolina (38–14); and Danville, California. State College Post 245 (52–9) came in through the New England Region after finishing second in its Pennsylvania state tournament. Cherryville Post 100 possessed a power pitcher-hitter in Ralph Roberts, who remains the career home run leader at Cherryville High School and Post 100 and number three in wins for both. He played six seasons in the Atlanta chain. Danville, California, Post 246 (56–10) had played together since 1991, when the Hoots Baseball Club was formed. This was their first time in the ALWS. Teams from Las Vegas and Excelsior, Minnesota, rounded out the eight-team field. Excelsior Post 259 (60–10) had the most wins of the eight. They had beaten the Omaha Blue Jays, a team from Creighton Prep, 6–1, in the regional finals to get to Las Vegas. It was, however, their first time in the Series. The host team, Las Vegas Post 8 (49–13) Knights, was composed of boys from Bishop Gorman High School.[78]

Team placement in pool play followed the logic of the Regionals. That is, Regions 1, 2, 3 and 4—State College, Brooklawn, Cherryville, and Jefferson City—the easternmost teams, were placed in the American Division. Regions 5, 6, 7, and 8, including Edwardsville, Excelsior, Danville, and Las Vegas, clustered together in the National Division.

On the first day of play, Edwardsville let it be known they were for real. Third baseman Chris McCoy led the way with a homer and four runs batted in as Edwardsville crushed Excelsior for a 13–2 victory. Ben Hutton was the winning pitcher. In the second game, State College surprised Brooklawn, 12–3. In exciting, close games with lots of scoring, Cherryville topped Jefferson City 13–12, and Danville slipped by Las Vegas, 14–13. The Cherryville-Jefferson City game set a record for most hits with 35 (19 by Cherryville, 16 by Jefferson City). Cherryville scored three runs in the ninth inning on big Ralph Roberts' home run.

On the second day, Edwardsville ran into a hot pitcher in Danville's Peter Dunkle, who threw a five-hitter with 12 strikeouts in Danville's 8–1 victory. Edwardsville would dust themselves off and keep going. Brooklawn, Jefferson City, and Excelsior lost for the second time; they would have been on the way home under the double-elimination format. Cherryville, behind Ralph Roberts' home run, beat Brooklawn, 16–9. Jefferson City committed six errors in losing, 14–6, to State College. Danville had little trouble with Excelsior, winning 13–2.[79]

Danville and State College finished pool play undefeated with 3–0 records. Danville had little trouble with Excelsior, a team without a win, beating them by a 13–2 score. State College and Cherryville were playing for first place in the American Division. State College hung on for a 14–12 victory and remained undefeated in Series play. In a meaningless game, played for pride, Brooklawn was embarrassed by Jefferson City, 25–8, in a game called after seven innings. Brooklawn relinquished eight unearned runs in the first inning. In three games, they committed 16 errors, not Brooklawn's style of play. The 25 runs scored by Jefferson City set a new record. In the final game of pool play, Edwardsville beat Las Vegas, 7–5, to earn a spot in the playoffs.[80]

The conclusion of pool play set up undefeated State College (3–0) to play Edwardsville (2–1), with Danville (3–0) against Cherryville (2–1) in the two semi-final games.

For Edwardsville, pitcher Ben Hutton had his good stuff. Chad Opel, the 5-foot-9, slick-fielding shortstop, continued his hitting, batting over .600 in national play. Right fielder Nick Seibert drove in four runs, and Edwardsville cruised to a 9–3 victory. Cherryville-Danville proved to be a much tighter game, with Cherryville prevailing, 5–4.[81]

Edwardsville spotted Cherryville an early 2–0 lead in the 1998 championship game, but then took command with three runs in the seventh inning. Seibert's single scored Todd Haug with the tying run. Seibert scored the go-ahead run on outfielder Bubba Turner's RBI single. McCoy's home run in the eighth added two more runs to up the final score to 9–3. Pitcher Jim Hutton pitched into the eighth inning to collect the win before giving way to brother Ben. Edwardsville collected 12 hits to maintain its status as the top-hitting team at the ALWS, finishing with a record .399 batting average and 262 total bases for the playoffs. Opel became only the third player in Legion history to bat over .600. His .632 mark ranked second to the .650 of Doug Palmer of New Ulm, Minnesota, in 1978. The players sat in a darkened stadium an hour after the awards ceremony, knowing that when they returned home, everyone would go their separate way.[82]

Opel earned the 1998 George W. Rulon Player of the Year honor. His .632 average obviously topped all hitters to take the Louisville Slugger Award. Ralph Roberts, Cherryville's hulking slugger, took the Big Stick Award with 34 total bases. Roberts also won the Bob Feller Award by striking out 41 batters, and he was voted the Sportsmanship Award. Chris Wright of State College took home the Cowger RBI Award by driving in 25 runs. Opel headed a group of four Edwardsville players in the All-Tournament Team. Outfielder Dave Crouthers and pitchers Jim and Ben Hutton joined Opel on the team selected by *Baseball America*. The remainder of the team were: catcher B. J. Vesce, Danville; first base Ryan Lee, Las Vegas; Brad Lane, second base, Cherryville; third base Matt Furman, Brooklawn; outfielders Ralph Roberts, Cherryville; Justin Alumbaugh, Danville; and Crouthers, Edwardsville. Rounding out the team were designated hitter, Chris Wright, State College; utility, Josh Reynolds, Jefferson City; pitchers Jim and Ben Hutton, Edwardsville.[83]

The 1998 Series drew a disappointing 22,000 to Cashman Field in Las Vegas. After the lighting at Middletown was deemed sub-par for TV cameras, Middletown responded to that affront by allocating $200,000 in the next city budget to upgrade the lighting. William Pomfret, chairman of the World Series Committee of Post 75 of Middletown, stick-handled the process through the shoals of local politics, and James Quinlan, baseball coordinator for the American Legion, supported Middletown within the Legion. Middletown was selected for 1999 over Corvallis, Oregon; Joliet, Illinois; Harrisburg, Pennsylvania; and Alton, Illinois. The Series was scheduled for August 20–24, 1999, at Middletown's Palmer Field.[84]

The teams that made it to Middletown included some familiar faces. Brooklawn was the only repeat from 1998. They had spun out last year, but the Brooks appeared more balanced this year. Their 43–6 record included an 8–3 win over State College in the Mid–Atlantic final. They again featured a running offense, lots of stolen bases, and taking the extra base. Tri-City Red Post 513 from New Brighton, Columbia Heights, and St. Anthony, Minnesota, were loaded with hitters. St. Anthony had last appeared in the 1997 ALWS, when they lost two straight games. The Red team set a Minnesota record of 126 home runs in 1999, and then raced through the Central Plains Regional, winning five straight games, including a 13–10 victory over Omaha Post 2. For the tournament, they batted .374 as a team. That and their 60–4 record made them, along with Brooklawn, one of the Series favorites. Minnesota had a second team in the Series, Bloomington (35–11). Second in the Minnesota State tourney, they slipped into the Great Lakes Regional, winning it with a 11–9 victory over Somerset, Kentucky. Portland, Maine Post 17 had become the first team from Maine to make the ALWS back in 1995. They beat South Attleboro, Massachusetts, 4–3, in 11 innings in the Northeast Regional to give them a record of 32–4. Gallatin, Tennessee, with a 48–15 record, won its way in by taking the Southeast Regional, beating Douglasville, Georgia, Post 145 by a 13–7 score. Edmond, Oklahoma, came in as a dark horse team. They went 5–0 in the Mid–South Regional, defeating Omaha Post 1, 4–0. Kennewick, Washington, Post 34 (50–13) came in as a power-hitting team. They had won five straight in the Northwest Regional, trouncing Danville, California, 18–7, in the final. In the Western Regional, Chatsworth, California, Post 582 lost to Nevada Post 76, but they came back to take the tourney by beating the Nevada team, 13–8.[85]

The pool parings placed the two pre-tourney favorites, Brooklawn and New Brighton, in the National Division with Edmonds and Chatsworth. The American Division consisted of Portland, Gallatin, Bloomington, and Kennewick. On the first day, New Brighton, Bloomington, Brooklawn, and Kennewick all won. New Brighton rolled over Edmonds, 8–2. Bloomington had an easy time, beating Gallatin, 13–3. Kennewick's Jason Smith pitched a four-hitter and slammed three homers in a 9–1 pasting of Portland. Brookland had the only close game, beating Chatsworth, 6–3. Pitcher Bob Sperone won his 13th game without a loss.

The second day, August 21, produced rain; all games had to be cancelled. When play resumed, Kennewick second baseman Dave Coogin drove in all of his team's runs in a 5–3 victory over Bloomington. Not to be outdone, New Brighton second baseman Billy Schneider drove in five runs in New Brighton's victory over Chatsworth. Poor Portland lost to Gallatin, 4–1. Brooklawn had a close 5–4 win over Edmond; shortstop Brad Reed collected three hits to pace the Brooks. In a crucial game on August 23, Brooklawn bested New Brighton, 11–5. Center fielder Paul Fayer and designated hitter Mike Ricci each had three hits to pace Brooklawn. At that point, Brooklawn was the only undefeated team and the odds-on favorite to take the Series. Kennewick lost to Gallatin, 7–6, in an upset. Edmond enjoyed a 6–2 victory over Chatsworth.[86]

The Brooks finished first in the National Division with a 3–0 record, followed by New Brighton at 2–1. In the American Division, Kennewick and Gallatin finished 2–1. That left Brooklawn to face Kennewick, and New Brighton to take on Gallatin in the semi-final games. Kennewick upset Brooklawn. The saddest part of the loss for Brooklawn was that their pitching ace, Bob Sherone, with 13 wins and no losses, took sick the night before the game and was unable to pitch. Still, Brooklawn led 6–4 after four innings. Kennewick scored three runs in the seventh inning to gain the victory, 9–8. Kennewick first baseman Donnie Watts drove in four runs, including a big three-run homer in the seventh inning. Brooklawn's John Oehler, the catcher, had three hits including a homer in a losing cause. New Brighton beat Gallatin, 9–6, in the second semi-final game, as first baseman Brian Paone collected three hits, three RBI, and his tenth home run of the Series. Gallatin catcher Darron Osborne went 4-for-4 with four RBI in a losing cause.[87]

The last championship game of the 20th century, between New Brighton and Kennewick, was played before a disappointing 2,691 fans and the nationwide ESPN telecast. The game was tight through seven innings, with New Brighton clinging to a 4–3 lead. In the eighth, a seven-run New Brighton explosion sealed the victory with a 11–5 score. Third

baseman Brad "Bags" Baglien wore the hero's cloak by going 5-for-5, the first time that
had been done in a championship game. He batted .478 with an ALWS-best six doubles.
Left-handed-hitting right fielder Peter Wiedewitsch had 23 hits, tops in the Series, and
batted .511, third best. First baseman Brian Paone set an ALWS record with 10 home runs
and 48 total bases. The Minnesota club scored 133 runs in ten ALWS games.[88]

There were plenty of awards for New Brighton players. Peter Wiedewitsch took
home the Most Valuable Player Award. Kenny Judd of Edmond, Oklahoma, took the
Slugger Award with a .552 batting average. Tyrel Davis of Kennewick finished second
with a .524 mark. Paone captured the Rawlings Big Stick Award for total bases with 48
and the RBI Award with 26. In an unusual selection, the James F. Daniel Sportsmanship Award went to Timothy Allen Brusseau, Jr., of Wood River, Vermont. He was the
first winner not to participate in the World Series. The Bob Feller Pitching Award went
to Steve Grasley of New Brighton, who struck out 43 batters in 33 innings. New Brighton coach Jeff Larson, of course, took home the Jack Williams Memorial Leadership
Award. The George W. Rulon Player of the Year Award, which now included a $5,000
college scholarship, went to Jeremy Roberts, of Rison, Arizona. The all-tournament
team, as selected by *Baseball America,* included: catcher Darren Osbourne, Gallatin;
first baseman Brian Paone, New Brighton; second baseman Billy Schneider, New Brighton; third baseman Tyrel Davis, Kennewick; shortstop Andy Kratz, Bloomington; outfielder Peter Wiedewitsch, New Brighton; outfielder Travis Lee, Edmonds; outfielder
Joel Keith, Bloomington; designated hitter Dave Coogan, Kennewick; utility, Anthony
Aquilino, Brooklawn; pitcher Steve Grasley, New Brighton; pitcher Ben Hendrickson,
Bloomington.[89]

As the 20th century came to an end, the American Legion could be proud of its
accomplishments in furthering baseball. Legion baseball was thriving and still growing. In the past decade, the number of sanctioned teams had increased from 4,135 to
5,192, a healthy 25.5 percent growth. Pennsylvania continued to have the most teams with
516 clubs, followed by Nebraska with 340, Minnesota with 331, California with 278, and
New Jersey with 229 teams. Legion graduates continued to be honored by election to the
National Baseball Hall of Fame. At the century's closing, these included Jim "Catfish"
Hunter (1987), Willie Stargell (1988), Carl Yastrzemski (1989), Johnny Bench (1989), Jim
Palmer (1990), Joe Morgan (1990), Gaylord Perry (1991), Rollie Fingers (1992), Hal New-
houser (1992), Tom Seaver (1992), Reggie Jackson (1993), Steve Carlton (1994), Richie
Ashburn (1995), Jim Bunning (1996), Earl Weaver (1996), Phil Niekro (1997), Nelson
"Nellie" Fox (1997), George Brett (1999), and Robin Yount (1999).[90]

The 20th century had been America's century. At the close of the millennium, the
United States reigned as the only major power in the world. Economically, Europe stag-
nated. Russia verged on total economic collapse. The American economy dwarfed that
of Japan and China. Militarily, spending by the United States exceeded that of the next
dozen nations. That the economic growth of the 1990s appeared to mark the beginning of
a new era of sustained growth based on new information industries including electronic
communications, software, personal computers, the World Wide Web, and cell phones
had become inescapable.

8

Storms on the Horizon, 2000–2010

Despite America's power and prestige, on September 11, 2001, Al-Qaeda terrorists hijacked four commercial passenger planes and turned them into instruments of terror. One crashed into the Pentagon, symbol of American military power, and two took out the twin towers of the World Trade Center, symbol of U.S. economic dominance. The fourth, heading for Washington, was brought down by its passengers in the mountains of Pennsylvania. The attack coordinated by Osama Bin-Laden killed some 3,000 people. This was not a major death toll compared to past battles Americans had fought, but it devastated the American psyche for at least two decades.

American Legion baseball entered the 21st century with little reason to be concerned about its future. The final decade of the 20th century had, after all, seen a 25.5 percent increase in the number of Legion teams. The total went from 4,135 in 1990 to 5,192 in 1999. Pennsylvania continued to field the greatest number of teams with 516. California, the largest state of the lower 48, fielded 278 post teams. The Midwest and Upper Midwest contained the largest regional grouping: Nebraska had 340, Minnesota 331, Wisconsin 196, Missouri 196, and Illinois 191. New Jersey, next door to Pennsylvania, had 229 post teams. Other states with significant numbers were Florida with 178, Washington 157, and New York 157.[1]

The Mississippi River town of Alton, Illinois, had long wanted to host the American Legion World Series. Its time came in the Millennial Year of 2000. Alton, a town of some 25,000, was in the hinterland of St. Louis, near the confluence of the Missouri and Mississippi Rivers. A new riverboat casino, the Argosy Casino Alton, brought new people and dollars into town. The ball field, Lloyd Hopkins Field, a tiny old wooden park with roofed stands behind home plate and bleachers down both foul lines, had been renovated in 1997 to make it the home of the Bluff City Bombers of the Central Illinois Collegiate League. The park was also home to Alton High School and American Legion Post 126. It seated about 3,500 fans. Dimensions were standard at 325 down both foul lines and 385 to dead center.[2]

Four clubs seemed to stand out from the pack in 2000. Brooklawn, New Jersey Post 72 (47–3) was appearing in its fourth straight World Series, and was the only returning team from 1999. The Brooks had to be one of the favorites. The bulk of their players came from Gloucester Catholic High School, which compiled a record of 33–1 in the spring. Dennis Barth coached both Gloucester Catholic High School and Brooklawn Legion. They had destroyed all comers in the Mid–Atlantic Regional, scoring over ten runs in

165

each of their five straight wins, culminating in a 14–0 thrashing of Muhlenberg, Pennsylvania. Five other teams had been to the Series three years in a row—Dave McNally's Billings team of 1960–1962, Rio Piedras, 1972–1974, Mike Boddicker's Cedar Rapids club of 1974–1976, Santa Monica 1976–1978, and Boyertown 1986–1988. No team before had made four consecutive appearances.

The Danville, California, Post 246 Hoots (52–9) had finished third in 1998. Danville, a small city of 40,484, was a farming community in the San Ramon Valley. Don Johns had coached the team since its founding in 1991. The Hoots qualified through Region 7 after Chino knocked them out of the California title. Chico had then lost the Western title to Taylorsville, Utah, in a surprise. The Paducah, Kentucky, Post 17 Chiefs brought a 49–5 record to the ALWS. They beat Libertyville, Illinois, 6–4, in the Great Lakes Regional. Omaha, Nebraska, Westside Post 1, aka Grubb & Ellis (41–16), did not have the best record, but they put on a hitting display at the Central Plains Regional, compiling a team batting average of .322. Their big bopper, Al Smith, batted .524 and led the Regional in RBI. Chris Knust and Fran Johnson also batted over .400. They beat Rapid City, 6–4, at Rapid City to earn their way to Alton. Other teams in the Series were Hamilton, New Jersey, Post 31 (33–2); Richland County Riders from Columbia, South Carolina, Post 6 (43–7); Texas City, Texas, Post 89 (33–8); and Taylorsville, Utah, Post 71 Warriors (37–4). At the Region 1 tournament, Hamilton beat New London, Connecticut, 8–0, thanks to Mike Rogers' shutout pitching. Richland County/Columbia had to beat a tough team from Bayamon, Puerto Rico, in a tight 2–1 game to make the Series. Texas City had to beat Senath, Missouri, 15–5, to punch their ticket to Alton. Finally, Taylorsville upset Chino, California, with its 32–2 record, by a 10–6 score.[3]

As tournament organizers were preparing for the opening ceremonies, an issue appeared that called upon Jim Quinlan's fast thinking. For the past 12 years, ESPN had televised the ALWS on a two-day delay. Now the television network demanded that the tape-delay telecast of the Series' final game be extended for a week. Jim Quinlan first announced that there would be no television coverage of the Series. Four days later, after lengthy negotiations, he managed to arrange for the American Legion to purchase a three-hour block of time from ESPN for $85,000 and sold commercials to Buick, Gatorade, and Major League Baseball to pay for the time.[4]

In the pool play, to the surprise of no one, Brooklawn and Danville went undefeated (3–0). Brooklawn opened with a 6–4 win over Texas City as Brad Reed garnered three RBI. Next, they won, 12–4, over Taylorville, with Matt Ryan collecting four hits and four stolen bases. The Brooks then shut out Richland County, 6–0. In that game, Josh Copskay pitched the shutout, and Mark Michael hit a two-run homer. Danville beat Omaha, 5–2, behind Mateo Miramontes' 12 strikeouts, then pounded Hamilton, 11–0, and Paducah, 9–3. Texas City and Paducah each finished second with a 2–1 record, thereby making the semi-final games.[5]

In the semi-final games, Paducah upset Brooklawn, 8–7, in a dramatic game. The Chiefs came back from being down, 4–0. Brandon Ladd's two-run single in the top of the ninth inning put the Chiefs ahead. In the bottom of the ninth, catcher Mike Ricci, with a chance to tie or win the game, instead grounded into a doubleplay to end the game and Brooklawn's hopes. Paducah ace Jerome King (11–0) pitched the final two innings to get credit for the win. In the other semi-final, Danville had to go 13 innings to beat Richland, 3–1. Mateo Miramontes struck out 11 in six-plus innings of relief, and Adam Ricks, with four hits, starred for Danville.[6]

In the 2000 final, played before a crowd of 3,225, Danville trotted out ace Matt Brown, a 6-foot-5 hurler, who tossed a three-hitter to lead the Hoots to a 2–1 victory. Paducah got on the board first in the second inning, aided by two Danville errors. Danville tied it on Tom Gilhooly's double. Shortstop Adam Ricks' RBI in the fifth was the difference in the game. Danville founder and manager Don Jones had brought the Hoots to the pinnacle of Legion ball, his goal since 1991. Danville became the 17th ALWS champion from California.[7]

Matt Brown deserved his selection as the Most Valuable Player of the Series. The University of California signee allowed only 11 hits and a single unearned run in 27 innings. Josh Zender of Deming, Washington, got the American Legion Player of the Year Award. Brown lost out in the Bob Feller Award, which went to Ben Thurmond of Richland County. Brown did, however, receive the Sportsmanship Award. Brooklawn slugger Matt Ryan won the Louisville Slugger Award for the highest batting average with a .547 mark. The RBI Award went to Al Smith of Omaha. Smith tied for the Big Stick Award with Mark Michael of Brooklawn and Ryan Lymangrover, the Danville first baseman. The all-tournament team consisted of: Tim Gilhooly, catcher, Danville; Ryan Lymangrove, first base, Danville; Eddie Hannan, second base, Paducah; Mark Michael, third base, Brooklawn; Adam Ricks, shortstop, Danville; Al Smith, outfield, Omaha; Matt Ryan, outfield, Brooklawn; Kevin Flaherty, outfield, Danville; Geoff Kirksey, designated hitter, Paducah; Mike Ricci, utility, Brooklawn; Matt Brown, pitcher, Danville; and Mateo Miramontes, pitcher, Danville.[8]

The Hoots entered the 2001 season with high hopes of winning back-to-back crowns. They sailed through the California tournament and then had little trouble in taking the Region 8 title. That punched their ticket to Yakima, Washington. Waiting on them and the other seven teams was Parker Field, where the view included Mount Adams to the southwest and Mount Rainier of the northwest. Danville, however, was running into history. Brooklawn came into the ALWS with a 52–4 record, the best among the final eight teams. It was the Brooks' 23rd New Jersey state title. They beat Rockland County, New York, OTB, 3–2, to earn the right to be in Yakima. Their coach, Joe Barth, Sr., was 83 and in his 54th season as Brooklawn coach. The players wanted desperately to win one for "Pops." He had tasted success in 1991 but failed in nine other trips to the ALWS. Assistant coach Dennis Barth, who also coached the highly successful program at Gloucester Catholic High School, ran the team. They had two outstanding pitchers: 6-foot-5 Andrew Noe owned a serious heater, and lefty Justin Mendek, a 6-foot-3 lefty, who owned a 10–1 record for the regular season.[9]

Other teams in the 2001 World Series were: Milford, Massachusetts, Post 59, the first Massachusetts team in a decade; Albany, Georgia, Post 15, who beat Sanford, Florida, 5–1, to get to Yakama; Midwest City, Oklahoma, Post 170 Outlaws (64–13); Napoleon, Ohio, Post 300 Bandits; Omaha, Nebraska Post 1, the team composed of boys from Creighton Prep; and Lewiston, Idaho, Lewis-Clark Post 13 Twins. The Eastern teams, except for Napoleon, were clustered in the American Division for pool play. Western teams, except Midwest City, lined up in the National Division.

Danville and Brooklawn both had to come from behind to win their opening games. Noah Albers' double in the seventh inning gave Danville the go-ahead run against Napoleon in the Hoots' 8–7 victory. Against Midwest City, Brooklawn came back from a 4–0 deficit to win, 9–6. The Brooks scored seven times in the eighth inning, sparked by center fielder Ryan Flynn's bases-clearing double.. Catcher Mike Ricci contributed a two-run

Joe Barth, Sr., an accountant who founded Brooklawn Post 72 baseball in 1951 and continued to make out the lineup card for 60 years, long after son Joe, Jr., and then son Dennis took over the day-to-day coaching duties. Brooklawn won its first national title in 1991 and again in 2013–2014 (photo by Bruce Darrow, CNBNews).

double in the win. Milford's 15–2 destruction of Albany was the first win by a Massachusetts team since 1978, breaking an 0–10 streak. Bob Kenny went 5-for-5 with five RBI for Milford. Lewiston, behind the pitching of lefty Julius Smith, had little trouble beating Omaha, 5–1. The big news from the second day of play was the disintegration of Danville. Omaha beat the Hoots, 8–7, in 11 innings. Jim Hinrichs, who got on base via an error, scored from third on Todd Jansen's squeeze bunt. The Hoots, however, committed four errors, including putting the winning run on base, and left a record 20 runners on base. Napoleon also lost because of shoddy fielding. The Naps blew a 10–7 lead in the bottom of the ninth inning by committing three errors. Albany suffered the same fate as Napoleon by recording seven errors in a 9–5 loss to Midwest City. Brooklawn, behind Andrew Noe's three-run homer and lefty Justin Mendek's pitching, had little trouble with Milford, winning 6–2.[10]

On the third and final day of pool play, Danville bit the dust, losing 9–6 to Lewiston. Left fielder Jake Rogers' two-run triple gave Lewiston the lead. Lewiston recorded a 3–0 record in pool play. Omaha hammered Napoleon, 10–0. Losing teams were showing exhaustion. Milford, one such team, committed seven errors in losing to Midwest City, 11–5. Brooklawn finished 3–0 in pool play, beating Albany, 11–8. Midwest City had two wins. In the National group, besides Lewiston's 3–0 record, Omaha made the semi-final with a 2–1 mark.[11]

The two semi-final games proved to be tight, one-run affairs. Lewiston slipped by Midwest City, 4–3. Jake Rogers broke a 2–2 tie by knocking in two runs. Midwest City threatened in the ninth inning, putting two runners on base with only one out. Lewiston brought in Joe Broemeling, who struck out the next two batters for the save. In the other game, Brooklawn went up, 4–1, on Ricci's home run, but Omaha tied the game in the third inning and took the lead in the eighth. Brooklawn was down, 9–6, with two outs and nobody on base in the ninth, when, as Joe Barth said later, "the baseball gods decided to smile on us." Shortstop Joe Lamb doubled, his fourth hit of the game, and came home on Mike Flasca's single. Kyle Davis and center fielder Ryan Flynn followed with singles. Ricci drove in the tying run. Then the Omaha shortstop booted Andrew Noe's ground ball, allowing the winning run to score.[12]

In the 2001 championship game, Lewiston took a 2–0 lead on four doubles in the third inning. After that, Brooklawn's big Andrew Noe allowed just two hits and struck out ten Twins. Brooklawn tied the game in the fourth inning. Third baseman Nate Schill singled, as did Noe, and scored on right fielder Bryan Ciconte's grounder to short that erased Noe at second. Ciconte came around to score on a muff by the shortstop. That tied the score. In the sixth inning, Ricci drove a fastball over the fence with a runner on base to break the 2–2 tie. Brooklawn provided the *coup de grace* in the ninth when Lamb doubled and Fakasca singled to provide an insurance run.[13]

The champion Brooks finished with a 51–4 record. They were tough enough to stage comebacks in three ALWS games, including a four-run comeback against Omaha. As a team, they batted .348 while compiling a 2.35 ERA. MVP Mike Ricci set a record by appearing in his fourth World Series. For Papa Joe Barth, it had been an exhilarating ride. For him, the championship provided a final validation of his approach, if that was needed.[14]

Baseball America again selected an all-tournament team. It included the following: first base, Dayton Ries, Midwest City; second base, Brendan Winn, Milford; third base, Allen Balmer, Lewiston; shortstop, Joe Lamb, Brooklawn; outfielder, John Devany, Danville; outfielder, Joe Pietro, Omaha; outfielder, Nate Marshall, Lewiston; catcher, Mike Ricci, Brooklawn; utility, Nate Schill, Brooklawn; pitcher, Julius Smith, Lewiston; pitcher, Andrew Noe, Brooklawn. Ricci, who batted .410 for the tournament, was selected as Most Valuable Player for the Series. Surprisingly, Jay Threet of Adrian, Michigan, a team that failed to make the World Series, nevertheless was selected American Legion Player of the Year for 2001. He batted .403 and had a pitching record of 10 wins and three losses. Richard Chinn of Danville won the Louisville Slugger Award for the highest batting average with a .538 mark. The Bob Feller Award was bestowed on Chad Billingsley of Napoleon, who had a 1.38 ERA for the Series. He played in the majors with the Dodgers, the team that drafted him, and the Phillies, making the National League All-Star team in 2009. The RBI Award went to Josh "Burto" Burton of Lewiston, while the Big Stick Award went to Nate Martin of Lewiston, who accumulated 34 total bases. Julius Smith of Lewiston was selected for the Sportsmanship Award. The Leadership Awards go to the winning coach and assistants, but it seemed especially appropriate to recognize Joe "Pop" Barth, Sr., who still made out the lineup card for each game, and son Dennis, who earlier in the year won a state championship as coach of Gloucester Catholic High School.,[15]

The 2002 American Legion season is best described by Shirley Povich's poignant article on Don Larsen's perfect game. He wrote: "The million-to-one shot came in. Hell froze over. A month of Sundays hit the calendar." A team called the Bryan Packers, representing West Point, Mississippi, Post 212, came out of nowhere to win the Legion title. They had not been to the ALWS before and had little expectation of returning. For August of 2002, however, the stars shone on them, and pixie dust doused them; they could do nothing wrong.

The Series was played at Danville, Virginia, from August 23–27, on 10-year-old American Legion Field. At the diamond, several disconnected seating units comprised stands between third and first bases. None had a roof. Officially, it seated 2,588. If the stands were asymmetrical, the playing field was a standard 330 down the lines. No team from either the 2001 or 2000 ALWS made the field of eight in 2002. Before the start of the Series, a decision was made about the 2004 ALWS. Corvallis got the nod; previously, Bartlesville, Oklahoma, had been selected to host the 2003 ALWS.[16]

Excelsior, Minnesota, Post 259 (49–15) and Rapid City, South Dakota, Post 22 (83–12) were pre-tournament favorites. Excelsior had been ranked number one in a pre-season poll of coaches, but Coach Jim Peck's team failed to live up to that hype. They came into the Series with the lowest winning percentage (49–15) of any team in the Series. They bragged about two players: shortstop Zack Peterson, who batted .421 on the season, and left-handed pitcher Mark McKenzie, who posted an 8–1 record. Rapid City, a long-time power in the upper Midwest, was coming off its 33rd state title. It entered the ALWS with 24 straight wins and a record of 83–12. They had beaten Overland Park, Kansas, 8–4, for the Region 6 title.[17]

It was hard to locate dark horses among the other teams. Dothan, Alabama, entered with a fine 60–10 record. They were the first Alabama team to make the ALWS since Tuscaloosa won it all in 1967. Strong pitching gave Dothan its chance to make waves in the Series. Their staff ERA of 2.51 attested to their pitching strength. Ace Ronnie Woods, with a 1.42 ERA, had been the Most Valuable Player in both the state and Southeast tourneys. The number two pitcher, Pat Kelly, possessed an even more impressive ERA of 1.35. Manchester, New Hampshire, Post 2 had few illusions about winning. Rockland County, New York, Post 1447, sponsored by Off-Track Betting (OTB) with a 58–12 record, had been to the ALWS before, and had some hope of making waves. The Bryan Packers, sponsored by Sara Lee Corporation from West Point, Mississippi, representing Post 212, brought a record of 47–13 to the Series. Mississippi had never won a game in the ALWS, let alone a title. In Josh Johnson, who had a 9–1 record, they had a fine pitcher, and in shortstop Corey Carter, a big bopper. Medford, Oregon, Post 15 Mustangs and Las Vegas Post 40, winner over Hawaii, 7–6, in the West Regional, hoped to avoid embarrassing themselves.[18]

Only Dothan managed to go undefeated in pool play. They opened with a 7–4 win over Rockland. Woods got the win, while Ben Tankersley led the way with three hits. In their second game, Dothan beat West Point, 8–6, as Clint Wade got two hits, two RBI, and scored two runs. Finally, Dothan clobbered Manchester, 13–4. West Point opened with a 5–2 win over Manchester. After the loss to Dothan, they beat Rockland, 9–5, to give them a 2–1 record in pool play. Favorites Rapid City and Excelsior also posted a 2–1 record in the West Division. Rapid City started out like gangbusters, destroying Excelsior, 18–7. Cody Moser had five hits, and Andy Shepherd had four. Pitcher Kasey Keller ran his record to 15–0 in that game. After beating Las Vegas, 6–2, their 27-game winning streak came to an end in a 7–2 upset loss to Medford. Following its opening-day loss to Rapid City, Excelsior beat Medford, 9–8, as Jake Williams banged out three hits and Zach Peterson drove in two runs. They secured a spot in the semi-finals by beating Las Vegas,

3–2. In the semi-finals, Excelsior continued its winning ways, handing Dothan a 7–3 loss, its first defeat in the Series. Zach Peterson (10–2) had two hits and pitched a complete game for Excelsior, giving up only one earned run. Rapid City, having suffered a devastating loss the day before, lost again to West Point by a 6–3 score. Packers catcher Brent Patton had a two-run double, while left fielder Brandon McGarity and right fielder Joby Garner contributed two hits each. Jeff Schafer scattered seven hits in pitching a complete game.[19]

Josh Johnson controlled the 2002 ALWS championship game as West Point climaxed its surprising run by beating Excelsior, 4–0, before a meager crowd of 1,715. He pitched a complete game, scattered seven hits, and struck out 11 batters. West Point got on the scoreboard in the fifth inning when Brandon McGarity slashed a double inside the left field foul line. They got a gift of two more runs in the seventh inning when the Excelsior center fielder dropped a fly ball. The final run came in the eighth inning on Johnson's sacrifice fly. Mississippi had its first ALWS championship. Johnson compiled a slick 1.15 earned run average for the tournament, and as a third baseman he fielded flawlessly and batted .469.[20]

Johnson and Matt Skundrick of Medford tied for the Bob Feller Award with 34 strikeouts for the tournament. West Point teammate Corey Carter took the Rawlings Big Stick Award with 31 total bases. Dothan's Josh Sowell captured the Louisville Slugger Award with a .553 average. The Dr. Irvin "Click" Cowger RBI Award went to Spenser Ingaldson of Rapid City. Dothan's fine pitcher, Ronnie Woods, took home the Sportsmanship Award. West Point coach Frank Portera and his assistant, Tyler Brahon, received the Jack Williams Leadership Award. The 2002 All-Tournament team consisted of catcher Spencer Ingaldson, Rapid City; first baseman Mike McKenzie, Excelsior; second baseman Cody Moser, Rapid City; third baseman Andy Shepherd, Rapid City; shortstop Pat Moran, Rapid City; outfielder Josh Sowell, Dothan; outfielder Jeff Engel, Excelsior; outfielder Corey Carter, West Point; designated hitter Dustin "Dusty" Snider, West Point; utility Josh Johnson, West Point; pitcher Jeff Shafer, West Point.[21]

In the early years of the new millennium, signs began to appear suggesting that down the road, the Legion and Legion baseball might be in trouble. World War II veterans, who made up the bulk of Legion membership, were beginning to die off. Veterans from the Korean and Vietnam Wars had not joined at the same rate as World War II vets had done. As an example, in southeastern Pennsylvania, the Ches-Mont League (Chester and Montgomery Counties) had only five of 11 teams with Legion sponsors. One team, organized by the Caln Athletic Association, called itself "Coatsville Post 6" in hopes of attracting a sponsoring post, but found that the post had only four members. Legion ball was experiencing competition from Babe Ruth League baseball, and from travel and showcase teams, which promised greater exposure for aspiring 18-year-olds. Major league scouts admitted that they found few big-time prospects at the ALWS anymore. Quinlan admitted, "the loyalty [to local teams] seems to be leaving. Parents will do whatever it takes to get their son a million-dollar contract," or even a Division I scholarship. Even so, he was quick to add, Legion baseball had 5,404 teams, up from 3,500 in 1986.[22]

The 2003 ALWS was scheduled for Bill Doenges Memorial Stadium in Bartlesville, Oklahoma. The local Legion powers there had bid on the 1998 World Series, but that bid had been rejected because of poor lighting on the playing field. After that disappointment, the local post allocated $100,000 in 1999 for a new lighting system and other stadium improvements. That won the day for Bartlesville. The little park sat only 2,500, just

1,500 under roof. Its dimensions, while symmetrical, 350–355–350, were short to center field.

The elite eight in the 2003 World Series included two teams from New Jersey. Haddon Heights Post 149 (49–9) won the New Jersey state title by beating West Deptford Post 100 by a 5–2 score. The Heights went on to take the Region 2, the Mid–Atlantic Regional, title. They beat Newburgh, New York, 5–0, in the finals. Andy Console captured the Most Valuable Player trophy for the Regional. West Deptford (36–9) shifted to the Northeast Regional at Torrington, Connecticut. With outfielder Andy Krumm batting .524 West Deptford (36–9) won the Region One tournament, beating Essex, Vermont, 5–1, in the final game. Cherryville, North Carolina, Post 100 (43–8) and the Rochester, Minnesota, A's of Post 96 (47–4) looked to be the powers of the Series. Cherryville beat a tough Tuscaloosa, Alabama, team, 4–0, in the finals of Region 3. Post 100 had the best pitcher in the tournament in Chris Mason. He owned a 13–1 record and had struck out 33 in 21 innings in the regionals. For the entire tournament, he posted a record 69 strikeouts. Most of the Rochester team (47–4), including coach Keith Kangas, came from Century High School, which had taken the Minnesota high school championship before the Legion season. They had beaten Eden Prairie, 4–3, to take the state title, and Bloomington Blue in 10 innings to take the Regional crown.[23]

The remainder of the elite eight were Blue Springs, Missouri, Post 499 (60–12), Whitehorse, Ohio (42–12), Richey's Market of Corvallis, Oregon, Post 11 (42–20), and Northridge, California (46–9), which had no post identification. Blue Springs had a 30-game win streak. They had beaten Midwest City, Oklahoma, 14–4, for the Regional crown. Whitehouse upset Mattoon, Illinois, 9–8, in their Regional final. Pitcher-outfielder Steve Calvero compiled a .550 batting average. The Marketmen of Corvallis were making their first appearance in the ALWS since 1990, thanks to Josh Brandt's fourth homer of the Regional that allowed them to beat Cheyenne, 7–2. Brandt was acclaimed as the Most Valuable Player for the Region 7 tournament. Northridge won Region 8 on Jose Carollo's walk-off home run for a 4–3 victory in 12 innings.[24]

For pool play, teams were assigned with no regard to geography. The American Division consisted of Haddon Heights, Cherryville, Blue Springs, and Northridge. The National Division had West Depford, Rochester, Whitehouse, and Richey's Market/Corvallis. Every team complained about the heat, which hit 100 degrees each day. In pool play, Richey's Market and Cherryville garnered the most excitement. Richey's beat West Depford, 9–5, behind Joey Briggs' two home runs. Then Corvallis put up 20 runs in destroying Whitehouse, 20–1, setting a record for most hits. The Marketmen closed out pool play with a 9–4 win over a tough Rochester, Minnesota, team. Cherryville started slowly, just getting by Blue Springs, 3–1, and then losing to Haddon Heights, 9–6. Andy Console of Haddon got the walk-off homer and collected three RBI in that game. The Heights came back from six runs down in the ninth inning to win. Cherryville came back to put a beating on Northridge, 12–4. Along the way the Carolina boys showed they knew the fundamentals of the game by establishing a record for highest fielding percentage (.978). Their pitching ace, Chris Mason, set a record by striking out 69 batters in the tournament. .[25]

Coming out of pool play, only Corvallis remained undefeated. The Rochester A's finished 2–1. In the American division, Haddon Heights and Cherryville finished with two wins and a loss. The semi-final games had Haddon Heights facing Rochester and Cherryville against Richey's Market. Although Haddon Heights outhit Rochester, the A's finished on the winning end of an 8–4 score. In the other semi-final game, Cherryville surprised Corvallis, and everyone else, by crushing a record seven home runs in destroying the Corvallis team, 14–1. Mason struck out 15 Marketmen.[26]

In the 2003 championship game, Rochester surprised Cherryville, 5–2. Aaron Craig scattered four hits in eight innings and was the winning pitcher, giving him a 12–0 record for the season. Michael "Hoss" Badger pitched the final inning in relief to pick up the save. It was his record eighth appearance in the tournament. Cherryville jumped out to a 2–0 lead in the first inning, but Rochester put up three runs in the third to take the lead they did not relinquish. Second baseman Lee Anderson's two-run single tied the game at 2–2. Anderson scored the go-ahead run on catcher Chris Collins' single to left. Mason came on to pitch for Cherryville in the fifth inning and struck out 10 in four-plus innings, but the damage had been done.[27]

Chris Mason of Cherryville won the Bob Feller Award, and he seemed to be the logical choice for Most Valuable Player in the ALWS. The George W. Rulon Player of the Year Award, however, went to Jared Willis of Post 19, Logan, West Virginia. Andy Console of Haddon Heights captured the Louisville Slugger Award with a .514 average. He tied Joey Briggs of Richey's Market for the RBI Award with 17. Briggs captured the Rawlings Big Stick Award with 41 total bases. Rochester's relief pitcher, Michael Badger, was selected for the Sportsmanship Award. Rochester did better in collecting all-tournament recognition than they did in the awards. Pitchers Aaron Craig and Mike Badger led the all-star delegation. Third baseman Justin Grant, outfielder Nathan Bowers, and designated hitter Ted Garry also garnered recognition. The remainder of the all-star team consisted of: first baseman Brett Brunner, Richey's Market; second baseman Chris Kunda, Richey's Market; shortstop Robert Marcial, Northridge; outfielder Andy Console, Hadden Heights; catcher David Wise, Cherryville; utility man Jay Heafner, Cherryville; and pitcher Chris Mason, Cherryville.[28]

Back in May 2002 Corvallis, Oregon, had been selected to host the 2004 World Series from August 20–24. The city beat out Rapid City, South Dakota, Alton, Illinois, and Charlotte, North Carolina. The park since 2002 was known as Hansen Stadium at Taylor Field, named after Gene and Helen Hansen. It had hosted the ALWS in 1990, drawing over 30,000 fans. Gene Hansen had been the long-time general manager of the Richey's Market team, from 1978 to 2003. Unfortunately, Gene Hansen died in March before the World Series. Hansen Stadium was wearing down, and there were open complaints, led by *Corvallis Gazette-Times* sports columnist Brooks Hatch, that Oregon State University's field, Goss Stadium, "had seating, lighting, locker rooms, parking and other amenities that far outclassed those at Hansen Stadium."[29]

Some familiar faces appeared at the 2004 World Series. Boyertown Post 471 Bears, the dominant team in the 1980s, returned to the ALWS for the first time since 1988. They defeated Chester, Pennsylvania, 7–1 and 4–1, for their eighth Regional title. With a record of 52–2, they appeared ready to reassert their dominance. Edmond, Oklahoma, Post 111 Stars (42–5) beat Enid, Oklahoma, by scores of 6–3 and 4–1 on their way to Corvallis. Paducah, Kentucky, Post 31(42–9) Pirates had been runner-up in 2000. Eden Prairie, Minnesota, Post 58 had long been a power. They won the state in commanding fashion, beating Apple Valley, 13–3. Kennewick, Washington, Post 34 (58–8) won the spot that local favorite Richey's Market had hoped would belong to the host Post.[30]

Three of the eight teams were in the ALWS for the first time. DeLand, Florida, Post 6 Sixers (43–7) was the most improbable team. They finished in a tie for third in the state tournament, but after two other teams turned down the opportunity, they were invited to the Southeast Regional in Tennessee, where they won their way to the Series. Niwot, Colorado, a tiny hamlet near Boulder, played as Boulder Post 10 (72–7). The Portland, Maine, Rams were sponsored by Nova Seafood (33–4) and composed of boys from the 2003 and 2004 state champion Deering High School. In the Northeast Regional, they lost, 15–3, to Bristol but came back to beat Bristol twice.[31]

In pool play, Portland, Maine, lined up with Edmond, Boyertown, and Niwot-Boulder. That left Paducah, DeLand, Kennewick, and Eden Prairie in Pool B. In the opening game, Edmond upset Boyertown, 4–3. Paul Boland homered in the seventh inning, and J. R. Goodman drove in the deciding run in the ninth. Portland beat Boulder, 10–9, as Jeff Skillin went 4-for-4. DeLand exploded for seven runs in the sixth to take an 11–8 win over Paducah. Justin Bass homered in the third inning and drove in a run in the seventh. Eden Prairie beat Kennewick, 7–4, to complete the first day of play. Portland was beginning to look like the team to beat. Against Edmond on day two, second baseman Scott Brown got four hits and Skillin drove in two runs. Boyertown got back on the winning track, beating Boulder, 7–3. Kennewick got the only shutout of the Series, winning 1–0 over Paducah. A sacrifice fly by Sam Sainz in the ninth inning accounted for the win. DeLand beat Eden Prairie, 12–2.[32]

On the final day of pool play, Portland made it 3–0, beating DeLand, 8–2, despite a triple play by DeLand. Boyertown beat Eden Prairie, 8–6. Chris Mackey was walked intentionally by Eden Prairie to set up a double play, but Brian Ernst doubled in the winning run, ending the Minnesota team's season. Kennewick beat Edmond, 7–5, to reach the semi-finals. Portland went 3–0 in pool play, while Boyertown, DeLand, and Kennewick went 2–1. In the semi-finals, Portland drew Boyertown and Kennewick lined up against DeLand. Portland score three runs in the eighth inning to tie the game and send it into extra innings. Portland loaded the bases in the tenth inning on a single, an error, a sacrifice, and an intentional walk. Walking a batter to get to Scott Brown proved problematic. He delivered the game-winning hit and a 4–3 win. The hit prompted coach Mike D'Andrea to state: "He's just a great ball player." In the other semi-final, Kennewick's Matt Crowe pitched a complete game, scattered seven hits, and struck out nine in a 4–3 victory. DeLand's Shane Schoenberg had two RBIs and Tyson Hicks another.[33]

In the championship game of 2004, Portland pitcher Mike Powers was the hero, allowing only one hit in eight innings. Ryan Reid doubled in the second inning and scored on a fielder's choice. In the eighth, Chris Burleson singled, stole second, and scored on Reid's double. Reid went to the mound in the ninth inning and, after two batters reached base, he struck out the side. Region one teams traditionally were early outs, but the Nova Seafood team gave Maine its first World Series title by a 2–0 final.[34]

Portland's Scott Brown was the Most Valuable Player of the 2004 World Series. The George W. Rulon Player of the Year Award, however, went to Nolan Gallagher of Red Lodge, Montana. The Slugger Award went to DeLand's Tommy Cauly, who accumulated a .500 batting average. The Rawlings Big Stick Award for total bases was won by Steve Marquardt of Kennewick with 29. The award for the most runs batted in, the Irwin "Click" Cowger Award, went to Zac Berg of Enid Prairie with 21. Portland's fine pitcher, Ryan Reid, won the Bob Feller Award and also the Sportsmanship Award. The All-Tournament team included only three players from Portland, pitcher Mike Powers, outfielder Scott Brown, and Ryan Reid, outfielder/pitcher. Others were Forrest Rice, pitcher, Kennewick; Nick Pugliese, pitcher, DeLand; Kody Gibson, first baseman, Edmond; Kody Kaiser, second baseman, Edmond; Shane Schoenberg, third baseman, Kennewick; Tommy Cauley, shortstop, DeLand; Matt Cotellese, outfielder, Boyertown; and Steve Marquardt, utility, Kennewick.[35]

Stagnant attendance at the World Series reinforced fears about the future of Legion ball. Bartlesville, Oklahoma, which hosted the 2003 series, drew a respectable 20,030 fans. The following year, Corvallis, Oregon, which had drawn over 30,000 fans in 1990, only attracted 11,905 paying fans.

The 2005 World Series went to Rapid City, South Dakota, which previously hosted the Series in 1975, 1986, and 1997. Floyd Fitzgerald Stadium had been built in 1957 and named Sioux Park Stadium. It had been rebuilt in 1972 following the Red River flood, and renamed Fitzgerald Stadium after the president of the Black Hills Sports, Inc. It now seats 5,000. The format for the ALWS shifted from pool play back to double elimination, which had been the format for many years. Jim Quinlan offered no explanation for the change, but it is reasonable to guess that it was at the request of ESPN.[36]

At the ALWS, the buzz about clubs dropping increased even though the actual statistics showed little change. There was plenty of anecdotal evidence of decline. Greenville County, South Carolina, once had eight teams, but was now down to two. George Mayfield, director of the Northeast Regional, was clear that "we're losing teams," and he offered three reasons. He cited high school teams joining Dizzy Dean Baseball to keep the high school team together. Second, he blamed football coaches for forbidding their players from playing American Legion ball so they did not have to skip crucial pre-season practice. Third, he cited the amount of paperwork in the American Legion.[37]

Rapid City fans were excited because their local Post 22 team managed to make the ALWS by beating Sioux Falls Post 15 East, 11–0, and Lawrence, Kansas, 8–6. They brought a 57–21 record to the Series. In Max Fenske, they had one of the leading hitters in Regional play, a .500 hitter. Brooklawn, back in the Series again with a 42–7 record, wanted to win another title for Joe "Pop" Barth, Sr., even though son Dennis was now officially the coach. Pop fell in the dugout the first day of play to add a seriousness of purpose to the team's goal. Their third baseman, Vince Mazzaccaro, was hitting .500. Bradford, Connecticut, Post 83 won its first state title and first Regional title, but they showed signs of developing a team capable of returning to the Series. Dothan, Alabama, Post 25 appeared in the ALWS in 2002, finishing third. Enid, Oklahoma, a city of 50,000, labeled itself "the wheat center of the U. S." Post 4 boasted a pitcher, Tyler Fleming, who had been selected Most Valuable Player in the state and the Regional tournaments. He had recorded a 10–2 high school record and was 17–2 in Legion play. Post 4 had been to the ALWS before, but not since 1995. Woodbury, Minnesota, Post 501 had finished second in the state to Eden Prairie, but were sent to the Great Lakes Regional, where they played their way into the Series by beating Rockport, Indiana, 19–3 and 3–0. Henderson, Nevada, Post 40 entered with a 41–15 record. Pasco, Washington, Twin Cities (Pasco and Kennewick) Post 34 had played in 2004 as Kennewick, finishing second. They were excited about pitcher Tyler Cheney, who led all pitchers with 26 strikeouts.[38]

In the opening round of play, Brookland, Twin Cities, and Bradford enjoyed blowouts. Brooklawn, behind the pitching of Kevin O'Hara, beat Sierra Vista of Henderson, 9–1. Twin Cities enjoyed the mercy rule to overwhelm Dothan, 12–0. Bradford used homers by Karl Derbacher, Connor Reardon, and Brian Monack to surprise Rapid City, 14–2. In the only close game of day one, Enid slipped by Woodbury, 6–4. To the dismay of the home fans, Rapid City found itself on the outside looking in after a 14–2 smack-down by Henderson. Richie Michelin and Kurt Temple had four RBI each. Brooklawn continued to roll with a 14–4 licking of Bradford. Joe Sacerdote led off the game with a homer to set the tone. Sean Curran's two-run double in the second inning plated two runs. Enid again played a close game, slipping by Twin Cities, 5–3.[39]

Enid and Twin Cities came to dominate the 2005 ALWS. Henderson and Woodbury departed the tournament on the third day. Henderson lost to Twin Cities, 8–4, while Woodbury fell to Bradford, 11–9. In the meeting of the undefeated, Enid showed it was for real by thumping Brooklawn, 10–5. Kurt Elliott and Zac Berg homered in that one. In the semi-final games, Twin Cities and Enid took out Brooklawn and Bradford. Twin Cities, led by Tyler Cheney, who went 3-for-3 with a home run, took out Brooklawn, 13–6. Enid scored two runs in the bottom of the ninth inning on Schyler Burns' base hit to finish off Bradford. That left Enid and Twin Cities in the final.[40]

Enid Post 4, the only undefeated team in the 2005 tournament, continued to roll in the final. They scored six runs in the third inning to take a commanding lead. Twin Cities chipped away at the lead, with one in the fourth inning followed by two in the eighth. In the top of the ninth inning, Twin Cities got three runs to tie the game. In the bottom of the ninth, Tyler Fleming singled and moved to second base on a sacrifice, followed by a walk to Tom Wilson. Zac Berg hit a grounder to third, with Fleming out on a fielder's choice. Burns was intentionally walked to make a play an any base possible. With Austin Box at bat, pitcher Jeremy Stumetz, thinking a pickoff play was called, turned to throw to first, but no one was there. A clear balk. That sent the winning run across home plate. Game and Series to Enid. The town that called itself "the wheat capital of the U.S." could now call itself the capital of American Legion baseball. Coach Bill Mayberry's Majors continued to rely on the heart of the order, center fielder Zach Burns, who led the ALWS in RBI and total bases, catcher Schyler Burns, and left fielder Austin Box. In addition, pitcher Tyler Fleming was the MVP in the Oklahoma state tourney and in the Regional. He went 17–2 on the season, winning two games in the ALWS. Enid became the first Legion national championship from the state of Oklahoma.[41]

The Most Valuable Player for the 2005 World Series was Zac Berg of Enid. The Timberlake High School grad batted .413 with 21 RBI to give him the Irvin "Click" Cowger Award for most in the Series, and the Rawlings Big Stick Award for most total bases with 40. Fernando Irizarry of Montero, Puerto Rico, was selected Player of the Year. The Louisville Slugger Award for highest batting average in the national tournament went to Mike Tamsin of Bradford with a .538 mark. The Bob Feller Award went to Tyler Cheney of Twin Cities; he accumulated 41 strikeouts. The Daniel Sportsmanship Award went to Tyson Seng of Enid. Coach Bill Mayberry and his Enid coaching staff won the Jack Williams Leadership Award. The 2005 All-Tournament team consisted of: Jeremy Stumetz, pitcher, Twin Cities; Matt Peck, pitcher, Enid; Michael Tamsin, first baseman, Bradford; Adam Tussey, second baseman, Brooklawn; Joe Bonfe, third baseman, Woodbury; Tyson Seng, shortstop, Enid; Schyler Burns, catcher, Enid; Kyle Conley, outfielder, Twin Cities; Paul Martin, outfielder, Twin Cities; Zac Berg, outfielder, Enid; Tyler Fleming, utility, Enid; and Tyler Roberts, designated hitter, Twin Cities.[42]

Even without local Post 22 as a drawing card for long, Rapid City drew 28,058 fans for the Series. That was the most since 1996, when the Series was held in Roseburg, Oregon. Writers for the *Rapid City Journal* could not resist a final plug for their city in the American Legion sweepstakes. When the Legion powers got around to selecting a permanent site for the ALWS, they should remember, "they will not find a better place than Rapid City."[43]

For 2006 the ALWS moved from Rapid City, South Dakota, to Cedar Rapids, Iowa, which had never hosted a Series. Prior to the 2006 Series, Midlothian, Virginia, out of the Mid–Atlantic Region, and Metairie, Louisiana, were thought to be favorites. Midlothian Post 284 entered with a nearly perfect 32–2 record. Midlothian had won it all back in 1985. Since then, Region Two had its share of winners—Boyertown, Mayo, Brooklawn, Yardley, and Brooklawn again. Metairie, Louisiana, is an unincorporated but census-designated place of 138,481 inhabitants, part of the greater New Orleans metropolitan area. Post 175 (40–6) won the state championship by beating Gauthier and Amedee of Gonzales, 13–1, behind the three-hit pitching of Dane Maxwell. They featured an outstanding pitcher in hard-throwing Bobby Broach, slick-fielding shortstop Mike Liberto, a .360 hitter, power-hitting Kirk Cunningham, and first baseman/pitcher Dale Maxwell, who hit .619 and garnered MVP honors at the Regional. Metairie drew its players from Archbishop Rummel High School, long a New Orleans-area baseball power.[44]

Of the other six teams in the Series, Wayne Newton Post 346 of Terra Haute, Indiana (35–5) looked the strongest. They got to the Series by beating Limestone, Illinois, 11–4, in 11 innings. Outfielder Brady Shoemaker batted .619 for the Regional. Outfielder Nick Ciolli hit .455. Catcher Josh Phegley had been selected Mr. Baseball in Indiana out of Terre Haute North High School. Milton, Massachusetts's, Post 114 entered with the same record as Midlothian, 32–2, but it was Milton's first trip to the ALWS. They pulverized Farmingham, 20–2, for the state title and slipped by Cumberland, Rhode Island, 15–14, in ten innings. The Lawrence, Kansas, Raiders (41–7) won their fourth straight state title but advanced to the ALWS for the first time. Sumter, South Carolina, Post 15 (32–6) and Henderson, Nevada (55–11), were just happy to be in the World Series. Lincoln, Nebraska, Southwest Post 3 (43–12), sponsored by Pinnacle Bank, beat Cheyenne, Wyoming, 6–3, for the Northwest Regional title. Ian Dike was the winning pitcher and contributed three hits, including a home run.

Games were played at Veterans Memorial Stadium, so named in 2001 after a new structure replaced the original 1949 park. It served as home for the Cedar Rapids Kernels of the Midwest League. The park favored right-handed hitters with a friendly left field fence just 315 feet away. Other dimensions were normal, 403 to dead center field and 325 down the right field line.[45]

In the opening round, a four-hour rain delay slowed play. Midlothian showed its "Yaw" by sailing through five Henderson errors to take an 8–2 victory. Sumter, in a mild upset, beat Lincoln, 7–5. Tony Micklon homered and drove in three runs for Sumter. In another surprise, Milton put it to Lawrence, 14–4. Mark Perdios went 4-for-4. In the real surprise of the day, Terre Haute pulled off a 6–3 win over Metairie. That loss did not prohibit the Louisiana club from claiming the title, but it made coming back problematic. Only four teams had lost their first game and come back to win—Baldwin, Missouri, in 1972, Yakima, Washington, in 1975, Boyertown in 1987, and Newbury Park in 1992.

On day two, Terre Haute showed that its upset of Metairie was not a fluke by winning the only shutout of the Series, a 6–0 win over Sumter. Cole Vicars pitched a nifty five-hitter. Nick Ciolli's homer sparked a four-run sixth inning for Terre Haute. Midlothian continued winning, beating Milton 5–3 as Josh Alford's triple in the eighth inning provided the big blow. The Lawrence Raiders eliminated Henderson, 9–8. In that game, Lawrence raced out to a 7–0 lead before six errors allowed Henderson to pull even. A Henderson error gave the game back to Lawrence. In an elimination game, Metairie sent

Lincoln back to Nebraska with a 7–6 victory. Kirk Cunningham had three hits, and Kevin Weidenbacker plated the winning run.[46]

At that point, Terre Haute looked to be the class of the tournament. In the battle of unbeatens, Terre Haute hammered Midlothian, 15–7. Josh Phegley led the way with two homers. The win guaranteed Terre Haute a place in the championship game. Metairie ousted Milton, 12–4. Brett Accirdo went 3-for-3 with a homer and five runs batted in. Sumter put an end to Lawrence's run with a 6–5 win in 13 innings. Travis Witherspoon provided the game-winning RBI. In what could be considered semi-final games, Midlothian ousted Sumter, and Metairie continued its winning ways beating Terre Haute 14–9 in a rematch of the first game of the Series. Mike Liberto collected four hits and drove in four runs. In Midlothian's 9–2 elimination of Sumter, David Coleman had four hits.[47]

In the championship game of the 2006 tournament, Terre Haute twice had leads over Metairie, 2–0 and 3–1. They took a 4–3 lead in the top of the eighth inning thanks to Nick Ciolli's rocket home run shot. Terre Haute, however, could not keep ahead. In the bottom of the eighth, Metairie took the lead on RBI singles by Kevin Weidenbacker, Dane Maxwell, and Brett Palermo. In the ninth, Terra Haute got a runner on base with one out, but Metairie turned a well-executed first-to-short-to-first double play to end the game. Matt Brown used his 90 mile per hour fastball to pitch a complete game for Metairie and get a 6–4 win. He scattered nine hits, striking out 11 and yielding only one earned run.[48]

Metairie shortstop Mike Liberto won the Most Valuable Player Award for the Series. Bobby Broach, Metairie pitcher, took home the Bob Feller Award with 30 strikeouts. He pitched four years for Tulane, but never tried pro ball. Terre Haute's Brady Shoemaker won the power hitting awards, Louisville Slugger for batting average with a .523 mark, Rawlings Big Stick Award for most total bases with 39, and the Dr. Irvin L. Cowger RBI Award with 18. In addition, Shoemaker won the Sportsmanship Award. The all-tournament team for 2006 included: pitchers, Bobby Broach, Metairie, and Cole Vicars, Terre Haute; first baseman Dan Gordon, Sumter; second baseman Kevin Weidenbacker, Metairie; third baseman Phil Cerreto, Midlothian; shortstop Taylor Cole, Las Vegas; outfielders Grayson Tanner, Sumter, Travis Witherspoon, Sumter, and Brady Shoemaker, Terre Haute; catcher Josh Phegley, Terre Haute; utility Mike Liberto, Metairie; and designated hitter Kirk Cunningham, Metairie.[49]

As far back as Lou Brissie's time as commissioner of American Legion baseball, there had been interest in playing the World Series in a single location. The College World Series had long been played in Omaha, and the Little League World Series was identified with its holy see, Williamsport, Pennsylvania. Attendance at the ALWS had long been unpredictable. Having the World Series provided obvious economic advantages to the local community. For this reason, there never was a problem in attracting applications to host. Locations wishing to host needed to gear up four years in advance. Organizing committees were usually stretched thin by the end of the Series. The Legion powers had tried different approaches in the hope that a consensus would coalesce in favor of a specific site. Brissie had favored Hastings, Nebraska, and had used his powers of persuasion to build attendance. He gave Hastings several opportunities to make its case.

Attendance had dropped in the decade of the 1980s. The bottom fell out in 1989 at Millington, Tennessee, where a mere 561 showed up for the final game. In the 1990s, a triumvirate of cities—Boyertown, Pennsylvania, Fargo, North Dakota, and Roseburg, Oregon—alternated as host. All three had a long tradition of supporting Legion baseball and had erected stadiums for their Legion team, and they were in small cities or towns.

Attendance averaged around 25,000 during those six years, higher than anything since, except Manchester, New Hampshire, in 1976–1977.

Without an announcement, Jim Quinlan and the Americanism Commission appeared again to be auditioning cities. Since the turn of the 21st century, the host sites had been Bartlesville, Oklahoma, Corvallis, Oregon, Rapid City, South Dakota, Cedar Rapids, Iowa, and now in 2007 it was Bartlesville again. Local organizers used Oklahoma's 100-year celebration of statehood to support their case. Rumors held that the permanent site was Bartlesville's to lose. When the ALWS was last played there in 2003, players had expressed unhappiness about the heat, which topped 100 degrees each day of the tourney. The ball carried well in the dry heat, so Doenges Memorial Stadium saw lots of runs and few pitching duels.

Boyertown (52–8), which was last in the Series in 2004, opened as the 2007 favorite. They won their second straight state title, 15–1 over North Chester, and took the Mid–Atlantic Regional from Morgantown, West Virginia, by a 7–0 score. They appeared to overwhelm opposing teams. Tucson Morgan McDermott Post 7 (35–10), however, was loaded with power hitters. Kevin Hussey batted .615 and won the MVP Award in the Region 8 tournament. They led all ALWS teams in home runs, RBI, and batting average. Bellingham, Washington, King Nissan Post 7 (64–6) came in with the best record and most wins, so they attracted a lot of attention. Bryant, Arkansas, Post 298 (41–9) brought the best pitcher in Legion ball in Aaron Davidson, a strikeout machine. Columbia, Tennessee, Post 19 (53–10) and Eden Prairie, Minnesota (41–9), had balanced teams capable of going deep in the playoffs. Columbia qualified for the tournament by beating Gaffney, South Carolina, 9–4, and Bayamon, Puerto Rico, 15–5. Bradford, Connecticut, Post 83 (31–8) and Rockford, Indiana, Post 254 (30–8) brought little or no hope of winning the title.[50] The 2007 Series was scheduled from Friday, August 24, to Tuesday, August 28. On the first day, Boyertown, behind the pitching of Garret Crable, who pushed his personal record to 13–2, beat Bryant 5–3. Eden Prairie hammered Tucson 19–5. The New England champion, Brantford, picked up a win, 13–12 over Bellingham in 13 innings when Ray Jones drew a bases loaded walk. Michael Olt had three hits including a two-run homer to tie the score at 12 in the 11th inning. That game set several records: Bradford got 56 at bats in the game, the two teams combined for 111 at bats. Columbia, Tennessee, won in dramatic fashion, beating Rockport 7–4 on Chris Lovett's three run, walk-off home run in the bottom of the ninth inning.

On the second day, Boyertown survived a close call against Eden Prairie, winning 11–10. In the losers' bracket, Tucson eliminated Bryant, beating them, 6–1. In the best pitching performance of a Series known for hitting, Tucson's Chris Moon pitched a one-hitter, striking out 10 and walking just two batters. Appropriately, the one hit came on a sixth-inning home run by Kaleb Jobe. Bellingham knocked out Rockport, 17–8. A tired Bradford squad lost to Columbia, 9–8, when catcher Cody Pomeroy hit a walk-off home run.[51]

In the feature game on Sunday, Columbia burst Boyertown's bubble with a convincing 16–5 victory. Eden Prairie kept pace by sending Bellingham home with a 7–3 win. J. T. Canakes had three hits for Eden Prairie. In the wildest game of the tournament, Tucson beat Bradford in a battle of one-loss teams, 7–9. That game broke more batting records. Tucson set a new mark by slamming seven home runs in the game. Marc Damon wrote his name firmly into the record book by becoming the first player to hit three homers in one game. Damon homered in the second, third, and seventh innings. He collected five runs batted in as well. He did not know it, of course, but that game was the high point of Damon's baseball career. He went on to play at community college for two years and then for Texas A&M. In his time with the Aggies, he hit a total of three home runs. Damon had one more shining moment. The following day, he took the mound and became the winning pitcher in Tucson's 13–6 upset of pre-tournament favorite Boyertown. Damon pitched a complete game to gain the victory and chipped in a home run of his own. Kevin Hussey and Aaron Tapia each drove in two runs. Columbia's reign as the only undefeated team proved to be short-lived. Now guaranteed a place in the finals, they fell to Eden Prairie, 8–5, in 10 innings. J. T. Canakes had three hits for the winners. With momentum on its side, Eden Prairie continued by knocking out slugging Tucson, 8–3. Danny Miller pitched the complete game for the winners.[52]

In the championship game of 2007, Columbia had relatively little trouble beating Eden Prairie, 11–4. Columbia jumped out to a 6–1 lead in the first three innings and never looked back. In the third inning, left fielder Holden Killen launched a two-run homer, and Chris Lovett hit a solo shot in the fourth inning. Scott Beasley entered in relief and picked up the victory, his record-setting third win in the ALWS. He went 5–0 in Regionals and the Series with a 0.72 ERA. The 2007 American Legion champion Columbia, Tennessee Post 19 finished with a 57–11 record.[53]

The Series would be remembered for hitting. There were no shutouts in the Series. There were a record 46 round-trippers, including Damon's three in one game. There was little complaint about the heat, but the total attendance of 23,220 fans would not be remembered. If Jim Quinlan had seen Bartlesville as his favorite to become the permanent site for the ALWS, he no longer had such confidence.

Tucson pulled in most of the awards. Kevin Hussey captured the Louisville Slugger Award with a mark of .533. The Dr. Irvin "Click" Cowger RBI Award was won by Aaron Tapia with 22. Marc Damon won the Rawlings Big Stick Award for total bases with 46. His nine home runs were also an ALWS record. The Bob Feller Award went to Aaron Davidson of Bryant with 31 strikeouts in 23 innings. The Sportsmanship trophy was awarded to outfielder Holden Killen of Columbia. The all-tournament team lined up as follows: pitchers Danny Miller, Eden Prairie, Chris Moon, Tucson, and Scott Beasley, Columbia; first base, Aaron Tapia, Tucson; second base, Alan Kennedy, Bellingham; third base, Chris Lovett, Columbia; shortstop, Mike Olt, Branford; outfielders J. T. Canakes, Eden Prairie, Holden Killen, Columbia, and James Balzano, Bradford; catcher Cody Pomeroy, Columbia; and designated hitter Marc Damon, Tucson. The Most Valuable Player Award went to Danny Miller, Eden Prairie pitcher.[54]

The 2008 ALWS had been scheduled for Shelby, North Carolina. The seat of Cleveland County is located in the Piedmont section of south-central North Carolina. The region had gone through a decline from 1970 to 2000 as the American textile industry went overseas and sank mill towns into depression. The recovery carried the population to just over 20,000 by 2008. In 2002, when Shelby became the venue for the Legion's Southeastern Regional tournament, the volunteer committee formed to coordinate the Regional continued to function. It guided the city through the state tournament in 2004. The committee morphed into the group responsible for getting the ALWS in 2008. Keener Stadium, built in 1976, served as home to the Post 82 team and local high school ball. It possessed reasonable dimensions, 330 down both foul lines but a short 365 to center field.

A team variously known as Bishop Gorman, Southern Nevada Titans, and Las Vegas Post 76 looked to be odds-on favorite before the ALWS began. Coach Chris Sheff, who had played on Pepperdine's 1992 NCAA champions, doubled as coach of Bishop Gorman High School, where he recruited most of his players. They were Nevada high school champions in 2006, 2007, and 2008, so Sheff's players came from a winning tradition. Southern Nevada/Gorman/Post 76 came in with a record of 70 wins against 7 losses, riding a 21-game winning streak. In the finals of the West Regional, they beat St. George, Utah, 11–2. Southern Nevada had a serious prospect in outfielder/pitcher Paul Sewald, who batted a team-leading .459, but who made it to the majors ten years later as a pitcher with the Mets.

Other teams hoped for the best but knew it would be a struggle to take down the powerful Nevada club. Sumter, South Carolina, Post 15 owned the next-best record, 34–3. Sumter played itself into the ALWS on Keener Field by beating Shelby in the Southeast Regional. They would have the advantage of being the fan favorites. The Pasco, Washington, Post 34 Sun Devils from the Tri-cities of Pasco, Kennewick, and Richland lacked the gaudy won-lost records, posting a 48–18 mark, but they passed the eye-test with scouts. They got to the ALWS by beating Boise, 6–4, in the Northwestern Regional. Max Garrett, MVP of the Regional, brought a .520 batting average to the ALWS. Bristol, Connecticut, Post 2 posted a 35–9 record, but was happy just to make the ALWS. South Richmond Post 137, with a sparkling 33–5 record, believed it could go deep in the tournament. Midland, Michigan, Berryhill Post 165 posted a 55–10 record; they beat DePere, Wisconsin, 8–6, to reach the World Series. Omaha, Nebraska, Post 375, with a 40–16 record, was composed of boys from always tough Creighton Prep. Jonesboro, Arkansas Post 21 (42–10) rounded out the field.[55]

On the opening day of the 2008 ALWS, Southern Nevada showed it was for real by beating Omaha, 7–5. First baseman Jeff Malm led the offense. Malm would go on to an eight-year minor league career. No surprises popped up as Sumter topped Bristol, 5–3, and Pasco, Washington, had no trouble with Jonesboro, winning 12–3. Sumter's pitching ace, Mathew Price, coming off a no-hitter, kept Bristol at bay. In a mild surprise, South Richmond beat Midland Berryhill, 5–2. Their fine pitcher, Blake Hauser, went the distance. On day two, in the losers' bracket Jordan Dean collected four hits and drove in five runs as Midland crushed Bristol, 15–5. Jonesboro surprised Omaha, 13–8, sending the Creighton Prep boys home early. Sumter whipped South Richmond, 9–6, and Southern Nevada continued its winning ways, 10–8 over Pasco. On Sunday, in elimination games, Pasco scored a 10–8 victory over Midland as Jameson Rowe pounded out four hits. South Richmond took out Jonesboro, 13–8. Southern Nevada, now guaranteed a spot in the finals, chose not to rest, eliminating Sumter, 11–9, and Richmond, 6–1. Pasco reached the championship game by taking out Sumter, 11–7.[56]

Southern Nevada rolled to the 2008 title. In the semi-final games, the Titans continued their undefeated run through the tournament by beating South Richmond, 6–1. In a close game, Pasco knocked out Sumter by the narrowest of scores, 8–7. After the semis, the weather took over. The final game had to be postponed a day because of the effects of Hurricane Fay. Southern Nevada claimed the title, winning its record 75th game, 5–1, over Pasco. Pitcher Stephen Manthei cruised to a complete-game, five-hit win. Outfielder Paul Sewald, who led the team during the ALWS with a .459 batting average, collected three hits. Third baseman Scott Dysinger, who hit .444 for the Series, chipped in two hits. Outfielder Neil Lawhorn made the defensive play of the game by leaping high to take away a Pasco home run.[57]

The champions were loaded with pro prospects. First baseman/pitcher Jeff Malm also gained recognition by being selected to the *USA Today* All-American high school team. He failed to live up to his clippings. After eight years knocking around the minors and two more in independent leagues, he retired without so much as a cup of coffee in the majors. A teammate, pitcher Matt Hall, pitched 25 games for Detroit and Boston from 2018–2020. Outfielder Paul Seweld went on to play for the University of San Diego, then six minor league seasons before playing for the New York Mets from 2017 to 2020. Pitcher Donn Roach made his major league debut in 2014 with the San Diego Padres. He pitched briefly for the Chicago Cubs and Seattle Mariners before going to Japan, where he finished his career. The Titans' cleanup hitter, outfielder Johnny Field, made it to the majors with Toronto in 2018, also playing for Tampa Bay and Minnesota that season. He finished with an unimpressive .222 lifetime batting average. Joey Rickard played outfield for the 2012 College World Series champion Arizona Wildcats, before making it to the majors with the Baltimore Orioles and San Francisco Giants from 2016 to 2020. In 317 games he batted .245. Second baseman/pitcher R. J. Santigate went to Central Arizona College and got drafted by the Los Angeles Angels, but he never made it above rookie league ball.

The attendance of 37,701 at the 2008 Series reflected the work of the organizing committee. Jim Quinlan, National Director of American Legion Baseball, termed it "a team effort," referring to the 100 or so local volunteers who worked to make it a successful event. That attendance was the highest mark since 1996, when the Series was played in Roseburg, Oregon, and the second-highest since 1954, when Yakima drew 40,269.

Nevada first baseman/pitcher Jeff Malm won the Most Valuable Player Award. As a pitcher, he posted a 1–0 pitching record, saved five games, and compiled an ERA of 0.00. In the field he was perfect, fielding 98 chances. At bat, he hit .300 with 14 runs scored, second in the ALWS. Patrick Singletary of Hendersonville, North Carolina, Post 77 was selected as Player of the Year. Brandon Bass of Omaha batted .576, the highest in ten years, to win the Louisville Slugger Award. Max Garrett of Pasco took the Rawlings Big Stick Award with 38 total bases and the RBI Award with 17. Cade Lynch of Jonesboro won the Bob Feller Award, striking out 33 batters. Las Vegas outfielder Paul Sewald was named recipient of the Sportsmanship Award. The Leadership Award went automatically to Chris Sheff, as coach of the championship team. The champs did not fare much better on the all-tournament team selected by Baseball America. They placed just three on the mythical squad: Jeff Malm at first base, Scott Dysinger at third base, and Matt Hall as a pitcher. Other selections were Brittan Hammer, Pasco, second base; Brad Shaban, shortstop, South Richmond; outfield, Travis Witherspoon, Sumter; outfield, Jamison Rowe, Pasco; outfield Thad Thornburg, Jonesboro; catcher Max Garrett, Pasco; utility Matt Talley, Sumter; designated hitter, Sam Key, Sumter; pitcher Matt Price, Sumter; and pitcher, Blake Hauser, South Richmond.[58]

In May 2009, the Legion announced that it was looking for a permanent site for the World Series. Cities had a year to make their pitch; bids were due at the Americanism Commission in May 2010. Bids were expected from Billings, Montana, Shelby, South Carolina, Bartlesville, Oklahoma, and Boyertown, Pennsylvania, but there might be more. Later in the summer, Jim Quinlan announced the decision to move the ALWS start up one week. Pressure from college coaches, both baseball and football, to get kids in school had finally become too loud to ignore. Legion coaches, whose teams went deep into the playoffs, had complained that they were forced to go without their whole team because players were leaving.[59]

Las Vegas/Southern Nevada (62–12) returned to the 2009 American Legion World Series to defend its title. Initially, the boys from Bishop Gorman were pre-tournament favorites. Before the Series got underway, the best Las Vegas player, Jeff Malm, signed a professional contract. Then Midland, Michigan, Berryhill Post 165 Bruins (49–8) appeared to be the logical choice to take the title. They were the only other 2008 team to return to the ALWS in 2009, and they made a credible choice with a balanced team of heavy hitters led by Garrett Yatch, sound fielding led by shortstop Jordan Dean, and big-time pitching headed by Kyle O'Boyle, who also brought a reputation as a slugger.[60]

The Series returned to Fargo, North Dakota, where it had been held in 1983, 1992, and 1995. Newman Outdoor Field on the North Dakota State University campus officially seated 4,513 fans. It had reasonable dimensions, although short down the foul lines— 318 feet to the left field fence, 408 feet to dead center, and 314 to right. The other six teams that qualified included teams with phenomenal records. Berlin, Connecticut, Post 68 (34–6), had beaten Portland's Nova Seafood, 9–4 and 8–5, at the Manchester Regional. Mid–Atlantic Region 2 always seemed to send strong teams, but Mount Airy, Maryland, Post 191 (38–15) looked to be an exception. They did beat Mt. Laurel, New Jersey, 8–1, to reach the ALWS. The Rowan County Lions, aka Salisbury, North Carolina, Post 342 (37–8), expected to go deep in the tournament. Texarkana, Texas, Post 25 (28–4) had the least experience of any team in the Series. Festus, Missouri, Post 253 (39–4) beat Pittsburg, Kansas, convincingly, 10–5 and 7–0, to reach Fargo. Medford, Missouri, Post 15 Mustangs (45–10) had hosted the Northwest Regionals, which they won. Las Vegas Post 76 remained a threat even without Jeff Malm. They beat Reno, 12–3, to win the West Regional.[61]

Lots of rain led organizers to cancel games on the second day and to reduce games on the first and third days to seven innings in order to speed them up. Midland, the opening favorite to win the tournament, began on the first day with a big win over Medford, Oregon Post 15, their biggest challenger, by a 4–2 score. Texarkana beat Mt. Airy, 3–2, behind the pitching of Michael Wacha. Shortstop John Stilson doubled home Duncan Collins with the winning run in the bottom of the ninth inning. Las Vegas slipped by Berlin, 8–7. Joe Balowski had four RBI for the winners, but it was T. J. White's single in the ninth inning that won the game.[62]

All games were cancelled by the rain on Saturday. When play resumed, Medford eliminated Berlin as Jordan Lewis pitched a 5–0 shutout. Jake Matuszah and Zach Parsons each got three hits for the winning Mustangs. Rowan County got back on the winning side, beating Mt. Airy, 8–3, sending the Maryland team home. Texarkana won its second game, beating Festus, 10–6, as Dylan Bigham collected three hits and four RBI. Midland looked to be the power, beating Las Vegas, 11–8; Alex Rapanos won in relief in a rain-soaked game. On the third day of the Series, Rowan County/Salisbury eliminated defending champion Las Vegas, 8–7. Medford destroyed Festus, 9–0. Medford had to return to the field on Monday and just managed to slip past Texarkana, 7–6. The Mustangs scored two runs in the bottom of the ninth inning to notch the win. Texarkana, forced to play a second game on the same day, squared off against Midland. Berryhill Post scored all the runs it needed when it got three runs across in the third inning. Texarkana picked up two runs in the bottom of the seventh, but Midland's Matt Creswell collected the save in the 3–2 win.[63]

The teams were reduced to four—Midland, Medford, Rowan County, and Texarkana. Midland gave Texarkana its first loss, 3–2. Sean Hartman got credit for the win, and

Matt Creswell picked up the save. The Medford Mustangs scored two runs in the bottom of the ninth to finish off Texarkana, knocking them out of the tournament by a 7–6 score. In the wildest game of the Series, Midland went up, 12–0, over Rowan County, only to see Salisbury get back in the game by scoring eight runs in the sixth inning. Midland came back with three runs in the seventh to give themselves a seemingly safe lead, 15–8, only to see the North Carolina team score five runs in the bottom of the seventh. Rowan County scored another run in the bottom of the ninth, but they could not get the tying run across the plate, losing 15–14.[64]

In the 2009 championship game against Medford, Midland again jumped out to a big lead, 8–0 after four innings. Medford picked up three runs in the sixth. Midland responded with three runs of its own in the eighth inning. Medford could not come back, and Midland won, 11–4. Kyle O'Boyle got the win with a three-hitter and chipped in three hits himself. Garret Yatch collected three hits and scored three runs for the winners. Midland finished with a 54–7 record and the 2009 championship.[65]

Midland's Jordan Dean, the slick-fielding, hard-hitting shortstop was selected Most Valuable Player in the Series. Teammate Kyle O'Boyle won the Irvin L. "Click" Cowger RBI Award with 19 runs batted in and Rawlings Big Stick Award with 40 total bases. Tyler Jacobson of Pulaski, Wisconsin, was picked for the George W. Rulon Player of the Year Award. The Louisville Slugger Award went to T. J. White of Las Vegas who batted .559 in the Series. The Bob Feller Award went to Matt Stiles of Festus, Missouri. He struck out 30 hitters. Midland's Garret Yatch was selected for the James F. Daniel Sportsmanship Award. Midland head coach Steven Cronkright received the Jack Williams Leadership Award. Shortstop Jordan Dean, infield partner third baseman Eric Dawson, and pitcher Chad Mayle were the only Midland representatives on the all-tournament team. The rest of the all-star squad consisted of: first baseman Trey Holmes, Rowan County; second baseman Jake Ringold, Mount Airy; outfielder T. J. White, Las Vegas; outfielder Johnny Fields, Las Vegas; outfielder Kendrid Henderson, Texarkana; catcher Lewis Sebrell, Medford; designated hitter Matt Maurer, Medford; pitcher Brad Shipley, Medford; and pitcher Michael Wacha, Texarkana.[66]

The big take-away from the 2009 Series was the rain. Downpours kept spectators away in droves. Only 1,867 turned up for the final. For the entire slate of games, the attendance was a disappointing 15,579. Back in 2004, Corvallis had drawn under 12,000, the worst crowds in the 21st century.

Eddie Holbrook and Jim Horn had been Shelby, North Carolina's, movers and shakers who organized the drive to get the 2008 World Series at Shelby, and they continued to organize and develop Shelby's bid to become the permanent home for the American Legion World Series. They had often expressed the vision that Shelby "could exceed anyone in volunteerism, community support and small-town pride." Their 16-member committee put together a 56-page proposal for the Legion's Americanism Commission. The bid document identified 400 volunteers willing to work at all sorts of jobs. Later, the volunteer staff increased to 500–600. The proposal offered upgrades to Keeter Stadium at a cost of $1.2 million; this figure turned out to be more like $2.5 million. Lowe's home goods donated $300,000 toward construction of a new headquarters for the ALWS. The committee proposed to increase seating at Keeter Stadium to 5,000 and to build a new scoreboard with an electronic message center and a high-definition video screen. Fearing the written proposal would not be enough, the committee chartered two buses to carry supporters decked out in orange tee-shirts to Indianapolis, Indiana, to deliver the bid proposal to Legion headquarters. Joe Caouette, Chairman of the Legion's Americanism Commission, announced that Shelby would be the home for the ALWS for four years beginning in 2011. Shelby beat out Bartlesville, Oklahoma, the too-hot spot where the World Series had been held in 2007. Upon hearing the announcement, the Cleveland County manager commented, "the World Series is going to be one of the biggest economic drivers we've had in a long time."[67]

Since the ALWS would not settle into Shelby until 2011, the 2010 Series would be played as far away from Shelby as possible, in Spokane, Washington, at Avista Stadium. During the season, the park was home to the Spokane Indians, a minor league team in the short-season Northwest League. It opened upon completion in 1958. It featured a short right field porch just 295 feet away from home that quickly became 356 feet in right-center, moving on to 398 in dead center and 331 down the left field line. It seated 6,803 spectators.

Most of the eight teams that made the 2010 World Series had been there before. Brantford, Connecticut (28–8), under coach Rich Balzano, last appeared in the 2005 and 2007 ALWS. Little was expected this year. They struggled to get past East Longmeadow, Massachusetts, 2–1, and were offensively challenged. Their team batting average of .235 was the only mark in the Series below .250. Chesapeake, Virginia, Post 280 (29–6) was in its first ALWS. They got to the Series by upsetting Brooklawn, 6–2, in the Mid–Atlantic Regional. Kernersville, North Carolina, Post 36 (34–15) was also making its first appearance in the Series. They beat Columbia, Tennessee, the 2007 national champions, by a 10–2 score to reach the ALWS. Midwest City, Oklahoma, Post 170 Outlaws (61–9) would have been odds-on favorite to win the Series had they not lost their

Keeter Stadium, in Shelby, North Carolina, opened in 1976 and served as home to various minor league teams. Beginning in 2000 it hosted various Legion tournaments. In 2008 it hosted the Legion World Series and won the right to host on a trial basis beginning in 2011. The Series proved so successful, breaking attendance records each year, that the Legion happily made Shelby and Cleveland County the home of its World Series. Player introductions are always a highlight of the event (courtesy Brittany Randolph, *Shelby Star*).

star, J. T. Realmuto, to the pros after the Regional, where he was the Most Valuable Player. The future MLB All-Star catcher got an $800,000 signing bonus. Midwest City came in with the lowest earned run average, an impressive 2.56 mark. Moline, Illinois, Post 246 (42–7) came in with the highest team batting average at .350, but their pitching faltered, giving up 5.16 runs per game. They struggled before getting past Terre Haute in the Regional. Eden Prairie, Minnesota (36–7), last appeared in 2007, when they finished second to Columbia, Tennessee. To make the Series, they had to beat Festus, Missouri, who appeared last year, 15–5. Roseburg, Oregon, Docs (33–14) won the Northwest Regional by beating Kelso, Washington, 6–3, behind the pitching of MVP Brandon Jackson. Las Vegas Post 40, aka Nevada Youth Association (47–15), continued a long line of Las Vegas-area representatives. They beat Hawaii, 15–4, to take the Western Regional crown.[68]

Only one of the opening-round games was close. Las Vegas gained a 6–5 win over Kernersville. Conner Klein homered for Vegas, and Alex Estrella had three hits, including the game-winning RBI in the bottom of the eighth inning. Midwest City hammered Chesapeake, 18–2, in a game shortened to seven innings by the mercy rule. Kevin Hill struck out 15 batters while allowing just three hits. Dalton Bernardi had three hits and three RBI. Moline left fielder Eric Ashcraft collected five hits, including a homer, and drove in five runs as his mates had little trouble crushing Bradford, 15–7. Moline tied the ALWS record with 22 base hits. Eden Prairie gave notice of its power in a 13–6 victory over Roseburg. Second baseman Tony Skjefte drove in five runs. In the second round, Kernersville eliminated Bradford, 8–6, as outfielder Brandon Harrison had a homer among his three hits. Roseburg overcame five errors and an outstanding performance by Chesapeake shortstop Matt Dickason, who had three hits, including two home runs, and three RBI. Despite that effort, Roseburg pulled out an 11–10 victory that eliminated Chesapeake. Las Vegas had no trouble against Moline in a mercy rule-shortened 12–2 game. Designated hitter Julian Cutolo had five RBI for Las Vegas. In the feature game of the tournament to date, Eden Prairie hung on to take Midwest City, 9–6. The Minnesotans led, 9–1, in the ninth, before the Outlaws staged a comeback. Midwest City shortstop Alex Polston had four RBI, but it was not enough.[69]

On day three, Vince Ampi hit a homer and drove in four of Roseburg's runs in their 9–7 elimination of Moline. Midwest City beat Kernersville, 6–1, eliminating the North Carolina team. Third baseman Josh Halbert had three of the Outlaws' hits. In Game 11, Eden Prairie put a 9–6 beating on Las Vegas. Second baseman Tony Skejefte had three hits and a couple of RBI. In battles of one-loss teams, Midwest City designated hitter Caleb Price homered and drove in three runs in a 7–1 thrashing of Las Vegas, while Eden Prairie won, 6–2, over Roseburg. Catcher Matt Halloran collected four hits and drove in three runs.[70]

That left Eden Prairie and Midwest City as the only teams standing. Eden Prairie needed just one win to go home with the championship trophy. However, Midwest City took the first game, 11–6. Third baseman Josh Halbert homered in the seventh inning and had four RBI and a steal of home to pace the Outlaws. Dalton Bernardi contributed three hits and three RBI. Four Eden Prairie errors contributed to Midwest City's victory. In the 2010 championship game, Midwest City left no doubt about which was the best team by clobbering Eden Prairie, 10–1. On this day it was second baseman Greg Nelson who played hero, slamming out four hits, including a home run, and driving in three runs. Bernardi also drove in three runs and collected three hits. Midwest City put pressure on their opponents by running. In the final two games against Eden Prairie, the Outlaws stole 13 bases.[71]

Dalton Bernardi, who compiled a .420 batting average, was selected Most Valuable Player of the Series. The Player of the Year Award went to Brandon Drozd of Genoa, Nebraska. Jake Hager of Las Vegas took the Louisville Slugger Award by batting .476 in national play. Kevin Hill of Midwest City captured the Bob Feller Award with 35 strike-outs. The Cowger RBI Award went to Vince Anpi of Roseburg with 19. The Rawlings Big Stick Award for total bases went to Matt Halloran of Eden Prairie with 34. Blake Schmit, Eden Prairie shortstop, got the Sportsmanship Award. The 2010 all-tournament team selected by *Baseball America* consisted of: first base, Tanner Hessman, Midwest City; second base, Tony Sjefte, Eden Prairie; third base, Josh Halbert, Midwest City; shortstop, Josh Hager, Las Vegas; outfield, Cameron Newell, Roseburg; outfield, Tom Miller, Eden Prairie; outfield, Turner Coon, Midwest City; catcher, Alex Swim, Kernersville; utility, Blake Schmit, Eden Prairie; pitcher, Dalton Bernardi, Midwest City; pitcher, Kevin Hill, Midwest City; and pitcher, Brandon Jackson, Roseburg.[72]

Attendance at Spokane was worse than the previous year had been at Fargo. An embarrassing 1,200 turned out for the final game. The reported attendance of 13,000 for the Series made Legion officials long for next year, when the Series would switch to Shelby, North Carolina. If the Legion was disappointed with attendance at the 2010 World Series, they had reason to be proud of the continuing Legion graduates who entered baseball's Hall of Fame. For the first decade of the 21st century, the HOF inductees with Legion backgrounds included George "Sparky" Anderson (2000), Carlton Fisk (2000), Dave Winfield (2001), Gary Carter (2003), Eddie Murray (2003), Paul Molitor (2004), Ryne Sandberg (2005), Wade Boggs (2005), Bruce Sutter (2006), Dick Williams (2008), Joe Gordon (2009), Jim Rice (2009), Whitey Herzog (2010), and Doug Harvey (2010).

Indeed, in 2010, America as a whole was just recovering from the Crash of 2008. Beginning in 2007, housing prices had plummeted. In 2008, rising unemployment reached above ten percent, and declining real estate prices threatened the entire financial structure of the country. The 2008 election of the first African American president, Barack Obama, created enormous excitement, but it was not until 2010 that he stabilized the economy and Congress made reforms that backers believed would forestall another recession.

9

Shelby:
A Home for the American
Legion World Series,
2011–2019

Before the 2011 American Legion World Series, the citizens of Shelby, North Carolina, and, indeed, all of Cleveland County pulsed with excitement. Eddie Holbrook, co-chair of Shelby's ALWS Committee, said, "We look forward to putting on the best World Series the Legion has ever had, becoming a complementary partner with them and making [the]Legion proud that they selected us." Shelby, a town of about 20,000, was the county seat of Cleveland County, nestled in the rolling hills of the Piedmont region of southern North Carolina. Gastonia to the east was the nearest city of any size, and Charlotte loomed just east of Gastonia. Shelby had won the right to host the ALWS for the next four years, and who knew beyond that. It had been a team effort for the 400 or so citizens who volunteered to work on the project, but now they had to put on the Series, in front of a national TV audience on ESPN. All 15 games would be shown live on ESPN3. Cleveland County manager David Dear's predictions about the economic benefits of hosting the Series appeared to be on its way to becoming reality. Shelby's organizers built in a significant military recognition which appealed to the national Legion staff. They promised Black Hawk and Apache flyovers, the 82nd Airborne Chorus, representatives from all three services, and the National Guard.[1]

The concerns about baseball below the professional level sounded much like those of 1924–1925. USA Baseball in Cary, North Carolina, reported that between 1990 and 2005, the number of kids playing amateur baseball dropped by 25 percent, from 16 million to 12 million. Those were worrisome numbers. On the other hand, Legion ball somehow grew by 180 teams. In North Carolina, the number of teams increased from 60 to 160. Shelby organizers pointed to the excitement sparked by the American Legion World Series coming to Cleveland County.

Most of the teams that made the 2011 ALWS had experienced the Series before. Region One winner Bedford, New Hampshire, Stevens-Buswell Post 54, was not one of those experienced teams. They had gone 5–0 in the New England tournament, beating Whitestown, New York, 10–0, for the title as Lucas Olen threw a tidy four-hitter. Third baseman Pat Parker hit .524 in the regional. Brooklawn, New Jersey Post 72 was getting to be a regular, having made the Series in 2000, 2001 and 2005, its 13th overall appearance. They came in with a 44–4 record. The Brookers survived Boyertown by scoring in the bottom of the ninth inning, after Boyertown had put up six runs in the top of the ninth to tie it, giving Brooklawn a 10–9 win in the Mid–Atlantic final. "We're in it to win it," exclaimed Brooklawn coach Dennis Barth. Gaffney, South Carolina, Post 109 beat Bradenton twice, 8–5 and 14–6, to win Region Three, the Southeast Regional. They were also new to the World Series. The representative of Region Four, Mid–South, came from Tupelo, Mississippi, Post 49 (32–11). The 49ers beat Columbia, Tennessee, the 2007 national champions, by a convincing 20–9 score. Drew Alford led the way with five RBI.[2]

Teams from the West had taken the past three Series and could reasonably expect a repeat. Region Five, Great Lakes, champion Midland, Michigan, Berryhill Post 165 had won the national crown as recently as 2009. In 2011, they beat Napoleon, Ohio, 2–0, to get to the Series. Region Seven, the Great Plains, sent the 2010 runner-up, Eden Prairie, Minnesota, Post 580. They brought a 43–8 record, having beat Carroll, Iowa, 8–2 and 11–9, in regional finals. Without question they were pre-tournament favorites along with Brooklawn. The Waipahu, Hawaii, Post 56 Marauders came out of the Northwest, Region Seven. They had played few games, bringing a 19–5 record to the Regional, but after winning five games in a row, the last a 7–0 victory over Billings, Montana, they began to establish some credibility. Las Vegas was a fixture in the ALWS. Post 40 from Henderson, Nevada, had appeared in 2002, 2005, 2006, and 2010. In 2008 and 2009, Post 76 of Las Vegas had represented the Western Region. In 2008, they won the national title with a final record of 70–7. The last two teams were composed of boys from Bishop Gorman High School, but known as the Nevada Youth Baseball Association Titans, as was the 2011 team, champions of Region Eight.[3]

The opening day featured a clash between Eden Prairie and Midland. In an upset, Midland pounded Eden Prairie pitching ace Adam Bray and went on to a shortened 14–3 win. Left fielder Alex Goodwin had four RBI. Kenton San Miguel was the winning pitcher. Brooklawn got a walk-off 3–2 win over Waipahu when second baseman Joe Brooks singled home the winning run in the bottom of the ninth. Cody Brown was the winning pitcher. Gaffney easily beat Bedford, 12–1, in seven innings. Third baseman Colby Painter had a homer and three RBI, and Kaleb Earls allowed no earned runs. In the final first-round game, Tupelo beat Las Vegas, 6–3, as ace Will Cox pitched a three-hitter and collected three hits and three RBI himself.[4]

In the losers' bracket, Waipahu and Bedford quickly succumbed to Eden Prairie and Las Vegas, respectively. Eden Prairie pitcher Tyler Ruemmele allowed just one earned run in a 10–2 victory. Center fielder Dave Belusiky and catcher Danny Blasy each had three hits, while first baseman Tyler Peterson and right fielder Lance Thonvold homered. Against Bedford, Las Vegas left fielder A. J. Van Meetren collected three hits, including a home run, as Vegas cruised to an 11–0 win. Midland broke opened a rain-delayed game, tied 4–4 in the eighth inning, against Brooklawn. Center fielder Larsen Cronkright drove in three runs, and designated hitter Alex Rapanos homered. The Gaffney-Tupelo game, scheduled last on day two, had to be suspended until the next day because of rain. It was a scoreless game until the seventh inning, when Tupelo shortstop Channing Nanney smashed a long double to left, scoring three runners. That was all Tupelo needed for a 3–1 win.[5]

In a battle to the death between once-beaten teams Las Vegas held on to beat Brooklawn, 14–10. Both teams collected 15 hits. Brooklawn center fielder Steve Wilgus collected four hits, including a home run, but it was not enough. Eric VanMeetren countered with four hits and four RBI for Las Vegas. The loss eliminated Brooklawn.

Eden Prairie had an easy time eliminating Gaffney, 12–2. Cameron Mingo pitched eight innings before Anthony King-Foreman finished up. First baseman Tyler Peterson collected four hits, while third baseman Ryan Maenke also had four hits and drove in four runs. Tupelo racked up an easy win over Midland by an 8–1 score. First baseman Cody Shrewsbury homered and drove in five runs. On Monday, Day Four of the Series, Las Vegas had an easy time beating Midland, 7–1. The loss eliminated Midland. Las Vegas pitcher Evan Dunn allowed no earned run in collecting the win. Erik VanMeetren, again, led the way with three hits, including a homer and three runs batted in. Eden Prairie enjoyed a 14–4, seven-inning laughter in knocking Tupelo from the undefeated ranks. Shortstop Blake Schmit, second baseman Tony Skjefte, and catcher Danny Blasy each drove in three runs.[6]

To get to the final game, one-loss Eden Prairie needed to beat Las Vegas, which they did in a 2–1 squeaker. The Series had not seen a pitching duel since the first day of competition, but now Eden Prairie's Adam Bray locked up against Adam Wozniak. Eden Prairie got on the board with two runs in the second inning. Bray, who had three hits on the day, singled, went to second on a wild pitch, and scored on left fielder Tyler Ruemmele's double. Ryan Maenke reached on an error by the third baseman and scored on center fielder David Belusky's double. That was all the scoring until the ninth inning, when Las Vegas picked up a run when T. J. White singled, stole second, and scored on a double by right fielder Kenny Meimerstorf. Bray struck out the final batter to end the threat. With Las Vegas eliminated, Eden advanced to the championship game against Tupelo.[7]

In the 2011 championship game, the two one-loss teams struggled for 13 innings before Eden Prairie emerged the 5–4 winner. Tupelo put up four runs in the first inning. Shortstop Channing Nanney doubled to the right field corner. Goss reached on a fielding error by the second baseman, and as Eden Prairie kicked the ball around, Nanney scored the first run. Goss advanced to third on a fielder's choice and scored as Brandon Woodruff grounded out to second. Catcher Ben Hudspeth kept the rally going by working a walk. Drew Alford singled to right field, and Cody Shrewsbury singled to load the bases. Left fielder Connor Carothers doubled to left-center, scoring two runs to give Tupelo a 4–0 lead after the first inning. Eden Prairie chipped away at the lead. They got two runs back in the second inning. Lance Thonvold and Jordon Smith walked before Ryan Maenke's double to left-center drove them both across the plate. Eden Prairie got another run in the fifth when Blake Schmit homered. In the eighth, Eden Prairie tied the game at 4–4. Schmit singled but was out at second on Skjefte's bunt. Skjefte came around to score on Peterson's double to right field. Both teams replaced their starting pitchers at that point. In the 13th inning, Eden Prairie's Tyler Peterson led off with a walk. Tupelo brought Drew Alford in from right field to pitch. Lance Thonvold reached on a fielding error by second baseman Kirk Roberts, which allowed Peterson to advance to third base. After Ruemmele struck out, Jordon Smith grounded to the shortstop who, hoping for a double play to end the inning, flipped to second, but they failed to turn the double play, allowing Peterson to score the go-ahead run. In the bottom half of the inning, Tupelo staged a rally. With one out, Cody Shrewsbury singled to right. Catcher Tyler Moore followed with a single up the middle. The game turned as Lance Thonvold, pitching his sixth inning of relief, picked Shrewsbury off at second. The next batter grounded out. Game and title to Eden Prairie.[8]

In the final game, Tupelo pitchers struck out 15 batters, ten by starter Will Cox. In eight innings of work, they gave up just six hits. Eden Prairie pitchers Ruemmele and

Thonvold allowed just one earned run in their 13 innings. Channing Nanney and Drew Alford each had three hits for Tupelo, while Blake Schmit had three for Eden Prairie. Runner-up Tupelo had the highest team batting average, .342, for the tournament, but Eden Prairie had a far better ERA, 3.09 to Tupelo's 4.41. The shame was that one team had to lose.

Few argued at the selection of Blake Schmit as Player of the Year. Schmit also won the RBI Award. Colton Loomis of Midland captured the Bob Feller Award for strikeouts. The Rawlings Big Stick Award for total bases went to Tony Skjefte. The Louisville Slugger Award for highest batting average was won by Dylan Huskey of Gaffney with a .500 average. The all-tournament team included the following: first base, Tyler Peterson, Eden Prairie; second base, Tony Skjefte, Eden Prairie; third base, T. J. White, Las Vegas; shortstop, Blake Schmit, Eden Prairie; outfield, Dillon Palencia, Gaffney; outfield, A. J. Van-Meetren, Las Vegas; utility, Channing Nanney, Tupelo; designated hitter, Alex Rapands, Midland; pitcher, Will Cox, Tupelo; pitcher, Kaleb Earis, Gaffney; and pitcher, Brandon Woodruff, Tupelo.[9]

Despite the rain that interrupted several games, total attendance reached a record high of 86,162, topping the previous mark set 75 years earlier in Spartanburg, South Carolina. Shelby pulled out all the stops for the Series. They offered a number of on-field tributes to veterans, music concerts, and other social gatherings. In 2012, the local organizers of the World Series were determined to put on a good showing, even though the 2011 ALWS set an all-time attendance record. Jackie Sibley, executive director of Tour Cleveland County, arranged for two concerts. The Christian rock band Mercy Me was scheduled for Sunday at the county fairgrounds, where they expected to draw 10,000 fans, along with a country duo, Montgomery Gentry. For unspecified reasons, they moved the start of the ALWS back from August 12 to 17.[10]

For the 2012 ALWS, Milford, Connecticut, Post 196 (30–7) was the only new face. It was also their first state title. From the state championship, they had gone on to beat Portland, Maine, 9–1, in the New England Regional. Shawn Cariglio led the way with five RBI. Brooklawn, New Jersey, Post 72 over the years seemed to have no problem getting to the ALWS; their problem was winning it. They had two trophies but lots of "what ifs." Coach Dennis Barth believed 2012 could be the year for the Brookers. They had sailed through the Mid–Atlantic Regional, going 5–0, beating Spring City, Pennsylvania, 9–8, in the final. With a record of 59–5, they appeared to be the team to beat in the ALWS. Florence, South Carolina, Post 1 (40–5) defeated Wilmington, North Carolina, 10–2, in the Southeast Regional. New Orleans Post 125 returned to the Series they last won in 1960. Jesuit High School again supplied the players, and Retif Oil sponsored the team. Jesuit, as they were known, went 5–0 in the Regional and polished off Columbia, Tennessee, 4–3. Designated hitter Matthieu Robert led Retif in virtually all offensive categories. Western teams in the final eight were Moline, Omaha, Bellevue, and Lakewood, California. Moline, Illinois (48–8), lost the opening game of the Great Lakes Regional to Adrian, Michigan, 4–2, but came back to win five straight, including a 4–1 rematch victory, and a 4–2 win over Terre Haute for the title. Omaha Post 1 (50–9) captured the Central Plains Regional by beating defending champion Eden Prairie, 6–1, after losing to them earlier in the tournament. That showing made Omaha one of the favorites. In the Northwest Regional, Bellevue, Washington (37–13), beat Waipahu, Hawaii, 15–4, for the title. As a team they batted .387 in the regional. Finally, in the Western Regional, Lakewood, California, Post 496 (24–8) beat Fairfield, California, 4–1.[11]

In the opening round, New Orleans and Brooklawn established themselves as the teams to beat. New Orleans had to go 11 innings before getting past Milford, 5–4 in dramatic fashion. Milford's Matt Ferraiota allowed just one earned run in nine innings. Emerson Gibbs, who had gone 10–1 for New Orleans, scattered six hits over ten innings. In the top of the 11th inning, Armand Daigle singled for New Orleans before Brady Williamson unloaded a mammoth home run for the win. Brooklawn was off and running, swiping six bases in their 9–6 win over Florence. Pat Kane, Steve Wilgus, and Brett Tenuto each collected three hits. Omaha beat Lakewood, 8–4, in a sloppy game that included nine errors. First baseman Zach Garrett batted in four Omaha runs. Bellevue catcher Jimmy Sinatro had three hits and four RBI as Bellevue rolled to an 11–4 win over Moline.

On the second day, Brooklawn and New Orleans continued to roll, although by the slimmest of margins. Brooklawn out-hit Bellevue, 7–4, but prevailed only by 3–2 in 10 innings. In the 10th inning, left fielder Pat Kane singled, went to second on a passed ball, stole third, and came home on the catcher's wild throw. New Orleans managed an 8–7 win over Omaha. Blue Jays first baseman Taylor Elman banged out four hits, including a home run, and second baseman Jonathan Lee had four RBI, three in their five-run eighth inning. Florence eliminated Moline, 10–8, as catcher Cameron McRae had a home run and four RBI and Carnell Montgomery had four hits. Lakewood pitchers Andrew Mendoza and Anthony Timmons combined on a three-hit shutout to beat Milford, 4–0. The loss eliminated Milford.[12]

On the third day, New Orleans and Brooklawn met in the featured Game 11, but rain was playing havoc with the games. Omaha scored five runs in the second inning and coasted to an 8–2 victory over Florence. Right fielder Evan Ryan picked up two hits and two RBI, and Mason Rudolph pitched seven innings without giving up an earned run. The loss eliminated Florence. Bellevue's Brandon Mahovlich scattered four hits over seven innings as Bellevue beat Lakewood, 4–1, in a game that eliminated the California team. Rain delayed the start of the Brooklawn-New Orleans game until well after 10:00 p.m. New Orleans managed a 6–5 win in the rain-shortened, seven-inning contest. Shortstop Anthony Fort-Bensen had a double, stolen base, and two RBI to pace New Orleans.[13]

With just four teams alive, New Orleans was guaranteed a spot in the finals. Bellevue, Brooklawn, and Omaha, the one-loss teams, needed to win their way into the final. Omaha came out tight and committed four costly errors in losing, 4–3, to Brooklawn. Bellevue knocked New Orleans from the unbeaten ranks with a 10–6 win in a game that mattered little. Right fielder Andrew Kemmerer had three runs batted in, and third baseman Aaron Sandefur homered for Bellevue. Bellevue's win set up a semi-final contest against Brooklawn. Lefty Cody Brown pitched a complete game for the Brookers and was never in trouble after the fourth inning, when Brooklawn scored three runs on its way to a 4–3 win. Left fielder Pat Kane starred for Brooklawn, bringing three runs home with a big double in the fourth inning. Brett Tenuto plated the final Brooklawn run.[14]

Rain delayed the start of the 2012 championship game until 11:00 p.m. The Blue Jays' starter, Tulane-bound Emerson Gibbs, was up to the task. He pitched a shutout, allowing just three hits, and walked none in a dominating performance. New Orleans had a 4–0 win over Brooklawn for the title. Designated hitter Matthieu Robert drove in three runs for New Orleans. The Blue Jays got on the board in the second inning thanks to a hit batter, three wild pitches, and three walks, the final one to Armand Daigle. They pieced together another run in the third on a single, stolen base, fielder's choice, and Robert's sacrifice fly. In the seventh inning, they got two runs on a hit batter, a fielding error, and a double by Robert. That made the score 4–0 and was the extent of the scoring. It was the first title game shutout since 2004. Blue Jays manager Joey Latino gave credit for the win to pitching and defense, saying, "It was great pitching, great defense, and we are just ecstatic." Despite the rain, and the fact that the game did not start until 11:00 at night and ended at 1:30 a.m., 5,468 fans braved the elements to see New Orleans win the title. New Orleans' big bopper, Matthieu Robert, finished with a .424 batting average for the Series.[15]

The 2012 awards should have included one for the Shelby/Cleveland County organizing committee for somehow attracting over 100,000 fans, officially 101,925, to the 15 games of the Series. That was despite the rain which plagued officials throughout the Series. The George W. Rulon Player of the Year Award went to Emerson Gibbs, the outstanding New Orleans pitcher, who went 10–1 during the regular season and 4–0 in national games with a 1.66 earned run average in the Series. Gibbs also took home the Bob Feller Award with 26 strikeouts in national play. Omaha slugger Evan Ryan took home nearly all the hitting awards: Louisville Slugger Award with a .571 batting average; Rawlings Big Stick Award for total bases; and tied for the Irvin "Click" Cowger RBI Award with Omaha teammate Taylor Elman and Matthieu Robert of New Orleans, with 16 apiece. Brooklawn's first baseman, John Brue, handled 123 chances in the field without a miscue to set a record. The all-tournament team included only three players from New Orleans, Emerson Gibbs, shortstop Anthony Fortier-Benson, and designated hitter Luke Voiron. Other selections were: first base, Taylor Elman, Omaha; second base, Joe Brooks, Brooklawn; third base, Brett Tenuto, Brooklawn; outfield, Pat Kane, Brooklawn; outfield, Evan Ryan, Omaha; outfield, Zach Shields, Florence; catcher, Jimmy Sinatro, Bellevue; utility man, Akeem Bostick, Florence; pitcher, Cody Brown, Brooklawn; and pitcher, Brandon Mahovlich, Bellevue. No one explained why Matthieu Robert failed to make the all-star team.[16]

After the 2012 ALWS, the newly elected Legion National Commander, Jim Koutz, announced that Shelby, which had won the bid to host the World Series for four years, 2011–2014, had been extended for another five years through 2019. Shelby had "surpassed all expectations, as well as embraced the Legion family, baseball players and fans with southern hospitality."

Despite the record attendance at the 2011 and 2012 American Legion World Series, concern about the future of American Legion baseball increased. The core of Legion baseball had always been local Legion posts sponsoring teams. Now, the posts increasingly found themselves in trouble. Jacob Bogage reported that in the 21st century, between 2000 and 2014, the American Legion lost 1,000 posts with two million members. He estimated this to be an 11 percent decline. The simple reason was that Vietnam vets had not joined up in the same proportion as those of World War I or World War II or even the Korean War. That meant the number of veterans in the United States was also shrinking; from 22.7 million in 2013 to an estimated 14 million in 2020.[17]

The long-term effect of this trend was obvious; nonetheless, baseball went on. The eight 2013 finalists included teams with mind-boggling records. The best belonged to Bradford, Connecticut, Post 83 with a 36–2 record. Bradford was no stranger to the ALWS; they had appeared in 2005, 2007, and 2010, but never went deep in the tournament. They punched their ticket by thumping Worcester, Massachusetts, 12–2. Wilmington, North Carolina, Post 10 won the Southeast Regional by beating Asheboro, North Carolina, 7–0. That win gave them a 34–2 record. Their shortstop, Steve Linkous, looked like a real prospect. Gonzales, Louisiana, Post 81, the Mid–South winner, was not far behind with a 46–4 record. They had to beat tough Midwest City, Oklahoma, the 2010 national champions, by a 5–1 score to reach the ALWS. Brooklawn Post 72 was back again, their 15th ALWS appearance and third in a row. The 2012 runner-up to New Orleans brought a 42–8 record. In the Mid–Atlantic Regional, they beat Funkstown, Maryland, 12–0, Boyertown, Pennsylvania, 6–4, New Castle, Delaware, 10–2, Twin Valley, Pennsylvania 12–6, and West Seneca, New York, 9–6. Newcomer first baseman Tony Harrold led the Brooklawn attack with a .529 batting average and .618 slugging average. Third baseman Nick Cieri followed with a .486 average and a Most Valuable Player trophy from the Mid–Atlantic tournament. Mike Shawaryn (2–0, 0.75 era), John Murphy (2–0, 1.72), and Tyler Mondile (2–0, 2.77) led the pitching staff. As always, they liked to run and force their opponents to make plays. They were greeted in Shelby by their host "family," a local church, which brought a delegation of 50 holding banners and greeting the Jersey boys with a loud ovation when they arrived.[18]

Of the rest, Waipahu, Hawaii, remained a bit of a mystery, and Petaluma, California, Post 28 loomed as a dark horse. Hawaii teams seldom played many games on the islands; they came to the mainland with an 18–3 record before going 5–1 in the Western Regional, beating Eugene, Oregon, 14–3, in the final. Third baseman Brent Sakurai supplied much of the offensive power with four hits. Petaluma, California, Leghorns of Post 28 (32–13) were from the Sonoma County wine country, 37 miles north of San Francisco. Their nickname, the "Leghorns," referenced a semi-professional football team of the post-war years. They won the Western Regional by beating Las Vegas, 18–4 and 9–0. Center fielder Charles Parnow homered and had three hits and four RBI. The Great Lakes and Central Plains teams were Napoleon, Ohio Post 300 (46–19) and Burnsville, Minnesota Post 1700 (36–10). Napoleon beat Edwardsville, Indiana, 3–1, to reach the ALWS. Burnsville knocked out Omaha, a strong team out of Creighton Prep, 15–5.[19]

The opening day 2013 action featured Brooklawn going 11 innings to get past Waipahu. Brooklawn's Mike Shawaryn pitched solid ball for nine innings, giving up two earned runs and striking out 12. In the 11th inning, an error by the third baseman got Brooklawn outfielder Jon Gonzalez on base. He stole second, went to third on a wild pitch, and scored on another wild pitch by Brent Sakurai. That gave Brooklawn a 5–4 victory. Gonzales got all eight of its runs in the third inning and coasted to an 8–5 win over favorite Petaluma. The highlight of that game came when Gonzales left fielder Robert Podorsky singled, stole second, stole third, and stole home. Burnsville shut out Napoleon, 4–0. Burnsville got all four of its runs in the seventh inning. Three of those runs came off the bat of catcher Camden Traetow. Behind the three-hit pitching of Joe O'Donnell, Wilmington shut out Bradford, 5–0. In second-round elimination games, Waipahu sent Napoleon home by a 9–5 score. Islanders third baseman Brent Sakurai had three hits, catcher Austyn Nagamine contributed three RBI, and right fielder Zach Fielder got credit for three RBI and four runs. Despite four errors, Petaluma managed to eliminate poor Bradford and its lofty expectations by a 6–3 score. Brooklawn got five runs in the fourth inning on its way to an easy 8–1 victory over Burnsville. Shortstop Phil Dickinson drove in three of those runs with a triple. Wilmington committed four errors, including one in the ninth inning that allowed the winning run to score, giving Gonzales a 6–5 win. For Gonzales, first baseman David Speligene had three RBI.[20]

On the third day, Petaluma pitchers Scott Hilbert and Jimmy Platt allowed just one run as the Leghorns eliminated Burnsville, 3–1. Third baseman Rob Busse's home run was the big blow for Petaluma. Waipahu batters had a field day as they destroyed Wilmington,

12–3, eliminating the North Carolina club. Center fielder Tanner Tokunaga had five RBI, catcher Austyn Nagamine chipped in three hits and three RBI, and shortstop Reid Akau had three hits and two RBI. In the final game of the day, Brooklawn scored a 7–2 win over Gonzales. First baseman Tony Harrold contributed three hits, and right fielder Fran Kinsey had two RBI.[21]

On the penultimate day of play, Petaluma, Waipahu, and Gonzales needed to win to stay alive. Waipahu, the crowd favorite in Shelby, got only five hits but managed to slip past Gonzales, 5–4, in 12 innings. They got three runs in the third inning on just one hit, thanks to two errors and two wild pitches. Gonzales second baseman Robert Podorsky drove in two runs in the bottom of the ninth inning to send the game to extra innings. In the 12th, Waipahu scored the winning run without benefit of a hit. Tanner Tokunaga was hit by a pitch, stole second, and came home on an error by the shortstop. Brooklawn, guaranteed a spot in the finals, let its foot off the gas. They seemed to just go through the motions in a 14–4 loss to Petaluma. The Brooks, usually steady in the field, committed four errors, but the most egregious shortcoming was their pitchers walking 17 batters to tie the all-time record for ineptitude set by Cedar Rapids in 1982.[22]

On the final day, Petaluma gained the final by taking out Waipahu, 8–2. Shortstop Anthony Bender had three hits, two of those doubles. Three Leghorns pitchers did not allow an earned run. Starter Jimmy Flatt earned the win. Before the 2013 championship game, Brooklawn players met. Assistant coach Josh Copskey reported that they said: "this is our moment, and we are going to walk this dream together." They did. Brooklawn avenged the earlier 14–4 drubbing and made clear they were the best team, by smashing Petaluma, 10–0, in a seven-inning game shortened by the mercy rule. Pitcher Mike Shawaryn gave up four hits, walked none, and struck out eight to give him a total of 33 for the tournament. Catcher John Theckston had three hits and three RBI, and third baseman Nick Cieri had three hits and two RBI to lead the Brooklawn attack.[23]

Brooklawn first baseman Tony Harrold finished with a .525 batting average for the tournament, good enough to win the Louisville Slugger Award. Teammate Nick Cieri finished second with a .486 average. Harrold also compiled the highest on-base percentage, .610. Petaluma could take plenty of pride in its hitting. They finished with the highest team batting average, .338. They were, also, highest in most other batting categories, including slugging average .473, on-base percentage .435, runs 100, runs batted in 89, walks 60, doubles 26, triples 3, home runs 7, and total bases 185. For his work, Harrold was selected Player of the Year on top of his Louisville Slugger Award. Brooklawn's Mike Shawaryn took home the Bob Feller Award for his 33 strikeouts. Petaluma's Anthony Bender won the Rawlings Big Stick Award with 28 total bases. Teammate Bob Busse took home the Click Cowger RBI award. Robbie Posorsky of Gonzales won the James F. Daniel, Jr., Award for Sportsmanship. The all-tournament team consisted of: Harrold, first base; second base Bob Podorsky, Gonzales; third base Nick Cieri, Brooklawn; shortstop Steven Linkous, Wilmington; outfield Colin Delaune, Gonzales; outfield Tanner Tokunaga, Waipahu; outfield Ryan Walsh, Petaluma; catcher Austyn Nagamine, Waipahu; utility Anthony Bender, Petaluma; pitcher Joe O'Donnell, Wilmington; pitcher Mike Shawaryn, Brooklawn; and pitcher Jimmy Flatt, Petaluma. There were many records in 2013. Fans purchased 104,726 tickets, a new attendance record for the third straight year. Brooklawn played in its 15th ALWS, the most by any post team. Teams from Cincinnati and New Orleans had played in 14 ALWS, but not all those teams were from the same post. For Brooklawn, it was their third championship, having won in 1991, 2001, and now in 2013. Fran Kinsey, the right fielder, said, "You look at talent and they [Petaluma] are probably better than us. We have a lot of new and younger guys on our team." Some 6,000 fans greeted the team when it returned home. Coach Dennis Barth, who had stayed back for years, giving the spotlight to his father, Joe "Pop" Barth, now took his place in the limelight; he had earned it.[24]

All sports willingly alter the way they do things, especially schedules, to accommodate television. In the case of the ALWS, ESPN 3 grew tired of games starting at 11:00 p.m. They wanted a predictable starting time for the championship game if they were to televise the game live. The way to accomplish that goal was to extend play by a day, so the 2014 World Series would be played from Thursday, August 14, to Tuesday, August 19, with the championship game starting at 7:00 p.m. on the final day. All other games would be streamed live. To make this work, the World Series would abolish the double elimination format, which required two games on the final day, and return to pool play. Teams were divided into two divisions, more or less by geography, with the East Division consisting of the Northeast, Mid–Atlantic, Southeast, and Great Lakes. That left the West Division with Mid–South, Central Plains, Northwest, and Western. Teams would play a round-robin in their Division from August 14–17. The team holding the best record in the East would play the West runner-up on, and the West winner would take on the East runner-up in semi-final games on August 18.[25]

Eddie Holbrook, co-chairman of Shelby's ALWS committee, announced, "one of our earliest goals for the ALWS was to make it more than just a baseball event." The featured non-baseball event in 2014 would be a concert by the popular Charlie Daniels Band. Country music performer Rodney Atkins would perform at the Celebration of Champions event held for players, their families, and the community on August 13 at Keeter Stadium. Singer-songwriter Corey Smith was scheduled to perform at the courthouse square on August 9, before games started on August 14, 2014.

Baseball remained the feature attraction. Defending champion Brooklawn Post 72 opened as the favorite to win back-to-back titles in 2014. Brooklawn won its fourth straight Mid–Atlantic Regional with a 10–0 victory over Cecil, Maryland. Repeating was no easy task, but as Brooklawn outfielder Fran Kinsey put it, "We don't rebuild, we reload." Before the start of the season, Brooklawn lost the team's founder and coach for 58 years, Joe "Pop" Barth, who died at age 91 on March 1. Players wore a patch on the front of their uniforms that said simply "Pop" to remind all of their loss and their commitment to "win this one for Pop." Barth had a reputation for being cantankerous and brusque, but as former Legion Player of the Year Mike Rucci put it, "He treated every one of us like his sons. We were all lucky to have played for him." The elder Barth, however, demanded commitment from his players. At the start of each season, he was fond of saying, "If you have a girlfriend, get rid of her. If you have a car, get rid of it." He wanted nothing to stand in the way of baseball. Brooklawn came in to the ALWS with a 49–7 record.[26]

Other teams in the East Division would be hard-pressed to knock off Brooklawn. A new face came out of New England, Rocky Hill-Cromwell-Portland, Connecticut's Carlson Sjvall Post 105 (aka RCT or Cromwell). They had beaten Milford, Massachusetts, in the Regional final, 5–4, on Tommy Seaver's walk-off single. Jacksonville, Florida, Post 88 won the Southeastern Regional, beating Randolph, North Carolina, Post 45 by the slimmest of margins, 8–7. They brought a 34–4 record to the ALWS. Traditional power Midland, Michigan Berryhill Post 165 represented the Great Lakes Regional. Midland Berryhill became a team to be recognized in the mid-1990s and had been to the ALWS in 1996, 2008, 2009, and 2011. They won the ALWS title in 2009. Midland came in with a 47–6 record, having beaten Napoleon, Ohio, a 2013 finalist, in the Regional title game. The West Division included Columbia, Tennessee, Omaha, Nebraska, Waipahu, Hawaii, and Chico, California. Columbia Post 19 had won the World Series in 2007. Their star, Bill Pilkinton, batted .421 in the Mid–South Region and led his team to two wins over Bryant, Arkansas, for the regional title. Omaha Westside had the best regular season record at 56–5. Over the years, Post 1 had been a national power. This year the team was sponsored by KB Building Services. Their hopes rested on pitcher Jake Meyers. The Waipahu Marauders from Ewa Beach had established themselves in Shelby as a fan favorite in 2013. They were making their third appearance in four years in the ALWS. They beat the Medford, Oregon, Mustangs, 8–6, in the Northwest final. Bryson Sasui had been the MVP in the Regional. Waipahu lacked a post to sponsor it; manager Kerry Kiyabu sponsored the team himself. With back-to-back California titles, the Chico Nuts brought confidence to Shelby. They beat Las Vegas for the Western crown.[27]

After the first two days day of play, Brookland, Omaha, and Midland looked to be the teams to beat. Brooklawn hammered Cromwell, 9–1. Right fielder Fran Kinsey and second baseman Sean Breen each had three hits for Brooklawn, and catcher Tre Todd drove in three runs. Omaha beat Columbia, 6–3, and Midland topped Jacksonville, 6–4. On the second day, Brooklawn and Omaha continued to roll. Brooklawn blasted Jacksonville, 9–2. First baseman Anthony Harold collected four hits, Breen got three hits again, and Tre Todd drove in three runs. Omaha's KB Builders experienced an easy time with Chico, winning 9–6. Waipahu announced to all the other teams that it needed to be reckoned with as it pounded Columbia, 14–1, in a seven-inning, mercy rule shortened game.[28]

The feature game on Saturday, day three, matched Brooklawn, 2–0 in pool play, against Midland, 1–0 in the East Division. Midland had leads of 5–0 after the second inning and 8–7 after six, but Brooklawn kept coming back. The Brookers scored in the eighth inning to tie the game. The Brookers' Johnny Malatesta scored the winning run on a wild pitch in the bottom of the ninth inning. Sean Breen had two hits and scored three runs for Brooklawn. In other games, Waipahu waltzed past Chico, 8–1. Kyle Parrsche of Jacksonville starred with four hits and three RBI as the Florida crew defeated Cromwell in ten innings by a 10–5 score. On the final day of pool play, Omaha beat Waipahu, 12–8, to lock up first place in the West Division with a 3–0 record. Will Patterson led KB with four hits and three RBI, and Matt Waldron chipped in three RBI. By beating Cromwell, 4–3, Midland assured itself of second place in the East and a spot in the semi-finals. Columbia salvaged a bit of pride by beating Chico, 3–1. Pool play ended with Brooklawn and Omaha undefeated at 3–0. In the East Division, Midland finished second with a 2–1 record, followed by Jacksonville 1–2 and Cromwell 0–3. The West finished Omaha 3–0, Waipahu 2–1, Columbia 1–2, and Chico 0–3.[29]

Both semi-final games were nail-bitters, one-run games. Brooklawn built a 6–0 lead after five innings. This time it was Hawaii coming back in the sixth, seventh, and eighth innings. Pitching in relief, Brooklawn's Kevin Terifay saved the day by slamming the door on Waipahu in the eighth and ninth, striking out the final batter in each inning to preserve Brooklawn's 7–6 victory. The Brookers' Fran Kinsey had three RBI. Midland upset Omaha, 4–3, in the other semi-final game. Omaha coach Bob Greco had saved his ace, Jake Meyers, to pitch this game, but he could not come through. Midland notched a 4–3 victory, making the final game an East Division final.[30]

Brooklawn left little doubt they were the best team in 2014 by pounding Midland,

18–0, in the most lopsided final in the 88 years of the ALWS. Midland fans showed up with loads of home-made signs supporting their team. Pre-game festivities included bringing the game ball to the mound by a parachutist carrying the American flag. Dale Earnhardt, Jr., brought greetings. When the game finally started before 7,907 fans, the most for a championship game since 1938, the game quickly became a mismatch. Brooklawn scored four runs in the first inning, including outfielder Pete Farlow stealing home. From there, it was a laughter for Brooklawn. Midland pitchers walked 15 batters, and the team behind them committed four errors. Brooklawn's Tyler Mondile pitched to contact with his mid-90s fastball to limit Midland to five harmless hits. Left fielder John Malatesta and catcher Tre Todd knocked in three runs each. Brooklawn had accomplished the seemingly impossible task of winning back-to-back championships. The last time a team won back-to-back titles was in 1973–1974, when Pio Piedras of Puerto Rico accomplished the feat. Others with consecutive titles had been West Covina, California, in 1970–1971, Cincinnati Bentley Post 50 in 1957–1958, and Oakland Bill Erwin Post in 1949–1950.[31]

For the fourth consecutive year, the ALWS set a new attendance record, attracting 110,036 fans. Brooklawn's Sean Breen reigned as the George W. Rulon Player of the Year. He won the Louisville Slugger Award with a .575 batting average and the Big Stick Award with 29 total bases. The Click Cowger RBI Award went to Jordan Mopas of Waipahu. Jake Meyers of Omaha took home the Bob Feller Award by collecting 29 strikeouts. Tanner Gross of Midland was selected to receive the Sportsmanship Award. Fittingly, Dennis Barth won the Jack Williams Leadership Award. Brooklawn first baseman Anthony Harrold was selected to the all-tournament team for the second straight year. Player of the Year Sean Breen held down the second base slot. Others included: Tanner Gross, Midland, third base; Matt Waldron, Omaha, shortstop; Tanner Tokunaga, Waipahu, outfield; Peter Farlow, Brooklawn, outfield; Adam Fitzgibbon, Midland, outfield; Kamalu Neal, Waipahu, catcher; Kyle Pausche, Jacksonville, designated hitter; Jonathan Hentschel, Midland, utility; Tyler Mondile, pitcher, Brooklawn; Evan Marquardt, pitcher, Midland; and Eric Schoor, Brooklawn, pitcher.[32]

Brooklawn set out to make it three in a row in 2015 in what would be their fifth consecutive trip to the American Legion World Series. Coach Dennis Barth had reason to believe his team could pull off the unprecedented feat. After all, he returned 2013 Player of the Year in first baseman Anthony Harrold, 2014 Player of the Year in second baseman Sean Breen, 2014 all-tournament shortstop Phil Dickinson, 2014 all-star outfielder Pete Farlow, and pitcher Tyler Mondile. Not many would bet against that group. They won their sixth consecutive state title and 29th overall state championship. For the state title, they beat Flemington, 9–6, at Ewing. Tyler Mondile was named Most Valuable Player of the New Jersey tournament. Right on track, the Brookers wrapped up the Mid–Atlantic Regional, taking their 18th championship by defeating Albemarle, Virginia, Funkstown, Maryland, Red Land, Pennsylvania, Leesburg, Virginia, and Red Land again, by a 7–3 score. Harrold had eight RBI, while Breen led with a .370 average. Brooklawn took a 45–6 record to Shelby.[33]

Awaiting Brooklawn was a Cinderella team from Chapin-Newberry, South Carolina, Post 193 that came to the ALWS undefeated in 29 games. Coach Don Gregory drew his players from four different high schools in the area: Clinton, Dutch Fork, Mid–Carolina, and Newberry. They had captured the state title in 2013, but no one expected this team to become transformed into a power. They won the South Carolina title by beating

Florence, 13–3, after putting away Gaffney, 8–5, and Union, 5–3. The MVP Award went to shortstop Justin Hawkins, while the award for outstanding pitcher went to Ryan Stoudemire. In the Southeast Regional at Asheboro, North Carolina, they beat Tallahassee, Florida, 4–3, Salisbury, North Carolina, 6–5, Asheboro, North Carolina, 3–2, Tallahassee again, 6–3, and host Asheboro for the second time, 7–4. Outfielder Danton Hyman was named MVP for the Regional.[34]

Waipahu Post 35 appeared for the fourth time in five years. They came with a gaudy 31–1 record, having captured the Western Regional by beating defending west champ Chico, 11–4, and Tucson, 10–7, after losing the first game, 6–3. Kody Cacal received MVP honors in the Regional. They finished third in 2013 and 2014. Two other strong teams were poised to make a run at the title. Midland, Michigan, Berryhill Post 165, from a city of 42,181 that boasted it was headquarters of Dow Chemical, and Corning, the 2014 runner-up to Brooklawn. They won the Great Lakes Regional by beating Metro East (St. Louis), 14–4; that win gave Midland a 47–6 record. New Orleans Post 125, known as Jesuit after the high school that most players attended, or Blue Jays, the Jesuit High School nickname, and Retif Oil, the team sponsor, had won the national title in 2012. They advanced to the ALWS by beating the Southwest Shockers of Lawton, Oklahoma, 7–6, in the Mid–South tournament. That gave Retif Oil a 32–7 record. The Medford, Oregon, Post 15 Mustangs captured the Northwest Regional by beating Gillette, Wyoming, 12–2, as catcher Austin Zavala led the Mustangs with three RBI. That win moved Medford's record to 42–13. Two teams with little chance of winning rounded out the field. Millard South, Nebraska, the 52 Patriots Post 374, had a record of 41–18 but struggled in the Central Plains Regional before beating Rapid City twice, 7–5 and 4–3. Rocky Hill-Cromwell-Portland, Connecticut, Post 105 won the New England Regional to get back to the ALWS. The last time a team won consecutive Region One titles was back in 1991–1992. New England teams never fared well, and this year seemed no exception despite their 37–5 record.[35]

For 2015, the Legion shifted the pool pairings around and renamed them. Instead of East and West, the divisions were now known as Stars and Stripes, reflecting the heavy military ethos of this year's Series. The Stars consisted of Brooklawn, Millard, Medford, and Waipahu. The Stripes included Cromwell, Chapin-Newberry, New Orleans, and Midland.

Brooklawn's hopes for making history took a severe blow from Medford on the opening day of World Series play. Pitchers Jordan Ragan and Tyler Mondile locked up in a 2–2 game until the seventh inning. The Brookers failed to adjust to Ragan's off-speed stuff. For Brooklawn, lefty Dante Scafidi replaced Mondile and was greeted by a Micah Brown triple, followed by Bryce Rogan's RBI single. That was all the scoring. Midland hammered Cromwell, 12–1. Right fielder Cole Brooks collected four hits including a homer for Midland. Waipahu got two runs in the fourth inning on Cameron Igarashi's hit and two Millard errors, and two more in the eighth on Tyler Yamaguchi's hit to take a 5–4 victory. On the second day, Cromwell almost got a win, but lost a tight game to New Orleans, 2–1. In the fourth inning, Retif Oil's right fielder, Ben Hess, doubled, followed by Hayden Fuentes' RBI double. In the seventh, Hess's RBI was the margin of victory for New Orleans. Mason Mayfield went the distance for New Orleans. Medford continued its surprising play, beating Millard, 3–2. Austin Zavala got two RBI and shortstop Micah Brown had the other. No one really knew if undefeated Chapin-Newberry was for real or not until they beat Midland, 2–1. Ryne Huggins, the winning pitcher, gave up no earned runs. Shortstop Justin Hawkins and left fielder Kevis Burton each had three hits for the winners.[36]

Medford went to 3–0 in pool play on the third day, surprising Waipahu, 2–1, in another low-scoring game. Medford got its first run in the seventh inning when Cole Carder drove home the tying run. The winning run came in the bottom of the ninth on a fielder's choice as right fielder Jared Evans got credit for the RBI. Micah Brown got the win in relief. Chapin-Newberry finally suffered a loss, falling to New Orleans, 5–2. For the winners, shortstop Nicholas Ray had three hits and right fielder Ben Hess drove in two runs. Brooklawn broke out with a 16–1 win over Millard, a game shortened to seven innings by the mercy rule. Sean Breen collected three hits, including a homer, and three RBI. Catcher Isaiah Easterling also had three hits and three RBI. A record 23,401 fans turned out for day three. The fourth day saw three one-run games to determine the semi-finalists. Cromwell appeared to have finally won a game, going up 6–0 on Chapin-Newberry after seven innings. That was when C-N pulled off a comeback not seen in 32 years, coming back to win, 8–7. Kevis Burton's three-run double was the big hit, but third baseman Landon Allison plated the game-winner. Brooklawn came through in the 11th inning for a 3–2 win over Waipahu. In the final frame, Brooklawn's Alex Krug beat out a bunt single. Outfielder Fran Kinsey, who had four hits on the day, had the walk-off single to win it. The win gave Brooklawn a 2–1 record in the pool round, which got the Brookers into the semis, and left Waipahu on the outside. New Orleans scored a 2–1 win over Midland. Davis Martin, the winning pitcher, exhibited dominating command. Retif got its two runs in the fifth inning thanks to two Midland errors. Right fielder Ben Hess had two hits for New Orleans.[37]

Both semi-final games ended 4–3. Chapin-Newberry topped Medford on a home run by shortstop Justin Hawkins and two runs in the ninth inning on Zach Ziesing's RBI single and a squeeze bunt by Danton Hyman. New Orleans and Brooklawn battled for ten innings. Brooklawn's Anthony Harrold had four hits, but it was not enough. Brooklawn appeared to win when in the top of the tenth inning, Sean Breen walked, Harrold singled, Rollins reached on an error, and catcher Brandon Gray laid down a successful squeeze bunt to take a 3–2 lead. In the bottom of the tenth, Retif's Nick Ray singled and moved to second on a wild pitch, Briuglio walked, and Ben Hess singled to load the bases. Trent Forshag banged a two-run single to crush Brooklawn's hopes of winning three straight World Series.

Chapin-Newberry won the 2015 title game over New Orleans with seeming ease, 9–3. Ben Hess drove in the first run in the opening inning. They scored three runs in the sixth inning and four in the eighth. Justin Hawkins plated two runs with a home run. Second baseman Peyton Spangler drove in two runs. Outfielder Kevis Burton drove in three runs on a bases-clearing double and had three hits, which gave him a .410 batting average for the tournament. The win by Chapin-Newberry gave South Carolina the first title by a state post since Spartanburg in 1936.[38]

Chapin-Newberry's Justin Hawkins earned the George W. Rulon Player of the Year Award, as well as the Rawlings Big Stick Award for total bases with 31 and the Irvin "Click" Cowger RBI Award with 12. Ben Hess of New Orleans led in batting with a .488 average. Jordan Ragan of Medford took the Bob Feller Award with 23 strikeouts. Ben Hess also received the James F. Daniel Sportsmanship Award winner. The 2015 Series brought in a record 117,072 fans in attendance. This was the fifth consecutive year that Shelby had established a new record. Brooklawn first baseman Anthony Harrold captured an unprecedented all-tournament first base award for the third time. Chapin placed four members on the all-star team: second baseman Peyton Spangler, shortstop Justin Hawkins, outfielder Danton Hyman, and pitcher Ryne Huggins. Others on the all-Series squad were: third baseman Hayden Fuentes, New Orleans; outfielder Cole Brooks, Midland; outfielder Dylan Sugimoto, Waipahu; catcher Keke Ross, Waipahu; designated hitter Ben Hess, New Orleans; utility Micah Brown, Medford; and pitchers Cody Coggins, Medford, and Lucas Rollins, Brooklawn.[39]

Unlike the 2015 World Series, which saw plenty of familiar faces, the 2016 Series filled up with many strange teams. In the New England Region, Rocky Hill-Cromwell-Portland (RCP), aka Cromwell, had represented the region in 2014 and 2015, but they fell, 5–0, to the Cumberland, Rhode Island, Upper Deck Post 86 (33–4). Drew Szafranski had the key hit to get them started. Previously, Cumberland had decimated Collette, 13–3, in the finals of the state tournament. The Mid–Atlantic Region belonged to Brooklawn in the 21st century. The Brookers took the title eight times. So there appeared to be little opportunity for any other team to take a title away. In 2016, however, the dynasty slipped. Brooklawn failed to win their state, losing to Flemington, 7–1. The open Regional gave an opportunity to the Leesburg, Virginia, Post 34 Rangers (20–8). They beat Flemington, 4–3, to take the title and move on to the World Series with a 20–8 record. Rowan County/Salisbury, North Carolina, Post 342 Lions (38–11) had been to the ALWS in 2009 and went 2–2, losing a semi-final game. This year they beat Florence, South Carolina, 3–1, to get to the Series. Rowan brought two .400 hitters in Lee Poteat and Jake Prichard. Like Rowan County, Texarkana, Arkansas, Post 58 Razorbacks (38–5) had been to the ALWS in 2009, where they lost in the other semi-final game. The Hogs brought a 37–5 record and hot prospect Blake Hall, who led the team in batting with a .419 average.[40]

The other four finalists in 2016 brought the gaudiest records. Rockport, Indiana, sported a 32–1 mark, and Omaha Post 1 came in with a 59–3 tally. Rockport Post 254 beat Edwardsville in the Great Lakes Regional. Pitcher Corey Ebelhar claimed MVP honors. Rockport coach Jim Haaff was finishing his 50th season as coach of Post 254. They had last been to the Series back in 2007. Omaha, Nebraska, Post 1 Vikings (59–3) were loaded with hitters out of Creighton Prep; Zack Luckey led the team with a .459 batting average, followed by Brett Vosik at .457 and Brandon Bena with a .400 average. Omaha got in by beating Rapid City, 5–2. The Kennewick, Washington, Outlaws, with a 54–14 record, had been to the Series before in 2004, when they finished second. They boasted three .400 hitters in Andrew Vargas (.435), Joshua Kutzke (.412), and Dillon Plew (.409). At the Northwest Regional final in Cheyenne, Kennewick beat the Medford Mustangs, 10–1. On the eve of the ALWS, San Mateo, California, Post 82 Shockers (36–5) learned of the murder of 2015 teammate Calvin Reilly. They turned the loss into motivation to win the West Regional, which they did by beating Tucson, 6–5, and Waipahu, Hawaii, 15–5. They entered with a 36–5 record.[41]

For pool play, the Stars Division consisted of Cumberland, Leesburg, Texarkana, and San Mateo. The Stripes Division had Salisbury, Rockport, Omaha, and Kennewick. The winner of the Stripes Division would play the second-place finisher in the Stars Division. In the other semi-final, the winner of the Stars Division would take on the second-place in the Stripes. As in 2015, both semi-finals and championship game were scheduled to be telecast live on ESPNU.

Rockport got off to a fast start, taking out Rowan County, 6–3. Rowan County jumped out to a 3–0 lead in the first inning, thanks to big hits by Hunter Shepherd and

Josh Prichard. Then the North Carolina boys from the Salisbury area showed their nerves by committing four errors which contributed to three unearned runs. In the sixth inning, Rockport combined three hits with two errors for a three-run rally. Spencer Deom doubled and scored on an error. After Grant Miller drove in a run, another error gave Rockport the 6–3 lead, which was all they needed. In the second game, shortstop Zack Luckey had three hits and four RBI as Omaha sailed to a 14–5 win over Kennewick. New England does not usually win games, but Cumberland roared past Leesburg, 9–2. Second baseman Josh Brodeur and third baseman Dante Donovan each had three RBI.[42]

On day two, Rockport continued its winning ways, beating Kennewick, 5–3, even though they were outhit, 9–3. Catcher Jacob Schuler knocked in three runs, and third baseman Trevor Zink plated two for the winners. San Mateo got two runs in the ninth inning to slip past Texarkana, 4–2. Center fielder Tyler Villareman was hit by a pitch to plate the go-ahead run. Angelo Bortolin's sacrifice fly brought in the final run. Rowan County jumped out to a 3–0 lead in the second inning on four hits and three walks. Trevor Atwood, Tanner File, and Chandler Blackwelder accounted for the RBI. Rockport punched their ticket to the semi-finals on the third day of pool play by beating Omaha, 8–3. The win gave Rockport a 3–0 finish in pool play. Jacob Shuter led the way with two hits and two RBI. Texarkana got back on the winning ways by beating Leesburg, 7–5. The Hogs fell behind, 3–0, before coming back thanks to two critical Leesburg errors and two RBI by Beau Burson. Reilly Orr and Matt Goodheart knocked in additional runs. San Mateo locked up a position in the semi-final round by shutting out Leesport, 8–0. Pitcher John Basse had the game under control the whole way. Felix Aberouette had three runs batted in, and Ramon Enriquez homered.[43]

On the final day of pool play, two places in the semi-finals remained to be earned. Rowan County grabbed the first slot by rolling over Kennewick, 12–0. Winning pitcher Hunter Shepherd and outfielder Lee Poteat each had three RBI. Texarkana gained the runner-up spot in the Stars Division by getting past Leesport, 7–5. The Hogs fell behind 3–0 in the first inning before coming back thanks to two crucial errors, and run scoring hits from Beau Burson, Reilly Orr and Matt Goodheart. San Mateo already assured a spot in the playoffs, remained perfect in pool play, beating Cumberland, 5–4. Felix Aberouette got the big blow for the Shockers in the sixth inning as they scored four runs, enough to hold on. He had two doubles and a home run.[44]

The semi-final games pitted San Mateo, 3–0 in the Stars Division, against Rowan County, runner-up in the Stripes Division. Undefeated Rockport took on Texarkana in the second game. In the first semi-final, San Mateo opened up a 2–0 lead over Rowan County, but pitching let them down in the second inning. Walk, walk, walk, and hit by pitch, followed by a ground out, spelled two runs. Rowan County did not stop there, piling up 13 runs to win, 13–4. Third baseman Juan Garcia had four RBI, while Hunter Shepherd, Rowan's RBI leader, and Lee Poteat, their batting leader, had three hits each. In the other semi-final game, Rockport's dream of a perfect Series came to an end at the hands of Texarkana, 4–1. Cole Boyd got the Razorbacks on the board with a home run in the first inning. Coach David Peavy said, "It's a momentum shift." In the third inning, Will Smith drove in two runs, and Beau Burson added a home run in the eighth. Rockport, despite their loss, could be proud of finishing with an impressive 35–2 record.[45]

The 2016 championship game proved worthy of its title as Texarkana and Rowan County battled 12 innings before the Hogs of Texarkana prevailed, 8–6. Rowan went up 4–0 after four innings. Shortstop Dalton Lankford drove in a run in the first inning.

Second baseman Tanner File doubled to start the home third, moved up on an error, and came in to score on center fielder Chandler Blackwelder's single. Another run scored on an error. In the fourth inning, File executed a perfect squeeze play to add the fourth run. Texarkana got all four runs back in the fifth. Parker Ribble doubled and came home on shortstop Riley Orr's single. The Hogs got their second run on Cole Boyd's fielder's choice. Orr scored on an error by the shortstop. The final run of the rally came when Matt Goodheart, who had walked, came home on a throwing error. After that, both teams settled in. The Hogs got two runners on in the seventh inning but could do no more damage. Rowan left two runners on base in the fifth, sixth, and tenth innings. The excitement fans had waited for arrived, giving the 8,496 spectators all they could hope for. Leading off for Texarkana, Matt Goodheart bunted his way on base. Center fielder Blake Hall unloaded a double down the left field to send Goodheart to third. Rowan intentionally walked Smith to load the bases. Nick Meyers singled up the middle scoring two runs. Parker Ribble followed with a double to left center, scoring two more runs. Texarkana would have been happy with one run; now they had four. The game appeared to be over, all except the shouting. Rowan, however, refused to die. In the bottom of the 12th inning, right fielder Lee Poteat led off with a double to left. He moved to third on a wild pitch and scored on Juan Garcia's fly to right. Brandon Walton singled to right, and Prichard reached when the pitcher threw wildly to second. Pitcher Austin Cross then hit Trever Atwood to load the bases. That brought Chandler Blackwelder to the plate, representing the go-ahead run. He worked a walk which brought in the third run. Now Rowan had the bases loaded, down by two runs, and a solid single would tie the score. Texarkana reached deep into its arsenal and brought in their top relief pitcher, Zac Harrington. Rowan shortstop Dalton Lankford hit back to Harrington, who ran halfway to first before easily tossing the ball to first to end the game and give the 2016 title to the deserving Hogs. Those who played in the game or just watched would never forget this game.[46]

Coach Dave Peavy's Razorbacks clearly deserved the title. All year, their pitching had been a marvel. Lefty Austin Cross (6–0, 1.19 era) and relief specialist Zac Harrington (4–1, five saves in the Series, 0.71 era) led the pitching staff. Pat Flanagan (9–1, 2.91) and Tanner Vaughn (8–1, 2.91) rounded out the pitching staff. Outfielder Blake Hall had the highest batting average with a .419 mark and the most RBI (49), Designated hitter Matt Goodheart followed Hall with a .412 batting average. Catcher Will Smith (.309) provided the team's glue.

Texarkana catcher Will Smith garnered the George W. Rulon Player of the Year honors. The Big Stick Award for total bases was shared by Zach Luckey of Omaha and Angelo Bortolin of San Mateo. Bortolin also won the Click Cowger RBI Award with 16. Gerald Hein of Kennewick captured the Bob Feller Pitching Award with 24 strikeouts. The Sportsmanship Award went to Logan Vidrine of Texarkana. The 14-man all-tournament team for 2016 had only three players from Texarkana. They were catcher Will Smith, outfielder Blake Hall, and pitcher Austin Cross. Others selected were: first baseman Nick Knecht, San Mateo; second baseman Tanner File, Rowan; third baseman Juan Garcia, Rowan; shortstop Zach Luckey, Omaha; outfielder Tyler Villaroman, San Mateo; outfielder Lee Poteat, Rowan; designated hitter Chris Right, Cumberland; utility Felix Aberouette, San Mateo; utility Jacob Shuler, Rockport; pitcher Hunter Shepherd, Rowan; and pitcher Sawyer Strickland, Rowan.[47]

The ALWS set yet another attendance record by attracting 121,197 patrons to the games. The vice president of tourism for Cleveland County reported that visitor spending brought $16.8 million to the region. Shelby City Manager Rick Howell noted the impact the Series had on the community: "That sense of pride in your community that you have been part of something, whether you're just a fan or one of the volunteers, that is the greatest value to me."[48]

The presence of San Mateo in the 2016 ALWS seemed to remind people of what Legion ball had lost without those great California teams of the past. California once dominated the World Series. No state came close to the Golden States in the number of appearances by a team from the state. California teams had been to the ALWS 53 times. New Jersey-based teams, mostly Brooklawn, appeared 27 times. California teams were national champions 17 times; Ohio lagged far behind with seven titles. Only one of those California champs came in the 21st century, that being Danville in 2000, and the Hoots left American Legion ball in 2005. What had happened got publicized in a seminal article in the Washington Post, titled "American Legion used to own summer baseball." Legion baseball remained strong in the upper Midwest, from which it had sprung. Minnesota still had 357 Legion teams, and Nebraska had 295. Pennsylvania had lost its lead in the number of teams but still reported 282. South Dakota, North Dakota, Montana, and Wyoming continued to run strong programs. Since 1997, the article estimated, Legion ball had lost 25 percent of its teams. The sunshine states, California, Florida, and Texas, plus Oklahoma and New Jersey, were the biggest losers, down nearly 80 percent since 2008. California was down to 51 teams, Florida could boast only 22 teams, and Texas a mere 10. New Jersey went from 336 teams in 2008 to 51 in 2017. The winners were travel and showcase teams.[49]

The explanation for this phenomenon was two-fold. First, Legion membership was on the decline. Between 2000 and 2014, nearly 1,000 posts had vanished. This constituted about 11 percent of the membership. Twenty years before, Legion membership stood at 3.1 million; by 2013, it declined to 2.4 million. Part of this decline came from the World War II veterans dying off and Korean and Vietnam War vets not joining in the same proportion as vets from World War II. It also was part of a declining membership in all fraternal organizations, part of the "bowling alone" phenomenon.[50]

The second factor in the decline was the explosion of travel or showcase teams. These teams, popular also in basketball and soccer, are essentially for-profit enterprises, designed to make money for the organizers. They manage to attract kids by maintaining that they offer more "face time" before college coaches and pro scouts. The dream of a college scholarship justifies whatever the cost to parents, and the costs can be steep. Club teams can cost as much as $2,000 or $3,000 per summer, and add to that travel, motel, and food costs. They do not take as much time as Legion teams do with working on team skills, such as sacrifice bunting, learning the strike zone, or command of pitches. They are individual rather than team-focused. Jason Queen noted that his town of Lexington, North Carolina, was once a hotbed of Legion baseball. In Legion ball, kids and parents came from different schools, but they came together as part of a team and remained close well past the summer.[51]

With decline as a background theme, the 2017 World Series seemed somehow less— less exciting, less majestic, less satisfying—than in past years. Certainly, it was more disrupted by rain than in the past. The death of Dave Ploof, coach of Rapid City from 1965 to 2011, cast a shadow over the proceedings. Ploof was the winningest coach in American Legion history with a 2,483–808 record. The Legion's National Executive Committee decided that all games in state tournaments through the World Series would be seven-inning games. They also approved tighter rules for pitch counts for pitchers, requiring four days between outings when a pitcher threw 81 pitches. Nonetheless, the eight teams represented the best out of 3,786 Legion teams. The three teams from the Eastern regionals, New England, Mid–Atlantic, and Southeast, appeared for the first time. Shrewsbury, Massachusetts, Post 397 came in with a 34–6 record. They beat another Massachusetts team, Braintree, by a 5–1 score to gain a trip to Shelby. Likewise, Hopewell, New Jersey, Post 339 took the Mid–Atlantic tournament for the first time by beating Ephrata, Pennsylvania, 8–6 and 10–6. Hopewell came in with a record of 38–9. In the Southeast Regional, Randolph County, North Carolina, Post 45 beat Tallahassee Post 13, the Florida champions, 5–4, to qualify. Overall, their record of 38–8 was less than stellar, but their three top pitchers posted an ERA of 0.00 in the Regional.[52]

Teams from middle-America all appeared poised to make a strong run at the title. Bryant, Arkansas Post 298 had been to the ALWS in 2007. In the Mid–South Regional, they beat Ada, Oklahoma, 5–2 and 3–0. That gave Bryant a 39–7 record. In Region Five, Great Lakes, Midland, Michigan Post 165 appeared on the verge of a dynasty. They had won the national championship in 2009, appeared in 2011, and finished second in 2014. Midland had the best record of the eight finalists, 40–2. They beat 2016 third-place finisher Rockport, Indiana, 9–4, to qualify. From the Central Plains Regional, Omaha, Nebraska Post 1, the Five Point Bank team comprised of boys from Creighton Prep, came in with a 54–6 record. They had to beat Johnston, Iowa, 7–2, to win the regional and a second consecutive trip to Shelby. One of the westernmost teams looked powerful, the other less so. Lewiston, Idaho, Post 13 was making its sixth trip to the ALWS, but last appeared in 2001. It topped off its 39–11 record by defeating Missoula, Montana, Post 14 in 15 innings by a 6–5 score. The final team to qualify, Henderson, Nevada, Post 40, aka Southern Nevada Blue Sox, last appeared in 2006. It accumulated a record of 54–7, including an 11–2 win over St. George, Utah, Post 90 to win the Western Regional. Shortstop Ryne Nelson batted .512 to capture the MVP Award at the regional. Henderson's play in the regional qualified them as one of the pre-tournament favorites. In the five regional games, they scored 66 runs and compiled a team batting average of .492. Lofty numbers, but pitching was their question mark.[53]

For pool play, the use of Stars and Stripes to connote divisions continued as it had the past several years. The Stripes Division contained three of the top favorites, Midland, Omaha, and Henderson, as well as Shrewsbury. The Stars Division consisted of Hopewell, Randolph County, Lewiston, and Bryant. Despite a forecast of rain, the Series would go on as scheduled from August 10–15.

Henderson's suspect pitching displayed itself the first day of the Series. Their bats did not come around, and the pitching stank, as they lost to Omaha by the embarrassing score of 9–1. Omaha's Joshua Culliver pitched two-hit ball, and Nebraska pounded out 21 hits, one shy of the record. Omaha did set one record by becoming the first team to have four players each with four hits. Tom Steier, Will Hanafan, Zach Luckey, and Cameron Blosson were the hot Omaha bats. Midland proved equally disappointing, losing to Shrewsbury, 3–2, in 10 innings. Matt Stansky pitched a two-hitter for Shrewsbury. Pat Galvin scored the winning run on an error. Bryant rolled, 4–0, over Lewiston. Julian Washburn threw a shutout for Bryant. Then the rains came, and the powers-that-be decided to make all additional games seven innings in hope of getting the Series finished in six days. The first day of play finished when Randolph County scored five runs in the sixth inning to put a 6–3 beating on Hopewell.[54]

Rain continued the second day, delaying the start of play for three hours, but officials managed to get two seven-inning games played. Omaha got six runs in the first inning and coasted to its second win, beating Midland, 6–3. The win virtually assured Omaha of a spot in the semi-finals. An answer to Henderson's pitching woes came from the arm of a 16-year-old Shane Spencer, who pitched a one-hitter in a 1–0 win over Shrewsbury. His counterpart, Kevin Hummer of Shrewsbury, allowed just four hits. In the bottom of the seventh inning, a double by Ryne Nelson, followed by a walk, a single, and Garrett Giles' sacrifice fly scored the only run of the game. After that game, rain discontinued play for the day. When play resumed on Saturday, Bryant got wind-aided home runs from Jake Wright, Logan Allen, and Seth Tucker to power the Hogs over Hopewell, 7–4. Randolph County picked up a 4–1 victory over Lewiston in a sloppy game full of walks and errors. Nonetheless, the win put Randolph County in the semi-finals. Omaha closed out its pool play with an 8–5 defeat of Shrewsbury to give Five Point Bank a perfect 3–0 mark in pool play. Henderson came in with suspect pitching and what was thought to be a high-powered offense, but it failed to score in a 1–0 loss to Midland. Shane Spencer pitched a one-hitter for Henderson. In a game to determine first and second place in the Stars Division, Bryant needed to win to stay alive, and it shut out Randolph County, 5–0.[55]

At the conclusion of pool play, Bryant stood at 2–1 in the Stars Division, Randolph County was runner-up at 2–1, Hopewell finished 1–2, and Lewiston brought up the rear at 1–2. In the Stripes Division, Omaha finished 3–0, while Shrewsbury, Henderson, and Midland all finished with one win and two losses. In a convoluted decision going to the third tie-breaker, Henderson qualified to play Bryant in one semi-final game. That game was played in a steady rain. The Blue Sox of Southern Nevada got on the board when catcher Roger Reilly doubled, shortstop Ryne Nelson singled, and first baseman John Thomas Wold got an RBI single. They got another run on a wild pitch. Bryant scored single runs in the third and fifth innings. Henderson's Nick Thompson, pitching in relief, got out of trouble with two on in the sixth inning, a bases loaded jam in the seventh, and a runner on third in the eighth. In the top of the ninth, Thompson doubled for the Blue Sox and Reilly followed with an RBI single. Then Bryant got sloppy, giving up three unearned runs. The Southern Nevada Blue Sox had managed a 7–3 win and a place in the final game. After one inning of the Omaha-Randolph County semi-final game, the sky opened up, causing umpires to suspend play for the day with Omaha leading, 2–1, on Zach Luckey's two-run single. Using helicopters to dry the field, play resumed the next day. Omaha managed to pick up another run on the sixth inning to beat Randolph County, 3–1.[56]

In the final, Southern Nevada pitched their young ace, Shane Spencer, who was up to the task. Spencer allowed only three Omaha hits. Omaha got on the board in the bottom of the first inning when Tom Steier walked, moved up on a single and sacrifice, and came home on Dylan Phillips' sacrifice fly. In the third inning, Henderson's Wold doubled to right field, the only extra-base hit of the game, and Garrett Giles singled in the run. In the sixth, the Southern Nevada boys continued to play small ball. J. J. Smith singled to left, stole second, went to third on a wild pitch, and came home on Nick Thompson's sacrifice fly. Henderson had a 2–1 win and a national title.[57]

For his part in Henderson Blue Sox's success, Shane Spencer was selected the George W. Rulon Player of the Year for 2017. Teammate John Thomas Wold won the American Legion Big Stick Award with 29 total bases. Jordan Patty of Midland batted .529 to take the Louisville Slugger Award. Patty also won the Bob Feller Award with 19 strikeouts. The Dr. Irvin L. "Click" Cowger RBI Award went to Zach Luckey of Omaha with 13. The Sportsmanship Award was awarded to Will Hanafan of Omaha. The Stat-Crew All-Tournament selections were headed by pitcher Shane Spencer and Blue Sox teammates John Thomas Wold, first base, and catcher Roger Reilly. Other all-stars were: Peyton Williams, Randolph County, second base; Tom Steier, Omaha, third base; Will Karp, Hopewell, shortstop; Will Hanafan, Omaha, outfield; Logan Allen, Bryant, out-field; A. J. Light, Lewiston, outfield; Zach Luckey, Omaha, designated hitter; Jordan Patty, Midland, utility; Matt Stansky, Shrewsbury, pitcher; and Josh Culliver, Omaha, pitcher. Diamond Sports announced its all-academic team. The player designated captain, Trace Henry of Tupelo, Mississippi, received a $2,500 college scholarship. Eight others received a $500 grant.[58]

Attendance at the World Series declined in 2017 for the first time since the Series moved to Shelby. The official figure of 120,924 still registered higher than in any year except 2016. The terrible weather got the blame for the decline.

The 2018 American Legion World Series was scheduled between Thursday, August 16, and Tuesday, August 21. All games were scheduled to be telecast on ESPN3 or ESPNU, and again all games would be seven innings. Each day had a special theme—August 16 was designated as Senior Citizens Day; August 17 was Youth Academic Achievement Day; August 18 was Military Appreciation Day; August 19 was Medical Community Day; and August 20 was Family Day. Even before teams arrived, there were scheduled events. Volunteer Appreciation Day was scheduled for August 7. The "Seventh Inning Stretch Festival" ran on August 11 from 3:00 to 10:00 p.m. As part of the Stretch, there were free concerts by the Dirty Grass Soul, a Shelby country group, Darrell Harwood, another North Carolina country singer, and Randy Owen, best known as the lead singer for Ala-bama. The day before games started, a parade went through town, and a concert by Sum-mer Brooke and the Mountain Faith Band got the place jumping.[59]

Half of the eight finalists in 2018 were making their first appearance in the Amer-ican Legion World Series. Braintree, Massachusetts, Post 86, with a 24–9 record, mas-tered last year's regional champion Shrewsbury, 7–4, in the New England Regional. In the Mid–Atlantic Regional, Wilmington, Delaware, Post 1 beat up on Leesburg, Virginia, 10–0. Their shortstop, Nate Thomas, batted .571 for the tourney. Delaware came in with a tidy 35–3 record. Randolph County, North Carolina, Post 45 posted a 29–18 record after beating Troy, Alabama, 3–2. They relied on the hitting of Dawson Painter, who bat-ted .529 in the Regional. Randolph County/Salisbury finished fourth in last year's Series, losing in a semi-final game. Gonzales, Louisiana, Post 81 had been a familiar face in the 1990s, but last appeared in 2013. They owned a 42–6 record after squeaking by Bryant, Arkansas, last year's third-place finisher. Midland, Michigan, Berryhill Post 165 appeared poised to become the next dynasty, making its fourth appearance in five years. The Ber-ryhills posted a 45–9 record after topping Danville, Illinois, 8–4. Their shortstop, Mar-tin Money, hit .500 in the Regional. Dubuque, Iowa, played only 16 games, winning 12, including Central Plains wins over West Fargo, 11–0 and 3–2. Meridian, Idaho, Post 113, with a 38–17 record, beat Yakima Valley, Washington, Peppers, 10–0, to qualify. Finally, defending champion Las Vegas/ Henderson Post 40 looked to repeat. They came with a 49–14 mark after beating League City, Texas, 11–1, and Tucson, 7–3, to finish off the West-ern Regional.[60]

Delaware looked to be the Cinderella team right off the bat as Post One beat yellow-clad Dubuque, 3–0. Chris Ludman pitched a three-hit shutout, while Jack Dubecq drove in two runs and shortstop Nate Thomas plated one. Game 2 provided an even tighter pitching duel between Gonzales' Jack Merrifield and Braintree's Kyle Gray. Gonzales got the only run of the game in the fourth inning when Merrifield drove in Preston Thrash, who had reached base on an error. Midland, looking for a championship, beat Randolph County, 7–2. Randolph got two runs in the fourth inning thanks to an error, a walk, an error, Adam Randall's RBI, and two batters hit by a pitch. Midland's Marty Money got those runs back in the fifth inning, and Midland continued to roll to a 7–2 victory. Henderson completed the first day of play by crushing Meridian, 10–0. Jimmy Gamboa pitched a two-hit shutout, and Chaison Miklich had three hits and three RBI.[61]

The second day of play began with Gonzales taking the wind out of Wilmington's sails by winning an exciting, nip-and-tuck game by a 5–4 score. Delaware got on the board first when shortstop Nate Thomas drove in a run. Gonzales tied the game in the bottom of the second inning on second baseman Brayden Caskey's single, and they went ahead in the third on catcher Reid Bouchereau's RBI hit. Wilmington came back to tie it on Jon Golebiowski's hit in the fourth inning. In the bottom of the inning, Gonzales got back on top when Carson Dabadie worked a walk with the bases loaded. In the Gonzales sixth, Dabadie drove in a run. In the seventh inning, Wilmington scored two runs on a Michael Cautillo hit to tie the game at 4—4. Gonzales won in the bottom of the ninth on Preston Thrash's squeeze bunt to score Reid Bouchereau. In the other game on day two, Dubuque hammered Braintree, 9–1. Dubuque scored five runs in the fifth inning on just two hits, aided by two errors.[62]

In day three action, Midland just got by Henderson in a tight game, 3–2. Berryhill got all its runs in the bottom of the third inning. Logan LaCourse singled to left and scored on a throwing error by the shortstop on a ball hit by Nick Dardas, who came home on Tyler David's single. Marty Money brought David home with a single of his own. The second game of the day was delayed two hours by rain. Meridian got four runs in the third inning and hung on to overcome Randolph County and win, 6–4. Bryce March of Randolph had three hits, including a double and home run, and three RBI. On Sunday, four games had been scheduled. Gonzales gained the top spot in the Stripes Division with a 3–2 win over Dubuque in one of strangest finishes in memory. All of Gonzales' runs came in the first inning. The three batters at the top of the order scored. Right fielder Carson Dabadie and designated hitter Reid Bouchereau each drove in a run. The third scored on an error. In the fifth inning, Dubuque staged a comeback. With runners on second and third, Wil Courtney lashed a drive to center that looked like two runs, but Gonzales center fielder Zane Zeppahar made a great diving catch. However, as Zeppahar lay on the turf injured, two runs came in to score. Unfortunately for Dubuque, the runner on second failed to tag up after the catch, so after a protest he was ruled out. Gonzales' win gave them a 3–0 record in pool play.[63]

Dubuque's loss opened the door for Wilmington, who needed a win over Braintree to advance to the semi-finals. In the top of the first inning, Jack Dubecq plated the first run. In the third, Dubecq's double scored Eric Ludman. Dubecq scored on a sacrifice fly by Matt Poma. Wilmington went up, 4–0, in the fourth when Nate Thomas' sacrifice fly scored Michael Cautillo. Braintree got one run back in the bottom of the fourth and mounted a serious threat in the seventh thanks to two Wilmington errors. With two runs across the plate and two runners on base, Matt Diaz induced a fly ball to left to end the rally. Post One assured itself of a spot in the semi-finals.

Midland already had a lock on first place in the Stars Division, but runner-up was wide open. Henderson, Meridian, or Randolph County still contended. A win by Meridian over Midland would give them a spot in the semi-finals. Midland, however, refused to let up. In the third inning, singles by Tyler David, Marty Money, and Seth Gowers brought one run in. Brandon Smith doubled to score two more runs. They got two more runs in the fifth inning on Logan LaCourse's homer, a hit that raised his batting average to .600. Midland ended with a 5–2 win and a 3–0 record in pool play. After a rain delay, Randolph County managed a 10–6 win over Henderson in the final pool game. Henderson got three runs in the fourth inning, but Randolph County scored five in the fifth thanks to four straight walks. Despite the loss and the ten runs allowed, Henderson survived the tie-breaker to advance to the 2018 semi-finals.[64]

None of Wilmington's games had been easy—3–0, 4–5, 4–3—so why would the semi-final contest be different? It was not. Post One's Jack Dubecq cruised into the seventh and scheduled final inning with a 4–0 lead, without giving up a hit. His team had scored two runs in the third inning without benefit of a hit. In the sixth, they scored two more thanks to Chris Ludman's single to left. In the seventh, Dubecq walked the leadoff batter. Then Money singled for the first Midland hit. Seth Gower's double drove the two runners home. Gower scored after LaCourse walked with the bases loaded. That was it for Debecq; Nate Thomas moved to the mound from shortstop. He walked Zach Nelson to force in the tying run. In the Wilmington tenth, Poma walked and later tried to score from second on Michael Cautillio's single up the middle. Poma slammed into catcher Nick Dardas, who dropped the ball for an error. In the bottom of the tenth, Marshall Awtry got two quick outs before Money singled. Awtry then got an easy ground out to second to end the game. Henderson, like Wilmington a second-place finisher in pool play, rolled over Gonzales, 6–1. Henderson pitcher Jimmy Gamboa was in command; he had a no-hitter going into the seventh. His mates did plenty of damage. Left fielder Chaisan Miklich homered and drove in three runs, and center fielder Jim Sharman had three hits. In the seventh inning, after two walks and a fielder's choice, light-hitting shortstop Preston Thrash singled in Gonzales' only run.[65]

Not surprisingly, the 2018 championship game went to extra innings before Wilmington won, 1–0. Pitcher Chris Ludman went the distance for Wilmington, allowing just four hits and walking none. Ludman said, "I didn't have my slider, so I was just trying to pound them across, throw strikes, pitch to soft contact and my defense did a great job behind me."[66] For Henderson, Josh Sharman, who relied on off-speed pitches, went seven innings, giving up just four hits and two walks while striking out eight and not allowing a run. In the top of the eighth inning, Wilmington shortstop Nate Thomas made the defensive play of the game. With a runner on first, Josh Sharman pounded one up the middle that looked for all the world like a clean hit. The runner on first had been moving, so Thomas was also headed for second, and his momentum allowed him to dive full-out, grab the ball, and throw a rainbow to first to nip the runner. In the bottom of the eighth, third baseman Michael Cautillo worked a leadoff walk. Chris Ludman sacrificed him to second. Austin Colmery singled up the middle, bringing Cautillo home. Cautillo remembered, "I saw the catcher's eyes get big so I knew I had to run hard and make a good slide." Delaware had its first American Legion championship.[67]

Wilmington Manager Brent Tremi said after the game, "It still feels like a dream.... I feel like I'm going to wake up any second." Pitcher Chris Ludman, the University of Delaware freshman, threw 15 scoreless innings in the World Series. That merited him being named the George W. Rulon Player of the Year. Ludman allowed that Post One's goal was to win the Mid–Atlantic Regional. "Winning the whole national championship, that's just crazy. I never in a million years thought that." Players on the team came from Conrad, Salesianum, St. Mark's, Delaware Military Academy, Wilmington Christian, and St. Elizabeth high schools.[68]

In addition to Ludman's Player of the Year Awards, Delaware's Austin Calmery, who batted .467 in the Series, won the Big Stick Award with 21 total bases. The Click Cowger RBI Award went to Bryce March of Randolph County with 15. The Louisville Slugger Award for highest batting average went to Sam Link, Dubuque, with a .555 mark. Sam Goodman of Dubuque was selected to receive the Sportsmanship Award. The Bob Feller Award went to Jimmy Gamboa of Henderson with 25 strikeouts. The Stat Crew all-tournament team consisted of four from Delaware and four from Henderson. Jack Merrifield of Gonzales was picked at first base. Others were: Brayden Caskey, Gonzales, second base; Edarian Williams, Henderson, third base; Nate Thomas, Wilmington, shortstop; Austin Colmery, Wilmington, outfield; Josh Sharman, Henderson, outfield; Trevor Marsh, Randolph County, outfield; Parker Schmidt, Henderson, catcher; Sam Link, Dubuque, utility; Eric Ludman, Wilmington, utility; Chris Ludman, Wilmington pitcher; Jimmy Gamboa, Henderson, pitcher; and Sam Goodman, Dubuque, pitcher.[69]

The American Legion celebrated its centennial year in 2019, although Legion baseball was celebrating just its 93rd season. The American Legion World Series for the second straight year saw a champion from a state that had never experienced the joy of winning a title. Not only had Idaho never won a championship before, but its team, Idaho Falls Bandits Post 56 (56–6), was making its first appearance in the ALWS. They got to the Series by beating Kennewick, Washington, 3–0, and Bozeman, 5–1, in the Section Seven finals at Lewiston, Idaho. They were a team without stars, although their double-play combo of Bruer Webster and Alex Cortez would make the all-tournament team, and 6-foot-6 pitcher Randon Hostert, drafted by the Texas Rangers, had thrown a no-hitter against Bozeman to get his team to the ALWS.[70]

Of the remaining seven teams, Fargo Post 2 (51–6) appeared the team to beat. No stranger to the Series, they had appeared in 1969, 1989, and 1992. They got to the Series by beating Excelsior, Minnesota, twice by scores of 8–0 and 3–2 in the Central Plains Regional at Sioux Falls. In the Mid–Atlantic Region, Randolph County, North Carolina, (34–10) beat defending champion Delaware on its way to the Regional title game, where it beat Vienna, Virginia, 3–0 and 3–2. Shrewsbury, Massachusetts (30–7), Post 397 beat Lawrence, 4–3 and 3–1, to win the Region One title. A team from the New Orleans area played a record 75 ALWS games. The Pedal Valve Cardinals of Destrehan Post 366 (35–8) were making their first ALWS appearance, having beaten Tupelo, Mississippi, 4–2, in the Southeast final. Festus, Missouri, Post 253 (36–12) beat Bryant, Arkansas, 8–3, to make the Series from the Mid–South Region. Danville, Illinois, Post 210 was making its first ALWS appearance, having beaten Beverly/Lowell, Ohio, 14–6. From the West, Albuquerque, New Mexico, Post 13 (30–2) struggled, despite its record, to make the Series. They beat Petaluma, California, 6–5, and Honolulu, 5–3, to make the Series. They took pride in being the first team from New Mexico to make the ALWS, and to give coach Daniel Gonzales the present in his 31st year of coaching Legion ball.[71]

On opening day, Destrehan served notice by pounding out a 12–1 win over Danville. They pounded four home runs, two by right fielder Stephen Kline. Brendan Smock pitched a two-hitter to lead Festus to a 4–1 win over Albuquerque. Idaho Falls rode first baseman Randon Hostert's homer to a decisive 7–3 victory over Fargo. As expected,

Randolph County had little trouble defeating Shrewsbury, 8–4. Center fielder Trevor Marsh collected three hits, and designated hitter Braxton Davis homered. On day two of the ALWS, Albuquerque displayed its weakness, losing to Danville, 13–2. Danville's Jacob Stipp homered, walked three times, and scored three runs to lead the onslaught. In game six, Destrehan looked to be a team to beat as it pounded Festus, 9–1. Ron Franklin and Nick Lorio each had two hits and two runs batted in. On Saturday, August 17, Idaho Falls used three pitchers to complete the first shutout of the Series, a 4–0 win over hapless Shrewsbury. Fargo took out tough Randolph County, 4–1. Designated hitter Cole Hage homered and drove in two runs. Zach Sandy drove in the other two runs. Destrehan enjoyed a laughter against Albuquerque, 14–6. Kolby Bourgeois homered and had four RBI, Kline tripled and drove in three runs, and shortstop TJ Thomas got three hits. The next day, rain reduced the schedule to one game. Danville advanced to the semi-finals by besting Festus, 7–5. Catcher Chase Rademacher also got three hits and the save. The rain pushed two games back a day.[72]

Pool play finished with those two games. Fargo had no trouble as it beat Shrewsbury, 9–1. Blake Anderson had four hits, including a homer, to lead Fargo into the semi-finals. A Randolph County upset of Idaho Falls would put them in the semis, but the Falls refused to give in, winning a tight 4–3 game. Webster and Cortez each had three hits at the top of the order for Idaho Falls, and Cortez drove in two runs. Idaho Falls completed pool play without a loss in the Stripes pool, as did Destrehan in the Stars pool. Fargo and Danville finished second, each with a 2–1 record.[73]

All the rain pushed the semi-final games to 4:00 and 7:00 p.m. on Tuesday, August 19. In a surprise, Fargo, 2–1 in pool play, upset 3–0 Destrehan with seeming ease by the score of 11–4. Post 2 pounded out 14 hits. Shortstop Zach Kluvers had four hits, two of them doubles, and drove in three runs to lead Fargo. It was the first time a team from North Dakota made the championship game. If the first semi-final game was one-sided, the second proved to be a nail-biter. Idaho Falls managed to pull out a come-from-behind, 4–3 victory in the bottom of the ninth inning on only two hits. After Danville scored in the first inning, Idaho tied it up in the third without benefit of a hit. A dropped third strike put the first runner on, followed by a walk, a hit by pitch, and a wild pitch. Then first baseman Randon Hostert doubled to left to score two runs. Danville tied the game in the seventh on Logan Spicer's two-run single. In the bottom of the ninth, center fielder Andrew Gregersen singled, stole second, advanced to third on a fielder's choice, and scored on a wild pitch.[74]

In the 2019 final, the Idaho Falls Bandits became the first Idaho team to win the Legion title by taking a 5–3 win over Fargo. In the top of the first inning, Brayden Koenig and Brandt Kolpack each drove in a run to give Fargo the lead. The Bandits got one run back in the bottom of the first on an error. Then the rain caused the suspension of play until 10 a.m. the next day. When play resumed, the Bandits went to work. A single and two walks loaded the bases for Alex Cortez, who got one run across the plate on a single to deep shortstop. Tavyn Lords brought two runs home with a single. Idaho tacked on another run in the third inning. The score remained unchanged until the seventh, when Fargo scored on Brandt Kolpack's single, but Bandits pitcher Andrew Gregersen closed the door. Idaho Falls finished the season with a 61–6 record and became the first team from Idaho to win an American Legion title.[75]

Despite winning, Idaho did not dominate the awards for the ALWS. Trevor Marsh of Randolph County gained the George W. Rulon Player of the Year Award. He also garnered the Big Stick Award with 26 total bases. Destrehan third baseman Ron Franklin walked away with the Louisville Slugger Award for batting .600 and the "Click" Cower RBI award with 15. Idaho Falls' big Randon Hostert took the Bob Feller Pitching Award with 23 strikeouts, and the Bandits' shortstop, Alex Cortez, took the Sportsmanship Award. Idaho did place four players on the all-tournament team, one fewer than Fargo. The team consisted of: designated hitter, Zach Sandy, Fargo; utility, Zack Kluvers, Fargo; catcher, Chandler Ibach, Fargo; first baseman, Blake Anderson, Fargo; second baseman, Bruer Webster, Destrehan; shortstop, Alex Cortez, Idaho; third baseman, Ron Franklin, Destrehan; outfielders Trevor Marsh, Randolph County, Andrew Gregerson, Idaho, and Kolby Bourgeois, Destrehan; and pitchers Caden Christenson, Idaho; Stephen Klein, Destrehan; and Taylor Parrett, Fargo.[76]

Back in 1925 at Milbank, North Dakota, Major John L. Griffith had argued that athletic competition teaches courage and respect for others, encouraging democratic living and overall character development. The initial drivers to create American Legion baseball, Griffith and Frank McCormack, wanted to revive baseball from the doldrums created, in part, by the Black Sox scandal of 1919. It is difficult to argue that American Legion ball should take all the credit for the revival of organized baseball in the 1920s; Babe Ruth and the end of the Deadball Era have a stronger claim for baseball's success. By the 1950s, when two-thirds of major league players came through Legion ball, it was easier to give credit to American Legion baseball for the long-term success of the professional sport. The success of former Legion players continued into the 21st century. Since Shelby became the home of the Legion World Series, the following Legion alumni were inducted into the National Baseball Hall of Fame: Roberto Alomar (2011), Bert Blyleven (2011), Pat Gillick (2011), Ron Santo (2012), Barry Larkin (2012), Bobby Cox (2014), Tom Glavine (2012), Tony LaRussa (2014), Greg Maddux (2014), Joe Torre (2014), Mike Piazza (2016), Jeff Bagwell (2017), Tim Raines (2017), Ivan Rodriquez (2017), John Schuerholz (2017), Chipper Jones (2018), Jack Morris (2018), Jim Thome (2018), Alan Trammell (2018), Harold Baines (2019), Roy Halladay (2019), Mike Mussina (2019), and Lee Smith (2019).

In the spring of 2020, the coronavirus pandemic, COVID-19, invaded the East and West Coasts and threatened to sweep through the entire country. Medical personnel who ought to know such things predicted that as many as 200,000 Americans could lose their lives by the end of the year. In April, the Legion National Commander, James William "Bill" Oxford, and Americanism Commissioner Richard Anderson announced the cancellation of all 2020 regional and national tournaments, including the American Legion World Series. The country was, indeed, facing unusual times.

Would American Legion baseball continue? Would it be the same? Dan Sowers, who back in the 1930s was called "the father of American Legion baseball," firmly held the belief that good sportsmanship acquired through baseball would mysteriously translate to good citizenship. That belief has become more difficult to confirm or dispute as the very values Sowers held dear—sportsmanship and good citizenship—have faded over time. Legion teams continue to mouth the "Code of Sportsmanship" before games, but few players even understand why they do so. It sounds hollow to today's teenage boys. The values contained in the Code—respecting rules, keeping faith with teammates, controlling one's temper, and controlling pride—no longer seem to apply to America's youth. Winning overrides all.

Can American Legion baseball continue without its guiding first principles? In the second decade of the 21st century, the American Legion World Series has stabilized and grown since the ALWS moved to Shelby. That is no longer the weakest link in Legion ball. On the other hand, it is hard to believe that Legion ball can survive the inevitable decline of the post system. Clearly, Legion ball is losing good players to travel teams and showcase teams, who have proven they can draw the best players away from Legion teams, and they can reasonably be expected to continue to do so. Town teams no longer have the aura they once possessed, except in places like Fargo, North Dakota, and Idaho Falls, Idaho, where the thrill of pulling on a uniform that represents the home town remains a powerful pull on the emotions.

Respected veteran sportswriter of the *Philadelphia Inquirer* Frank Fitzpatrick penned an obituary for Legion ball in summer 2019. American Legion baseball once provided fans and scouts an opportunity to watch a community's best players, he wrote. From the mid–1930s until the mid–1990s, all the best teenage boys wanted to play Legion ball. "In the past decade or so," he opined, "this summertime tradition has experienced the summertime blues."[77]

Chapter Notes

Chapter 1

1. David Gropman, *Say It Ain't So, Joe! The True Story of Shoeless Joe Jackson* (New York: Citadel Press, 1979), xvi.

2. Benjamin G. Rader, *Baseball: A History of America's Game* (Urbana: University of Illinois Press, 1992), 112–129.

3. Robert Obojski, *Bush League: A History of Minor League Baseball* (New York: Macmillan, 1975), 18–19.

4. Neil Lanctot, *Negro League Baseball: The Rise and Ruin of a Black Institution* (Philadelphia: University of Pennsylvania Press, 2004); Robert Peterson, *Only the Ball is White* (New York: McGraw Hill, 1970), 83–87.

5. *Chicago Tribune*, December 8, 1944; *Clarksburg [WV] Telegram*, June 10, 1925.

6. Ray Schmidt, "Major John Griffith," *College Football Historical Society* XIII (February 2000): 1–3; Matthew Lindaman, *Fit for America: Major John L. Griffith and the Quest for Athletics and Fitness* (Syracuse: Syracuse University Press, 2018), 38–60.

7. *Allentown Morning Call*, December 28, 1925.

8. Harold Seymour, *Baseball: The People's Game* (New York: Oxford University Press, 1990), 84–85; Lindaman, 66–80.

9. Jack W. Berrymands, "From the Cradle to the Playing Field: America's Emphasis on Highly Organized Sport for Preadolescent Boys," *Journal of Sport History* 2 (Fall 1975): 115–116.

10. Emphasis added. Steven A. Reiss, *Sport in Industrial America, 1850–1920* (Wheeling, IL: Harlan Davidson, 1995), 139; Seymour, 120.

11. Tris Speaker, "Diamonds in the Rough," *Rotarian* 54 (April 1939):, 24

12. Seymour, *Baseball: The People's Game*, 85.

13. Thomas A. Rumer, *The American Legion: An Official History, 1919–1989* (New York: M. Evans, 1990), 16–19.

14. Marquis James, *A History of the American Legion* (New York: William Green, 1923), 16–18; George Seay Wheat, *The Birth of the Legion* (New York: G. P. Putnam's Sons, 1919), 207–208.

15. http://www.alpost66.org/Four Pillars; William Pencak, *For God and Country: The American Legion, 1919–1941* (University of Michigan Press, 1989), 58–59.

16. Tom Copeland, *The Centralia Tragedy of 1919: Elmer Smith and the Wobblies* (Seattle: University of Washington Press, 1993), 50–55, 82–83.

17. M. J. Heale, *American Anticommunism: Combating the Enemy Within, 1830–1970* (Baltimore: Johns Hopkins University Press, 1990), 85–86.

18. Rumer, 206.

19. *Sioux Falls Argus-Leader*, July 17, 1925; Raymond Moley, Jr., *The American Legion Story* (New York: Duell, Sloan and Pierce, 1966), 10.

20. John L. and William Pencak, *For God and Country; The American Legion, 1919–1941* (Boston: Northeastern University Press, 1989), 21–22; sonsdny.org, Sons of the American Legion, Detachment of New York.

21. Moley, 143, 213.

22. *Indianapolis News*, August 10, 1925; *New York Times*, December 30, 1925.

23. Ibid.

24. Armand Peterson and Tom Tomashek, *Town Ball: The Glory Days of Minnesota Amateur Baseball* (Minneapolis: University of Minnesota Press, 2006), x–xi.

25. *Louisville Courier-Journal*, May 25, 1926, October 1, 1926; *Brooklyn Times Union*, July 4, 1926; Jacob J. Bustad, "One-hundred Per Cent American: Nationalism, Masculinity, and American Legion Junior Baseball" [M. A. Thesis, University of Kansas, 2009], 11.

26. *Bridgewater (NJ) Courier-News*, July 3, 1926.

27. Dan Sowers, "Batter-Up," *American Legion Monthly* (February 1929), 26–27.

28. *Wilmington Morning News*, July 14, 1926.

29. *Philadelphia Inquirer*, October 13, 1926; *Wilkes-Barre Evening News*, October 14, 1926.

30. *Wilmington News Journal*, September 27, 1926.

31. *Philadelphia Inquirer*, October 13, 1926; *Hutchinson News*, May 24, 1926.

32. *Salt Lake Telegram*, October 13, 1926.

33. Martin W. Wilson, "Sesquicentennial International Exposition (1926)," in *The Encyclopedia of Greater Philadelphia*. www.philadelphiaencyclopedia.org.

34. Thomas Keels, *Sesqui! Greed, Graft, and the*

Forgotten World's Fair of 1926 (Philadelphia: Temple University Press, 2017).

35. *Ibid.*

36. *Philadelphia Inquirer,* October 12, 1926.

37. *Philadelphia Inquirer,* October 13, 1926.

38. *Philadelphia Inquirer,* October 11–13, 1926.

39. *Manti [Utah] Messenger,* December 10, 1926.

40. Moley, 213.

41. Dan Sowers, "Junior Baseball Launched into second big year," *New York Times,* April 9, 1928; Rumer, 208.

42. James Shutts, "Youth Goes to Bat," *The Rotarian* 47 (July 1935): 18–21; *Reading Times,* February 15, 1928.

43. Dan Sowers, "Batter Up," *American Legion Magazine* (February 1929), 26–27, 52–58; *New York Times,* May 8, 1928; Rumer, 207–208; *Los Angeles Evening Express,* April 19, 1928; *Wilmington (DE) News-Journal,* May 19, 1928.

44. "Batter Up!" *The American Legion Monthly* 4 (June 1928): 32.

45. *Ibid.; Lafayette Journal and Courier,* June 14, 1928.

46. "Margaret Gisolo—Pies and Home Runs," *American Legion Monthly* 5 (October 1928); T. Ladd, "Sexual Discrimination in Youth Sport: The Case of Margaret Gisolo, in Reed Howell, ed., *Anthology of Women in Sports* (West Point, NY: Leisure Press, 1982), 570–589.

47. *Arizona Republic,* November 8, 2009 (0bit).

48. *Chicago Tribune,* September 8, 1928; *Boston Globe,* September 7, 1928.

49. "Ward's Team Wins Title Junior World Championship," *Forward* (October 1928): 7.

50. *Shreveport Times,* August 29—31, 1928.

51. *Bridgewater (NJ) Courier-News,* September 7, 1928.

52. *Chicago Tribune,* September 2, 1928; *Tucson Daily Star,* September 2, 1928.

53. *Oakland Tribune,* September 10, 1928.

54. *Jackson [MS] Clarion-Ledger,* January 1, 1929.

55. Kent M. Krause, "From Americanism to Athleticism: A History of the American Legion Junior Baseball Program" (PhD dissertation, University of Nebraska, 1998), 52–58, 209.

56. Alexander Gardiner, "Everybody Up!" *American Legion Monthly* 7 (November 1929): 21–22; *Plainfield (NJ) Courier-News,* August 6, 1929.

57. *Shreveport Times,* August 17, 19, 1929; *Los Angeles Times,* August 23, 1929.

58. *Burlington Free Press,* August 22, 1929.

59. *Alexander (LA) Town Talk,* September 7, 1929; *Boston Globe,* September 5, 1929.

60. "Everybody Up," *American Legion Monthly* 7 (November 1929): 21–22, 71; *New York Times,* May 8, 1944.

61. *Louisville Courier Journal,* November 23, 1929; Philip M. Callaghan, "Legionaries, The First Generation: Dan Sowers," *American Legion Magazine* 48 (August 2009): 48; *Richmond Palladium-Item,* February 8, 1930.

62. *Indianapolis Star,* November 16, 1929; *Louisville Courier-Journal,* November 23, 1929; Rumer, 194.

63. Harold M. Sherman, *Batter Up! A Story of American Legion Junior Baseball* (New York: Grossest and Dunlap, 1930), 304.

64. *Baltimore Sun,* August 19, 1930; *Shreveport Times,* August 30, 1930.

65. *Shreveport Times,* August 28, 30, 1930.

66. *Baltimore Sun,* August 25, 1930.

67. *Cincinnati Enquirer,* August 18, 1930; *Los Angeles Times,* August 23, 1930; *Atlanta Constitution,* August 26, 1930.

68. *Shreveport Times,* August 28, 30, 1930; *Cincinnati Enquirer,* August 30, 1930.

69. *Battle Creek Enquirer,* August 28, 1931; *Chicago Tribune,* August8, 1931.

70. *Sioux Falls Argus-Leader,* August 23, 1931.

71. *Asheville Citizen,* September 27, 1931; Mike Vance, *Houston Baseball: The Early Years, 1861–1961* (Houston: Bright Sky Press, 2014), 167, 173; *Minneapolis Star Tribune,* August 29, 1931.

72. Ralph Berger, "Kirby Higbe," https:SABR.org/ Bioproject.

73. *Oakland Tribune,* August 29, 30, 1931; *San Bernardino County Sun,* August 30, 1931.

74. *Pottsville Republican,* February 4, 1932; Kirby Higbe, *The High Hard One* (Lincoln: University of Nebraska Press, 1998), 14–18.

Chapter 2

1. Charles C. Alexander, *Breaking the Slump: Baseball in the Depression Era* (New York: Columbia University Press, 2002), 14–15.

2. *Ibid.,* 6.

3. Dan Sowers, "On to Manchester," *American Legion Monthly* 12 (June 1932): 4–5.

4. *Monroe (LA) News Star,* August 1, 1932; *Shreveport Times,* August 18–19, 1932.

5. *Boston Globe,* August 18, 26, 27, 1932; *Burlington Free Press,* August 19, 1932.

6. Alexander Gardiner, "Won in the 10th," *American Legion Monthly* 13 (November, 1932): 4; *Chillicothe Constitution-Tribune,* August 31, 1932.

7. Gardiner, 4; *St. Louis Star and Times,* September 1, 1932.

8. *Alexandria Town Talk,* September 3, 1932; *Racine Journal Times,* September 3, 1932; Gardiner, 56.

9. *Monroe News Star,* September 3, 1932.

10. Benjamin G. Rader, *Baseball: A History of America's Game* (Urbana: University of Illinois Press, 1992), 136.

11. Dan Sowers, "Big League Stuff," *American Legion Monthly* 9 (November 1933): 4, 48–49; *Greenfield [IN] Daily Reporter,* August 29, 1933.

12. *The Sporting News,* August 3, 1933; *St. Louis Post-Dispatch,* August 2, 1933.

13. *Greenfield (IN) Daily Reporter,* September 29, 1933; Sowers, "Big League Stuff," 48–49.

14. Sowers, "Big League Stuff, 48–49.

15. *Nashville Tennessean,* September 2, 1933; Philip J. Lowry, *Green Cathedrals: The Ultimate Celebration of Major League and Negro League Ballparks* (New York: Walker), 144–145.

16. Lawrence Baldassaro, "Cavarretta," http// www.SABR*Bioproject*.

17. Peter Golenbock, *Wrigleyville: A Magical History Tour of the Chicago Cubs* (New York: St. Martin's Press, 1996), 300–309.

18. Kent M. Krause, "From Americanism to Athleticism: A History of the American Legion Junior Baseball Program" (PhD dissertation, University of Nebraska, 1998), 209–210.

19. Richard Anderson, *A Home Run for Bunny* (Bellevue, Washington: Illumination Arts, 2013), 7–8.

20. Richard Andersen, *We Called Him Bunny* (Amherst, MA: Levellers Press, 2014); *Salisbury (MD) Post,* July 21, 1935.

21. Andersen, *A Home Run for Bunny*, 17–18, 20; *Fitchburg Sentinel,* August 24, 1934.

22. *Ibid. Boston Globe*, August 24, 1934.

23. *Palm Beach Post,* August 26, 1934; *Nashville Tennessean,* August 24, 1934; *Hartford Courant,* August 31, 1934.

24. *Boston Globe*, August 24, 1934.

25. *Nashville Tennessean*, September 24, 1934; *American Legion Monthly* 17 (November 1934): 26; *Tampa Tribune*, October 26, 1934.

26. *Springfield Republican*, July 17, 2014.

27. *Shreveport Journal,* August 21, 1934; *Bluefield Telegraph,* August 29, 1934.

28. *Shreveport Times,* August 30, 1934; *Chicago Tribune,* August 31, 1934; *Baltimore Sun,* September 2, 1934.

29. Joseph K. Shepard, "Foe of All 'Isms," *Indianapolis Star,* December 13, 1952.

30. *Hammond Times,* June 15, 1935; *Pittsburgh Press,* June 19,1935; John A. Salmond, *Gastonia 1929: The Story of the Loray Mill Strike* (Chapel Hill: The University of North Carolina Press, 1995); Janet Irons, *Testing the New Deal: The General Textile Strike of 1934 in the American South* (Urbana: University of Illinois Press, 2000), 116–117.

31. Richard Goldstein, "Crash Davis, 82, 'Bull Durham' Model, Dies," *New York Times,* September 4, 2001.

32. David Christman, "Howie Moss: Minor League Slugger," *SABR Research Journal* (1982), 145–150.

33. *Indianapolis Star,* January 4, 1935.

34. *Arizona Daily Star,* August 18, 1935; *San Francisco Examiner,* August 23, 1935.

35. Alexander Gardiner, "Champion of Champions," *American Legion Monthly* 19 (November 1935): 32–33, 44.

36. *Charlotte News,* August 27–28, 1935.

37. H. L. Bob A. Nestor, *Baseball in Greenville and Spartanburg* (Charleston, SC: Arcadia, 2004; Benson, 374–375; *Los Angeles Times,* August 17, 1936; *Miami News,* August 29, 1936.Chaillaux, "It's True About the South," *American Legion Monthly* 21 (November 1, 1936): 34–36; *San Francisco Examiner,* September 1–4, 1936.

38. Terry Radtke, *The History of the Pennsylvania American Legion* (Mechanicsburg: Stackpole Books, 1993), 63–64, 131–133, 150.

39. *Shreveport Times,* September 3, 1937; *Boston Globe*, September 25–26, 1937.

40. *Birmingham News*, September 3–4, 1937; *Charlotte Observer*, September 5–6, 1937.

41. *Charlotte Observer*, September 5–6, 1937.

42. Saul Wisnia, "Clint Conaster," www. sabrbioproject.com.

43. *Tulare (CA) Advance-Register,* September 6, 1938.

44. Kent M. Krause, "From Americanism to Athleticism: A History of the American Legion Junior Baseball Program" (PhD dissertation, University of Nebraska, 1998), 218–229.*Gaffney Ledger,* August 28–30, 1938.

45. H.L. Chaillaux, "American Legion Tournament, 1938," *Spalding Official Base Ball Guide* (1939), 419; *Passaic Herald-News,* August 30, 1940; *Los Angeles Times,* August 29–30, 1940.

46. *New York Daily News*, September 3, 1938; *Lincoln Journal Star*, September 4–5, 1938.

47. *Louisville Courier Journal,* September 4, 1939, 1939.

48. *Muscatine Journal and News-Tribune,* September 2–3, 1939; *Columbus Telegram,* September 4, 1939, August 4, 1939.

49. *Asheville Citizen Times,* August 30, 1940; *Oakland Tribune,* September 27, 1940.

50. *Passaic Herald-News,* August 30, 1940; *Los Angeles Times,* August 29–30, 1940.

51. *Asheville Citizen-Times,* August 3, 1940; *Munster (IN) Times,* September 3, 1940.

52. *Los Angeles Times,* September 9, 1940.

53. *Oakland Tribune,* September 27, 1940; H. L. Chaillaux, "American Legion Tournament, 1940," *Spalding-Reach Official Baseball Guide, 1941* (New York: American Sports Publishing, 1941), 462–463.

54. Amy Essington, "Segregation, Race, and Baseball: The Integration of the Pacific Coast League, 1948–1952," PhD dissertation, Claremont Graduate University, 2009; *Los Angeles Times,* January 25, 2003 (obit).

55. *Des Moines Register,* August 10, 1941.

Chapter 3

1. John Fletcher, "The Boys of Summer of '42," *Los Angeles Times,* August 9, 1992.

2. *Los Angeles Times,* August 16, 22, 1941; *Visalia Times-Delta,* August 19, 1941.

3. *Bend (OR) Bulletin,* August 25, 1941; *Casper Star-Tribune,* August 29–30, 1941; *Tucson Arizona Republic,* August 30, 1941.

4. *Chicago Tribune,* August 30, 1941; *Allentown Morning Call,* September 8, 1941; *Los Angeles Times,* September 6, 8, 1941; *Salt Lake City Tribune,* September 7, 1941.

5. Office of the Commissioner, *Baseball: Official Major and Minor League Records* (Chicago: Office of the Commissioner, 1943) p. 195; for President Roosevelt's "Green Light" see *The Sporting News,* January 1, 1942.

6. John Fletcher, "The Boys of Summer of '42," *Los Angeles Times,* August 9, 1992.

7. *Los Angeles Times*, August 3, 1942.

8. *Los Angeles Times*, August 31, 1942, September 3, 1942.

9. *Chicago Tribune*, August 31, 1942; *St. Louis Star and Times*, August 27, 1942; Lesley O'Connor, ed., *1943 Baseball* (Chicago: Baseball Commissioner, 1943), 196–197.

10. *Los Angeles Times*, August 2, 7, 1942; *Honolulu Advertiser*, September 7, 1942; *Boston Globe*, September 5–7, 1942; *Butte Standard*, August 18, 1942.

11. *The Sporting News*, January 21, 1943; *Arizona Republican (Phoenix)*, April 11, 1943; Louis F. Grill, "Junior Baseball Carries On," *American Legion Magazine* 36 (February 1943): 38.

12. *Minneapolis Star Tribune*, August 28, 30, 1943.

13. *Great Falls Tribune*, August 21, 1943; *Mansfield News-Journal*, August 25, 1943.

14. *Ogden Standard*, August 14, 1943; *Greenville News*, August 29, 1943; *Billings Gazette*, August 28, 30, 31, 1943, September 1, 1943; *Minneapolis Star Tribune*, August 28, 1943; *Missoula Missoulian*, August 30, 1943.

15. *Minneapolis Star Tribune*, September 5, 1943.

16. *Minneapolis Star Tribune*, August 29, 1943.

17. *Western Hills High School Alumni.com*; *Cincinnati Enquirer*, December 22, 1991.

18. *St. Louis Star and Times*, August 16, 1944.

19. *Tucson Daily Citizen*, August 29, 1944; *Minneapolis Star Tribune*, August 27, 1944.

20. *Cincinnati Enquirer*, September 3, 1944; *Minneapolis Star Tribune*, September 2, 1944.

21. *Cincinnati Enquirer*, September 3, 1944.

22. Jonathan Zimmerman, *Whose America? Culture Wars in the Public Schools* (Cambridge: Harvard University Press, 2002), 67–70; *San Bernardino County Sun*, October 28, 1945; *New York Times*, February 20, 1946; *Seymour (IN) Tribune*, May 5, 1945; *Indianapolis News*, August 27, 1945.

23. *Shelby Star.com*

24. *Missoula Missoulian*, August 20, 1945; *Butte (MT) Standard*, August 20, 1945.

25. *Rocky Mount Telegram*, August 15, 1945; *Munster IN) Times*, August 23–24, 1945.

26. *Tucson Arizona Daily Star*, August 29, 1945; *Phoenix Republic*, August 30, 1945; *Harrisburg Evening News*, September 1, 1945.

27. *Hartford Courant*, August 15–16, 1945; *Allentown Morning Call*, September 7, 1945; *Mount Carmel Item*, August 28, 1945; *Tucson Arizona Daily Star*, August 30, 1945.

28. *Billings Gazette*, September 1, 1945; *Minnesota Star-Tribune*, September 2, 1945.

29. *Decatur (IL) Herald*, January 26, 1946.

30. *Ibid.*; Dawn Watts Perez, "Moon Landrieu: Reflections of Change," University of New Orleans, Master's Thesis, 1996.

31. *Ibid.*

32. *St. Louis Star*, August 17, 1946.

33. *Oklahoma City Daily Oklahoman*, August 27, 1946; *Cincinnati Enquirer*, August 28, 1946; *Bridgewater (NJ) Courier News*, August 28, 1946; *Florence Morning News*, September 1,1946.

34. *Bridgewater Courier News*, August 30, 1946; *Brooklyn Eagle*, August 31, 1946; *Los Angeles Times*, August 30, 1946; *Philadelphia Inquirer*, August 30, 1946.

35. *Los Angeles Times*, February 29, 1947.

36. Marshall Smelser, *The Life That Ruth Built* (Lincoln: University of Nebraska Press, 1975), 532–534, 538; *Ogden Standard-Examiner*, April 8, 1947.

37. Smelser, 536–537; *Indianapolis Star*, August 5, 1947; *Cincinnati Enquirer*, August 1, 1947.

38. Erik Barnouw, *Tube of Plenty: The Evolution of American Television* (New York: Oxford University Press, 1975), 112–113.

39. *Longview (TX) News-Journal*, April 10, 1947; *Shreveport Times*, July 10, 1947; *Los Angeles Times*, August 29, 1947; *Los Angeles Times*, July 17, 1947.

40. *Cincinnati Enquirer*, August 22–23, 1947, September 4, 1947.

41. *Jackson (MS) Clarion-Ledger*, August 18–19, 1947.

42. *The Sporting News*, September 3, 1947; *Nashua Telegraph*, August 15, 1947.

43. *San Bernardino County Sun*, August 17, 1947; *Billings Gazette*, August 21–22, 1947.

44. *Los Angeles Times*, August 29, 1947.

45. *Reno State Journal*, August 29, 1947; *Berkshire (MA) Eagle*, August 30, 1947.

46. *Cincinnati Enquirer*, September 4, 1947; *The Sporting News*, September 3, 1947; *Los Angeles Times*, September 1, 1947.

47. *westernhillsalumni.com*.

48. David L. Lewis, *The Public Image of Henry Ford: An American Folk Hero and His Company* (Detroit: Wayne State University Press, 1976), 385–386.

49. *The Sporting News*, September 8, 1948.

50. *Indianapolis Star*, September 6–10, 1948.

51. *Wilmington News Journal*, August 23, 31, 1948.

52. Joe Logue, "History on Post 31's Side: Schroths of 1948," *The Trentonian News*, August 17, 2000; *Statesville (NC) Daily Record*, September 10, 1948; *Camden Courier-Post*, September 11, 1948; *Chicago Tribune*, September 8, 1948.

53. Benson, 289.

54. *American Legion World Series 2014 Record Book*, 5, 26.

55. Al Stump, "Legion Baseball's Storybook Champs," *American Legion Magazine* 48 (May 1950): 17–18, 57.

56. William E. Akin, *West Virginia Baseball* (Jefferson, NC: McFarland, 2006), 56, 171; *Atlanta Constitution*, September 1, 1949.

57. *Mason City (LA) Globe-Gazette*, September 2, 1949.

58. *The Sporting News*, September 7, 1949; *Quad-City Times*, July 12, 1932.

59. George Ross, "All-Time Legion Team? Oakland Draws Support," *The Sporting News*, August 22, 1964.

60. *St. Louis Post Dispatch*, April 28–29, 1950; *Beatrice (NE) Daily Sun*, August 28, 1950; *Lincoln Nebraska State Journal*, August 29, 1950; *The Sporting News*, August 22, 1964.

61. *The Sporting News,* September 20, 1950; *Neenah (WI) News-Record,* September 8, 1964.

62. *The Sporting News,* August 22, 1964.

63. John C. Skipper, *Frank Robinson: A Baseball Biography* (Jefferson, NC: McFarland, 2015), 15–17; William M. Simons, *The Cooperstown Symposium, 2009–2010* (Jefferson, NC: McFarland, 2010), 3–4.

64. *Great Falls (MT) Tribune,* September 6, 1950.

65. *Oakland Tribune,* September 11, 1950.

66. Al Stump, "He Didn't Know What He was Buying," *American Legion Magazine* 52 (March 1952): 13–14.

67. Rick Oband, "The Sandlot Mentors of Los Angeles," *The National Pastime* (Phoenix: SABR, 2011), 23–27.

68. Joan Hulbert, "Bill Consolo," *SABR Bioproject.*

69. Sparky Anderson and Dan Ewald, *Sparky!* (New York: Prentice Hall, 1990).

70. Kevin Nelson, *The Golden Game: The Story of California Baseball* (Lincoln: University of Nebraska Press, 2004), 246–249.

71. *Los Angeles Times,* August 22, 26, 1951, September 1, 1952.

72. J. G. Taylor Spink, ed., *Baseball Guide and Record Book 1951* (St. Louis: The Sporting News, 1951), 166–167.

73. *Burlington (NC) Daily Times,* August 30, 1951; *Tampa Times,* September 1, 1951; *Tampa Tribune,* September 3, 1951.

74. *Detroit Free Press,* September 5, 1951.

75. *Detroit Free Press,* September 6, 1951; *The Sporting News,* September 18, 1951.

76. *Cincinnati Enquirer,* August 24, 1951; *Detroit Free Press,* August 6, 1951.

77. *Los Angeles Times,* September 8–10, 1952; *Detroit Free Press,* September 9, 1951.

78. Al Stump, "He Didn't Know What He Was Buying," *American Legion Magazine* (March 1952): 14; Carl Paul Maggio, *Swinging for the Fences: How American Legion Baseball Transformed a Group of Boys into a Team of Men* (Los Angeles: Wheatmark, 2013), 272.

79. *Los Angeles Times,* July 17, 1947.

Chapter 4

1. Mark Schmetzer, "Glory Days," *Cincinnati Enquirer,* April 19, 2018.

2. Bill Nowlin, "Russ Nixon," www.sabr.org/sabr.bioproj; *Cincinnati Enquirer,* November 10, 2016.

3. J. G. Taylor Spink, ed., *Baseball Guide and Record Book, 1952* (St. Louis: The Sporting News, 1952), 161.

4. *The Sporting News,* September 24, 1952; *Bend Bulletin,* August 28–29, 1952; *Fremont (NB) Tribune,* August 29, 1952.

5. *Bend Bulletin,* August 28–29, 1952; *Fremont (NE) Tribune,* August 29, 1952; *Waco News-Tribune,* August 30, 1952; *Kokomo Tribune,* August 29, 1952.

6. *Bloomington Pantagraph,* August 29, 1952; *San Bernardino County Sun,* September 1, 1952.

7. *The Sporting News,* September 17, 1952.

8. *The Sporting News,* September 24, 1952.

9. *Ibid.*

10. *Gaston Gazette,* November 5, 2012, September 15, 2013.

11. Benson, *Ballparks of North America,* 228.

12. *Oakland Tribune,* August 10, 1953; *Reno Gazette-Journal,* August 14, 1953; *DeKalb Daily Chronicle,* August 27, 1953; *Greenville (SC) News,* August 28–29, 1953.

13. Krause, 225–226; *The Sporting News,* September 16, 1953; *St. Louis Post-Dispatch,* September 4, 1953.

14. *St. Louis Post-Dispatch,* September 4–5, 1953.

15. *Miami News,* August 8, 1953.

16. *The Sporting News,* March 24, 31, 1954, April 7, 1953; *St. Louis Post-Dispatch,* January 23, 1955.

17. *The Sporting News,* April 7, 1954; Ira Berkow, *The Corporal Was a Pitcher: The Courage of Lou Brissie* (Chicago: Triumph Books, 2009), 200–204.

18. *Baltimore Sun,* September 2, 4, 1954; *St. Louis Post-Dispatch,* September 2–4, 1954; *Greenwood (SC) Index-Journal,* September 5, 1954.

19. *The Sporting News,* September 15, 1954; *St. Louis Post-Dispatch,* August 27, 1954.

20. *Greenwood (SC) Index-Journal,* September 5–6, 1954; *St. Louis Post-Dispatch,* September 11, 1954.

21. Peter Rowe, "Winning Streak: Baseball Has Been Very, Very Good to Billy Chapps for 50 Years" *San Diego Union Tribune,* May 30, 2004.

22. *Cincinnati Enquirer,* May 6, 1955.

23. *Helena Independent-Record,* August 16, 1955; *Lincoln Journal Star,* August 31, 1955.

24. *Lead (SD) Daily Call,* August 25, 1955; *Lincoln Star,* September 10, 1955; *Gastonia Gazette,* August 22, 1955; *Orangeburg Index-Journal,* August 27, 1955; *Florence (SC) Morning News,* August 28, 1955.

25. *Lincoln Journal Star,* August 31, 1955.

26. *American Legion World Series 2014 Record Book,* 26.

27. Berkow, *The Corporal Was a Pitcher,* 214;

28. *Kingston (NY) Daily Freeman,* August 31, 1956; *Rocky Mount Telegram,* August 27, 1956; *Roseburg News Review,* August 25, 31, 1955; *Bloomington Pantagraph,* August 30, 1955. *St. Louis Post Dispatch,* January 23, 1955.

29. *Rocky Mount Telegram,* August 27, 1956.

30. *Kingston (NY) Daily Freeman,* August 31, 1956; *Rocky Mount Telegram,* August 27, 1956; *Roseburg News Review,* August 25, 31, 1955; *Bloomington Pantagraph,* August 30, 1955.

31. *St. Louis Post-Dispatch,* September 5–6, 1956; *Bloomington Pantagraph,* September 6, 1956.

32. *St. Louis Post-Dispatch,* September 8, 1956; *Bloomington Pantagraph,* September 9, 1956.

33. *Bloomington Pantagraph,* September 9, 1956.

34. *Albany Democrat,* September 7, 1956.

35. *Bismarck Tribune,* August 31, 1956.

36. *Benton-Harbor News-Palladin,* September 7, 1957.

37. *Oklahoma City Daily Oklahoman,* August 20, 1955; *Bismarck Tribune,* August 19–20, 1955.

38. *Beatrice (NE) Daily Sun,* August 30, 1957; *Bloomington Pantagraph,* September 3, 1957 *Great Falls Tribune,* September 4, 1957.

39. *Oklahoma City Daily Oklahoman,* August 27, September 1, 1957; *Medford Mail Tribune,* August 29–30, 1957; *Baltimore Sun,* August 30, 1957.

40. *Bloomington Pantagraph,* September 6, 1957.

41. *Great Falls Tribune,* September 9, 1957; *Benton Harbor News-Palladium,* September 7, 1957.

42. Michael Sokolove, *Hustle: The Myth, Life and Lies of Pete Rose* (New York; Simon & Schuster, 1990), 162–163.

43. *Cincinnati Enquirer,* August 1, 1958, September 15, 1958.

44. David M. Jordan, *Pete Rose: A Biography* (Westport, CT: Greenwood Press, 2004), 6–7.

45. *Kingston Daily Freeman,* August 25–27, 1958.

46. *The Sporting News,* September 24, 1958.

47. *St. Louis Post-Dispatch,* August 22, 1958; *The Sporting News,* September 24, 1958.

48. *The Sporting News,* September 6, 1958; *Billings Gazette,* August 22, 1958; *Greenwood Index-Journal,* September 25, 1957.

49. Berkow, *The Corporal Was a Pitcher,* 210.

50. *The Sporting News,* August 24, 1958; *Official Baseball Guide and Record Book, 1958* (1958), 189.

51. *Jackson (MS) Clarion-Ledger,* December 12, 1958; *Lincoln Journal Star,* February 17, 1959.

52. Andy Romey, "American Legion Base Ball World Series: Edison Post 187, The 1959 National Champ!" *American Legion Magazine; Detroit Free Press,* September 11, 1959.

53. *Ibid.;* Sean Shapiro, "Michigan's only American Legion champ reuniting," *Oakland Press,* July 25, 2009.

54. J. G. Taylor Spink, ed., *Baseball Guide and Record Book 1959* (St. Louis: The Sporting News, 1959), 189.

55. *Newport News Daily Press,* September 8, 13, 1959.

56. *Newport News Daily Press,* September 7, 1959; *Detroit Free Press,* September 9, 1959.

57. *Detroit Free Press,* September 11, 1959; *Hartford Courant,* September 9, 1959; *Billings Gazette,* September 8, 1959.

58. *Bend Bulletin,* September 1, 1959.

59. *Jefferson City Tribune,* February 18, 1960; *Rapid City Journal,* February 11, 1960; *Bend Bulletin,* April 7, 1960.

60. *The Sporting News,* September 14, 1960.

61. *Ibid.*

62. *Klamath Falls Herald and News,* August 30, 31, 1960.

63. *Ibid.,* August 30, 1960

64. Mark Armour, "Dave McNally" *www.sabr.org/bioproject*; Ed West, "Montana's Greatest Athlete Falls to Cancer at Age 60," *Billings Gazette,* December 3, 2002.

65. Norm King, "Rusty Staub," *www.sabr.org/bioproject.*

66. *Klamath Falls Herald and News,* August 30, 1960.

67. *The Sporting News,* September 14, 1960; *Klamath Falls Herald and News,* September 4, 1960.

68. *Passaic Herald-News,* September 2, 1960.

69. *The Sporting News,* September 3, 1960; *Klamath Falls Herald and News,* September 14, 1960.

70. *archives.jesuitnola.org.*

71. *Greenville News,* March 7, 14–15, 1961; *Indianapolis Star,* March 7, 1961; *The Sporting News,* March 22, 1961.

72. *The Sporting News,* March 21, 1961, May 10, 1961; *Oshkosh Northwestern,* March 16, 1961.

73. *Greenville News,* May 10, 1961, June 7, 1961; *The Sporting News,* May 10, 1961, June 7, 1961; *Augusta Chronicle,* November 26, 2013.

Chapter 5

1. *The Sporting News,* May 10, 1961.

2. *The Sporting News,* June 7, 1961.

3. Gerry Brown, "Al Stanek's 22-strikeout game remains an American Legion Regional Record." *Springfield Republican,* June 19, 2011.

4. *Billings Gazette,* September 5, 1961.

5. *Richmond (IN) Palladium-Item,* August 24, 1961.

6. *Petersburg (VA) Progress-Index,* August 30, 1961; *Butte (MT)Standard,* August 29, 1961.

7. *Beatrice (NE) Daily Sun,* August 30, 1961; *Sioux City Journal,* August 29, 1961; *Jackson (MS) Clarion-Ledger,* August 30, 1961.

8. *Salem (OR) Statesman-Journal,* August 29, 1961; *Janesville (WI) Daily Gazette,* August 30, 1961; *Arizona Republican (Phoenix),* September 6, 1961; *Lincoln Star,* August 31, 1961; *Janesville Daily Gazette,* September 1, 1961.

9. *Janesville Daily Gazette,* September 1, 1961; *Arizona Republic,* September 5–6, 1961; *Lincoln Star,* September 4, 1961.

10. *Arizona Republic,* September 10, 1961.

11. *The Sporting News,* June 9, 1962.

12. See Tom Dunkel, *Color Blind: The Forgotten Team that Broke Baseball's Color Line* (New York: Grove Press, 2013).

13. *St. Louis Post-Dispatch,* August 31, 1962.

14. *Helena Independent Record,* August 20, 1962.

15. *Monroe (LA) News-Star,* August 29, 1962; *Helena Independent Record,* August 20, 1962; *St. Louis Post-Dispatch,* August 31, 1962; *Rochester Democrat and Chronicle,* August 31, 1962.

16. *St. Louis Post-Dispatch,* September 1, 1962; *Newport News Daily Press,* September 3, 1962.

17. *Honolulu Star-Bulletin,* September 2–3, 1962; *Huron Daily Plainsman,* September 4, 1962.

18. *Honolulu Advertiser,* September 5, 1962.

19. Bob Feller, "Bob Feller and American Legion Baseball," *American Legion Magazine* 74 (June, 1963): 14–15.

20. *The Sporting News,* August 15, 1963.

21. *The Sporting News,* August 24, 1963.

22. *Ibid.*

23. Bob Keisser, *Baseball in Long Beach* (Charleston, SC: History Press, 2013).

24. *Roseburg News-Review,* August 28, 1963; *Long Beach Independent,* March 30, 1963.

25. *St. Louis Post-Dispatch,* September 1, 1963.

26. *Bridgeport Post,* September 1, 1963; *Chicago Tribune,* September 2, 1963; *St Louis Post-Dispatch,* September 1, 1963.

27. J. G. Spink, ed., *Official Baseball Guide and Record Book* (St. Louis: The Sporting News, 1964), 249.

28. *Blytheville (AR) Courier News,* August 25, 1964.

29. *Waterloo Courier,* August 27, 1964; *Blytheville (AR) Courier-News,* August 25, 1964; *Des Moines Tribune,* August 29, 1964.

30. *Los Angeles Times,* August 30, 1964.

31. *Detroit Free Press,* August 29, 1964; *Shamokin Dispatch,* August 31, 1964.

32. *Gaston Gazette,* August 9, 1964; *Salisbury Post,* February 27, 2015.

33. Bensen, *Ballparks of North America,* 1–2.

34. *The Sporting News,* September 18, 1965.

35. *Passaic Herald News,* September 1, 1965; *Chicago Daily Herald,* August 2, 1965; *El Paso Herald-Post,* August 26, 1964.

36. *Moline Dispatch,* August 6, 1965; *Chicago Daily Herald,* September 9, 1965; *El Paso Herald-Post,* August 26, 1964.

37. *Reno Nevada State Journal,* September 9, 1965.

38. *The Sporting News,* August 17, 1966; *Newport News Daily Press,* August 25, 1966; *Enid (OK) News and Eagle,* August 19, 1966; *Tucson Daily Star,* August 23, 1966.

39. *Orangeburg Times and Democrat,* August 30, 1966; *The Sporting News,* September 1, 1966.

40. *The Sporting News,* September 1, 1966; *Orangeburg Times and Democrat,* September 4, 1966.

41. *Ibid. Greenville (SC) News,* September 5, 1966.

42. *The Sporting News,* September 19, 1966.

43. Terry Radtke, *The History of the Pennsylvania American Legion* (Mechanicsburg, PA: Stackpole Books, 1993), 131; *The Sporting News,* August 27, 1966; *New Castle News,* August 21, 1966.

44. *The Sporting News,* September 2, 1967.

45. *Wilmington Morning News,* September 1–2, 1967.

46. *Wilmington Morning News,* September 4, 1967; *Carbondale Southern Illinoisan,* September 3, 1967.

47. *Tuscaloosa News,* September 6, 1967; *Mt. Vernon Register-News,* September 6, 1967.

48. *La Crosse Tribune,* September 10, 1967.

49. *The Sporting News,* September 21, 1968.

50. *Hartford Courant,* August 27, 1968; *South Bend Tribune,* August 26, 1968; *Billings Gazette,* August 27, 1968; *Odessa American,* August 26, 1968.

51. *Wilmington News Journal,* August 30, 1968; *Nashua Telegraph,* August 31, 1968.

52. *The Sporting News,* September 21, 1968; *New York Daily News,* September 3, 1968.

53. *New York Daily News,* September 3, 1968.

54. *The Sporting News,* September 20, 1969.

55. *Ibid.*

56. *Lincoln Star,* August 29, 1969; *Bismarck Tribune,* September 2, 1969; *Palm Beach Post,* August 30, 1969.

57. *St. Louis Post Dispatch,* August 31, 1969; *Hartford Courier,* September 1, 1969.

58. *Mason City Globe-Gazette,* September 1, 1969; *Baltimore Evening Sun,* September 1–2, 1969.

59. *St. Louis Post-Dispatch,* September 3, 1969; *Baltimore Evening Sun,* September 3, 1969.

60. *Portland Mercury,* June 21, 2017.

61. *Bismarck Tribune,* August 27,1970; *Wilmington Morning News,* September 2, 1970; *Corvallis Gazette-Times,* September 3, 1970.

62. *Corvallis Gazette-Times,* September 3, 1970.

63. *Wilmington Morning News,* September 7, 1970.

64. *Orangeburg Times and Democrat,* September 8, 1970; *Salem Capital Journal,* September 9, 1970; *Arizona Republic,* September 8, 1970; *San Rafael Independent Journal,* September 9, 1970.

65. *Albany Democrat Herald,* September 10, 1970; *Salem Statesman Journal,* August 10, 1970.

66. *Ibid.*

67. *The Sporting News,* September 4, 1971.

68. *Los Angeles Times,* September 9, 1971.

69. *Salem Statesmen Journal,* August 30, 1971; *Pomona Progress Bulletin,* September 1, 1971.

70. *Tucson Daily Citizen,* September 1, 1971.

71. *Tucson Daily Citizen,* September 4–6, 1971; *Burlington Free Press,* September 4, 1971.

72. *Ibid.*

73. *Ibid.,* September 8, 1971.

74. *Ibid.*

75. *Tucson Arizona Daily Star,* September 9, 1971.

76. *The Sporting News,* December 16, 1972; Bensen, *Ballparks,* 227.

77. *Blytheville Courier News,* August 31, 1971.

78. *Sikeston (MO) Daily Standard,* August 28, 1972.

79. *Orangeburg Times and Democrat,* September 1, 1972; *Circleville Herald,* September 1, 1972.

80. *St. Louis Post-Dispatch,* September 7, 1972.

81. *Springfield Leader and Press,* September 10, 1972.

82. *The Sporting News,* September 20, 1973; *Jackson Clarion-Ledger,* August 30, 1973.

83. Benson, *Ballparks,* 206.

84. *Van Nuys News,* August 24, 1973.

85. *Spokane Chronicle,* August 31, 1973; *Pocatello Idaho State Journal,* September 2, 1973.

86. *The Sporting News,* September 20, 1973; *Salem Statesman Journal,* September 5, 1973.

87. *Great Falls Tribune,* September 5, 1973.

88. *Columbus Telegram,* August 21, 1974.

89. Thomas Rumer, *The American Legion,* 209, 265.

90. *Stevens Point Journal,* August 13, 1974.

91. *Coos Bay World,* August 24, 1974; *Bismarck Tribune,* August 24, 1974.

92. *Corvallis Gazette-Times*, August 26, 1974; *Naupa (ID) Free Press*, August 27, 1974; *Coos Bay World*, August 28, 1974.

93. *Nampa (ID) Press-Tribune*, August 27, 1974; *Corvallis Gazette-Times*, August 28, 1974.

94. *Salem Capital Journal*, August 28, 1974.

95. *Rapid City Journal*, August 15, 1975; Benson, *Ballparks of North America*, 328.

96. *Rapid City Journal*, August 27–30, 1975.

97. *Rapid City Journal*, August 27–28, 1975.

98. *Rapid City Journal*, August 29, 1975, September 2, 1975.

99. *Ibid.; Pocatello (ID) State Journal*, September 2, 1975.

100. *Cedar Rapids Journal*, September 2, 1975.

101. *Ibid.*

Chapter 6

1. *Arlington Heights (IL) Daily Herald*, June 18, 1976, September 3, 10, 1976.

2. *Chicago Daily Herald*, September 3, 1976; *Des Moines Register*, September 3, 1976.

3. *Chicago Tribune,* September 4, 1976; *Bridgeport Post*, September 5, 1976; *Wilmington News Journal*, September 4, 1976.

4. *Carbondale Southern Illinoisan*, September 5, 1976; *Detroit Free Press*, September 5, 1976.

5. *Arlington Herald*, September 1, 1976.

6. *Arlington Herald*, September 7, 1976; *White Plains Journal News*, September 7, 1976.

7. Mel Machuca and Will Shepherd, *An Inning at a Time: An American Legion Baseball National Championship Story* (Portland, OR: Inkwater Press, 2010) provides a detailed summary of the year.

8. *Lafayette (IN) Journal and Courier*, August 15, 1977; *Nashua Telegram*, August 31, 1977.

9. *Berkshire Eagle*, September 2, 1977; *Hattiesburg American*, September 3, 1977.

10. *Palm Beach Post*, September 4, 1977; *Rapid City Journal*, September 5, 1977.

11. *Hattiesburg American*, September 6, 1977; Machuca and Shepherd, *An Inning at a Time*, 139.

12. Machuca and Shepherd, 171.

13. *The Sporting News*, September 24, 1977.

14. *Berkshire Eagle*, September 8, 1977.

15. *St. Petersburg Times*, August 22, 1978.

16. *Miami News,* August 28, 1978.

17. *Salem Statesman Journal*, September 1, 1978; *Albany (OR) Democrat-Herald*, September 2, 1978; *Rapid City Journal*, September 2, 1978.

18. *Corvallis Gazette-Times*, September 3, 1978; *Salem Capital Journal*, August 5, 1978.

19. *Ibid.*

20. *Miami News*, august 6, 1978.

21. *Hattiesburg American*, June 2, 1979.

22. *Yakima Herald-Republic*, April 5, 2013.

23. *North Hills (PA) News Record*, September 7, 1979.

24. *Rapid City Journal*, August 31, 1979.

25. *Clarksdale Press*, August 31, 1979; *Mattoon (IL) Journal Gazette*, August 31, 1979; *Bismarck Tribune*, September 1, 1979.

26. *Bismarck Tribune*, September 1, 1979; *Chicago Tribune*, September 2–4, 1979.

27. *Vincennes Sun-Commercial,* September 4, 1979.

28. *St. Louis Post-Dispatch,* August 4, 1979.

29. *Billings Gazette,* August 25, 1980.

30. *Minneapolis Star*, September 2, 1980.

31. *Helena Independent-Record*, August 27, 1980.

32. *Honolulu Star-Bulletin*, August 31, 1980.

33. *Honolulu Star-Bulletin, September* 1, 1980; *Minneapolis Star Tribune*, September 1, 1990.

34. *Minneapolis Star Tribune*, September 2, 1980.

35. *Honolulu Star-Bulletin*, September 2, 1980.

36. *Ibid.*

37. *Sumter Daily Item,* September 3, 1981; Benson, *Ballparks*, 384.

38. *Hartford Courant*, August 31, 1981; *St. Cloud Times*, August 31, 1981; *Owensboro Messenger-Inquirer*, September 1, 1981.

39. *Louisville Courier-Times*, September 5, 1981; *Orangeburg Times and Democrat*, September 4, 1981; *Hartford Courant*, September 5, 1981; *Great Falls Tribune*, September 6, 1981.

40. *Palm Beach Post*, September 8, 1981.

41. *Tampa Times*, September 8, 1981.

42. *Trophies and Awards* (Indianapolis: The American Legion, 2008), 10–34.

43. Darryl Grumling, "1969 Bears Pioneered Boyertown's Storied Tradition," *Pottstown Mercury,* July 28, 2009.

44. *Reading Eagle*, July 6, 2016; Tom McNichol, "Bear Stadium," *1994 American Legion World Series Program; Philadelphia Inquirer*, September 9, 1982.

45. *Somerset (PA) Daily American*, June 15, 1982.

46. *St. Cloud Times*, August 30, 1982.

47. *Reading Eagle,* July 6, 2016.

48. *Pottstown Mercury,* July 28, 2009.

49. *Indianapolis Star*, September 6, 1982; *Philadelphia Inquirer*, September 6, 1982.

50. *Philadelphia Daily News*, September 7, 1982.

51. *Philadelphia Inquirer*, September 7, 9, 1982.

52. https://www.post2baseball.com/page/show/279977-jack-williams-stadium.

53. *Edina Magazine* (August 2013), p. 1.

54. "Edina's American Legion Baseball," *EdinaMagazine.com*, August 2013; Darryl Grunning, "1983: The One that Got Away," *Pottstown Mercury*, August 6, 2013.

55. *Minneapolis Star Tribune*, September 2, 1983; *Rapid City Journal*, September 4, 1983; *Bismarck Tribune*, September 3, 1983.

56. *Bismarck Tribune*, September 3–4, 1983; *Jackson (MS) Clarion-Ledger*, September 5, 1983.

57. *Allentown Morning Call*, September 6, 1983; *Minneapolis Star Tribune*, September 6, 1983.

58. *Trophies and Awards* (Indianapolis: The American Legion, 2008), 10–34.

59. *Kokomo Tribune,* July 23, 1985.

60. *Rapid City Journal*, August 31, 1984.

61. *Philadelphia Inquirer*, June 29, 1986.

62. *Rapid City Journal*, August 31, 1984.

63. *Rapid City Journal*, September 2, 4, 1984.

64. *Hartford Courant*, September1, 1984; *Rapid City Journal*, August 31, 1984, September 2, 1984.

65. *Rapid City Journal,* September 5, 1984.
66. *Trophies and Awards* (Indianapolis: American Legion, 2008), 9–31.
67. *Kokomo Tribune,* July 23, 1985.
68. *Rapid City Journal,* September 1, 1985.
69. *Rapid City Journal,* August 31, 1985; *Hartford Courant,* August 31, 1985.
70. *Ibid.,* September 1, 1985; *Tucson Arizona Daily Star,* September 1, 1985.
71. *Logansport Pharos-Tribune,* September 3, 1985; *Rapid City Journal,* September 3, 1985.
72. *Rapid City Journal,* August 26, 1986.
73. *Ibid.*
74. *Los Angeles Times,* August 6, 16, 1986.
75. *Los Angeles Times,* August 27, 1986.
76. *Rapid City Journal,* August 29–30, 1986.
77. *Palm Beach Post,* September 1, 1986.
78. *Palm Beach Post,* September 2, 1986; *Rapid City Journal,* September 2–3, 1986.
79. *Rapid City Journal,* August 28, 1986; *Indianapolis News,* January 24, 1989.

Chapter 7

1. *Stevens Point Journal,* April 15, 1986, September 8, 1987.
2. *Stevens Point Journal, September* 8, 1987; *Pottstown Mercury,* August 8, 2012.
3. *Tampa Tribune,* September 3, 1987.
4. *Stevens Point Journal,* September 8, 1987.
5. *Stevens Point Journal,* September 5, 1987; *La Crosse Tribune,* September 5, 1987.
6. *Stevens Point Journal,* September 5, 1987.
7. *Tampa Bay Times,* September 8–9, 1987; *Camden Courier-Post,* September 8, 1987.
8. *Tampa Tribune,* September 9, 1987.
9. Ted Mexell, "Boyertown Opens Defense of Legion Crown Baseball," *Allentown Morning Call,* August 25, 1988.
10. *Hartford Courant,* August 24, 1988.
11. *Ibid.,* August 24–25, 28, 1988.
12. *Ibid.,* August 25, 1988.
13. *Ibid.,* August 26–27, 1988.
14. *Hartford Courant,* August 27, 1988.
15. *Cincinnati Enquirer,* August 29, 1988; Bill Siebert, "Kessler's Hurling, Hitting Lead Cincinnati to Title," *American Legion Magazine* 125 (November 1988): 50.
16. *Hartford Courant,* August 29, 1988; *Cincinnati Enquirer,* August 29, 1988.
17. *Los Angeles Times,* August 19–21, 1989.
18. *Germantown (TN) News,* August 24, 1989.
19. *Los Angeles Times,* August 23, 1989.
20. *Los Angeles Times,* August 26–28, 1989.
21. *Los Angeles Times,* August 28, 1989; *Madison (WI) State Journal,* August 28, 1989.
22. *Madison State Journal,* August 28, 1989; *Wisconsin Rapids Daily Tribune,* August 28, 1989.
23. Bill Siebert, "Marine Leads Charge to Series Title," *American Legion Magazin,* 127 (November 1989): 58.
24. *Corvallis Gazette-Times,* August 22, 1990.
25. *Ibid.*
26. *Ibid.,* August 24–25, 1990; *Salem Statesman Journal,* August 24, 1990.
27. *Corvallis Gazette Times,* August 25–26, 1990.
28. *Corvallis Gazette Times,* August 27, 1990.
29. *Ibid.; Baltimore Sun,* August 29, 1990.
30. *Ibid.; Hartford Courant,* August 24, 1991.
31. *Allentown Morning Call,* August 21, 1991.
32. *Camden Courier-Post,* August 23, 1991; *Sudbury (PA) Daily Item,* August 22, 1991; *Tampa Tribune,* August 22, 1991.
33. *Hartford Courant,* August 24, 1991; *Camden Courier-Post,* August 24–25, 1991.
34. *Camden Courier-Post,* August 27, 1991; *Philadelphia Inquirer,* September 5, 1991.
35. *Newark Advocate,* August 26, 1991; *Coshocton Tribune,* August 26, 1991.
36. *Allentown Morning Call,* September 12, 1991.
37. *Los Angeles Times,* July 13, 1994.
38. *Hartford Courant,* August 27–28, 1992.
39. *Bridgewater Courier-News,* August 29, 1992; *Hackensack Record,* August 29, 1992.
40. *Chicago Tribune,* August 31, 1992; *Philadelphia Inquirer,* August 31, 1992.
41. *Los Angeles Times,* August 31, 1992, September 1, 1992.
42. Anthony Miller, "Newbury Park Hits It Big: California Team Wins Legion World Series," *American Legion Magazine* 133 (November 1992): 14–15.
43. *Sioux Falls Argus Leader,* September 2, 1993.
44. *Billings Gazette,* July 1, 2006, September 27, 2017.
45. *Rapid City Journal,* August 30, 1993.
46. *Corvallis Gazette Times,* August 28, 1993.
47. *Ibid.; Coos Bay World,* August 29–30, 1993.
48. *Billings Gazette,* September 1–2, 1993; *Rapid City Journal,* August 31, 1993.
49. *White Plains Journal News,* September 3, 1993; *Sioux Falls Argus Leader,* September 3, 1993.
50. *Rapid City Journal,* September 5, 1993.
51. *Camden Courier-Post,* August 26, 1994; *Allentown Morning Call,* August 27, 1994; *Roanoke Times,* October 23, 2006.
52. *Camden Courier-Post,* August 26, 1994.
53. *Camden Courier-Post,* August 26–28, 1994; *Allentown Morning Call,* August 27, 1994.
54. *Allentown Morning Call,* August 28–29, 1994.
55. *Camden Courier-Post,* August 31, 1994.
56. *Ibid.*
57. *Bismarck Tribune,* June 19, 1995.
58. *Minnesota Star-Tribune,* August 23, 1995; *Oklahoma City Daily Oklahoman,* August 24, 1995; *Honolulu Advertiser,* August 23, 1995; *Fremont (NE) Tribune,* August 23, 1995.
59. *St. Cloud Times,* August 25, 1995; *Bismarck Tribune,* August 26–27, 1995; *Honolulu Advertiser,* August 27, 1995.
60. *Bismarck Tribune,* August 29, 1995; *Sioux Falls Argus-Leader,* August 28, 1995.
61. T. Douglas Donaldson, "Hawaiian Heat: Led by an overpowering pitcher, Aiea wins the American Legion World Series," *American Legion Magazine* 139 (November 1995): 18–20; *Honolulu Star-Bulletin,* August 30, 1995.
62. *Ibid.*

63. *Hartford Courant,* August 16, 1996.

64. Andy Vineberg, "Recalling a Team for the Ages," *Bucks County Courier Times,* August 4, 2011; *Brunswick (NJ) News Tribune,* August 21, 1996.

65. *White Plains Journal News,* August 25–26, 1996; *Philadelphia Inquirer,* August 28, 1996.

66. *Sioux Falls Argus Leader,* August 26, 1996.

67. *Philadelphia Inquirer,* August 30, 1996.

68. *Ibid.; Rapid City Journal* August 30, 1996.

69. *Ibid.,* September 2, 1996.

70. *Quad-Cities Times,* August 22, 1997; *Rapid City Journal,* August 21, 1997.

71. *Annapolis Capital,* August 20, 1997; *Moline Dispatch,* August 22, 1997.

72. *Moline Dispatch,* August 24, 1997; *Rapid City Journal,* August 23–24, 1997.

73. *Hartford Courant,* August 26, 1997; *Orlando Sentinel,* August 27, 1997.

74. *Ibid.*

75. *Rapid City Journal,* August 27, 1997.

76. *Hartford Courant,* December 16, 1998.

77. *Camden Courier Post,* August 18, 1998; *Edwardsville Intelligencer,* August 4, 2015.

78. *Lincoln Journal-Star,* August 18, 1998; *Gastonia Gazette,* June 10, 2016.

79. *St. Louis Post-Dispatch,* August 23, 1998; *Philadelphia Inquirer,* August 22, 1998; *Camden Courier-Post,* August 22–24, 1998; *St. Cloud Times,* August 22, 1998.

80. *Camden Courier-Post,* August 24, 1998.

81. *St. Louis Post-Dispatch,* August 26, 1998.

82. *Ibid.,* August 26–27, 1998.

83. *Rapid City Journal,* August 18, 2005.

84. *Hartford Courant,* December 12, 1998.

85. *Minneapolis Star Tribune,* August 19, 1999.

86. *Camden Courier-Post,* August 21, 24–25, 1999.

87. *Hartford Courant,* August 25, 1999.

88. *Ibid.; Camden Courier-Post,* August 24–25, 1999.

89. *Ibid.*

90. *St. Louis Post-Dispatch,* December 13, 1999.

Chapter 8

1. *St. Louis Post-Dispatch,* December 13, 1999.

2. *St. Louis Post-Dispatch,* August 17, 2000.

3. *St. Louis Post-Dispatch,* August 17, 21, 2000.

4. *Ibid.*

5. *St. Louis Post-Dispatch,* August 18–20, 2000; *Camden Courier-Post,* August 20–21, 2000.

6. *Paducah Sun,* August 22, 2000.

7. *Paducah Sun,* August 22–23, 2000.

8. *St. Louis Post-Dispatch,* August 24, 2000.

9. *Camden Courier-Post,* August 30, 2000.

10. *Camden Courier-Post,* August 25–26, 2001; *Ukiah (CA) Daily Journal,* August 26, 2001.

11. *Camden Courier-Post* August 27, 2001.

12. *Ibid.,* August 28, 2001.

13. *Ibid.,* August 29–30, 2001; *Boston Globe,* August 30, 2001.

14. Jeff Stoffer, "The Power of Perseverance: The Brooklawn, New Jersey Team Shows What It Takes to Win the American Legion Baseball World Series," *American Legion Magazine* 151 (November 2001): 38.

15. *Ibid.*

16. *Corvallis Gazette-Times,* May 8, 2002.

17. *Rapid City Journal,* August 23, 2002.

18. *Ibid.*

19. *Minneapolis Star Tribune,* August 27, 2002; *Jackson Clarion-Ledger,* August 27, 2002.

20. *Minneapolis Star Tribune,* August 28, 2002.

21. *Rapid City Journal,* August 18, 2005.

22. *Philadelphia Inquirer,* June 18, 2002, August 24, 2003.

23. *Ibid.*

24. *Camden Courier-Post,* August 23, 2003; *Oklahoma City Daily Oklahoman,* August 22, 2003.

25. *Camden Courier-Post,* August 23–27, 2003; *Corvallis Gazette-Times,* August 29, 2003; *Philadelphia Inquirer,* August 24, 2003.

26. *Salem Statesmen Journal,* August 26, 2003; *Philadelphia Inquirer,* August 26, 2003.

27. *Billings Gazette,* August 28, 2003.

28. *Rapid City Journal,* August 18, 2003.

29. *Corvallis Gazette-Times,* May 8, 2002, August 20, 2004.

30. *Corvallis Gazette-Times,* August 20, 2004.

31. *Albany Democrat-Herald,* August 21, 2004.

32. *Corvallis Gazette-Times,* August 21–22, 2004; *Albany Democrat-Herald,* August 21, 2004.

33. *Salem Statesman Journal,* August 23–24, 2004.

34. *Bangor Daily News,* August 25, 2004; *Corvallis Gazette-Times,* August 25, 2004.

35. *Rapid City Journal,* August 18, 2005.

36. *Rapid City Journal,* May 11, 2005.

37. *Greenville News,* July 10, 2005.

38. *Rapid City Journal,* August 18, 2005.

39. *Camden Courier-Post,* August 20, 2005; *Sioux Falls Argus-Leader,* August 21, 2005.

40. *Sioux Falls Argus-Leader,* August 21, 2005; *Philadelphia Inquirer,* August 23, 2005.

41. *Oklahoma City Daily Oklahoman,* August 25, 2005.

42. *Rapid City Journal,* August 24, 2005.

43. *Ibid.*

44. *Cedar Rapids Gazette,* August 18, 2006.

45. *Ibid.;* Benson, *Ballparks of North America,* 74–75.

46. *Lincoln Journal Star,* August 19, 2006; *Cedar Rapids Gazette,* August 19, 2006; *Rapid City Journal,* August 22, 2006.

47. *Boston Globe,* August 20, 2006; *Lincoln Journal Star.* August 20–21, 2006; *Cedar Rapids Gazette,* August 22–23, 2006.

48. *Rapid City Journal,* August 23, 2006.

49. *Cedar Rapids Gazette,* August 23, 2005.

50. *Mt. Carmel (IL) Daily Republican,* August 24, 2007.

51. *Philadelphia Inquirer,* August 26, 2007; *Hartford Courant,* August 25–26, 2007; *Nashville Tennessean,* August 27, 2007.

52. *Arizona Daily Star,* August 27–28, 2007.

53. *Arizona Daily Star,* August 28–29, 2007; *Minneapolis Star Tribune,* August 29, 2007.

54. *Minneapolis Star Tribune,* August 29, 2007.

55. *Hartford Courant,* August 22, 2008.

56. *Hartford Courant,* August 23, 2008.

57. *Hartford Courant,* August 26, 28, 2008.

58. *American Legion Magazine* 165, October 28, 2008.

59. *Boston Globe,* July 26, 2009.

60. *Battle Creek Inquirer,* August 21, 2009.

61. *Hartford Courant,* August 11, 2009; *Camden Courier-Post,* August 11, 2009.

62. *Hartford Courant,* August 15, 2009; *Billings Gazette,* August 18, 2009.

63. *Hartford Courant,* August 16–17, 2009; *Corvallis Gazette,* August 18, 2009.

64. *Great Falls Tribune,* August 19, 2009; *Corvallis Gazette,* August 18, 2009.

65. *Coos Bay World,* August 19, 2009; *Bismarck Tribune,* August 20, 2009.

66. *Bismarck Tribune,* August 20, 2009.

67. Cameron Richardson, "A Team Effort: The American Legion World Series now has a Permanent Home," *American Legion Magazine* 171 (August 2011): 36–37.

68. *Rock Island Argus,* August 13, 2010; *Oklahoma City Daily Oklahoman,* August 13, 2010; *Spokane Spokesman-Review,* August 13, 2010.

69. *Oklahoma City Daily Oklahoman,* August 14, 2010; *Minneapolis Star Tribune,* August 18, 2010; *Rock Island Argus,* August 15, 2010.

70. *Oklahoma City Daily Oklahoman,* August 14–15, 2010.

71. *Ibid.,* August 18–19, 2010; *Minneapolis Star Tribune,* August 18, 2010.

72. *Spokane Spokesman-Review,* August 18, 2010.

Chapter 9

1. Cameron Richardson, "A Team Effort: The American Legion World Series now has a permanent home," *American Legion Magazine* 171 (August 2011): 36–40.

2. *Philadelphia Inquirer,* August 11, 2011; *Camden Courier-Post,* August 12, 2011; *Gaffney Ledger,* August 12, 2011.

3. www.legion.org/baseball/tournaments/regional/2011; *Bismarck Tribune,* August 24, 2011.

4. *Philadelphia Inquirer,* August 13, 2011; *Camden Courier-Post,* August 13, 2011.

5. *Camden Courier Post,* August 15, 2011.

6. *Gaffney Ledger,* August 17–18, 2011; *Camden Courier-Post,* August 15, 2011.

7. *Billings Gazette,* August 15, 2011.

8. *Gaffney Ledger,* August 17, 2011.

9. *2017 American Legion World Series Record Book,* 10–14, 40.

10. *Hartford Courant,* August 14, 2012.

11. *Rock Island Argus,* August 17–18, 2012.

12. *Ibid.,* August 18–19, 2012.

13. *Camden Courier-Post,* August 20, 2012.

14. *Ibid.,* August 21–22, 2012.

15. *Ibid.,* August 22–23, 2012;

16. www.legion.org/baseball, 2012 world series, August 22, 2012.

17. *Fremont (OH) News-Messenger,* August 7, 2013; Jason Queen, "Legion baseball on decline," *Lexington (NC) Dispatch,* June 21, 2012; www.legion.org, October 23, 2012.

18. *Hartford Courant,* August 16, 2013.

19. *Moline Dispatch,* August 16, 2013; *Camden Courier Post,* August 16, 2013; *The American Legion. org.* "2013 World Series field set."

20. *Hartford Courant,* August 18, 2013; *Camden Courier Post,* August 18, 2013.

21. *Philadelphia Inquirer,* August 18–19, 2013.

22. *Camden Courier-Post,* August 20, 2013; *Honolulu Star-Advertiser,* August 20, 2013.

23. *Camden Courier-Post,* August 21–22, 2013.

24. *Ibid.,* August 21, 2013; *Shelby Star,* August 20, 2013; Cameron Richardson, "New Jersey wins 87th Legion World Series," www.legion.org, August 23, 2013.

25. www.legion.org/baseball/ "American Legion World Series to be broadcast on ESPNU."

26. *Philadelphia Inquirer,* March 3, 2014.

27. *Hartford Courant,* August 14, 2014.

28. *Camden Courier-Post,* August 15–16, 2014; *Hartford Courant,* August 15, 2014; *Great Falls Tribune,* August 15–16, 2014.

29. *Hartford Courant,* August 15–17, 2014; *Camden Courier-Post,* August 17–19, 2014.

30. *Camden Courier-Post,* August 19, 2014; *Philadelphia Inquirer,* August 19, 2014.

31. *Philadelphia Daily News,* August 20, 2014; *Camden Courier-Post,* August 20, 2014.

32. *Camden Courier-Post,* August 20, 2014.

33. *Camden Courier-Post,* August 10, 2015.

34. *Columbia (SC) Cola Daily,* August 11, 2015.

35. *Hartford Courant,* August 13, 2015; www.legion.org/baseball/2015 "world series field set," August 10, 2015.

36. *Ibid.,* August 14–15, 2015; *Camden Courier-Post,* August 14, 2015; *HonoluluStar-Advertiser,* August 15, 2015; *Salem Statesman Journal,* August 15, 2015.

37. *Hartford Courant,* August 14, 2015; *Honolulu Star-Advertiser,* August 15, 2015; *Camden Courier-Post,* August 16–18, 2015.

38. *Greenwood (SC) Index-Journal,* August 19, 2015.

39. *The State (Columbia, SC),* August 18, 2015.

40. *Hartford Courant,* August 8, 2016.

41. *Princeton (IN) Daily Clarion,* August 9, 17, 2016; *Jasper (IN) Herald,* August 9, 2016.

42. *American Legion World Series Journal,* August 2016; *Princeton (IN) Daily Clarion,* August 12, 2016.

43. *Princeton (IN) Daily Clarion,* August 13, 2016; *American Legion World Series Journal,* August 12–13, 2016.

44. *Lincoln Journal Star,* August 14, 2016; *American Legion World Series Journal,* August14, 2016.

45. *Princeton (IN) Daily Clarion,* August 16, 2016; *American Legion World Series Journal,* August 14, 2016.

46. *Princeton (IN) Daily Clarion,* August 17,

2016; *American Legion World Series Journal,* August 15, 2016.

47. *americanlegion.org/Award winners, all-tournament team announced,* August 16, 2016.

48. *Shelby Star,* August 16, 2017.

49. *Washington Post,* July 26, 2017; Phil Miller, "The Future of American Legion Baseball," *thesportseconomist.com,* October 2, 2017.

50. Sandra Constantine, "American Legion posts see national trend of declining membership," *Springfield (MA) Republican,* July 8, 2013.

51. Miller, "The Future of American Legion Baseball," *thesportseconomist.com;* Jerry Smith, "In the End, it will be Worth It," *Wilmington (DE) Sunday News Journal,* June 25, 2017; Joe Strupp, "Bases Empty," *New Jersey Monthly* (March 2018), 28–31.

52. *Sioux Falls Argus-Leader,* May 29, 2017; *St. Cloud Times,* October 13, 2017.

53. *Rapid City Journal,* August 10, 2017.

54. *Lincoln Journal Star,* August 11, 2017; *American Legion World Series Journal,* August 10, 2017.

55. *American Legion World Series Journal,* August 11, 14, 2017; *Lincoln Journal Star,* August 13, 2017.

56. *Ibid.,* August 15, 2017.

57. *Lincoln Journal Star,* August 16, 2017.

58. www.americanlegion.org/Legion Baseball awards presented at ALWS.

59. *Greenville News,* August 10, 2018.

60. www.americanlegion.org/2018 American Legion World Series, August 13, 2018.

61. *American Legion World Series Journal,* August 16, 2018.

62. *www.americanlegion.sportngin.com.*

63. *Ibid.*

64. *Ibid.*

65. *Ibid.*

66. *Wilmington News Journal,* August 17, 2018.

67. *Wilmington News Journal,* August 17, 23, 2018.

68. *Wilmington News Journal,* January 24, 2019.

69. *www. americanlegion.org/2018American Legion World Series/awards.*

70. *www.americanlegion.org.* "Eight teams punch ticket to 2019 ALWS.'

71. *Ibid.*

72. *Ibid.; Albuquerque Journal,* August 16, 2019.

73. *Ibid.*

74. *Bismarck Tribune,* August 21–22, 2019; *Twin Falls Times-News,* August 21, 2019.

75. *Twin Falls Times-News,* August 22, 2019.

76. *www.americanlegion.org/2019baseball awards.*

77. Frank Fitzpatrick, "Legion Baseball Is Slowly Fading Away." *Philadelphia Inquirer,* July 28, 2019.

Bibliography

Books

Alexander, Charles C. *Breaking the Slump: Baseball in the Depression Era*. New York: Columbia University Press, 2002.

American Legion. *The American Legion, Good Sportsmanship, Good Citizen, Good Soldier: A History of the American Legion Junior Baseball Program*. Indianapolis: American Legion, 1944.

_____. *Junior Baseball, 1926–1951: Silver Anniversary*. Indianapolis: American Legion, 1951.

Anderson, Richard. *A Home Run for Bunny*. Bellevue, WA: Illumination Arts Press, 2013.

_____. *We Called Him Bunny*. Amherst, MA: Levellers Press, 2014.

Anderson, Sparky, and Dan Ewald. *Sparky!* New York: Prentice Hall, 1990.

Barnouw, Erik. *Tube of Plenty: The Evolution of American Television*. New York: Oxford University Press, 1975.

Bensen, Michael. *Ballparks of North America: A Comprehensive Historical Reference to Baseball Grounds, Yards and Stadiums, 1845 to Present*. Jefferson, NC: McFarland, 1989.

Berkow, Ira. *The Corporal Was a Pitcher: The Courage of Lou Brissie*. Chicago: Triumph Books, 2009.

Cohen, Marilyn. *No Girls in the Clubhouse: The Exclusion of Women from Baseball*. Jefferson, NC: McFarland, 2009.

Copeland, Tom. *The Centralia Tragedy of 1919: Elmer Smith and the Wobblies*. Seattle: University of Washington Press, 1993.

Crepeau, Richard C. *Baseball: America's Diamond Mind, 1919–1941*. Orlando: University of South Florida Press, 1980.

DiNunno, Vin. *Spartan AC: An American Legion Baseball Team United Through Adversity*. Rayham, MA: Sports Playbook Publishing, 2008.

Dunkel, Tom. *Color Blind: The Forgotten Team That Broke Baseball's Color Line*. New York: Grove Press, 2013.

Gellerman, William. *The American Legion as Educator*. New York: Teachers College, 1938.

Golenbock, Peter. *Wrigleyville: A Magical History Tour of the Chicago Cubs*. New York: St. Martin's Press, 1996.

Gropman, David. *Say It Ain't So! The True Story of Shoeless Joe Jackson*. New York: Citadel Press, 1979.

Higbe, Kirby, with Martin Quigley. *The High Hard One*. Lincoln: University of Nebraska Press, 1998.

Howell, Reet, ed. *Her Story: A Historical Anthology of Women in Sports*. West Point, NY: Leisure Press, 1989.

Irons, Janet. *Testing the New Deal: The General Textile Strike of 1934 in the American South*. Urbana: University of Illinois Press, 2000.

Jones, Richard S. *A History of the American Legion*. Indianapolis: Bobbs-Merrill, 1946.

Jordan, David. *Pete Rose: A Biography*. Westport, CT: Greenwood Press, 2004.

Keels, Thomas. *Sesqui: Greed, Graft, and the Forgotten World Fair of 1926*. Philadelphia: Temple University Press, 2017.

Keisser, Bob. *Baseball in Long Beach*. Charleston, SC: History Press, 2013.

Lanctot, Neil. *Negro League Baseball: The Rise and Ruin of a Black Institution*. New York: McGraw-Hill, 1970.

Lewis, David L. *The Public Image of Henry Ford: An American Folk Hero and His Company*. Detroit: Wayne University Press, 1987.

Lindaman, Matthew. *Fit for America: Major John L. Griffith and the Quest for Athletes and Fitness*. Syracuse: Syracuse University Press, 2018.

Loosbrock, Richard J. *The History of the Kansas Department of the American Legion, 1919–1968*. Topeka: Kansas Department of the American Legion, 1968.

Lowry, Philip J. *Green Cathedrals: The Ultimate Celebration of Major League and Negro League Ballparks*. New York: Walker Publishing, 2006.

Machuca, Mel, and Will Shepherd. *An Inning at a Time: An American Legion Baseball National Championship Story*. Portland: Inkwater Press, 2010.

Maggio, Carl Paul. *Swinging for the Fences: How American Legion Baseball Transformed a Group of Boys Into a Team of Men*. Los Angeles: Wheatmark Press, 2013.

Moley, Raymond, Jr. *The American Legion Story*. New York: Duell, Sloan and Pearce, 1966.

Nelson, Kelvin. *The Golden Game: The Story of California Baseball*. Lincoln: University of Nebraska Press, 2004.

Nester, Bob A. *Baseball in Greenville and Spartanburg*. Charleston, SC: Arcadia Press, 2004.

Obojski, Robert. *Bush League: A History of Minor League Baseball.* New York: Macmillan, 1975.

O'Connor, Lesley, ed. *1943 Baseball.* Chicago: Baseball Commissioner, 1944.

Pencak, John L., and William Pencak. *For God and Country: The American Legion, 1919–1941.* Boston: Northeastern University Press, 1989.

Peterson, Armand, and Tom Tomashek. *Town Ball: The Glory Days of Minnesota Amateur Baseball.* Minneapolis: University of Minnesota Press, 2006.

Peterson, Robert. *Only the Ball Was White.* New York: McGraw-Hill, 1970.

Rader, Benjamin G. *Baseball: A History of America's Game.* Urbana: University of Illinois Press, 1992.

Radtke, Terry. *The History of the Pennsylvania American Legion.* Mechanicsburg, PA: Stackpole, 1993.

Reiss, Steven A. *Sport in Industrial America, 1850–1920.* Wheeling, IL: Harlan Davidson, 1995.

Rumer, Thomas A. *The American Legion: An Official History, 1919–1989.* New York: M. Evans, 1990.

Salmond, John A. *Gastonia 1929: The Story of the Lorey Mill Strike.* Chapel Hill: University of North Carolina Press.

Seymour, Harold, and Dorothy Seymour Mills. *Baseball: The Golden Age.* New York: Oxford University Press, 1989.

Seymour Mills, Dorothy, and Harold Seymour. *Baseball: The People's Game.* New York: Oxford University Press, 1990.

Sherman, Harold M. *Batter Up! A Story of American Legion Junior Baseball.* New York: Grosset and Dunlap, 1930.

Simons, William M. *The Cooperstown Symposium, 2009–2010.* Jefferson, NC: McFarland, 2010.

Skipper, John C. *Frank Robinson: A Baseball Biography.* Jefferson, NC: McFarland, 2015.

Smelser, Marshall. *The Life That Ruth Built.* Lincoln: University of Nebraska Press, 1975.

Sokolove, Michael. *Hustle: The Myth, Life and Lies of Pete Rose.* New York: Simon & Schuster, 1990.

Spalding-Reach Official Baseball Guide, 1941. New York: American Sports Publishing, 1941.

Spink, J. G. Taylor, ed. *Baseball Guide and Record Book, 1951, 1952, 1958, 1959, 1964.* St. Louis: Sporting News, 1951, 1952, 1958, 1959, 1964.

Sullivan, Dean A. *Middle Innings: A Documentary History of Baseball, 1900–1948.* Lincoln: University of Nebraska Press, 1998.

Vance, Mike. *Houston Baseball: The Early Years, 1861–1961.* Houston: Bright Sky, 2014.

Zimmerman, Jonathan. *Whose America? Culture Wars in the Public Schools.* Cambridge: Harvard University Press, 2002.

Articles

Adams, Franklyn J. "Legion Raised." *American Legion Magazine* 23 (August 1937): 12–13, 55–57.

Armour, Mark. "Dave McNally." www.https://sabr.org, bio project.

Baldassaro, Lawrence. "Phil Cavarretta." www.https://sabr.org, bio project.

Barry, Dan. "Not I but We." *American Legion Magazine* 27 (November 1939): 26–27, 56.

Berger, Ralph. "Kirby Higby." www.https: //sabr.org. Bio Project.

Berryman, Jack W. "From the Cradle to the Playing Field: America's Emphasis on Highly Organized Sport for Preadolescent Boys." *Journal of Sport History* 2 (Fall 1975): 112–131.

Brown, Gerry. "Al Stanek's 22 Strikeout Game Remains an American Legion Regional Record." *Springfield Republican,* June 19, 2011.

Callaghan, Philip M. "Legionnaires, the First Generation: Dan Sowers." *American Legion Magazine* 167 (August 2009): 48.

Chaillaux, Homer L. "American Legion Tournament, 1938." *Spalding Official Baseball Guide, 1939.* St. Louis: Sporting News, 1940.

_____. "American Legion Tournament, 1940." *Spalding Baseball Guide.* New York: American Sports Publishing, 1941.

_____. "It's True About the South." *American Legion Magazine* 13 (November 1935): 32–33.

_____. "Winner Take All." *American Legion Magazine* 23, November 193, 38–39, 57–58.

Christman, David. "Howie Moss, Minor League Slugger." *SABR Research Journal* 1982: 145–150.

Constantine, Sandra. "American Legion Posts See National Trend of Declining Membership." *Springfield Republican,* July 8, 2013.

Donalson, T. Douglas. "Hawaiian Heat: Aiea Wins American Legion World Series." *American Legion Magazine* 139 (November 1995): 18, 22.

Epler, Eric F. "Summers in Boyertown Mean American Legion Baseball: Going Deep." Penn Live, July 4, 2010. www.eepler@pennlive.com.

Feller, Bob. "Bob Feller and American Legion Baseball." *American Legion Magazine* 74 (June 1973): 14–15.

Fitzpatrick, Frank. "Legion Baseball Is Slowly Fading Away." *Philadelphia Inquirer,* June 28, 2019.

Fletcher, John. "The Boys of Summer, '42." *Los Angeles Times,* August 9, 1942.

Gardiner, Alexander. "Champion of Champions." *American Legion Magazine* 19 (November 1935): 32–33, 44.

_____. "Everybody Up! *American Legion Magazine* 7 (November 1929): 21–22.

_____. "Won in the 10th." *American Legion Magazine* 13 (November 1932): 4–5.

Goldstein, Richard. "Crash Davis, 82, 'Bull Durham Model' Dies." *New York Times,* September 4, 2001.

Gould, James. "The President Says Play Ball." *Baseball Magazine,* January 1942.

Grill, Louis F. "Junior Baseball Carries On." *American Legion Magazine* 36 (February 1944): 24–25, 38.

Grumling, Darryl. "1983: The One That Got Away." *Pottstown Mercury,* August 6, 2013.

_____. "1969 Bears Pioneered Boyertown's Storied Tradition." *Pottstown Mercury,* July 28, 2009.

Hulbert, Joanne. "Bill Consolo." www.http://sabr.org. bio project.

James, Marquis. "777 North Meridian." *American Legion Magazine* 12 (June 1932): 20.

King, Norm. "Rusty Staub." www.http://sabr/org. bio project.

Ladd, T. "Sexual Discrimination in Youth Sport: The Case of Margaret Gisolo." *Anthology of Women in Sports,* edited by Reed Howell. West Point, NY: Leisure Press, 1982.

Logan, Joe. "History of Post 31's Side: Schroths of 1948." *Trentonian News,* August 17, 2000.

Mexell, Ted. "Boyertown Opens Defense of Legion Crown." *Allentown Morning Call,* August 25, 1988.

Miller, Anthony. "Newbury Park Hits It Big." *American Legion Magazine 133* (November 1992): 14- 16.

Miller, Phil. "The Future of American Legion Baseball." www.thesportseconomist.com, October 2, 2017.

Nolin, Bill. "Russ Nixon." www.http://sabr.org//bio project.

Oband, Rick. "The Sandlot Mentors of Los Angeles." *The National Pastime.* Phoenix: Society for American Baseball Research, 2011.

Pitkin, Robert B. "The Biggest League: Things You Didn't Know About Junior Baseball." *American Legion Magazine* 99 (July 1975): 20, 56–59.

Queen, Jason, "Legion Baseball on the Decline." *Lexington (NC) Dispatch,* June 21, 2012.

Randolph, Jennings. "The Sportscope." *Clarksburg Telegram,* June 10, 1925.

"Remembering Coach Powles." In *Cooperstown Symposium, 2009–2010,* edited by William M Simons. Jefferson, NC: McFarland, 2010.

Richardson, Cameron. "A Team Effort: The American Legion Baseball World Series Now Has a Permanent Home." *American Legion Magazine* 171 (August 2011): 36–40.

Romey, Andy. "American Legion Baseball World Series: Edison Post 187 the 1959 National Champ." *Gloucester City News,* August 12, 2010.

Ross, George. "All-Time Legion Team; Oakland Draws Support." *The Sporting News,* August 22, 1964.

Rowe, Peter. "Winning Streak: Baseball Has Been Very Good to Billy Chapps for 50 Years." *San Diego Union-Tribune,* May 30, 2004.

Rulon, George W., and R.B. Pitkin. "50 Years of American Legion Baseball." *American Legion Magazine* 99 (July 1975): 14–17, 39–40.

Schlesinger, Arthur. "Biography of a Nation of Joiners." *American Historical Review* (October 1944): 1–25.

Schmetzer, Mark. "Glory Days." *Cincinnati Enquirer,* April 19, 2018.

Schmidt, Ray. "Major John Griffith." *College Football Historical Society* 13 (February 2000): 1–3.

"Scrub Baseball Now Has a League." *New York Times,* May 2, 1926.

Seibert, Bill. "Kessler's Hurling, Hitting Lead Cincinnati to Title." *American Legion Magazine* 125 (November 1988): 50.

_____. "Marine Leads Charge to Series Title." *American Legion Magazine* 127 (November 1989): 58.

Shapiro, Sean. "Michigan's Only American Legion Champ Reuniting." *Oakland Press,* July 25, 2009.

Shepard, Joseph K. "Foe of All Isms." *Indianapolis Star,* December 13, 1952.

Shutts, James. "Youth Goes to Bat." *Rotarian* 47 (July 1935): 18–21.

Sowers, Dan. "Baseball Revival Planned Among Boys of the Nation." *New York Times,* April 9, 1928.

_____. "Batter Up!" *American Legion Magazine* 6 (February 1929): 28–29, 52–58.

_____. "Big League Stuff." *American Legion Magazine* 15 (November 1933): 4, 48–49.

_____. "Junior Baseball Launched Into Second Big Year." *New York Times,* April 9, 1928.

_____. "On to Manchester." *American Legion Magazine* 12 (June 1932): 4–5.

Speaker, Tris. "Diamonds in the Rough." *Rotarian* 54 (April 1939): 22–25.

"Sportsmen All: Victory and Defeat Are Not Everything in Legion Little World Series." *American Legion Magazine* 17 (November 1934): 26.

Staffer, Jeff. "The Power of Perseverance: The Brooklawn, New Jersey Team Shows What It Takes to Win the American Legion Baseball World Series." *American Legion Magazine* 151 (November 2001): 38–39.

Strupp, Joe. "Bases Empty." *New Jersey Monthly* (March 2018): 28–31.

Stump, Al. "He Didn't Know What He Was Buying." *American Legion Magazine* 52 (March 1952): 13–14.

_____. "Legion Baseball's Storybook Change." *American Legion Magazine* 48 (May 1950): 17–18, 57.

Sullivan, Dean. "Margaret Gisolo, Baseball Star." In *Middle Innings: A Documentary History of Baseball, 1900–1918.* Lincoln: University of Nebraska Press, 1998.

Vineberg, Andy. "Recalling a Team for the Ages." *Bucks County Courier-Times,* August 4, 2011.

Voss, Dale. "Rollie Fingers." www.http//sabr.org bio project.

"Ward's Team Wins Title in Junior World Championship." *Forward* (October 1928): 7.

West, Ed. "Montana's Greatest Athlete Falls to Cancer at Age 60." *Billings Gazette,* December 3, 2002.

Wilson, Martin W. "Sesquicentennial International Exposition, 1926." *The Encyclopedia of Greater Philadelphia.* www.philadelphiaencyclopedia.org.

Dissertations

Bustad, Jacob J. "'One Hundred Per Cent Americanism': Nationalism, Masculinity and American Legion Junior Baseball in the 1920's" MA Thesis, University of Kansas, 2009.

Essington, Amy. "Segregation, Race and Baseball: The Integration of the Pacific Coast League, 1948–1952." PhD dissertation, Claremont Graduate University, 2009.

Krause, Kent M. "From Americanism to Athleticism: A History of the American Legion Junior Baseball Program." PhD dissertation, University of Nebraska at Lincoln, 1998.

Perez, Dawn Watts. "Moon Landrieu: Reflections of Change." University of New Orleans, Master's Thesis, 1996.

Newspapers

Albany Democrat
Alexander (LA) Town Talk
Allentown Morning Call
Appleton Post-Crescent
Arizona Daily Star (Tucson)
Arizona Republican (Phoenix)
Arlington Heights (IL) Daily Herald
Asheville Citizen
Atlanta Constitution
Baltimore Sun
Bangor Daily News
Battle Creek Enquirer
Bend (OR) Bulletin
Billings Gazette
Bismarck Tribune
Bridgeport (CT) Post
Bridgewater (NJ) Courier-News
Brooklyn Times Union
Burlington (VT) Free Press
Butte Standard
Camden Courier-Press
Carbondale (IL) Southern Illinoisan
Cedar Rapids Journal
Chicago Daily Herald
Chicago Tribune
Chillicothe Constitution-Tribune
Cincinnati Enquirer
Clarksburg (WV) Telegram
Clarksdale (MS) Press Register
Coos Bay World
Corvallis Gazette-Tribune
Decatur (IL) Herald
Des Moines Tribune
Detroit Free Press
Edwardsville Intelligencer
El Paso Herald
Fitchburg (MA) Sentinel
Gaffney (SC) Ledger
Gaston (SC) Gazette
Great Falls (MT) Tribune
Greenburg (IN) Gazette
Greenville (SC) News
Harrisburg Evening News
Hartford Courier
Hattiesburg American
Helena Independent-Record
Honolulu Star-Bulletin
Huron (SD) Daily Plainsman
Hutchinson (KS) News
Idaho State Journal (Pocatello)
Indianapolis News
Indianapolis Star
Jackson (MS) Clarion-Ledger
Jasper (IN) Herald
Jefferson City Tribune
Kinston (NC) Daily Freeman
Klamath Herald and News
Kokomo (IN) Tribune
Lafayette (LA) Journal and Courier
Logansport (IN) Pharos-Tribune
Long Beach Independent

Los Angeles Times
Louisville Courier-Journal
Madison (WI) Statesman
Mansfield (OH) News-Journal
Manti (UT) Messenger
Mason City (IA) Globe Gazette
Medford (OR) Mail Tribune
Miami News
Minneapolis Star Tribune
Missoula Missoulian
Monroe (LA) News-Star
Nampa (ID) Free Press
Nashua Telegram
Nashville Tennessean
New York Daily News
New York Times
North Hills (PA) Record
Oakland Tribune
Ogden Standard-Examiner
Omaha World-Tribune
Orangeburg Index-Journal
Oshkosh Northwestern
Owensboro Messenger-Inquirer
Paducah Sun
Palm Beach Post
Philadelphia Inquirer
Pittsburgh Press
Plainfield (NJ) Courier-News
Pomona Progress Bulletin
Portland (OR) Mercury
Pottstown Mercury
Pottsville Republican
Quad-Cities Times
Rapid City Journal
Reading Times
Reno State Journal
Richmond (IN) Palladium-Item
Rochester (NY) Times-Democrat
Rocky Mount Telegram
Roseburg (OR) News-Review
St. Louis Post-Dispatch
St. Louis Star-Times
Salem (OR) News-Review
San Bernardino County Sun
San Diego Union-Tribune
Seymour (IN) Tribune
Shelby Star
Shreveport Times
Sioux Falls (SD) Argus-Leader
The Sporting News
Stevens Point Journal
Sumter (SC) Daily Item
Tampa Times
Tampa Tribune
Tucson Daily Citizen
Tulare Advance-Register
Tuscaloosa News
Visalia Times-Delta
Waterloo Courier
White Plains Journal News
Wilkes-Barre Evening News
Wilmington Morning News
Yakima Herald-Republican

Index